International Macroeconomic Interdependence

World Scientific Studies in International Economics

(ISSN: 1793-3641)

World Scientific Studies in International Economics includes works dealing with the theory, empirical analysis, and evaluation of international economic policies and institutions, with topics covering international macroeconomics and finance, international trade theory and policy, as well as international legal and political economy. Monographs and edited volumes will comprise the core of the publications.

Vol. 60 *International Macroeconomic Interdependence*
by Paul R. Bergin (UC Davis)

Vol. 59 *Contributions to the Economics of International Labor Standards*
edited by Arnab K. Basu (Cornell) & Nancy H. Chau (Cornell)

Vol. 58 *International Economic Integration and Domestic Performance*
edited by Mary E. Lovely (Syracuse University, USA)

Vol. 57 *Trade Policies for Development and Transition*
by David G. Tarr (The World Bank, USA)

Vol. 56 *Nontariff Measures and International Trade*
edited by John Christopher Beghin (Iowa State University, USA)

Vol. 55 *The Future of Large, Internationally Active Banks*
edited by Asli Demirgüç-Kunt (World Bank, USA),
Douglas D. Evanoff (Federal Reserve Bank of Chicago, USA) &
George G. Kaufman (Loyola University Chicago, USA)

Vol. 54 *Globalization: The Macroeconomic Implications of Microeconomic Heterogeneity*
by Andrei A. Levchenko (University of Michigan, USA)

Vol. 53 *Multinational Enterprises and Host Country Development*
by Holger Görg (Kiel Institute for the World Economy, Germany)

Vol. 52 *Microeconometrics of International Trade*
by Joachim Wagner (Leuphana University Lueneburg, Germany)

Vol. 51 *The Political Economy of Trade Policy: Theory, Evidence and Applications*
by Devashish Mitra (Syracuse University, USA)

The complete list of the published volumes in the series can be found at
http://www.worldscientific.com/series/wssie

60 World Scientific Studies in International Economics

International Macroeconomic Interdependence

Paul R Bergin
University of California, Davis, USA

World Scientific
NEW JERSEY • LONDON • SINGAPORE • BEIJING • SHANGHAI • HONG KONG • TAIPEI • CHENNAI • TOKYO

Published by

World Scientific Publishing Co. Pte. Ltd.

5 Toh Tuck Link, Singapore 596224

USA office: 27 Warren Street, Suite 401-402, Hackensack, NJ 07601

UK office: 57 Shelton Street, Covent Garden, London WC2H 9HE

Library of Congress Cataloging-in-Publication Data

Names: Bergin, Paul R., author.
Title: International macroeconomic interdependence / Paul R. Bergin (UC Davis).
Description: New Jersey : World Scientific, [2017] | Series: World scientific studies in international economics ; volume 60 | Includes bibliographical references and index.
Identifiers: LCCN 2017023349 | ISBN 9789813224599 (hc : alk. paper)
Subjects: LCSH: International finance. | International trade. | Macroeconomics. | Economic policy. | Business cycles.
Classification: LCC HG3881 .B4648 2017 | DDC 332/.042--dc23
LC record available at https://lccn.loc.gov/2017023349

British Library Cataloguing-in-Publication Data

A catalogue record for this book is available from the British Library.

Desk Editors: Herbert Moses/Lum Pui Yee

Typeset by Stallion Press
Email: enquiries@stallionpress.co

Printed in Singapore

About the Author

Paul Bergin is a professor of economics at the University of California at Davis, as well as a research associate at the National Bureau of Economic Research. He is an editor of the *Review of World Economics/Weltwirtschaftliches Archiv* and an associate editor of the *Journal of International Economics*. He has published articles in prominent academic journals such as the *American Economic Review*, *Economic Journal*, and *Journal of Monetary Economics*. His research investigates topics such as exchange rate determination, international financial imbalances, and international monetary policy cooperation

Contents

CHAPTER 1

International Macroeconomic Comovement: The Role of Globalization in Goods and Asset Markets

Paul R. Bergin

Department of Economics, University of California at Davis,
One Shields Ave., Davis, CA 95616, USA
prbergin@ucdavis.edu

1. Introduction

The US Great Recession of 2007–2009 has been dubbed as the first truly "global recession" of recent times, in that the severe economic downturn starting in the US coincided with downturns in many other countries. As the world struggles to recover from the global recession, this is an opportune time to reflect on the nature and mechanisms of *International Macroeconomic Interdependence.* This episode provides new evidence, as well as new urgency, regarding a set of questions long debated in the macroeconomics literature. To what degree do national economies move together in their cycles of recession and recovery? Does the trend of greater international integration in goods and asset markets provide greater opportunity for transmission of shocks from one country to another? In terms of policy implications, does greater comovement imply greater benefit from countries coordinating together with their domestic macroeconomic policies?

This chapter brings to bear updated empirical evidence and novel model simulations to provide a new perspective on these fundamental questions.

Data indicate that the Great Recession was truly an unusual episode. Prior to it, business cycle comovement between the US and its major trading partners was moderately positive but far from perfect. During the Great Recession, the correlation of national gross domestic product (GDP) fluctuations was nearly complete, with recessions experienced by all the major trading partners. However, this does not appear to be a new norm, as the US recovery from the recession was not experienced universally, and the correlation of national GDP levels subsequently moved to low levels.

Can this episode of high international comovement be attributed to trends of globalization in goods and asset markets? I do document a long-run trend of rising integration, which appears to have accelerated in the decade prior to the crisis, both in terms of goods trade and asset trade. Both types of trade reversed trend and dropped significantly during the Great Recession, and even though both have since recovered their previous levels, the trends of rapid growth in both goods and asset trade of the pre-crisis period have not returned. To focus on how goods and asset trade affect business cycle comovement, rather than the reversed direction of causality, we look at the cross sectional experience of the US main trading partners in the year prior to the crisis, and see how this related to the varying degrees of GDP comovement with the US among these countries. One finds suggestive evidence that greater integration in both goods and asset markets promoted greater business cycle comovement during the particular episode of the Great Recession.

To understand better the mechanisms by which goods and asset trade can transmit shocks across countries, I construct a simple dynamic stochastic general equilibrium model with two countries, two goods, and two assets. Two countries are needed as a minimum, of course, to study transmission across a border. Two goods are needed if one wants to consider integration in goods markets separately from asset markets, so that a country trades one good for another good under the condition of balanced trade. Finally, two internationally tradable assets are needed to consider the hypothetical case of international integration in asset markets, where there is no trade in goods, but only trade of one asset exchanged for another asset. I believe this is the first paper of to study separate goods and asset market integration in this manner.

Stochastic simulations of the model indicate that the greatest transmission occurs when both goods and asset integration are operative, so that a country may trade assets to finance a level of expenditure on goods different from domestic production. Financing of a trade imbalance thus allows for a large effect on the level of domestic demand for foreign goods, and hence induces the greatest spillover to the level of foreign production. This transmission typically takes place through changes in the world interest rate, which has direct effects on foreign consumption, investment, and production decisions. Transmission via the goods market alone, in isolation from asset market trade, can also be fairly large, but the transmission there takes place largely via the terms of trade, the relative price of the two country's export goods. Changes in the relative value of foreign exports also affects the consumption and production decision in the foreign country. Finally, we find that integration in asset markets alone, in isolation from goods trade, does not provide a transmission channel for the usual supply or demand shocks, but can provide a potent transmission channel for shocks hitting the financial market of one of the countries. This last result may offer insight into the mechanisms by which the financial crisis in the Great Recession in the US could be transmitted so strongly to other countries.

The model also makes clear that, even while greater international market integration can strengthen spillovers of shocks, these spillovers can make foreign output either move the same direction as home output or in the opposite direction. The sign of the spillovers depends on the shocks involved and the structure of the economies. In general, comovement will be positive in the case of demand shocks like government spending, or in a case when home and foreign goods are viewed by demanders as more complementary.

This chapter contributes to a large body of research on international business cycle comovement. Backus, Kehoe, and Kydland (1992) first showed that comovement can be negative in theory, using a simple one good business cycle model. This chapter differs in modeling the asset trade explicitly, rather than assuming complete asset markets operating in the background, so as to be able to track the asset trades that underlie shock transmission. I also extend the analysis to study the possibility of asset trade in isolation of goods trade. Early theoretical work actually had difficulty demonstrating a strong linkage between trade and positive business cycle comovement (see Kose and Yi, 2006). Burstein, Kurz, and Tesar (2008) showed that international trade linkages can promote positive output comovement, depending on the complementarity of home and foreign goods. But they interpret their comovement in terms of production rather than consumption, and again, they do not consider the separate role of asset market integration.[1]

There is also mixed evidence regarding the relationship between financial integration and business cycle comovement. Among limited empirical evidence, some work has found financial market integration can either promote positive comovement (see Kose, Prasad, and Terrones, 2004), and other work finds negative comovement (see Kalemli-Ozcan, Papaioannou, and Peydró, 2013). In theoretical work, Heathcote and Perri (2002) find that a business cycle model with financial autarky does a better job matching certain features of the data than a model with complete asset markets. Recent business cycle research has focused on shocks to the financial market that can generate recession, which one might think is particularly relevant to the Great Recession. Perri and Quadrini (2016) find that in this context financial integration can potentially contribute to positive output comovement. One paper that focuses on the Great Recession episode is Imbs (2010), which finds empirical evidence that asset market integration promotes output comovement during this particular event. We differ, among other things, in that our more updated data covers both the recession period and the recovery afterward, which gives a very different perspective, as will be explained below.[2]

The next section of this paper presents empirical methodology and stylized facts regarding international output comovement. Section 3 constructs a novel theoretical framework, and Section 4 presents simulation results. Section 5 concludes, and summarizes the contribution of the other chapters in this volume to the constellation of questions raised in this chapter.

2. Empirical Motivation

This section will document several empirical regularities regarding international comovement in real GDP. Data come from the International Financial Statistics collected by the International Monetary Fund. As standard in

[1] Recent research has extended the logic of Burstein, Kurz, and Tesar (2008) to model internationalized production more explicitly in terms of offshoring (see Zlate, 2016; and Arkolakis and Ramanarayanan, 2009).

[2] This allows me to use GDP data, which is more comprehensive than the industrial production data Imbs needed to use due to its higher reporting frequency and his short sample.

business cycle research, data are quarterly and HP-filtered to remove long run trends. Countries were chosen because they are the ten largest trading partners of the US, excluding India due to lack of data availability. In sum, the list consists of the G-7 countries plus three emerging markets, Mexico, China, and Korea.

Table 1 lists the correlation of each country's GDP with the US for the sample period 1980:1–2016:3, along with the standard deviation of that country's GDP. Note that all correlations are positive, indicating positive comovement in the business cycles of these countries with the US on average. But the value of comovement varies widely by country, with Canada the most correlated with the US, and Korea the lowest.

Comovement also varies over time. Figure 1 reports correlations computed over a five-year rolling window. Two averages are plotted, one for the G-7 countries and the other for the three emerging markets. While correlation with the US generally is positive, there are periods of negative correlation, notably during the middle of the sample in the 1990s. This seems to belie the perception of a growing trend of globalization, in which the world's economies are becoming ever more integrated. A singular event, however, is immediately obvious toward the end of the sample. The US Great Recession of 2007–2009 appears to have been mirrored in downturns in all of the trading partners. This is reflected in a near perfect correlation

Table 1. Real GDP moments

	Standard deviation	Correlation with US
US	0.94	—
Canada	1.03	0.79
France	0.82	0.58
Germany	1.53	0.33
Italy	1.16	0.53
Japan	1.27	0.50
UK	1.07	0.71
China	1.03	0.79
Mexico	1.66	0.57
Korea	1.10	0.18

Source: International Financial Statistics, IMF. Quarterly real GDP, 1980:1–2016:3. Seasonally adjusted, logged and HP-filtered.

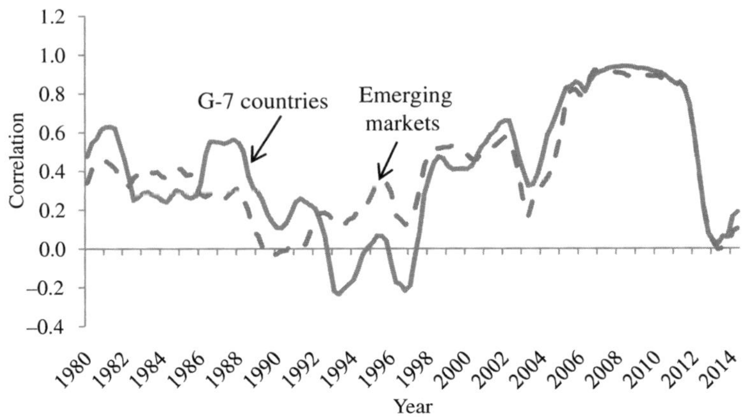

Figure 1. Correlation of GDP with US in rolling five-year window

Note: Solid line represents average among G-7 countries (excluding US), which includes Canada, France, Germany, Italy, Japan, and United Kingdom. Dashed line represents average among emerging markets countries in our sample, which includes China, Korea, and Mexico.

Source: International Financial Statistics, IMF. Quarterly real GDP, 1980:1–2016:3. Seasonally adjusted, logged and HP-filtered.

in GDP movements during this sample window. Correlations appear to be high both in developed and emerging market trading partners of the US. While the correlation in the early part of the crisis was somewhat lower than that in the G-7, we do not see strong evidence of the "decoupling" hypothesis of Kose, Otrok, and Prasad (2012), in which recessions in developed economies have smaller spillovers to emerging markets than in past decades. Nonetheless, the very high international correlation during the Great Recession appears to have been a one-off event, rather than indicating a new status quo of increased globalization and comovement, as in the aftermath of the Great Recession the correlations fall to near zero. This reflects recovery in the US, while there was new weakness in the economies of Europe and other trading partners.

Whether one takes the extremely high correlation of GDPs during the Great Recession as evidence of international integration, one readily can point to other indicators. While later chapters in this volume will discuss various ways of measuring goods market integration in terms of international convergence of prices, one crude but simple way to gauge integration is in terms of goods flows. Figure 2 plots trade volume (exports plus

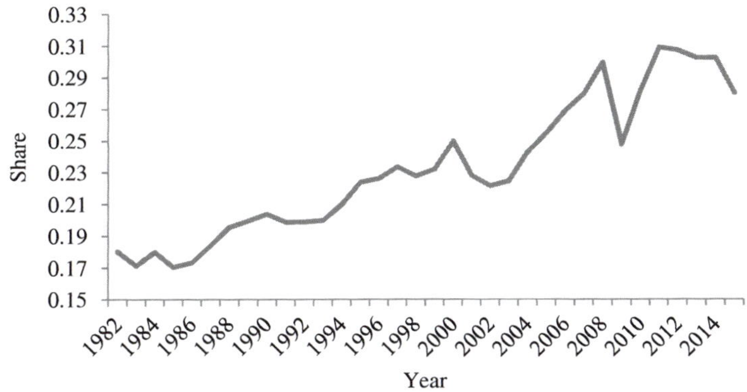

Figure 2. US goods trade volume (exports plus imports) as a share of US GDP
Source: Comtrade.

imports) of the US as a share of GDP. Data are taken from Comtrade from the United Nations. One observes a steady rise in trade share in the first half of the sample, with a rapid rise in the early 2000s. This often is taken as indication of progressive integration of the goods markets among countries. But one notes a sudden drop-off during the Great Recession, indicating that as real GDP fell in the period, trade volume fell even more rapidly. This "trade collapse" often is attributed to the fact that a disproportionate share of trade consists of durable and investment goods, which comprise a particularly volatile component of GDP (see Alessandria, Kaboski, and Midrigan, 2010; Engel and Wang, 2011; Eaton *et al.*, 2016). What is less well understood is the fact that in the aftermath of the Great Recession, while trade volume recovered to its pre-recession level, the rapid rate of growth in trade did not resume.

Asset markets also show signs of growing international integration. Figure 3 plots the volume of US cross-border trade in portfolio investment assets. Data come from the Coordinated Portfolio Investment Survey (CPIS) of the International Monetary Fund (IMF), for which data begin in 2001. As with goods trade, one observes a rapid rise in the first decade of the 2000s, and a sudden drop-off during the Great Recession. The level of asset trade recovered afterward, but again showed a slower rate of growth.

It has been conjectured that the progression toward greater international integration in both goods and asset markets provides channels of cross-border transmission of shocks, hence engendering greater macroeconomic

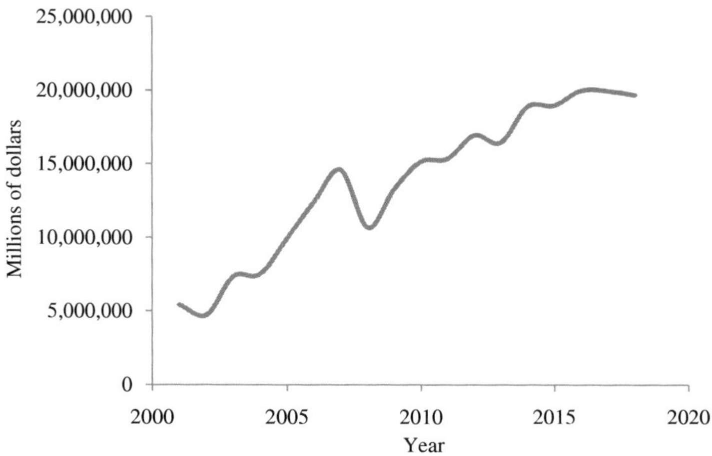

Figure 3. US bilateral portfolio investment with the world (mill. $)

Source: Coordinated Investment Portfolio Survey, IMF. Quarterly real GDP, 1980:1–2016:3.

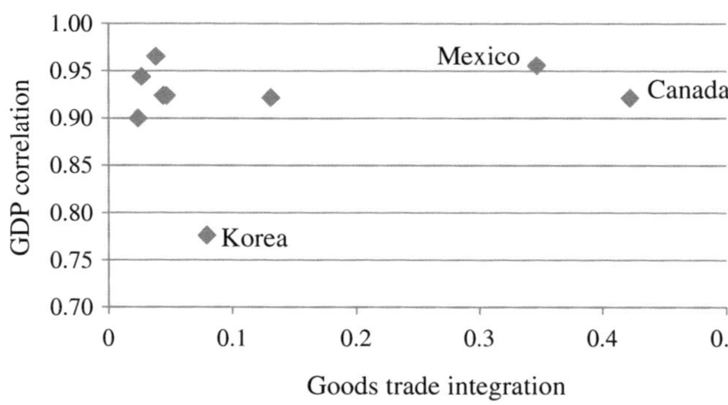

Figure 4. Bilateral GDP correlation with US in 2009 plotted against bilateral trade volume with US in 2006 as a share of country's GDP

interdependence. As measured by correlations in Fig. 1, we see that the one period of significantly higher international comovement was during the Great Recession. We here briefly use this episode to investigate if there is any relationship between GDP comovement and the degree of integration in asset or goods markets, using the cross-sectional variation among the nine countries. Given the small sample, we do not conduct formal econometric analysis, but present some simple plots.

Figure 4 plots a measure of GDP correlation against a measure of trade integration. For the vertical axis, I use the correlation of GDP with the US computed over the five-year window centered on 2009:1 for each of the nine countries. For the horizontal axis, I compute the volume of bilateral trade with the US in 2006 as a share of that country's GDP. Trade from a year prior to the onset of the crisis is used, in order to reduce problems of endogeneity. Recall that countries experienced a significant drop-off in trade volume with the US, ostensibly resulting from the onset of the Great Recession starting in 2007. I measure bilateral trade relative to GDP, rather than relative to total trade, in order to gauge not only the bilateral relationship with the US compared to other trading partners, but also the overall importance of trade for GDP in a country. The smattering of points seems to indicate a weak positive correlation between trade volume in 2006 and the correlation of GDPs in 2009. For example, note that the two counties far to the right on the graph with the greatest trade shares, Mexico and Canada, had GDP correlations above the average for the sample.

Similarly, Fig. 5 plots the GDP correlation centered on 2009:1 for each of the nine countries, against the volume of bilateral investment asset trade with the US in 2006 as a share of that country's GDP. Again there is substantial randomness, but one can see some support for a positive relationship, in that the country with the greatest investment trade, the United Kingdom, also happens to be the country with the highest GDP correlation during this period.

Overall, one concludes that there is on average positive comovement in business cycles across countries in our sample, but that this varies greatly

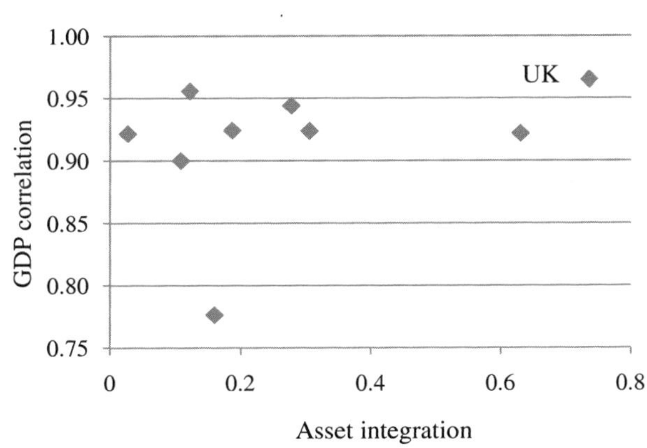

Figure 5. GDP correlation with US in 2009 plotted against bilateral trade volume in investment assets with US in 2006 as a share of country's GDP

over time and by country. The recent Great Recession is a singular episode of positive comovement. Greater integration in goods and asset markets seems to contribute at least somewhat to greater comovement.

3. A Framework to Organize Concepts

To explore the logic of how international trade in goods markets and asset markets can affect the transmission of macroeconomic shocks, I next construct a theoretical model that can be used to simulate relevant scenarios. The model consists of two counties, which is the minimum required to study cross-border transmission. It also features two tradable goods as well as two tradable assets. Again, this is the minimum requirement to study the relevant scenarios of integration in both goods and asset markets, as well as integration in each market alone. For example, to allow integration in goods market only, counties will trade one good for another. And to allow for integration in assets markets only, counties will trade one asset for another. The two goods will be country specific, standard in the business cycle literature. The two assets will be a global noncontingent nominal bond and money. For simplicity, both countries use the same money, that is, they are part of a monetary union. This provides a common numeraire for measuring variables throughout the model. Experiments will focus on two shocks, a standard supply shock in the form of a rise in total factor productivity, and a standard demand sock in the form of a rise in government expenditure.[3]

3.1. *Households*

Each country is population by a representative household, which derives utility from consumption (C), holding real money balances (M/P), and disutility from labor (L). P is the overall consumption price index. The household derives income by selling labor at the nominal wage rate (W), renting capital (K) to firms at the real rental rate (r), and interest (i) income

[3]One could also considered introducing a simple financial shock, in the form of an exogenous rise in money demand, but this would have minimal impacts on output in the absence of price rigidities.

on holding nominal bonds (B). Households decide the level of investment (I) in creating new capital each period, subject to a rate of depreciation (δ) and a quadratic adjustment cost (AC). Lump sum taxes fully fund government expenditures (G) each period.

More formally, household optimization for the home country may be written:

$$\max E_0 \sum_{t=0}^{\infty} \beta^t U\left(C_t, L_t, \frac{M_t}{P_t}\right)$$

subject to the budget constraint:

$$\begin{aligned} &P_t(C_t + I_t +_t G_t) \\ &\quad + (M_t - M_{t-1}) + B_t - (1 + i_{t-1})B_{t-1} = W_t L_t + P_t r_t K_{t-1} \end{aligned} \quad (1)$$

and law of motion for capital:

$$I_t = (K_t - (1 - \delta)K_{t-1}) + \mathrm{AC}_t \quad (2)$$

$$\mathrm{AC}_t = \frac{\xi}{2} \frac{(K_t - K_{t-1})^2}{K_{t-1}}, \quad (3)$$

where utility is defined by

$$U_t = \frac{\sigma}{\sigma - 1} C_t^{\frac{\sigma-1}{\sigma}} + \ln \frac{M_t}{P_t} - \frac{1}{1+\psi} L_t^{1+\psi}.$$

Optimization implies an intertemporal Euler equation:

$$1 = \beta(1 + i_t)E_t \left[\frac{P_t C_t^{\frac{1}{\sigma}}}{P_{t+1} C_{t+1}^{\frac{1}{\sigma}}}\right] \quad (4)$$

which indicates that households try to smooth marginal utility of consumption across time periods, unless a high interest rate convinces them to raise saving and postpone consumption to the future. For reference, we can define rr as a home-country *ex-ante* real interest rate, adjusting the nominal rate for expected inflation:

$$1 + rr_t = (1 + i_t)E_t\left[\frac{P_t}{P_{t+1}}\right].$$

Optimization also implies a labor-supply condition:

$$W_t = P_t C_t^{\frac{1}{\sigma}} L_t^{\psi} \tag{5}$$

which indicates that households equate the benefit of working more, in terms of marginal utility of extra consumption, to the marginal disutility of working.

A money demand condition:

$$M_t = P_t C_t^{\frac{1}{\sigma}}\left(\frac{1 + i_t}{i_t}\right) \tag{6}$$

indicates that households wish to hold more real money balances when consumption is high or the nominal interest rate is low.

An optimal capital accumulation decision:

$$\left(1 + \frac{\xi(K_t - K_{t-1})}{K_{t-1}}\right) = \beta E_t\left[\frac{P_t C_t^{\frac{1}{\sigma}}}{P_{t+1} C_{t+1}^{\frac{1}{\sigma}}}\left(r_t + (1 - \delta) + \left(\frac{1}{2}\xi\frac{K_{t+1}^2 - K_t^2}{K_t^2}\right)\right)\right] \tag{7}$$

indicates that households equate the benefit of more capital, in terms of the marginal utility of higher rental income less depreciation and lower future adjustment cost, to the cost of investment, including the current adjustment cost.

The foreign household has an analogous problem and optimality conditions.

3.2. *Firms*

Firms are perfectly competitive price takers. They hire labor and rent capital as inputs in production, with a multiplicative technology term (A) subject to exogenous shocks:

$$Y_t = A_t K_{t-1}^{\theta} L_t^{1-\theta}. \tag{8}$$

The objective of the firm is to maximize profits,

$$\pi_t(h) = P_H Y - W_t L_t - r_t K_{t-1},$$

where P_H is the producer price of home goods. This implies factor demands:

$$W_t = P_{H,t}(1-\theta) A_t K_{t-1}^{\theta} L_t^{-\theta} \tag{9}$$

$$r_t = P_{H,t} \theta A_t K_{t-1}^{\theta-1} L_t^{1-\theta}, \tag{10}$$

where firms hire workers and rent capital up to the point that the marginal cost of the factor equals the value of the marginal product of hiring an extra unit in terms of extra revenue from selling the additional output.

Foreign firm have an analogous problem and optimality conditions.

3.3. *Goods market structure*

Each of the components of final demand $D = \{C, I, G\}$ is an aggregate of the good produced in the home country and the good produced in the foreign country, with elasticity between home and foreign goods aggregates (ϕ), and a share ν indicating home bias:

$$D_t = \left(\nu^{\frac{1}{\phi}} (D_{H,t})^{\frac{\phi-1}{\phi}} + (1-\nu)^{\frac{1}{\phi}} (D_{F,t})^{\frac{\phi-1}{\phi}} \right)^{\frac{\phi}{\phi-1}}. \tag{11}$$

The corresponding price index is

$$P_t = \left(\nu (P_{H,t})^{1-\phi} + (1-\nu)(P_{F,t})^{1-\phi} \right)^{\frac{1}{1-\phi}}, \tag{12}$$

where P_F is the price of the imported foreign good. These definitions imply demand for a good that falls as its price relative to the average rises:

$$D_{H,t}/D_t = \nu (P_{H,t}/P_t)^{-\phi} \tag{13}$$

$$D_{F,t}/D_t = (1-\nu)(P_{F,t}/P_t)^{-\phi}. \tag{14}$$

For reference, define net exports as

$$NX_t = P_{H,t}(C_{H,t}^{*} + I_{H,t}^{*} + G_{H,t}^{*}) - P_{F,t}(C_{F,t} + I_{F,t} + G_{F,t}), \tag{15}$$

where * indicates foreign country variables.

3.4. *Market clearing and shock processes*

Market clearing for the home goods market requires

$$C_{H,t} + C^*_{H,t} + I_{H,t} + I^*_{H,t} + G_{H,t} + G^*_{H,t} = Y_t, \tag{16}$$

and for the home bond market:

$$B_t + B^*_t = 0. \tag{17}$$

The world supply of money is assumed constant and normalized:

$$M_t + M^*_t = 1. \tag{18}$$

The home balance of payments condition may be derived by combining the budget constraint of the home household and firms, with goods market clearing conditions:

$$NX_t + i_{t-1}B_{t-1} = (B_t - B_{t-1}) + (M_t - M_{t-1}). \tag{19}$$

This indicates that a country can finance a current account, which is the sum of net exports with asset income, by trading assets in the international asset market.

The shocks, to technology and government expenditure, will be log-normally distributed:

$$(\log A_t - \log \overline{A}) = \rho_A(\log \theta_{t-1} - \log \overline{A}) + \varepsilon_{At}$$
$$(\log A^*_t - \log \overline{A}^*) = \rho^*_A(\log \theta^*_{t-1} - \log \overline{A}^*) + \varepsilon^*_{At}$$
$$(\log G_t - \log \overline{G}) = \rho_G(\log G_{t-1} - \log \overline{G}) + \varepsilon_{Gt}$$
$$(\log G^*_t - \log \overline{G}^*) = \rho^*_G(\log G^*_{t-1} - \log \overline{G}^*) + \varepsilon^*_{Gt}$$
$$[\varepsilon_{At}, \varepsilon^*_{At}, \varepsilon_{Gt}, \varepsilon^*_{Gt}] \sim N(0, \Sigma).$$

3.5. *Simulation setup*

See Table 2 for values of parameters, generally taken from the business cycle literature. In particular, the intertemporal elasticity is set at $\sigma = 0.5$, and the intratemporal elasticity at $\phi = 1.5$, both values from Backus, Kehoe, and Kydland (1992). Shock processes are specified so there is no contemporaneous correlation across countries, or exogenous lagged spillovers. This specification is chosen simply to focus on the endogenous international transmission via goods and asset markets.

Table 2. Benchmark parameter values

Preferences	
Intertemporal elasticity	$\sigma = 0.5$
Elasticity of intratemporal substitution	$\phi = 1.5$
Time preference	$\beta = 0.99$
Labor-supply elasticity	$\psi = 0.5$
Home bias share	$\nu = 0.8$
Technology	
Capital share	$\theta = 0.3$
Investment adjustment cost	$\xi = 0.1$
Depreciation rate	$\delta = 0.025$
Shocks:	
$\rho_A = \rho_A^* = \rho_G = \rho_G^* = 0.9$	
$\sigma_A = \sigma_A^* = \sigma_G = \sigma_G^* = 0.00852$	

As is standard, the model is linearized around a determinist steady state, then simulated under a sequence of random draws from the shock processes. The artificial data thus generated are then HP-filtered and used to compute moments such as standard deviations and correlations.

4. Simulation Results

A series of simulations are conducted to investigate the international transmission of shocks. Special attention will be focused on the roles that international integration in goods and asset markets play, separately and in combination. The key lessons to emerge are as follows. First, it is not inevitable that international integration promotes greater positive comovement in the recessions of countries, since greater integration can lead to either positive or negative spillovers to a foreign country, depending on the type of shock and the characteristics of the economy. Second, both goods market and asset market integration contribute to international transmission, with asset markets tending to work primarily through the interest rate and goods market integration through the terms of trade. Goods market integration, on its own, can generate substantial international transmission of shocks, even in the absence of asset trade. Integration in asset markets alone, in isolation from goods trade, does not provide a transmission channel for the usual supply or demand shocks, but can provide a potent transmission channel for other types of shocks hitting the financial market of one of the countries.

4.1. *Integration in both goods and asset markets*

The first experiment considers productivity shocks in the benchmark model with both trade in goods and assets. Column (1) of Table 3 shows that the correlation of home and foreign GDP is negative, suggesting negative business cycle comovement. The negative cross-country correlation applies also to employment and investment, but not to consumption. Intuition can be gained from impulse responses to a shock raising home productivity 1%, reported in Fig. 6. The largest response is in investment, with a large rise at home and large fall abroad. We also see a rise in home output on impact and a negative movement in foreign output that is two orders of magnitude smaller. The fall in foreign output results from the fall in foreign labor inputs, and is compounded in later periods by the fall in capital inputs due to low investment. The shift in investment expenditure away from foreign toward home is reflected in a home trade deficit.

The logic is similar to that in Backus, Kehoe, and Kydland (1992), although our model tracks explicitly the asset trade, in terms of non-contingent one period bonds, rather than assuming a complete set of state-contingent securities operating in the background. The rise in home marginal product of capital raises the benefit of owning capital and stimulates significant investment. This rise in the demand for goods for investment expenditure beyond the rise in goods supply raises the real interest rate in both countries. This rise in interest rate enters the capital accumulation equation of the foreign country, discouraging investment abroad. The home country finances its additional investment expenditure by selling bonds to foreign, which finances a home trade deficit during the initial period of investment. In later periods, as the investment demand returns to normal, world demand falls below the supply of goods, and the trade deficit reverses to a surplus. This surplus is used to pay the interest on the bonds that have been accumulated by the foreign households. The drop in foreign labor input observed in Fig. 6 results in large part from the fact that foreign consumption rises along with home consumption, not shown in the figure, due to the improving foreign terms of trade. A rise in consumption induces a desire for more leisure, and in the absence of a

Table 3. Bu iness cycle moments from model simulations

	Both goods and asset trade			Only goods trade			Only asset trade		
	(1) Productivity shock, benchmark parameters	(2) Productivity shock, alternate parameters	(3) Government spending shock	(4) Productivity shock, benchmark parameters	(5) Productivity shock, alternate parameters	(6) Government spending shock	(7) Productivity shock, benchmark parameters	(8) Government spending shock	(9) Financial shock
Standard deviations:									
Output	0.0130	0.0132	0.0041	0.0125	0.0117	0.0048	0.0126	0.0052	0.0016
Employment	0.0028	0.0032	0.0059	0.0023	0.0035	0.0069	0.0026	0.0073	0.0023
Consumption	0.0027	0.0046	0.0062	0.0028	0.0036	0.0080	0.0032	0.0082	0.0002
Investment	0.0605	0.0557	0.0538	0.0445	0.0469	0.0729	0.0501	0.0681	0.0071
Net exports	0.0075	0.0129	0.0159	0.0000	0.0000	0.0000	—	—	—
Real interest rate	0.0004	0.0004	0.0003	0.0000	0.0000	0.0000	0.0042	0.0122	0.0005
Terms of trade	0.0070	0.0171	0.0960	0.0097	0.0634	0.0037	—	—	—
Correlations between home and foreign variables:									
Output	−0.0440	0.1107	0.4044	0.0290	0.4127	0.0542	0.0000	0.0000	0.4697
Employment	−0.1096	0.6181	0.36[illegible]7	0.2429	0.3756	0.0507	0.0000	0.0000	0.4697
Consumption	0.4306	−0.0799	0.5844	0.3095	0.5225	−0.0160	0.0000	0.0000	0.4711
Investment	−0.3139	−0.0282	0.6951	0.2650	0.3728	−0.0795	0.0000	0.0000	0.4694

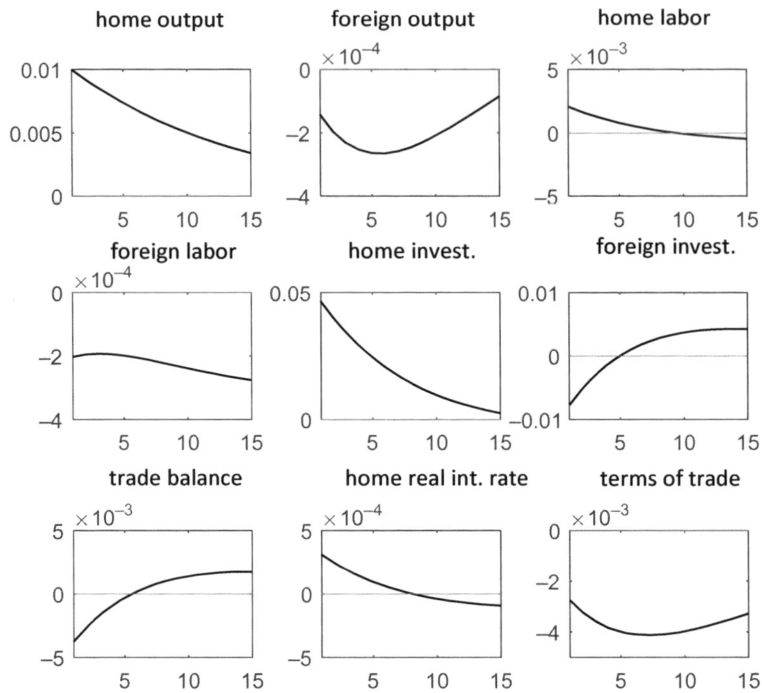

Figure 6. Impulse response to a positive home productivity shock in benchmark model

Note: Vertical axis is percent deviation (0.01 = 1%) from steady state levels. Horizontal axis is time (in quarters).

productivity shock raising the real wage, results in a fall in the quantity of labor supplied.

In sum, this simulation illustrates the lesson that international integration can transmit a productivity shock negatively via a rise in the real interest rate if the home investment response is large, reducing international comovement rather than raising it. Further we see that this effect involves trade of assets for goods, as observed in the balance of payments condition, as home exports bonds (fall in B_t) in order to finance a net import of goods (fall in NX_t) to use for investment purposes.

We next demonstrate that international integration can generate positive international comovement, depending in certain key characteristics of the goods market. In the benchmark model above, home and foreign goods were assumed to be substitutes for each other, with an elasticity of intratemporal substitution greater than unity ($\phi = 1.5$). But suppose now instead a case where home and foreign goods are complementary, with an intratemporal elasticity less than unity ($\phi = 0.5$). Change also the elasticity summarizing substitutability across time from a value greater than one in the benchmark case ($\sigma = 0.5$) to a value greater than unity ($\sigma = 1.5$). Importantly, this indicates that agents are more willing to substitute across time than across goods within a period.

Column (2) of Table 3 now shows that the cross-country correlations of output as well as labor are positive, indicating positive international comovement for productivity shocks. This is confirmed in Fig. 7, showing that a positive home productivity shock leads to a positive spillover on foreign output and labor. The fundamental logic is that when home output

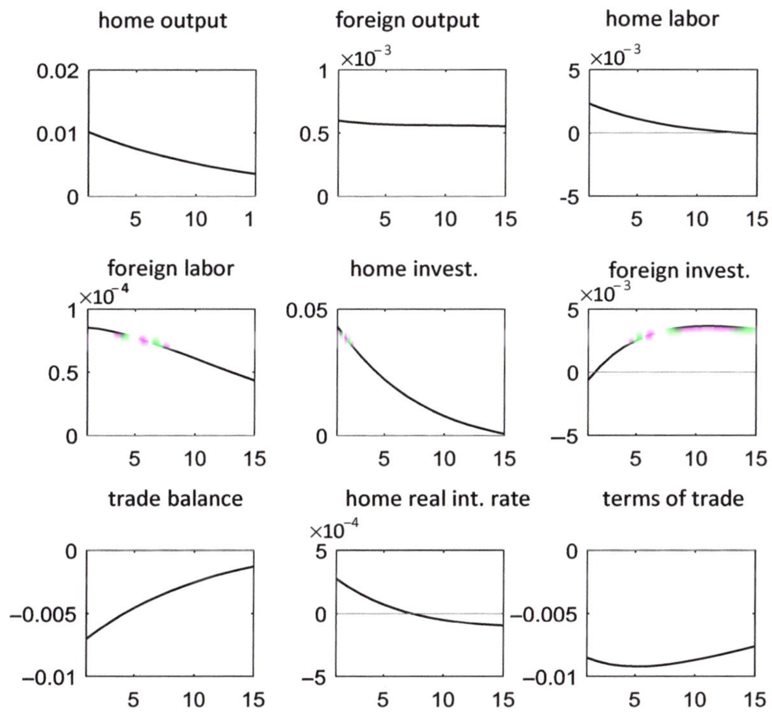

Figure 7. Impulse response to a positive home productivity shock in model with alternative parameter values

Note: Vertical axis is percent deviation ($0.01 = 1\%$) from steady state levels. Horizontal axis is time (in quarters).

rises, home goods are more useful in combination with foreign goods, so foreign production must also rise. Incidentally, this case is useful for suggesting a resolution to another puzzle in the international business cycle literature. Data suggest a lower cross-country correlation in consumption levels than for outputs, whereas the benchmark calibration implies the opposite. However, the case with alternative parameter values implies a negative consumption correlation at the same time as a positive output correlation. The logic is that if the home country needs foreign as well as home goods for its rise in investment expenditure, it imports more foreign goods, driving down foreign consumption. This is reflected in a larger home trade deficit than for the benchmark case.

The direction of comovement also depends on the nature of the shock. Column (3) in Table 3 reports moments for simulations involving shocks to government expenditure instead of productivity (for the original parameter settings).[4] The table shows a marked positive international comovement, with a correlation between home and foreign output of 0.40. Figure 8 shows the effect of a rise in home government expenditure, indicating a rise in output and employment in both countries. This illustrates the idea that, in contrast with supply shocks, demand shocks tend to generate large positive spillovers and substantial cross-country comovement in business cycles.

4.2. *Integration in goods market only*

Next isolate the role of goods market integration in transmitting shocks, by repeating the simulations above, but shutting down international asset trade. This takes the form of specifying that the net bond position of the home country is zero, and that each country has a separate money supply that his held constant and cannot be traded internationally. This also implies that a nominal exchange rate be introduced in the model to convert all foreign prices from foreign money units to home money units. The fact that no asset trade can be used to finance a trade imbalance implies that the balance of payment condition reduces to a requirement that net exports equal zero.

---

[4]The role of demand shocks in an international business cycle model first was demonstrated by Stockman and Tesar (1995) using taste shocks.

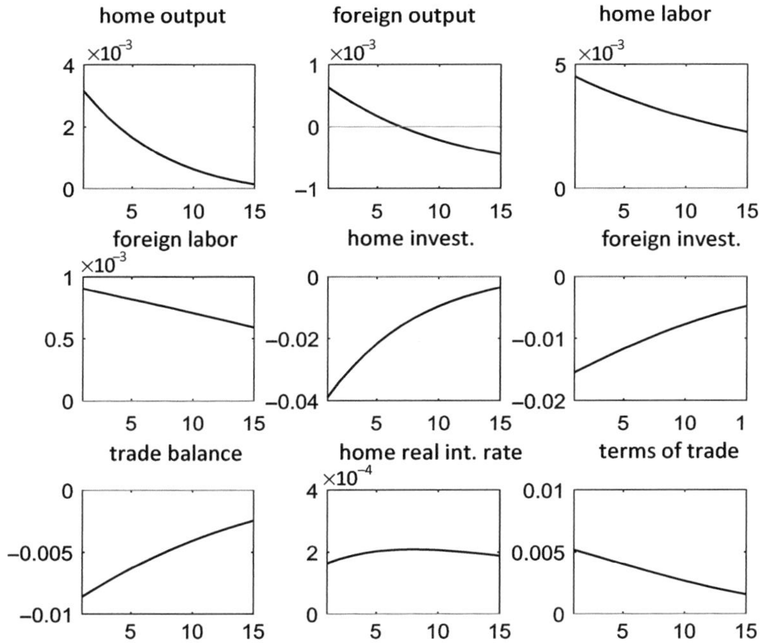

Figure 8. Impulse response to a positive home government expenditure shock

Note: Vertical axis is percent deviation (0.01 = 1%) from steady state levels. Horizontal axis is time (in quarters).

Shutting down the asset market has a significant effect on the transmission of a productivity shock. Column (4) of Table 3 shows that the output correlation switches sign relative to column (1), to become a small positive correlation. It no longer is possible for the home country to finance a large expansion of investment spending by borrowing abroad and forcing the foreign county to cut back on expenditure, since trade is now limited to be balanced period by period. As a result, home investment expenditure rises less than in the case with asset trade, and the foreign counterpart now rises rather than falls. While there is no longer transmission via asset trade and the associated interest rate, transmission is possible via the terms of trade, the relative price of home goods in terms of foreign goods. The rise in supply of home goods makes them relatively cheaper, which lowers the overall price index in the foreign country. This is equivalent to a rise in the real wage, which induces a rise in labor supply, and hence production. These effects are visible in the impulse responses shown in Fig. 9.

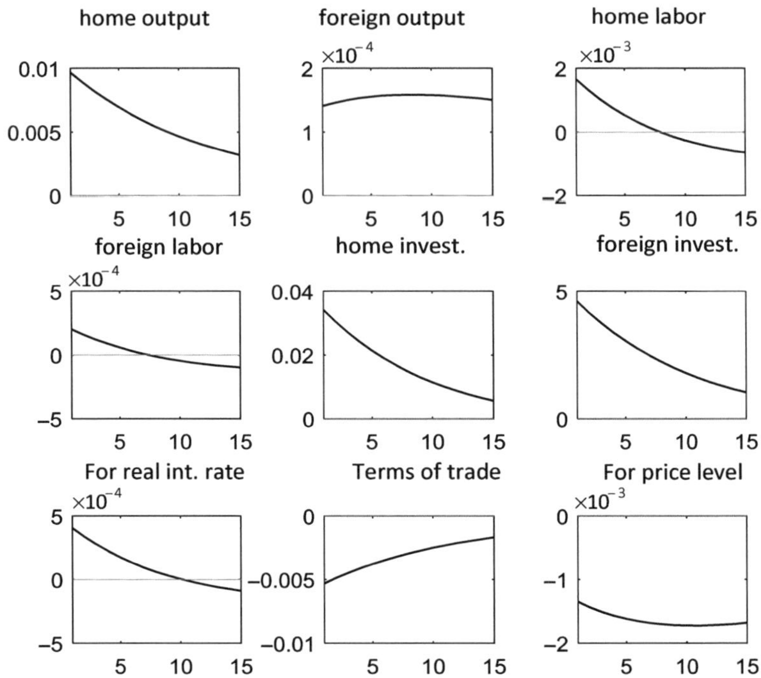

Figure 9. Impulse response to a positive home productivity shock, under no asset trade

Note: Vertical axis is percent deviation (0.01 = 1%) from steady state levels. Horizontal axis is time (in quarters).

In the case where home and foreign goods are complements, column (5) of the table show that the cross-country correlation rises even higher in the absence of asset trade than the level in column (2) in the case with asset trade. Impulse responses are qualitatively similar to those in Fig. 7 but with magnified values, and hence are not reported. The terms of trade improvement here is quite strong, leading to a very large fall in foreign price index. Again, this implies a rise in the foreign real wage, leading to a rise in labor supply and production.

Recall that the case of government demand shock, positive transmission relied upon the home country borrowing abroad and raising demand for foreign goods. This channel is shut down in the absence of the asset market. So it is not a surprise that the positive comovement in column (6) is much smaller than in column (3). Impulse responses are generally qualitatively similar to those in Fig. 8, and are not reported here.

4.3. *Integration in asset market only*

We finally investigate the role of asset market integration on its own, by repeating the simulations above, but shutting down all international goods trade. This takes the form of assuming households have preferences for only their domestic goods and no desire for imported goods, by setting the home bias parameter $\nu = 1$. With no trade in goods, the balance of payments condition indicates that bonds are traded only in exchange for money, that is, an international swap of one asset for another. So again it is not possible to run a trade deficit, because this would imply consumption of imported goods. In this setting neither the home productivity shock nor the government spending shock leads to any spillover to foreign output. Table 3 reports the zero comovement in columns (7) and (8). It appears that asset market integration in the absence of goods market integration does not support international transmission of the real shocks considered so far.

So we now extend the model to consider a financial market shock. Consider a simple example, a money demand shock that takes the form of a multiplication of the utility benefit of money, χ_t. Generalize the utility function to also specify an interest elasticity of money demand, μ:

$$U_t = \frac{\sigma}{\sigma - 1} C_t^{\frac{\sigma-1}{\sigma}} + \frac{\mu}{\mu - 1} \chi_t \left(\frac{M_t}{P_t} \right)^{\frac{\mu-1}{\mu}} - \frac{1}{1+\psi} L_t^{1+\psi}.$$

This implies a revised money demand condition:

$$M_t = P_t \chi_t^{\mu} C_t^{\frac{\mu}{\sigma}} \left(\frac{1+i_t}{i_t} \right)^{\mu}. \tag{20}$$

Further, in order to give nominal shocks potency over real variables, introduce a nominal rigidity in the form of a labor-supply condition that needs to preset the wage four quarters ahead of time based upon expectations for the future state of the economy.

$$W_t = E_{t-4} \left(P_t C_t^{\frac{1}{\sigma}} L_t^{\psi} \right). \tag{21}$$

Simulations reported in the last column of Table 3 show substantial positive comovement arising from money demand shocks. Intuition comes from Fig. 10, showing that when the home country experiences a shock raising demand for money balances, it acquires more by exchanging bonds

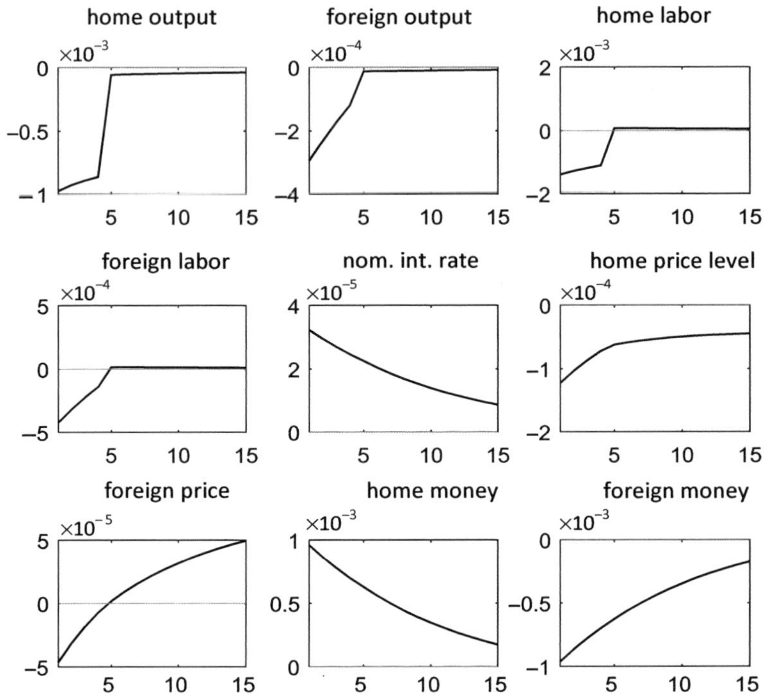

Figure 10. Impulse response to a positive home money preference shock, under no goods trade

Note: Vertical axis is percent deviation (0.01 = 1%) from steady state levels. Horizontal axis is time (in quarters).

for money with the foreign country. The shock is transmitted abroad in part via the rise in the interest rate, which helps lower foreign money demand and induce the foreign country to give up some of its money holdings to the home country. The shortfall of money supply relative to money demand in each of the counties leads to a drop in price levels. Given the predetermined nominal wages, this implies a rise in real wages in both countries, and hence a fall in labor demand and production. This process is an example where financial integration transmits a financial shock to generate strong international output comovement. While the money preference shock is a particularly simple version of a financial shock, it offers insight into the mechanisms by which the financial crisis in the Great Recession in the US could be transmitted so strongly to other countries.

5. Contributions of Chapters in This Volume

The main message of this study of business cycle comovement is that greater integration in goods and asset markets tends to imply more extensive transmission of business cycle shocks across borders. Globalization makes countries more interdependent in terms of macroeconomic cycles, and this may have implications for the conduct of domestic macroeconomic policies. But the experience of comovement can vary widely over time and among countries, depending on the nature of shocks and the characteristics of the economy. The Great Recession episode in the US is a recent example of how linkages in goods and financial markets can produce a truly global recession.

The chapters of this volume will revisit contributions to the literature addressing the fundamental questions raised above. The first section (Section I) addresses the question of when comovement is positive. Chapters 2 and 3 study the interesting case of Mexico, where US recessions seem to be transmitted with strong amplification. This positive comovement seems to be associated with the rise of offshoring production, and a theoretical model shows how this channel provides particularly potent transmission, whereby the effect of a US shock on Mexican employment in the offshoring sector can actually be larger in magnitude than the effect on employment in the corresponding sector in the US. While these two chapters were motivated by earlier episodes of recession, the lessons appear to apply well to the extensive transmission of the US Great Recession to Mexico. Among major trading partners, Mexico had the second highest correlation in GDP levels with the US during the Great Recession period.

Chapters 4 and 5 present among the earliest examples of modern business cycle models estimated econometrically as a structural dynamic system. Such models have since become widespread tools used by policy makers at central banks. The lessons arising from these chapters point to the importance of asset market shocks driving international financial flows. At the time, this stood in contrast to the view that financial flows were driven mainly by optimal saving and investment decisions. The empirical relevance of financial market shocks is a conclusion made all the more relevant by later experience with the financial crisis underlying the Great Recession.

Section II of this volume focuses on evidence of international integration in goods markets, which was seen above to be one prominent mechanism transmitting macroeconomic shocks. While one obvious metric of goods market integration is the quantity of goods traded, arguably a better metric is the degree of price convergence across national goods markets. If two countries function as a single market, arbitrage should enforce the convergence of prices across the two countries. Such arbitrage may not necessarily require a large volume of cross-border trade.

Chapters 6–8 of this volume offer explanations for several puzzling aspects of the deviation in overall price levels between countries, measured by the real exchange rate. Chapter 6 offers an explanation for the high persistence and volatility of real exchange rates, Chapter 7 for the fact that real exchange rates are more volatile than the corresponding relative price between a country's exports and nontraded goods, and Chapter 8 for why the association of real exchange rates with relative income between countries appeared to have strengthened over time. These chapters also contributed for some methodological innovations. Chapter 6 introduced the use of translog preferences to explain why firms choose different price markups in different countries, which is a tool that subsequently has become widespread in the international trade literature. Chapter 7 was one of the first two chapters to introduce endogenous tradability to the macroeconomic literature to explain international relative prices.

Chapter 9 differs in studying the international differences in prices of individual goods rather than the overall price level. Again harnessing the idea endogenous tradability, it shows that depending on whether goods market integration expands trade at the extensive margin of previously nontraded goods, integration can actually lead to greater average price deviations across countries rather than convergence.

Section III studies integration in asset markets, the other channel of international transmission demonstrated above. How has asset integration contributed to the development of unprecedentedly large global financial imbalances? Chapter 10 estimates when these imbalances can be justified in terms of rational economic behavior, suggesting they are not a problem for policy to solve. Chapter 11 discusses the role of equity rather than bond markets, providing an explanation for how one can reconcile extensive integration in terms of trading volume of equity assets, with a low degree of diversification in terms of asset holdings.

The final section (Section IV) explores policy implications of globalization and macroeconomic comovement, in terms of the conduct of a country's monetary and fiscal policies. Chapter 12 raises the question of how countries sharing a common currency need to coordinate their fiscal policies in light of their integrated monetary policy. While this chapter was written in 2000, when monetary union in Europe was viewed with significant optimism, the issues first raised here came to the fore in recent years as causes of disintegration and financial crisis in Europe. Chapter 13 shows theoretically under what conditions it is optimal for monetary policy in a global environment to formally respond to international variables such as the exchange rate. We identify cases where it is important for policy makers to take an international view, rather than focus just on domestic economic conditions. Chapter 14 finds evidence that countries often implicitly coordinate their monetary policies with other countries, regardless of an official stance of policy independence.

References

Alessandria, G., J. Kaboski, and V. Midrigan. 2010. The great trade collapse of 2008–09: An inventory adjustment? *IMF Economic Review*, 58: 254–294.

Arkolakis, C. and A. Ramanarayanan. 2009. Vertical specialization and international business cycle synchronization. *Scandinavian Journal of Economics*, 111: 655–680.

Backus, D. K., P. J. Kehoe, and F. E. Kydland. 1992. International real business cycles. *Journal of Political Economy*, 100: 745–775.

Burstein, A., J. Kurz, and L. Tesar. 2008. Trade, production sharing, and the international transmission of business cycles. *Journal of Monetary Economics*, 55: 775–795.

Eaton, J., S. Kortum, B. Neiman, and J. Romalis. 2016. Trade and the global recession. *American Economic Review*, 106: 3401–3438.

Engel, C. and J. Wang. 2011. International trade in durable goods: Understanding volatility, cyclicality, and elasticities. *Journal of International Economics*, 83: 37–52.

Heathcote, J. and F. Perri. 2002. Financial autarky and international business cycles. *Journal of Monetary Economics*, 49: 601–628.

Imbs, J. 2010. The first global recession in decades. *IMF Economic Review*, 58: 327–354.

Kalemli-Ozcan, S., E. Papaioannou, and J. L. Peydró. 2013. Financial regulation, financial globalization and the synchronization of economic activity. *Journal of Finance*, 68: 1179–1228.

Kose, A. M., C. Otrok, and E. Prasad. 2012. Global business cycles: Convergence or decoupling. *International Economic Review*, 53: 511–538.

Kose, M. A., E. S. Prasad, and M. E. Terrones. 2004. Volatility and co-movement in an integrated world economy: An exploration, in Siebert, H. (ed.) *Macroeconomic Policies in the World Economy*, Springer-Verlag, Berlin, pp. 89–122.

Kose, M. A. and K.-M. Yi. 2006. Can the standard real business cycle model explain the relation between trade and comovement? *Journal of International Economics*, 68: 267–295.

Perri, F. and V. Quadrini. 2016. International Recessions. Federal Reserve Bank of Minneapolis Working Paper.

Stockman, A. C. and L. L. Tesar. 1995. Tastes and technology in a two-country model of the business cycle: Explaining international comovements. *American Economic Review*, 85: 168–85.

Zlate, A. 2016. Offshore production and business cycle dynamics with heterogeneous firms. *Journal of International Economics*, 100: 34–49.

Section I
Business Cycles in a Global Context

CHAPTER 2

Offshoring and Volatility: Evidence from Mexico's Maquiladora Industry*

Paul R. Bergin,[†,§] Robert C. Feenstra[†,¶]
and Gordon H. Hanson[‡,||]

[†] *Department of Economics, University of California at Davis, One Shields Ave., Davis, CA 95616, USA*

[‡] *University of California, San Diego, 9500 Gilman Dr., MC: 0519 La Jolla, CA 92093-0519, USA*

[§] *prbergin@ucdavis.edu*

[¶] *rcfeenstra@ucdavis.edu*

[||] *gohanson@ucsd.edu*

This chapter addresses the question of what promotes international macroeconomic spillovers by studying the particular case of Mexico, where recessions arising in the US seem to be transmitted with amplification. This particularly strong positive comovement is associated with the rise of offshoring production, the arrangement whereby firms carry out particular stages of production abroad. Comparing employment in the offshoring sectors across countries, shocks arising in the US generate fluctuations in Mexico twice as large as in the US.

Offshoring has grown over time to become an important part of the trade relationship between the US and Mexico. It is also of growing

*This article originally appeared in *American Economic Review* (2009), 99(4), 1664–1671.

importance for trade between the EU and emerging economies in Europe, and in global trade with China. In Mexico, employment in export-assembly plants engaged in production for foreign firms grew 10-fold from 0.12 million in 1980 to 1.2 million in 2006. The sector accounts for just under 3% of Mexico's total GDP, 20% of Mexican manufacturing value-added, and nearly half of the country's exports. While Mexican officials have hailed the export-assembly plants for their contribution to economic growth, some have also complained that the sector is fickle and subject to excessive volatility.[1] The assembly plants, known as *maquiladoras*, are seen as a channel by which the US exports to Mexico a portion of its employment fluctuations over the business cycle. This phenomenon is beginning to be investigated in the literature on real business cycles across countries. This chapter is unique in focusing on the maquiladora sector and on cross-country comparisons of volatility.[2]

We begin by documenting the variance in offshoring industries in Mexico. These industries are composed of maquiladoras which US and other foreign firms use to assemble inputs into final outputs. The data cover Mexico's four largest offshoring industries, which together account for three quarters of maquiladora production in the country: apparel, transportation equipment, computers and electronics, and electrical machinery. We match these industries to their counterparts in the United States. The main empirical result is that in all four maquiladora industries the volatility of economic activity in Mexico is significantly higher than in the US; averaging over the four industries, volatility in Mexico is twice as high as in the US.

One might suspect that this finding simply reflects higher volatility in the overall Mexican economy. That conjecture is not true for employment

[1]See for example the news account of how the Mexican car industry is highly susceptible to fluctuations in demand for American brand automobiles in Dickerson (2005).

[2]Burstein, Kurz, and Tesar (2008) study the implications of multinational production for international macroeconomic comovement; as such, their focus is on covariances across countries, rather than on comparing variances, which is our focus. For other work on intermediate inputs and business cycle synchronization, see Kose and Kei-Mu Yi (2001, 2006) and Ambler, Cardia, and Zimmerman (2002). See also Thesmar and Thoenig (2007) on vertical separation and employment and sales volatility in French firms.

volatility, which is lower in Mexico. A second conjecture might be that higher volatility in Mexico reflects the smaller size of industries in Mexico. However, our results are robust to comparing Mexican industries with the more similarly sized industries of US border states.[3]

Finally we decompose this effect into its extensive and intensive margins, where the extensive margin is measured using data on the number of plants operating each month in the maquiladora sector, and the intensive margin is measured using data on average employment per plant. Volatility is present along both of these margins.

Section 1 of this chapter describes relevant background of the maquiladora sector. Section 2 presents the main results characterizing employment volatility. Section 3 decomposes the effect into intensive and extensive margins, and Section 4 concludes.

1. The Maquiladora Sector

Offshoring by the US to Mexico generally takes the form of US firms producing parts and components, exporting these intermediate inputs to Mexico to be assembled or processed into final goods, and re-importing the finished products. US firms tend to specialize in R&D, component production, marketing, and other headquarters activities, while Mexican

[3]A third conjecture might be that labor-market institutions differ between the countries, such that it is easier to hire and fire employees in Mexico. However, when Botero *et al.* (2004) rank countries in terms of job security laws restricting the hiring and firing of workers, Mexico ties for the most regulated among the 85 countries in the sample, whereas the US ranks as the fifth least regulated economy in this respect; these data are used in the analysis of volatility and comparative advantage by Cunat and Melitz (2007). We also see this contrast in labor market flexibility reflected in our employment data discussed below, in which volatility of employment in overall Mexican manufacturing is lower than that for US overall manufacturing. In Mexico, labor unions are active in maquiladoras and other manufacturing establishments, both of which are subject to Mexican labor law (Otero and Pagan, 2002). In practice, collective bargaining agreements in maquiladoras are seen as less restrictive than in the rest of Mexican manufacturing, in that job classifications tend to be wider and firms tend to have greater leeway in establishing pay-for-performance schemes (Fairris, 2003). At the same time, the decline in unionization in Mexican manufacturing, which has been ongoing since the 1980s, is less evident among maquiladoras. The net effect of more flexible collective bargaining agreements but more stable union presence appears to be that differences in labor relations between maquiladoras and other Mexican manufacturing firms are relatively small.

plants — the maquiladoras — tend to specialize in assembly services.[4] Mexico is among the most important locations for offshoring by US firms and the US is by far and away Mexico's largest trading partner. Over the period 2000–2003, the United States was the source country for 73.4% of the inputs imported by maquiladoras in Mexico and maquiladora exports back to the United States were equal to 5.3% of US industry shipments (US International Trade Commission, 2005).[5] Maquiladoras have become an integral part of the Mexican economy, with their share of national manufacturing employment rising from 4.1% in 1980 to 24.5% in 2004 (Hanson, 2007).

Mexico first began to allow export-assembly plants to operate in the country in the 1960s. The maquiladora sector did not reach an appreciable size until the government relaxed restrictions on inbound foreign investment in the 1980s. Initially, US firms offshoring to Mexico received favorable tariff treatment under the HS9802 provision of the US tariff code (Feenstra, Hanson, and Swenson, 2000). Under HS9802, US firms that manufacture components at home and have them processed into final goods abroad pay duties on the foreign value-added only when the goods are brought back into the United States. The North American Free

[4]The Mexican government measures imports and exports by registered export-assembly plants in Mexico. Under Mexican trade policy, firms that export their output do not have to pay duties on any imported intermediate inputs used in production. To obtain duty-free status, a firm must register with the government. While under the North American Free Trade Agreement, imports from the United States are not subject to duties in Mexico but imports from most other countries are. As a result, the vast majority of export-assembly plants in Mexico are registered. (Strictly speaking, export-assembly plants in Mexico may be registered either as maquiladoras or as PITEX (Program for Temporary Imports of Articles to be Exported) companies (see http://www.economia.gob.mx/). Only the former appear in our data. In 2003, maquiladora exports to the United States were 2.2 times those by PITEX companies.)

[5]These figures apply to the four core offshoring industries, described in the text. Comparing US imports from Mexico to US industry output may give a deceptive sense of the size of Mexico's maquiladora sector relative to US manufacturing. US imports from Mexico include a substantial component of US value-added, in the form of the intermediate inputs produced in the United States and sent to Mexico for further processing. As an alternative measure of relative size, one might examine value-added in the two countries. Over the period 2000–2003, the ratio of value-added in Mexico's maquiladoras to value-added in US manufacturing was 0.034 in the four core offshoring industries, based on annual data (US International Trade Commission, 2005).

Trade Agreement (NAFTA) ended special tariff treatment for US firms offshoring to Mexico. But it did not slow growth in production sharing. Growth in real value added by maquiladoras accelerated after NAFTA was implemented, roughly tripling between 1994 and 2005. Far from removing the incentive for Mexico to specialize in assembly services, NAFTA freed resources that Mexico had devoted to domestic production to move into export assembly.

Most offshore production by US firms in Mexico occurs in one of the four industries: apparel, electronic accessories (including computer parts and electronic circuitry), electrical machinery (including televisions and other small domestic appliances), and transport equipment and parts (primarily motor vehicles). Over 1990 to 2005, these four industries accounted for three quarters of employment in the maquiladora sector. These industries are amenable to global production sharing because firms need not perform all stages — R&D, component production, final assembly — in the same location, and the stages vary in their factor intensities, giving multinational firms an incentive to locate labor-intensive activities in low-wage countries.

2. Volatility in Employment

As a measure of volatility, we shall focus on the relative variance of employment in US manufacturing industries and the plants to which they offshore production in Mexico.[6] This variance is computed using the monthly employment of production workers, which is available for both countries. We match Mexico's four primary maquiladora industries (assembly of apparel items; electronic materials and accessories, including computer parts; assembly of electrical machinery and equipment; and construction and assembly of transport equipment and parts) with their closest US three-digit industry matches (apparel manufacturing, NAICS 315; computer and electronic product manufacturing, NAICS 334; electrical equipment, appliance, and component manufacturing, NAICS 335; and transportation equipment manufacturing, NAICS 336). Data are

---

[6]In results available on request, we have confirmed that similar findings obtain when using the wage bill for production workers instead of employment.

available beginning in 1993.[7] However, in late 1994, there was a large depreciation of the peso, as capital fled Mexico, and in 1995 aggregate output dropped sharply. Given the exposure of the maquiladora sector to exchange rate fluctuations, including the peso crisis years in our sample could make volatility in Mexico's maquiladora industries seem artificially high. To avoid this problem, the analysis is limited to the period 1996–2005.

To provide a visual sense of the relative variation in industrial activity in the two countries, Fig. 1 plots the production worker employment for the four core maquiladora industries over the sample period. To remove seasonal fluctuations and time trends, each series is seasonally adjusted and HP-filtered (with smoothing parameter 14,400). In each industry, employment in Mexico is substantially more volatile than in the United States. Table 1, which shows the ratio of the standard deviations for the production worker employment in Mexican and US industries, reinforces this perception. In each industry, the standard deviation of Mexican employment is greater than in the United States, with the Mexico–US ratio averaging 2.2 over the four industries.

One simple reason that employment in Mexican industries could be more volatile than their US counterparts is because at an aggregate level the Mexican economy is also more volatile than the US economy. That reasoning does not apply for employment, however, since as shown in Table 1, employment of production workers in all manufacturing in Mexico has a *lower* monthly standard deviation than in the United States.[8] This may reflect the finding in Botero *et al.* (2004) that Mexico has more restrictive laws regarding employment security (see footnote 3).

A second reason for volatility to be higher in the Mexican maquiladora industries is that they are smaller than the US industries, so with idiosyncratic shocks across plants, US employment may be smoothing out shocks. To investigate the size differences between the Mexican and US industries,

[7]Data for Mexico's maquiladora industries go back to 1990. However, data on Mexico's overall manufacturing sector is only available from 1993 forward, owing to a change in the construction of the series in that year.

[8]This conjecture does hold for the wage bill, but the extra volatility found in the wage bill for Mexican maquiladora industries exceeds that found in Mexican manufacturing. The ratio of the wage bill in Mexico to that in the US is 2.0 for offshoring industries and 1.5 for manufacturing overall.

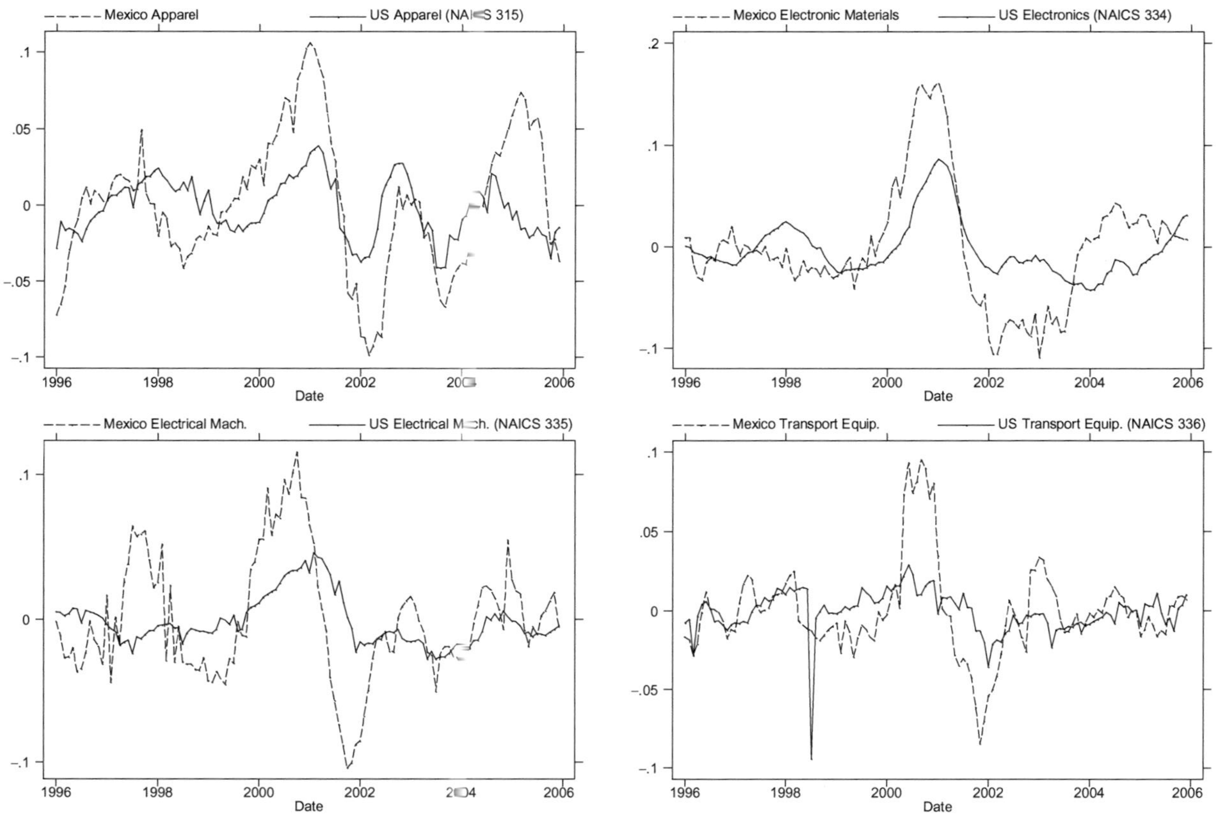

Figure 1. Employment for production workers in Mexico and US offshoring industries (log values, seasonally adjusted and HP-filtered)

Table 1. Relative volatility in Mexico and US offshoring industries: Production worker employment

	Apparel	Electrical machinery	Computer & electronics	Transport equipment	Average
Standard deviations, employment (%)					
$\sigma(L_i^*)$ (Mex. industry)	4.52	4.34	5.95	2.96	4.44
$\sigma(L_i)$ (US industry)	1.89	1.79	3.06	1.42	2.04
$\sigma(L^*)$ (Mex. aggregate manufacturing)	0.89	0.89	0.89	0.89	0.89
$\sigma(L)$ (US aggregate manufacturing)	1.15	1.15	1.15	1.15	1.15
$\sigma(L_i^*)/\sigma(L_i)$	2.39	2.42	1.94	2.08	2.21
$\sigma(L^*)/\sigma(L)$	0.77	0.77	0.77	0.77	0.77
Correlations, employment					
$\text{corr}(L_i^*, L_i)$	0.49	0.43	0.66	0.45	0.51
$\text{corr}(L^*, L)$	0.78	0.78	0.78	0.78	0.78
$\text{corr}(L_i^*, L^*)$	0.56	0.71	0.62	0.68	0.64
$\text{corr}(L_i, L)$	0.66	0.86	0.88	0.63	0.76

Notes: The top portion of the table shows standard deviations (in %) for the production worker employment in specific Mexico and US offshoring industries, and in Mexico and US aggregate manufacturing, and the ratios of these standard deviations. Each series is in log values, seasonally adjusted, and HP-filtered. Data are monthly from 1996 through 2005. The bottom portion of the table shows correlations between the various employment series.

Table 2 reports employment in each industry, showing that in two of the four industries the US is indeed much larger. We can deal with these size disparities by reducing the geographic coverage of the US series. The vast majority of maquiladoras in Mexico are located in Mexican border cities and many are linked to production operations on the US side of the border (Feenstra, Hanson, and Swenson, 2000). This makes US border states a natural geographic unit in comparison with Mexican maquiladora industries.

In Tables 2 and 3, we compare Mexican industries to their counterparts in California and Texas, the two US border states for which industry data are available.[9] At the state level, the only series available for three-digit

[9]The small number of plants in three-digit manufacturing industries in Arizona and New Mexico makes industry-level data for these states subject to disclosure restrictions.

Table 2. Size of offshoring industries in Mexico and the US

NAICS	Industry	Thousands of employees (mean 2000–2005)			
		Mexico	US	Texas	California
	All maquiladoras (Mexico)	1,151.00	—	—	—
	All manufacturing (United States)	—	15,336.70	955.5	1,649.00
315	Apparel	230.8	356.9	—	97.4
334	Computer and electronics	265.6	1,512.30	132.9	366.6
335	Electrical machinery	100.2	497.5	20.0	38.5
336	Transport equipment	240.7	1,855.80	85.2	137.5

Source: US Bureau of Economic Analysis, Regional Economic Information System, https://www.bea.gov/regional/; Mexico's National Institute for Statistics, Geography, and Informatics (INEGI), https://www.bea.gov/regional/.

industries is *total* employment, including production and nonproduction workers. Table 2 shows that employment in industries in California and Texas is similar in scale to Mexican industries. Table 3 shows that standard deviations and their ratios based on state employment data are broadly similar to those obtained for national data: the four offshoring industries are at least 75% more volatile in Mexico than in California, and 66% more volatile than in Texas, whereas overall Mexican manufacturing employment is less volatile than in either state. We conclude that regardless of the comparison case, the maquiladoras have substantially greater volatility than their corresponding industries in the US, or than overall manufacturing.

3. Volatility in the Extensive Margin

We next investigate how volatility in maquiladora employment is allocated between the intensive and extensive margins. The greater relative volatility in employment in Mexico's maquiladora industries could be due to changes in scale in existing plants or to plants entering and existing production. We use data on the number of plants operating each month in the maquiladora sector and the average employment per plant. Research on exporting plants in other countries has found that the sunk costs of becoming an exporter are quite high, with much smaller continuation costs of exporting. For example, Das, Roberts, and Tybout (2007) estimate that the sunk costs of becoming

Table 3. Relative volatility in Mexico and US offshoring industries: Total employment at the US state level

	Apparel	Electrical machinery	Computer and electronics	Transport equipment	Average
National level					
$\sigma(L_i^*)$ (Mex. industry)	4.48	4.11	5.50	2.73	4.21
$\sigma(L_i)$ (US industry)	1.63	1.52	2.47	1.07	1.67
$\sigma(L^*)$ (Mex. aggregate manufacturing)	0.77	0.77	0.77	0.77	0.77
$\sigma(L)$ (US aggregate manufacturing)	1.01	1.01	1.01	1.01	1.01
$\sigma(L_i^*)/\sigma(L_i)$	2.75	2.70	2.23	2.55	2.56
$\sigma(L^*)/\sigma(L)$	0.76	0.76	0.76	0.76	0.76
California					
$\sigma(L_i^*)$ (Mex. industry)	4.48	4.11	5.50	2.73	4.21
$\sigma(L_i)$ (US industry)	2.25	2.35	2.62	1.31	2.13
$\sigma(L^*)$ (Mex. aggregate manufacturing)	0.77	0.77	0.77	0.77	0.77
$\sigma(L)$ (US aggregate manufacturing)	1.40	1.40	1.40	1.40	1.40
$\sigma(L_i^*)/\sigma(L_i)$	1.99	1.75	2.10	2.08	1.98
$\sigma(L^*)/\sigma(L)$	0.55	0.55	0.55	0.55	0.55
Texas					
$\sigma(L_i^*)$ (Mex. industry)	4.48	4.11	5.50	2.73	3.09
$\sigma(L_i)$ (US industry)	n.a.	2.48	3.12	1.66	2.42
$\sigma(L^*)$ (Mex. aggregate manufacturing)	0.77	0.77	0.77	0.77	0.77
$\sigma(L)$ (US aggregate manufacturing)	1.16	1.16	1.16	1.16	1.16
$\sigma(L_i^*)/\sigma(L_i)$	n.a.	1.66	1.76	1.64	1.69
$\sigma(L^*)/\sigma(L)$	n.a.	0.66	0.66	0.66	0.66

Notes: The table follows the same format as the top portion of Table 1, but uses total employment rather than production worker employment. n.a. indicates this industry is not available for that state.

an exporter for Colombian plants are on the order of $1 million, or between 20% and 40% of the annual export value (with continuation costs around 1%). Those values suggest that movement in and out of exporting status would operate in a lumpy fashion, and only in response to large shocks. Our data on the maquiladora plants differs from other country samples in that *all* of these plants are involved in export assembly for foreign firms, so plant entry and exit is the same as the exporting decision.

The monthly standard deviation in the number of plants (logged, deseasonalized, and HP-filtered) ranges between 2.1% for electrical machinery and 5.2% for apparel, with an average of 3.1% over the four industries. That variation is about two-thirds as much as the monthly standard deviation in employment, and there is a positive correlation between the number of plants and employment. We can evaluate the relationship between aggregate employment and the number of plants more formally along the lines of Eaton, Kortum, and Kramarz (2004), using the identity:

$$N_{it} \times \frac{E_{it}}{N_{it}} \equiv \frac{E_{it}}{E_t} \times E_t, \tag{1}$$

where E_{it} is employment in industry i at time t, N_{it} is the number of plants in industry i at t, and E_t is aggregate employment in Mexico at t. From this identity, we specify two regression equations:

$$\ln N_{it} = \alpha_0 + \alpha_1 \ln \frac{E_{it}}{E_t} + \alpha_2 E_t + \varepsilon_{it} \tag{2}$$

and

$$\ln \frac{E_{it}}{N_{it}} = \beta_0 + \beta_1 \ln \frac{E_{it}}{E_t} + \beta_2 E_t + \varepsilon_{it}. \tag{3}$$

By the logic of least squares, $\alpha_0 + \beta_0 = 0$, $\alpha_1 + \beta_1 = 1$ and $\alpha_2 + \beta_2 = 1$. The relative magnitude of the coefficients identifies how aggregate shocks affect the number of plants (the extensive margin) and employment per plant (the intensive margin).

Table 4 reports results for this decomposition exercise. All series have been deseasonalized and HP-filtered and data are pooled across the four offshoring industries. Controls for industry fixed effects are included in the estimation. In column (1), the estimate for α_1 is 0.38 and for α_2 is 0.49, where both are statistically significant. In response to an increase, the share of aggregate employment in an offshoring industry (holding aggregate employment constant) over one-third of adjustment in industry employment occurs at the extensive margin, and in response to an increase in aggregate employment (holding the industry employment share constant)

Table 4. Adjustment in the Maquiladora industry: Extensive margins

	Number of plants (1)	Employment per plant (2)
Industry share of aggregate employment	0.376 (0.163)	0.624 (0.163)
Aggregate employment	0.494 (0.052)	0.506 (0.052)
R^2	0.303	0.513
N	480	480

Notes: Columns (1) and (2) show regressions of either the number of plants or employment per plant on total Mexican manufacturing employment and the industry share of manufacturing employment. The sample is the four maquiladora industries in Mexico, with data at a monthly frequency from 1996:1 to 2005:12. Regressions include controls for industry fixed effects, which are not shown. Standard errors (clustered by industry) are in parentheses.

nearly one-half of adjustment in industry employment occurs at the extensive margin.

4. Conclusion

Global production sharing is responsible for a substantial portion of world trade and is the primary means through which many developing countries engage in international commerce. While the expansion of export assembly operations have led to impressive rates of employment growth in China, Eastern Europe, Mexico, and elsewhere, the implications of global production sharing for the volatility of economic activity has only recently attracted scholarly attention.

In the case of Mexico, we document that the country's maquiladora industries experience fluctuations in economic activity that are twice as volatile as the corresponding industries in the US. These fluctuations are not simply byproducts of higher volatility in the overall Mexican economy, nor are they the product of the smaller size of the Mexican industries compared to their US counterparts. We also document that adjustments in the extensive margin account for one-third to one-half of this employment volatility.

The robust empirical regularity that this chapter identifies indicates that offshoring has implications for recipient economies not previously considered. Further, this finding presents a new fact useful for guiding and evaluating theoretical research on offshoring.

Acknowledgment

We thank Thomas Chaney, Fabio Ghironi and seminar participants at the NBER Summer Institute 2007, ASSA 2007 meetings in Chicago, UC San Diego, Carnegie Mellon University, Princeton University, University of Colorado, University of Paris, University of Southern California, and the International Monetary Fund for helpful comments. Financial support was provided by the National Science Foundation grant SES-031769.

References

Ambler, S., E. Cardia, and C. Zimmerman. 2002. International transmission of the business cycle in a multi-sectoral model. *European Economic Review*, 46(2): 273–300.

Botero, J. C., S. Djankov, R. L. Porta, F. L. de Silanes, and A. Schleifer. 2004. The regulation of labor. *Quarterly Journal of Economics*, 119(4): 1339–1382.

Burstein, A., J. Kurz, and L. Tesar. 2008. Trade, production sharing, and the international transmission of business cycles. *Journal of Monetary Economics*, 55(4): 775–795.

Cunat, A. and M. J. Melitz. 2007. Volatility, labour market flexibility, and the pattern of comparative advantage. NBER Working Paper 13062.

Das, S., M. J. Roberts, and J. R. Tybout. 2007. Market entry costs, producer heterogeneity, and export dynamics. *Econometrica*, 75(3): 837–873.

Dickerson, M. 2005. Big 3's woes migrate: Mexico's dependence on assembling cars for U.S. automakers puts pressure on its economy as Detroit loses market share to foreign competitors. *Los Angeles times Business Section*, 21: 1.

Eaton, J., S. Kortum, and F. Kramarz. 2004. Dissecting trade: Firms, industries, and export destinations. *American Economic Review*, 94(2): 150–154.

Fairris, D. 2003. Unions and wage inequality in Mexico. *Industrial and Labor Relations Review*, 56(3): 481–497.

Feenstra, R. C., G. H. Hanson, and D. Swenson. 2000. Offshore assembly from the United States: Production characteristics of the 9802 program. In *The Impact of International Trade on Wages*, ed. Robert C. Feenstra, ed., Chicago: University of Chicago Press and the National Bureau of Economic Research, pp. 85–128.

Hanson, G. H. 2007. Globalization, labor income, and poverty in Mexico. In *Globalization and Poverty*, ed. Ann Harrison, Chicago: University of Chicago Press and the National Bureau of Economic Research, pp. 417–456.

Kose, M. A. and Kei-Mu Yi. 2001. International trade and business cycles: Is vertical specialization the missing link? *American Economic Review*, 91(2): 371–375.

Kose, M. A. and Kei-Mu Yi. 2006. Can the standard real business cycle model explain the relation between trade and comovement? *Journal of International Economics*, 68(2): 267–295.

Otero, R. and J. A. Pagan. 2002. Unions and job queuing in Mexico's maquiladoras. *Eastern Economic Journal*, 28(3): 393–407.

Thesmar, D. and M. Thoenig. 2007. From flexibility to insecurity: How vertical separation amplifies firm-level uncertainty. *Journal of the European Economic Association*, 5(6): 1161–1202.

U.S. International Trade Commission. 2005. *Industry Trade and Technology Review*, USITC Publication 3762, December/January.

CHAPTER 3

Volatility Due to Offshoring: Theory and Evidence*

Paul R. Bergin,[†,§] Robert C. Feenstra[†,¶]
and Gordon H. Hanson[‡,‖]

[†] *Department of Economics, University of California at Davis, One Shields Ave., Davis, CA 95616, USA*

[‡] *University of California, San Diego, 9500 Gilman Dr., MC: 0519 La Jolla, CA 92093-0519, USA*

[§] *prbergin@ucdavis.edu*

[‖] *gohanson@ucsd.edu*

[¶] *rcfeenstra@ucdavis.edu*

1. Introduction

This chapter develops a theoretical explanation for the empirical finding in the preceding chapter, which showed that offshoring production transmits business cycle shocks from high wage countries like the US to low-wage countries like Mexico, with an amplified effect on employment in the low-wage country.

International trade is being transformed by offshoring, the arrangement whereby firms contract to carry out particular stages of production abroad. US, European, and Japanese firms that conduct product design and the production of sophisticated components at home use factories in Asia, Eastern Europe, and Latin America to assemble inputs into final outputs for

*This article originally appeared in *Journal of International Economics* (2011), 85, 163–173.

delivery to consumers. Offshoring is common, especially, in apparel, auto parts, electronics, and machinery, which are industries whose production stages are physically separable (such that they can be performed in different locations) and differ sharply in their factor intensities (such that fragmenting production across borders is attractive). A substantial portion of the recent growth in global trade is tied to offshoring (Hummels, Ishii, and Yi, 2001). The literature on global production sharing is expanding rapidly, with recent work examining which firms choose to engage in offshoring (Antras and Helpman, 2004), how global production sharing affects the relative demand for skilled labor (Feenstra and Hanson, 1999; Ebenstein, *et al.*, 2010) and the productivity of domestic factors (Grossman and Rossi-Hansberg, 2008), and the expansion of offshoring into services (Amiti and Wei, 2006).[1]

One consequence of global production sharing that has received relatively little attention is the effect of offshoring on the volatility of production. As US firms have expanded the number of export-assembly plants in Mexico, for instance, Mexican industry has become more tied to the US economy. This outcome is consistent with Burstein, Kurz, and Tesar (2008), who develop a real business cycle model in which global production sharing leads trading economies to have more synchronized business cycles.[2] A distinct and important feature of offshoring is excess volatility in the low-wage trading partner. Mexico's maquiladoras, as its assembly plants are known, exhibit swings in activity that are more exaggerated than in the United States.[3] Employment in Mexican maquiladoras that produce

---

[1]The papers listed are a subset of a much larger body of work. See Feenstra (2009) for a discussion of the literature.

[2]In related work, Zlate (2008) develops a dynamic model to study the effects of offshoring on international business cycle correlations and real exchange rate dynamics. Other work on intermediate inputs and business cycle synchronization include Kose and Yi (2001, 2006) and Ambler, Cardia, and Zimmerman (2002).

[3]We measure US production sharing in Mexico using data on maquiladoras. These export-assembly plants capture a large share of US offshoring to Mexico. However, Burstein, Kurz, and Tesar (2008), using BEA data on the foreign-owned affiliates of US multinationals, document that US offshoring to Mexico involves non-maquiladora establishments, as well. US firms license technology, subcontract production, and share distribution networks with a range of Mexican businesses. Three features make the maquiladora data, rather than BEA multinational data or other sources, suitable for our purposes. First, as explained by Burstein, Kurz, and Tesar (2008), the intensity of production sharing (measured as the share

auto parts declined by 13.8% in the 2001 recession, after expanding by 88.4% in the 1991–2001 expansion. US employment in auto parts, in contrast, contracted by only 9.9% in 2001, after 33.9% growth from 1991 to 2001. Bergin, Feenstra, and Hanson (2009) document that maquiladora industries in Mexico associated with US offshoring have fluctuations in employment that are twice as volatile as the corresponding industries in the US, a finding based on matching Mexico's four largest offshoring industries (apparel, transportation equipment, computers and electronics, and electrical machinery) to their US counterparts at the three digit level.[4] The pattern of greater relative volatility in Mexico appears also to be present in the most recent recession starting in late 2007. Comin *et al.* (2009) document that while the Mexican recession started subsequently to that in the US, it was significantly more severe, with a drop in output more than three times that in the US.

Why would outsourcing industries in Mexico have higher volatility than their US counterparts? One conjecture is that high volatility in Mexican maquiladoras simply reflects higher volatility in the overall Mexican economy. However, employment volatility for aggregate manufacturing in Mexico is actually lower than in the US (Bergin, Feenstra, and Hanson, 2009). A second conjecture is that labor-market institutions differ between the countries, such that it is easier to hire and fire employees in Mexico. Yet, when Botero *et al.* (2004) rank countries in terms of job security laws restricting the hiring and firing of workers, Mexico ties for the most regulated among the 85 countries in the sample, whereas the US ranks as the

---

of exports to the US in establishment total sales) is much higher in maquiladoras (90%) than in non-maquiladoras (21%). Second, Bureau of Economic Analysis (BEA) data are limited to affiliates in Mexico owned by US multinationals, whereas our maquiladora data include both US owned affiliates and arms-length suppliers to US firms. Third, maquiladora data are available at a monthly frequency, permitting us to examine the business cycle characteristics of offshoring, whereas BEA data are available only every five years.

[4]The next two largest industries in terms of maquiladora employment in Mexico are miscellaneous industries (11.3% of employment) and furniture (4.9% of employment). We exclude miscellaneous industries because we cannot match them to specific US sectors (miscellaneous industries in Mexico are distinct from those in the US) and furniture, owing to inconsistencies in the data series for the industry in Mexico. Other manufacturing industries (chemicals, toys, tools, food, and footwear) collectively account for just 6.2% of maquiladora employment.

fifth least regulated economy, a finding consistent with Mexico having lower aggregate employment volatility.[5]

In this chapter, we offer an explanation for the offshoring employment volatility puzzle by developing a model of global production sharing in which the decisions of firms respond to macroeconomic shocks. The offshoring sector consists of a continuum of products with heterogeneous unit labor requirements, along the lines of Dornbusch, Fisher, and Samuelson (1977) and Eaton and Kortum (2002). This sector is embedded in a two country, general equilibrium macroeconomic model, which also includes a homogeneous traded good in each country. Labor supply is endogenous and the wages of each country are determined in a general equilibrium that is affected by shocks to aggregate demand and supply. The model is stochastic and results for second moments are derived in a calibrated simulation exercise.

A key feature of the model is that the point along the product continuum at which firms in the home country begin to offshore production to the foreign country is endogenously determined as firms compare unit labor costs across borders. When the home country has a boom in demand, the fact that home wages tend to be procyclical alters the offshoring decision of some firms.[6] Since home workers become relatively more expensive to hire, firms that previously had not offshored any production now find it profitable to do so. This shift in the extensive margin acts as a powerful mechanism for the international transmission of shocks, whereby US producers shift disproportionately high levels of production abroad during a domestic economic boom, and the reverse during a recession. Numerical examples, by way of stochastic simulation under demand and supply shocks, indicate

[5]The labor regulations evaluated by Botero *et al.* (2004) apply to the formal sector in the countries considered. In Mexico, there is substantial employment (largely in services) in the informal sector, in which the enforcement of labor laws is relatively lax. The data we use on maquiladoras are limited to plants in the formal sector and the data we use on aggregate Mexican manufacturing are limited to plants with more than 15 employees (which account for over 80% of total sales in manufacturing), the large majority of which are in the formal sector (see http://www.inegi.org.mx/prod_serv/contenidos/espanol/bvinegi/productos/encuestas/establecimientos/eim/mensual/eim.pdf). While there is employment in Mexico subject to lax labor regulation, it is largely absent in our data.

[6]Huang, diu, and Phaneuf (2004) survey recent evidence confirming procyclicality of wages in the US in the postwar period, unconditionally as well as conditional on demand shocks.

that the mechanism provides a potential explanation for the extra volatility in Mexican offshoring, relative to the US Even when the shock is a purely domestic one (e.g. specific to the US), it is amplified in its transmission abroad, such that it has a greater impact on the offshoring industries in the low-wage foreign country than on the domestic counterpart industries.

There are two reasons why in our model shocks to home demand are amplified in their effect abroad. First, the foreign offshoring sector (e.g. maquiladoras in Mexico) has smaller total employment than in the home country (e.g. the US). Any given shift in an absolute amount of employment therefore has an amplified effect on foreign volatility. Second, because procyclical domestic wages induce more offshoring during domestic demand booms, the rise in domestic employment due to the boom and the fall in domestic employment due to greater offshoring counteract each other. In contrast, the foreign country experiences the effect of offshoring unmitigated by a counteracting effect. Because production in Mexican Maquiladoras is substantially directed toward US demand, a prominent role for US demand shocks gives this mechanism potency for Mexican offshoring employment.

To examine a key implication of the theory for the offshoring margin, we collect data on Mexican exports at US ports of entry associated with offshoring, which record both the value of exports and the number of product classifications exported. We find that at a monthly frequency there are substantial changes in the extensive margin of offshoring, consistent with our theory. Further, the degree of volatility of this margin observed in the data matches well the degree of volatility implied by the calibrated theoretical model, and it is quantitatively sufficient to explain the volatility puzzle in employment data.

The next two sections present the theoretical model and analytical results. Simulation results follow in Section 4. Section 5 presents empirical support, followed by a concluding summary.

2. Theoretical Model

We embed a model of offshoring in a simple dynamic stochastic general equilibrium model of two countries. Label the two countries as home and foreign, with foreign variables denoted by an asterisk. The offshoring relationship involves the home country offshoring to the foreign country, so that home may be thought of as representing the US and foreign as representing Mexico. We will scale the quantity variables coming from the foreign country by its relative size: if the share n of the world population resides at home and $1 - n$ in the foreign country, then we scale foreign quantities by $(1 - n)/n$.

2.1. *Pricing and product variety in the offshoring sector*

Each country has two sectors. The first is a standard homogeneous good whose production is specific to that country; this country-specific sector will be subscripted by H for the home produced good and F for the foreign produced good. The second sector consists of differentiated products that are multinational, subscripted by M, in that they can be produced using factors in either country. This sector will be referred to as the offshoring sector. There is a continuum of products in this sector indexed by $z \in [0, 1]$.[7]

Production in the offshoring sector involves a unit labor input requirement that differs by product. To characterize the distribution of the relative unit labor requirement function between countries, we follow Eaton and Kortum (2002, footnote 15), who develop a Ricardian model of trade in which firms randomly draw their productivities and countries differ in their average sectoral efficiency level. In a two country context, their model implies a function for the relative unit labor requirement resembling that of Dornbusch, Fisher, and Samuelson (1977),[8]

$$A(z) = \frac{a_{Mt}(z)}{a^*_{Mt}(z)} = \left(\frac{T}{T^*}\right)^{\frac{1}{\theta}} \left(\frac{1-z}{z}\right)^{\frac{1}{\theta}}. \tag{1}$$

In the formulation used here, T and T^* scale the unit labor requirement levels of the home and foreign country respectively, and θ characterizes the

[7] See the working paper version Bergin, Feenstra, and Hanson (2007) for an expanded version of the model with free entry of firms into each industry.

[8] Footnote 15 of Eaton and Kortum (2002) derives the following function $A(x)$, where x is the fraction of goods for which the ratio of home (country 1) to foreign (country 2) efficiency is at least A: $A(x) = (T_1/T_2)^{\frac{1}{\theta}}((1 - x)/x^{\frac{1}{\theta}}$. Our distribution, $A(z)$ is a direct transformation of this function in terms of relative unit labor costs, where z is the fraction of goods for which the ratio of home to foreign *unit labor cost* is *less* than A. In this transformation, the heterogeneity parameter θ is exactly the same as in Eaton and Kortum (2002, footnote 15), but the efficiency constants are replaced by unit labor cost constants: $T = 1/T_1$ and $T^* = 1/T_2$.

curvature of the distribution of productivities. By ordering of the products z, we assume that $A(z)$ is decreasing in z, i.e. products are arranged by increasing order of home comparative advantage. It follows that those offshoring activities below some cutoff z_t' will be produced in the foreign country, while those activities above z_t' will be done at home. The cutoff activity z_t' is determined by the equality of unit labor costs in the two countries, or given the wages W_t and W_t^*, by[9]

$$A(z_t') = \frac{W_t^*}{W_t}. \tag{2}$$

Overall home demand in this multinational sector is specified as

$$\ln D_{Mt} = \int_0^1 \ln d_{Mt}(z)dz, \tag{3}$$

where $d_{Mt}(z)$ is the demand for a product z. The market for each z is assumed to be perfectly competitive. The composite multinational good D_{Mt} will serve as the numeraire. The price index of multinational goods is computed by integrating over the distribution of unit costs in each country over the relevant range, where we split the relative unit cost distribution (1) into a home and foreign component: $a_{M,t}(z) = \left(\frac{T}{z}\right)^{\frac{1}{\theta}}$ for home, and $a_{M,t}^*(z) = \left(\frac{T^*}{1-z}\right)^{\frac{1}{\theta}}$ for foreign. The price index for these goods is computed as (see the appendix) follows:

$$\begin{aligned}\ln P_{Mt} &= \int_0^{z_t'} \ln(W_t^* a_{M,t}^*(z_t))dz + \int_{z_t'}^1 \ln(W_t a_{M,t}(z_t))dz \\ &= \ln(W_t^* T^{*\frac{1}{\theta}})z_t' + \ln(W_t T^{\frac{1}{\theta}})(1-z_t') + \frac{1}{\theta}((1-z_t')\ln(1-z_t')) \\ &\quad -\frac{1}{\theta}(z_t' \ln z_t') + \frac{2}{\theta}z_t' + \frac{1}{\theta}. \end{aligned} \tag{4}$$

The overall labor demand in the multinational sector at home, L_{Mt}, consists of labor used for activities not offshored ($z_t > z_t'$); labor demand abroad includes offshored activities ($z_t < z_t'$). The appendix derives these

[9]Our model abstracts away from overtime pay, which contributes to the procyclicality of wages (see, e.g. Bils, 1987). Unfortunately, there is scant literature comparing the prevalence of overtime pay in the US and Mexico.

labor demands:

$$L_{Mt} = \left(\frac{D_{Mt} + D^*_{Mt} \left(\frac{1-n}{n} \right)}{W_t} \right) (1 - z'_t), \tag{5}$$

$$\left(\frac{1-n}{n} \right) L^*_{Mt} = \left(\frac{D_{Mt} + D^*_{Mt} \left(\frac{1-n}{n} \right)}{W^*_t} \right) z'_t. \tag{6}$$

2.2. *Production in the rest of the economy*

The offshoring model is embedded in a general equilibrium setting that is standard in the open macroeconomy literature. The country-specific sector in the home country is a perfectly competitive market for the homogeneous traded good with production function:

$$Y_{Ht} = \frac{L_{Ht}}{a_{Ht}}, \tag{7}$$

where L_{Ht} is labor in the home country-specific sector and a_{Ht} is its unit labor input requirement. Prices in a competitive equilibrium are

$$p_{Ht} = W_t a_{Ht}, \tag{8}$$

where p_{Ht} is the relative price of the home domestic good in terms of the multinational good numeraire. Analogous conditions apply to the foreign country's homogeneous good.

2.3. *Households*

Household preferences in the home country are represented by an instantaneous utility function of consumption (C_t), which is a Cobb–Douglas composite of goods in the three sectors, and overall labor (L_t):

$$U_t = \frac{1}{1-\phi} C_t^{1-\phi} - \frac{1}{1+\mu} L_t^{1+\mu}, \tag{9}$$

where

$$C_t = (C^{\alpha}_{Mt} C^{1-\alpha}_{Ht})^{\omega_t} C^{1-\omega_t}_{Ft}$$

C_M denotes consumption by home private households of the multinational good, C_H home private consumption of the home good, and C_F home private consumption of the foreign good. As private consumption is the only form of expenditure in the benchmark version of the model, C_M is identical for the time being to overall demand in the M sector, D_M, defined earlier.

The implications of uncertainty in the model will be dealt with in a simple manner by assuming complete asset markets, as commonly assumed in the international macroeconomic literature (see Chari, Kehoe, and McGrattan, 2002). In each period t, the economy experiences one of finitely many events, s_t. We denote by $s^t = (s_0, \ldots, s_t)$ the history of events up through and including period t. All variables referred to so far are implicitly functions of the states of nature in period t (e.g. $Y_{Ht} \equiv Y_H(s^t)$). In period t, consumers in either country purchase state-contingent assets in units of the numeraire good, denoted by $B_{t+1} \equiv B(s^{t+1})$, which bear a return of exactly one unit of the numeraire good in period $t+1$ if state s^{t+1} occurs. They purchase these assets at the prices $V(s^{t+1}|s^t)$, which denotes the price of one unit of the numeraire good at s^{t+1} in units of the numeraire good at state s^t. The budget constraint facing the home household in period t is therefore:

$$P_t C_t + \sum_{s^{t+1}} V(s^{t+1}|s^t) B(s^{t+1}) = W_t L_t + B_t,$$

where P_t is the price index of the home country consumption basket in terms of the numeraire good.

Labor is mobile between sectors within a country, but there is no labor mobility between countries, meaning each country has a single but distinct equilibrium wage rate.

Households maximize the expected discounted sum of current and future instantaneous utility defined above, using the discount factor β, subject to the budget constraint.[10] The first-order conditions for this problem imply the following. Risk-sharing equates nominal marginal utilities of consumption apart from a constant of proportionality,

$$\frac{P_t C_t^{\phi}}{P_t^* C_t^{*\phi}} = \zeta, \tag{10}$$

[10]As the discount factor β is assumed identical across countries, it cancels out of the risk-sharing condition (16), and does not appear in the other equations of the model.

where ζ is a constant indicating the relative per capita wealth of the home country in the initial asset allocation. Demands for the goods are

$$C_{Mt} = \alpha\omega\left(\frac{P_t}{P_{Mt}}\right)C_t \tag{11}$$

$$C_{Ht} = (1-\alpha)\omega\left(\frac{P_t}{P_{Ht}}\right)C_t \tag{12}$$

and,

$$C_{Ft} = (1-\omega)\left(\frac{P_t}{P_{Ft}}\right)C_t. \tag{13}$$

Labor supply is

$$L_t^{\mu} = \frac{W_t}{P_t}C_t^{-\phi}. \tag{14}$$

Corresponding conditions apply for the foreign country.

2.4. *Market clearing and equilibrium*

Market clearing in the home goods market requires:

$$D_{Ht} + \left(\frac{1-n}{n}\right)D_{Ht}^{*} = Y_{Ht}, \tag{15}$$

where D_{Ht} and D_{Ht}^{*} are home and foreign demands for the home good. Again, because consumption is the only source of demand in the benchmark model, we may substitute C_{Ht} for D_{Ht} and C_{Ht}^{*} for D_{Ht}^{*}. There is an analogous condition for the foreign good.

Equilibrium in the labor market requires that overall labor supply equal the sum of labor demands across sectors:

$$L_t = L_{Ht} + L_{Mt}, \tag{16}$$

$$L_t^{*} = L_{Ft}^{*} + L_{Mt}^{*}. \tag{17}$$

The general equilibrium is a sequence of 17 endogenous variables: L_t, L_t^{*}, L_{Ht}, L_{Ft}^{*}, L_{Mt}, L_{Mt}^{*}, W_t, W_t^{*}, C_{Ht}, C_{Ht}^{*}, C_{Ft}, $C_{Ft}^{*} C_{Mt}$, C_{Mt}^{*}, P_{Ht}, P_{Ft}, and z_t', where we have used the fact $D_{it} = C_{it}$ and $D_{it}^{*} = C_{it}^{*}$ for $i = M, H, F$. These variables are determined by the labor-supply condition (14), demand for the multinational and home country-specific goods (11) and (12), labor demand for the country-specific sector (5) and the multinational sector

(7), the market clearing condition for the country-specific sector (15), the market clearing condition for labor (16), and the foreign counterparts for each of these. In addition, there is the marginal offshoring condition (2), the risk-sharing condition in (10), and the normalization of the price of the numeraire good $P_{Mt} = 1$.

3. Analytical Results

While a closed-form analytical solution is not possible for this model, we can solve for relative country ratios, which is helpful in providing intuition for the main result. Taking the ratio of labor demand conditions for the multinational sector, (5) and (6), and substituting for relative wages using condition (2):

$$\frac{L_{Mt}^{*}}{L_{Mt}} = \left(\frac{z_t'}{1-z_t'}\right)^{1+\frac{1}{\theta}} \left(\frac{T^{*}}{T}\right)^{\frac{1}{\theta}} \left(\frac{n}{1-n}\right). \tag{18}$$

This condition makes clear that if the offshoring margin, z, were not endogenous but instead assumed to be fixed, then the labor demands in the offshoring sectors of the two countries would be exactly proportional to each other. Since all other terms in the expression are constants, the standard deviations in log terms of offshoring employment in each country would be identical, $\sigma(L_{Mt}^{*}) = \sigma(L_{Mt})$, and it would be impossible to replicate the stylized fact of higher volatility in Mexican offshoring employment. This result points to the essential role played by an endogenous offshoring margin in explaining the volatility puzzle. The shock considered initially will be a demand shock in the form of a rise in the preference parameter ω_t, which increases demand for home and multinational goods relative to foreign goods. Let deviations of ω_t from its mean follow an iid log-normally distributed process. Assume that the foreign household has identical preferences.

Given the important role of endogenous changes in the offshoring margin, we solve for the equilibrium response of z' to the exogenous shock to demand ω_t. To solve the model, we start with the relative wage, which equates the ratio of total labor demands in the overall economies to the ratio of their labor supplies. Begin with total home labor demand, using the production function (7) and goods market clearing (15) for labor demand in the home goods sector, L_{Ht}

$$L_t = L_{Mt} + L_{Ht} = \left(\frac{C_{Mt} + C^*_{Mt}\left(\frac{1-n}{n}\right)}{W_t}\right)(1 - z'_t)$$
$$+ a_H\left(C_{Ht} + C^*_{Ht}\left(\frac{1-n}{n}\right)\right).$$

Use demand conditions (11) and (12), along with price setting for the home good and the normalization for the price of the multinational good, and do likewise for the foreign country:

$$L_t = \omega_t\left(1 - \alpha z'_t\right) P_t\left(\frac{C_t + C^*_t\left(\frac{1-n}{n}\right)}{W_t}\right)$$

and

$$L^*_t = L^*_{Mt} + L^*_{Ft}$$
$$= (\alpha\omega_t z'_t + (1 - \omega_t))P_t\left(\frac{C_t + C^*_t\left(\frac{1-n}{n}\right)}{W^*_t}\right)\left(\frac{n}{1-n}\right).$$

Set the cross-country ratio of these labor demands equal to the ratio of labor supplies from condition (14):

$$\left(\frac{\frac{W^*_t}{P^*_t}C^{*-\phi}_t}{\frac{W_t}{P_t}C^{-\phi}_t}\right)^{\frac{1}{\mu}} = \frac{L^*_t}{L_t} = \left(\frac{W_t}{W^*_t}\right)\frac{\alpha\omega_t z'_t + (1 - \omega_t)}{\omega_t\left(1 - \alpha z'_t\right)}\left(\frac{n}{1-n}\right). \tag{19}$$

Use the complete asset markets condition (10), along with the technology distribution (1) and marginal offshoring condition (2):

$$(\zeta)^{\frac{1}{\mu}}\left(\frac{T}{T^*}\right)^{\frac{1}{\theta}\left(1+\frac{1}{\mu}\right)}\left(\frac{1-n}{n}\right)$$
$$= \left(\frac{z'_t}{1-z'_t}\right)^{\frac{1}{\theta}\left(1+\frac{1}{\mu}\right)}\left(\frac{\alpha\omega_t z'_t + (1 - \omega_t)}{\omega_t(1 - \alpha z'_t)}\right) = 0. \tag{20}$$

This is an implicit function for z'_t as a function of the preference and technology parameters.

Let us consider the effects of a demand shock that takes the form of a rise in the share of consumption expenditure allocated to home and multinational goods and away from foreign goods, a rise in ω_t. We can find the comparative static effect on the offshoring margin, z'_t, as follows. By differentiating over the implicit function above, labeled as $F = 0$, it is easy to verify that $\frac{dz'_t}{d\omega_t} = -\frac{dF}{d\omega_t} / \frac{dF}{dz'_t} > 0$ (see the appendix for the derivation). A rise in demand ω_t leads to an increase in the margin of offshoring. Combined with the marginal offshoring condition (2), this immediately implies a rise in the relative home wage, W_t/W^*_t. And Equation (19) implies a rise in relative home total employment, L_t/L^*_t. Together, these results imply the following story: a demand shock biased toward home goods raises relative demand for home labor and hence raises home relative wages. This induces firms to offshore a greater range of goods in the offshoring sector to the foreign country.

Returning to Equation (18), the systematic movement in the offshoring margin has implications for the relative volatilities in employment in the two countries' offshoring sectors.

Taking natural logs of (18) and differentiating with respect to the demand shock ω_t

$$\frac{d \ln L^*_{Mt}}{d\omega_t} = \frac{d \ln L_{Mt}}{d\omega_t} + \left(1 + \frac{1}{\theta}\right) \frac{1}{(1 - z'_t)} \frac{d \ln z'_t}{d\omega_t}. \tag{21}$$

Variances can be computed for a log linear approximation around the mean values of $\overline{z}'$:

$$\begin{aligned} \operatorname{var}(\ln L^*_{Mt}) = \operatorname{var}(\ln L_{Mt}) + \left(1 + \frac{1}{\theta}\right)^2 \left(\frac{1}{1 - \overline{z}'}\right)^2 \operatorname{var}(\ln z'_t) \\ + 2\left(1 + \frac{1}{\theta}\right)\left(\frac{1}{1 - \overline{z}'}\right) \operatorname{cov}(\ln L_{Mt}, \ln z'_t). \end{aligned} \tag{22}$$

As shown in the appendix, this may be rewritten as

$$\begin{aligned} \operatorname{var}(\ln L^*_{Mt}) = \operatorname{var}(\ln L_{Mt}) + 2\left(1 + \frac{1}{\theta}\right) \\ \times \left(\frac{1}{1 - \overline{z}'}\right) \operatorname{cov}\left(\ln L_{Mt} + \ln L^*_{Mt}, \ln z'_t\right). \end{aligned} \tag{23}$$

Thus, a necessary and sufficient condition to have $\operatorname{var}(\ln L^*_{Mt}) > \operatorname{var}(\ln L_{Mt})$ is that

$$\operatorname{cov}(\ln L_{Mt} + \ln L^*_{Mt}, \ln z'_t) > 0. \tag{24}$$

There are two effects that can be seen at work. First, for a given share of offshoring, a rise in demand for multinational goods forces an equal percentage rise in employment in this sector in both countries. Second, since the rise in demand coincides with a rise in the share z'_t of goods offshored, there is a further effect raising employment abroad, but a negative effect counteracting the rise in employment in this sector at home. On net, foreign offshoring employment rises more than at home, implying greater foreign volatility in the face of such home demand shocks. Is it in fact the case that $\text{cov}(\ln L_{Mt} + \ln L^*_{Mt}, \ln z'_t) > 0$? The simulation section below will verify that this condition is satisfied in our calibrated model, and the following empirical section will verify that this positive correlation is satisfied in US and Mexican data.

Equation (21) also reveals that when relative foreign volatility is higher, the smaller will be the mean level of the offshoring margin, $\bar{z}'$. The relative size of the two countries in the offshoring sector matters because when a movement in the margin shifts an industry from the US to Mexico there is a larger percentage change in Mexico than in the US sector. Note, however, that relative country size in terms of overall population, n, cancels out from the above expression when taking log changes. It is sized specifically in the offshoring sector that matters for the volatility puzzle.

4. Numerical Experiment

4.1. *Model calibration*

To conduct a quantitative experiment, we calibrate the parameters to represent the US and Mexican economies. To permit calibration of demand shocks to data, these must be reinterpreted somewhat. Recall that the analytical results considered a shock to the home bias parameter, ω, raising the share of demand allocated to home and multinational goods relative to foreign goods. For a quantitative experiment, it is not entirely clear what shock in the data such a preference shift would correspond to or how we would calibrate it. The calibrated model instead will study the effect of an equivalent additive shock to government demand, for which data are available. Denoted G and G^*, government expenditure is allocated among the goods using the same demands as the private consumption as in

Equations (11)–(12), except that it is assumed that government has complete bias toward home goods: $\omega_G = \omega^*_G = 1$ for government preferences.[11] In addition to reflecting the stylized fact of greater home bias in government spending data, this specification allows government spending shocks to resemble the taste shocks assumed in the analytical results. Because government home bias is greater than private home bias ($\omega_G > \omega$), a shock raising the role of government demand in overall US demand will raise the share of overall home demand allocated to home and multinational goods rather than foreign goods, similar in spirit to the analytical result. The definitions of demands used previously must be expanded to account for government demand along with consumer demand: $D_{Mt} = C_{Mt} + G_{Mt}$, $D_{Ht} = C_{Ht} + G_{Ht}$, and $D^*_{Ft} = C^*_{Ft} + G^*_{Ft}$.

To deal with aggregate output fluctuations, the model will allow for supply shocks to the technology in the production functions: a_{Ht} and a^*_{Ft}. We do not compute a separate set of Solow residuals for the offshoring sector of each country, as this might replicate the higher volatility in the Mexican offshoring sector in a purely mechanical way. Instead, we consider two cases of how a country's domestic technology shocks affect the offshoring sector. One case simply assumes that unit labor requirement moves proportionately in the domestic and offshoring sectors within each country: $\tilde{a}_{Mt}(\bar{z}') = \tilde{a}_{Ht}$, $\tilde{a}^*_{Mt}(\bar{z}') = \tilde{a}^*_{Ft}$, where tildes indicate log deviations from means. This specification implies that the relative cost schedule $A(z)$ shifts in response to technology shocks. The other case differs in that it holds the $A(z)$ schedule fixed, assuming that technology shocks in a country's offshoring sector are perfectly transmitted to the other country's offshoring sector: $\tilde{a}_{Mt}(\bar{z}') = \tilde{a}^*_{Mt}(\bar{z}') = \tilde{a}_{Ht} + \tilde{a}^*_{Ft}$. Such a specification is similar to that assumed in Burstein, Kurz, and Tesar (2008), and is also consistent with Berman, Bound, and Machin (1998) who argue that technology shocks spread quickly to other countries. We take this second specification as our benchmark, although we shall report results for the first case as well.

[11] This implies the following particular government demands: $G_{Ht} = (1 - \alpha)(P_t/P_{Ht})G_t$, $G_{Mt} = \alpha(P_t/P_{Mt})G_t$, $G^*_{F,t} = (P^*_t/P^*_{Ft})G_t$, and $G_F = G^*_H = G^*_M = 0$.

Both demand and supply shocks are specified as first-order autoregressions in log deviations from their respective means:

$$\begin{bmatrix} \log(a_{Ht}) - \log(\overline{a_H}) \\ \log(a^*_{Ft}) - \log(\overline{a^*_F}) \end{bmatrix} = \rho_a \begin{bmatrix} \log(a_{Ht-1}) - \log(\overline{a_H}) \\ \log(a^*_{Ft-1}) - \log(\overline{a^*_F}) \end{bmatrix} + \begin{bmatrix} \varepsilon_{aHt} \\ \varepsilon_{aFt} \end{bmatrix},$$

$$\text{where} \begin{bmatrix} \varepsilon_{aHt} \\ \varepsilon_{aFt} \end{bmatrix} \sim \mathrm{N}\left(\begin{bmatrix} 0 \\ 0 \end{bmatrix}, \sigma_a^2 \right)$$

$$\text{and:} \quad \begin{bmatrix} \log(G_t) - \log(\overline{G}) \\ \log(G^*_t) - \log(\overline{G^*}) \end{bmatrix} = \rho_G \begin{bmatrix} \log(G_{t-1}) - \log(\overline{G}) \\ \log(G^*_{t-1}) - \log(\overline{G^*}) \end{bmatrix} + \begin{bmatrix} \varepsilon_{Gt} \\ \varepsilon_{G*t} \end{bmatrix},$$

$$\text{where} \begin{bmatrix} \varepsilon_{Gt} \\ \varepsilon_{G*t} \end{bmatrix} \sim N\left(\begin{bmatrix} 0 \\ 0 \end{bmatrix}, \sigma_G^2 \right). \tag{25}$$

Model parameters are calibrated to monthly data for the US and Mexico, and values are summarized in Table 1. To calibrate the steady state level of the offshoring share, the ratio of (6) and (5) indicates that $\bar{z}'$ can be calibrated to match the Mexican share of production labor earnings in the offshoring sector.

$$\frac{(1-n)W^*_t L^*_{Mt}}{nW_t L_{Mt}} = \frac{z'_t}{1-z'_t}. \tag{26}$$

Averaging over our data for earnings in the four offshoring industries at the end of our sample indicates a share of 0.06.

Calibrating the relative unit labor requirement distribution $A(z)$ involves three parameters. The curvature parameter θ is calibrated at 8.28 based upon the estimation by Eaton and Kortum (2002).[12] The level parameter for technology in the US offshoring sector, T, is calibrated so that the unit labor requirement at the steady state margin in this sector is the same as the unit labor requirement in the domestic goods sector: $a_{M,t}(\overline{z'}) = \left(\frac{T}{\overline{z'}}\right)^{\frac{1}{\theta}} = \overline{a}_{H,t} = 1$, so $T^{1/\theta} = \overline{z'}^{1/\theta} = 0.712$. Finally, the foreign technology level in the offshoring sector, T^*, is calibrated so that the relative unit labor requirement, which determines the relative wage

[12]Their estimates are based upon bilateral import shares and price differences for 50 manufactured products, most of which coincide with offshoring industries.

Table 1. Calibration of model parameters

Preferences		
ω	Home bias in US	0.88
ω^*	Home bias in Mexico	0.71
α	Offshoring expenditure share	0.24
μ	Labor-supply elasticity	1
ϕ	Risk aversion	2
n	Relative size of US	0.74
ζ	Relative wealth of US	31.3
$\overline{G}$	US mean government demand	0.164
$\overline{G^*}$	Mexican mean government demand	0.00382
Technology		
$\overline{a_H}$	US steady state unit cost	1
$\overline{a_F^*}$	Mexican steady state unit cost	3.15
$\bar{z}'$	Offshoring margin	0.06
θ	Curvature of distribution	8.28
$T^{1/\theta}$	US offshoring technology term	0.71
$T^{*1/\theta}$	Mexican offshoring technology term	7.94

Shock processes

$$\sigma_a^2 = \begin{bmatrix} 6.42 \times 10^{-5} & -4.67 \times 10^{-6} \\ -4.67 \times 10^{-6} & 1.87 \times 10^{-4} \end{bmatrix} \qquad \rho_a = \begin{bmatrix} 0.931 & -4.02e^{-2} \\ 7.38e^{-3} & 0.961 \end{bmatrix}$$

$$\sigma_G^2 = \begin{bmatrix} 7.69 \times 10^{-3} & 4.02 \times 10^{-3} \\ 4.02 \times 10^{-3} & 2.36 \times 10^{-2} \end{bmatrix} \qquad \rho_G = \begin{bmatrix} -0.0549 & 0.379 \\ -0.368 & 0.424 \end{bmatrix}$$

across countries, equals the relative wage in our data set, which is 1/8: $A(z') = \left(\frac{T}{T^*}\right)^{\frac{1}{\theta}} \left(\frac{1-z'}{z'}\right)^{\frac{1}{\theta}} = \frac{\overline{W^*}}{\overline{W}} = 1/8$ so $T^{*1/\theta} = (8)(1-0.06)^{1/8.28}$.

The relative wealth parameter ζ is chosen to imply a ratio of per capita consumption of the US to Mexico in steady state that matches the data, which the Penn World Tables indicates is 4.3 in 2000. The parameter n is calibrated to reflect the 74% share of the US in the combined population of the two countries. Calibrations of standard preference parameters are taken from the business cycle literature. The labor-supply elasticity is set at unity, $\mu = 1$, and the curvature parameter is set at $\phi = 2$, as is common in the business cycle literature.

The remaining preference parameters are calibrated to reflect the relationship between US and Mexican aggregates. The home bias parameters reflect the share of import expenditures in a gross domestic product (GDP), $\omega = 0.88$, and $\omega^* = 0.71$. The four US industries classified as offshoring industries in the data set used by Bergin, Feenstra, and Hanson (2009) to document the offshoring volatility puzzle (apparel, electrical machinery, computer and electronics, and transport equipment) represent 24% of total US manufacturing, so the offshoring share parameter is calibrated at $\alpha = 0.24$. The steady state levels of the additive consumption terms ($\overline{G}$ and $\overline{G^*}$) are calibrated at values that imply the share of government consumption in total demand is 17% in steady state equilibrium, which is the share of government purchases in US gross national expenditure data during our sample range.

The mean unit labor requirement in Mexico's domestic sector ($\bar{a}_F$) is calibrated to imply a steady state of the model consistent with the assumption above that the Mexican wage is 1/8 that of the US Unit labor requirement shock parameters are estimated from a first-order autoregression on the reciprocal of Solow residuals, computed from monthly manufacturing data from our sample range.[13] Regarding demand shocks, since there is no monthly series available for government consumption, total government spending from IFS is used. Linear trends are removed from the log of each series before fitting it to the first-order autoregressive processes used for all shocks above. See Table 1 for exact values.

4.2. *Numerical results*

Simulations involve solving the model numerically in its original nonlinear form for 120 periods of random draws of shocks. The first 20 periods are dropped, and the remaining 100 periods are HP-filtered and used to compute moments. This process is repeated 1,000 times, and we report the average of moments over the replications.

---

[13]We follow the convention in Glick and Rogoff (1995) of computing Solow residuals by setting the labor share at 0.6 and assuming a constant capital stock. Resulting estimates are almost identical if we assume a labor share of unity, as implied by the production function in the model above.

Table 2. Model simulation for production worker employment

	(1) Mexican or US data	(2) Bench-mark model	(3) US demand shock	(4) Mexico demand shock	(5) US supply shock	(6) Mexico supply shock	(7) High elasticity (χ =2)
			Std. devs. (%)				
$\sigma(L_M^*)$	4.44	5.18	4.66	2.17	0.97	0.03	5.05
$\sigma(L_M)$	2.04	0.99	0.65	0.12	0.40	0.31	1.63
$\sigma(L^*)$	0.89	0.81	0.38	0.28	0.37	0.33	0.81
$\sigma(L)$	1.15	1.13	0.82	0.03	0.43	0.30	1.14
$\sigma(L_M^*)/\sigma(L_M)$	2.21	5.26	7.17	17.70	2.40	0.09	3.15
$\sigma(L^*)/\sigma(L)$	0.77	0.72	0.47	9.65	0.86	1.10	0.71
			Correlations				
$\mathrm{corr}(L_M^*, L_M)$	0.51	0.80	1.00	−1.00	1.00	0.99	0.63
$\mathrm{corr}(L^*, L)$	0.78	0.93	1.00	1.00	1.00	1.00	0.94
$\mathrm{corr}(L_M^*, L^*)$	0.64	0.61	1.00	−1.00	1.00	0.99	0.57
$\mathrm{corr}(L_M, L)$	0.76	0.99	1.00	1.00	1.00	1.00	0.34
			Margins (%)				
$\sigma(z')$	3.61	3.71	3.36	1.93	0.48	0.23	3.54
$\mathrm{corr}(z', L_M^* + L_M)$	0.22	0.97	1.00	1.00	1.00	−1.00	0.87

Note: All variables are in natural logs.

Results for the benchmark case of the model are summarized in column (2) of Table 2; actual moments for Mexico and the US are in column (1), taken from Bergin, Feenstra, and Hanson (2009). Although the focus of this study is on the offshoring sector, it is reassuring for our general calibration of shocks that the volatilities for overall manufacturing employment are in the neighborhood of what is observed in the aggregate data, including the fact that overall employment volatility is somewhat higher in the US than in Mexico. Of primary interest is the fact that the calibrated model can easily generate a high degree of volatility in the offshoring sector of Mexico relative to the corresponding US sector, and relative to the overall Mexican economy. The standard deviation of employment for Mexican offshoring, 5.2%, is close to that in the data at 4.4%, and is far greater than the volatility in the US offshoring sector in the simulation, 0.99%, or overall Mexican economy, 0.81%. While the model succeeds in generating the greater volatility in the Mexican offshoring sector, it actually underestimates the degree of volatility in the US offshoring sector, a fact which will be discussed later in the Chapter.[14]

The model implies a standard deviation of the margin z' of 3.7%. The empirical section below will provide an empirical estimate for this volatility of 3.6%, which is remarkably close to the value generated by the benchmark simulation. This result lends support to the way we model the offshoring decision, and the role it plays in generating volatility. In particular, the theoretical model did not include a sunk cost of engaging in offshoring, which could reflect difficulties one might imagine in establishing new offshoring relationships with foreign producers. In practice, offshoring in Mexico seems to exhibit a fairly high degree of fluidity, with arms-length relationships starting and stopping fairly easily. This may be specific to the US–Mexico offshoring relationship. In any case, one might expect such sunk costs to dampen the response in offshoring to transitory shocks, as producers would not pay a significant sunk cost to engage in offshoring that generates benefits for a short period of time. Given that the standard deviation of the offshoring margin in the benchmark case is close to that in the data, there appears to be little empirical motivation for introducing such an adjustment cost in this model for the case of Mexican offshoring. See the empirical section below for further discussion of volatility in this margin.

The correlations of employment across sectors and across countries all are positive, as is seen also in the US Mexican data in the table. The positive comovement between the offshoring employment of both countries, $\text{corr}(L_M, L_M^*)$, and between US offshoring employment and the offshoring margin, $\text{corr}(z', L_M)$, coincide with the intuition provided in the analytical results section, regarding how demand shocks should generate extra volatility in the Mexican offshoring sector.

---

[14]The model also does not replicate the volatility of the wage-based real exchange rate across countries. The standard deviation of log W^*/W in the simulation is 0.48; in data, the standard deviation of log sw^*/w, where s is the nominal exchange rate and w and w^* are wage indexes from IFS, is 4.22 for our sample range. The failure to explain volatility of real exchange rates of various types is common to our class of models that exclude nominal shocks and nominal rigidities. This property is not a result of endogenous offshoring dampening relative wage volatility, as the volatility of the relative wage is likewise small, 0.87, when we suspend the $A(z)$ schedule and hold z' fixed.

Columns (3)–(6) of Table 2 report the results when just one of the four shocks is used. These results reveal that the US demand shock is the most important driver of the amplified volatility in the Mexican offshoring sector.

One feature of the data that the benchmark model failed to match was the fact that employment in the US offshoring sector is more volatile than in the overall US economy. Even if this contrast in volatility between offshorable and nonoffshorable sectors of the US is much less dramatic than in the Mexican economy, it is a failing, and potentially could reflect the presence of additional shocks specific to the offshoring sector that are shared by both countries. However, another potential explanation is that our specification of Cobb–Douglas preferences implying constant expenditure shares is too simple to capture the relationship among the three classifications of goods. Given that only a fraction of the goods that we classify as offshorable (autos, electronics, etc.) are actually offshored, and the large majority are actually produced entirely at home, one might conjecture they are more similar to the goods we classify as home goods in the model relative to those we classify as foreign goods. As a result, one might conjecture a nested CES consumption aggregator, permitting the elasticity of substitution between home and offshorable goods, χ, to be greater than unity:

$$C_t = \left(\left(\alpha^{\frac{1}{\chi}} C_{Mt}^{\frac{\chi-1}{\chi}} + (1-\alpha)^{\frac{1}{\chi}} C_{Ht}^{\frac{\chi-1}{\chi}}\right)^{\frac{\chi-1}{\chi}}\right)^{\omega_t} C_{Ft}^{1-\omega_t} \tag{27}$$

We have no compelling way of calibrating such an elasticity, but column (7) reports an experiment where the elasticity assumed in the benchmark simulation is doubled (from a value of 1 to 2), implying that home goods that can be offshored are twice as substitutable with other home goods than with foreign goods. Simulation results reported in column (7) indicate that the volatility of employment in Mexican offshoring and in the overall US and Mexican economies are unaffected by this change in calibration. However, the standard deviation of employment in the US offshoring sector increases from 0.99% to 1.6%, which is much closer to the 2.0% value observed in data. Recall that a shock raising overall US demand raises relative US wages and hence relative production costs and prices of US goods. The price rise is smaller for offshorable goods, because part of the labor and production costs are in Mexico. The higher elasticity implies that

Table 3. Robustness checks in model simulations: Production worker employment

	(1) Bench-mark model	(2) Fixed z'	(3) $\overline{z'} = 0.5$	(4) High M share ($\alpha = 4.8$)	(5) Low Mex M share ($\alpha^* = 0$)	(6) Altern. supply shocks	(7) Uncor. shocks
			Std. devs. (%)				
$\sigma(L_M^*)$	5.18	1.72	2.01	4.11	5.20	15.83	5.24
$\sigma(L_M)$	0.99	1.14	0.65	1.11	1.00	1.22	0.84
$\sigma(L^*)$	0.81	0.74	0.96	0.94	0.81	1.09	0.68
$\sigma(L)$	1.13	1.15	1.11	1.18	1.13	1.10	0.97
$\sigma(L_M^*)/\sigma(L_M)$	5.26	1.51	3.10	3.72	5.21	13.22	6.31
$\sigma(L^*)/\sigma(L)$	0.72	0.65	0.87	0.79	0.71	1.00	0.70
			Correlations				
$\text{corr}(L_M^*, L_M)$	0.80	0.97	0.74	0.85	0.80	−0.32	0.73
$\text{corr}(L^*, L)$	0.93	0.83	1.00	0.97	0.93	0.70	0.87
$\text{corr}(L_M^*, L^*)$	0.61	0.67	0.94	0.74	0.62	0.79	0.44
$\text{corr}(L_M, L)$	0.99	1.00	0.88	1.00	0.99	0.75	0.99
			Margins (%)				
$\sigma(z')$	3.71	0.00	0.71	2.70	3.72	15.78	3.92
$\text{corr}(z', L_M^* + L_M)$	0.97	0.00	0.90	0.96	0.97	0.98	0.98

Note: All variables are in natural logs.

more of the demand increase will shift from home goods to offshorable goods, enough that US production of goods in that sector rises more than under a unitary elasticity that implies a constant expenditure share for offshorable goods.

Table 3 reports results from a series of robustness checks, with other variations of the model specification. Column (2) confirms the analytical claim above that our main result depends crucially on endogenous movement in the offshoring margin. When the offshoring margin, z_t', is held fixed, Mexican employment volatility in the offshoring sector falls sharply, down to a level not much greater than in the US. Column (3) shows that Mexican offshoring employment also loses more than half of its volatility if the mean offshoring share is raised from 0.06 to 0.5. This numerical result coincides with the analytical result that country size in the offshoring sector contributes to higher Mexican volatility.

The four industries we classify as offshorable are not exhaustive, and some degree of offshoring exists in other sectors. To allow for a larger share of goods that are offshorable, column (4) reports results of a model simulation where the share of offshorable goods (α) is doubled from the benchmark calibration (4.8 instead of 2.4). Results are similar to the benchmark calibration, but with some moderation of the Mexican offshoring employment volatility. Next, it is also true that nearly the entirety of goods produced through offshoring by US firms in Mexico is intended for export back to the US for final consumption. The model can be altered to reflect this by specifying a separate expenditure share (α^*) for Mexican preferences in consuming offshorable goods, and setting this expenditure share to zero. Column (5) shows that results are nearly identical to the benchmark calibration.

We also consider an alternative specification of the supply shock. The benchmark case holds fixed the $A(z)$ schedule. In that case, supply shocks in the homogeneous goods turn out to have minimal impact on the offshoring margin z', relative wages, or other endogenous variables. This finding follows from a little-known result in the international macro literature. Consider our model without the offshoring sector, so that it is a two-good Ricardian model with complete asset markets, and assume Cobb–Douglas preferences over the homogeneous goods from each country. Then it turns out that the technology shocks have no impact at all on relative wages. The reason is that a positive supply shock to, say, the home good, will reduce its price on international markets but increase its demand by the same percentage amount, so the implied relative labor demand across countries is unchanged. Relative labor supply is also unchanged due to complete asset markets, so the equilibrium relative wage does not change.[15] Adding the

[15]The result that neutral technology shocks have no impact on the relative wage in a two-sector model with large countries and Cobb–Douglas preferences is noted by Krugman (2000), in a model with fixed labor endowments. Using labor choice and complete asset markets, Devereux and Engel (2001) obtain a factor-price equalization result under the assumption that labor enters the utility function linearly. Our assumptions are weaker, since labor enters utility with a power. Combining (16) and (19) we readily obtain $(L_t/L_t^*)^\mu = (W_t/W_t^*)$, which is the relative labor-supply schedule. Relative labor demand in the two-sector Ricardian economy is obtained by combining (14) with Cobb–Douglas preferences, $L_{Ht}/L_{Ft}^* = a_{Ht}Y_{Ht}/a_{Ft}^*Y_{Ft}^* = (a_{Ht}/a_{Ft}^*)(p_{Ft}/p_{Ht})$. Then substituting for prices from (15) we have, $L_{Ht}/L_{Ft}^* = (a_{Ht}/a_{Ft}^*)(a_{Ft}^*W_t^*/a_{Ht}W_t) = (W_t^*/W_t)$. In a standard model without an offshoring sector ($L_{H,t} = L_t, L_{F,t}^* = L_t^*$), this proves that both relative labor demand and supply do not depend on the technology shocks, so neither does the equilibrium relative wage.

offshoring sector but with a fixed $A(z)$ schedule leads to nearly the same result.

Column (6) of Table 3 considers the case where the $A(z)$ schedule responds to technology shocks, where T moves in proportion with a_H and T^* in proportion with a_F^*. While results show an impressive degree of volatility in Mexican offshoring employment, the correlation between Mexican and US employment in the offshoring sector is negative for this experiment, which is clearly counterfactual. Numerical results show that a rise in home supply shifts the $A(z)$ schedule down compared to a given relative wage, inducing a fall in offshoring. This "in-sourcing" behavior implies a negative correlation between employment in the home and foreign offshoring activity, which is counterfactual. Therefore, we conclude that our benchmark specification with supply shocks internationally transmitted in the offshoring sector is a better representation of reality, at least in this model.

Lastly, we check whether the international correlation structure of shocks is important to the result, by conducting a simulation where all off-diagonal elements of $\sigma_a, \sigma_G, \rho_a$, and ρ_G are set to zero. Column (7) shows that simulation results are almost the same as for the benchmark calibration.

5. Empirical Evidence Regarding the Offshoring Margin

The theoretical model developed in the preceding section implies that changes in employment by offshoring industries are driven in part by adjustment at the extensive margin. If such a mechanism is operative, we should see entry and exit among the assembly plants in Mexico that produce intermediate goods and services for US industry. There is abundant anecdotal evidence of such plant turnover. During the US economic expansion of the 1990s, the number of maquiladoras in Mexico grew from 1,600 to 3,700. Delphi Automotive Corp., a large US manufacturer of auto parts, expanded its operations in Mexico to include six assembly plants. As US economic growth slowed in 2001 and 2002, over 700 Mexican maquiladoras closed shop.[16] Delphi shut down two of its Mexican maquiladoras, leaving

[16]See "The Decline of the Maquiladora: The Government Isn't Moving to Rescue a Troubled Industry," *Business Week*, April 29, 2002.

the other four in operation, thereby reducing employment in the country by 28%.[17] Around the same time, Delphi also contracted production in its US plants, reducing domestic employment by a comparatively modest 5%.[18] Similar expansions and contractions in Mexican assembly plants are evident among firms that produce TV sets, cell phones, computer printers, and other manufacturing goods.[19]

More formal evidence of adjustment at the extensive margin comes from examining data on the number of products that Mexico exports to the US We use the Harmonized System (HS) import data for the US, at a monthly frequency, and focus on the three largest land border crossings: Laredo, El Paso, and San Diego. Table 4 summarizes the average number of HS 10-digit products crossing at each location per month in the four offshoring industries identified above. For example, there are 300 or more types of apparel items being imported at Laredo and San Diego each month, and a smaller number of items in other offshoring industries. We also report the mean number of months that HS products in each industry are exported each year, ranging from 5.8 months for apparel items in El Paso, to 9.0 months for transport equipment in Laredo.

These summary statistics show that there are many "zeros" in the data, i.e. many instances where an HS product is not exported some month. That fact is also illustrated by Fig. 1, which graphs the log number of HS products per month, after deseasonalizing and HP filtering. The standard deviation of these series (reported in Table 3), averaged across industries is 3.6%. This empirical volatility is very similar to the volatility of 3.7% found for the benchmark calibration of margin z' in the theoretical model. This indicates that the mechanism used in the theoretical model to explain the employment volatility puzzle requires a degree of movement in the offshoring margin that is modest and plausible.

[17]See Victoria Hirshberg, "Delphi to Consolidate Reynosa, Mexico, Operations," *Texas Knight Ridder/Tribune Business News*, July 23, 2004.

[18]See "Delphi Announces Plans to Cut 8,500 Jobs," *Associated Press*, December 12, 2004. Further, the absolute number of jobs reduced in the US (3,000) was less than the jobs lost overseas (5,500).

[19]See Mary Jordan, "Mexican Workers Pay for Success," *Washington Post*, June 20, 2002; Elizabeth Malkin, "A Boom along the Border," *The New York Times*, August 26, 2004; and Diane Lindquist, "Slight Gain in Output Cheers Mexico's Beleaguered Maquiladora Industry," *San Diego Union-Tribune*, March 11, 2004.

Table 4. US harmonized system imports from Mexico, 1996–2006

	Apparel	Electrical machinery	Computer & electronics	Transport equipment
	Laredo, TX			
Mean Number of HS products	384.0	219.2	258.6	140.5
Mean number of months a HS product is imported per year[a]	6.9	8.9	7.5	9.0
Std. dev. log number of HS products[b]	2.64	2.14	3.10	2.94
Correlation of number of HS products and US manufacturing employment[c]	0.28	0.32	0.07	0.31
Correlation of number of HS products and sum of US and Mexican employment in the industry	0.365	0.406	0.052	0.078
	El Paso, TX			
Mean number of HS products	162.6	137.0	208.3	53.4
Mean number of months a HS product is imported per year[a]	5.8	8.9	7.8	7.8
Std. dev. log number of HS products[b]	4.99	2.43	2.60	5.66
Correlation of number of HS products and US manufacturing employment[c]	0.05	0.04	0.12	0.30
Correlation of number of HS products and sum of US and Mexican employment in the industry	0.122	0.130	0.067	0.435
	San Diego, CA			
Mean number of HS products	299.8	129.6	237.0	53.2
Mean number of months a HS product is imported per year[a]	6.3	8.3	7.5	7.0
Std. dev. log number of HS products[b]	3.38	3.86	3.39	6.18
Correlation of number of HS products and US manufacturing employment[c]	−0.01	0.28	0.25	0.12

(*Continued*)

Table 4. (*Continued*)

	Apparel	Electrical machinery	Computer & electronics	Transport equipment
Correlation of number of HS products and sum of US and Mexican employment in the industry	0.067	0.420	0.225	0.305

Notes: [a]Averaged over HS products and over the years 1996–2006. [b]The log number of HS products has been deseasonalized and HP-filtered, and the standard deviation is multiplied by 100. [c]The number of HS products and US, manufacturing employment are in logs, and are deseasonalized and HP-filtered.
Source: Bureau of the Census, 1996–2006, *US Exports and Imports of Merchandise on CD-ROM* [machine-readable data file], Washington, D.C.

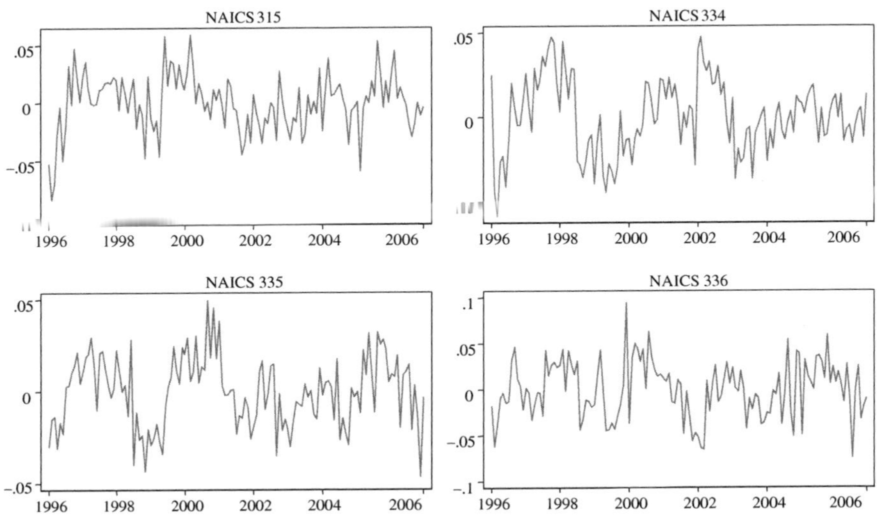

Figure 1. The number of HS products over years (average over 3 ports; Log values, seasonally adjusted, HP-filtered)

Some of the fluctuation in the number of HS products will reflect products that are exported at irregular intervals during the year. But we also expect that some fluctuation is systematic: visually, there appears to be a fall in the number of HS products in 2002, at the time when employment in both Mexico and the US fell substantially. That impression is confirmed by the correlations between the number of HS products and US manufacturing employment reported in Table 3, which are nearly all positive and often exceed 0.25. Further, the correlation between the offshoring margin and total employment in the offshoring industry summed across countries, corr($\ln L_{Mt} + \ln L^*_{Mt}, \ln z'_t$), is positive for all cases, and averages 0.22 across industries and locations. Recall from Equations (23) and (24) that this positive correlation (or its corresponding covariance) was shown in the analytical solution above to be necessary and sufficient in our theoretical model to explain the volatility puzzle. This finding lends empirical support for this theoretical condition.

6. Conclusions

Global production sharing is responsible for a substantial portion of world trade and is the primary means through which many developing countries engage in international commerce. While the expansion of export assembly operations have lead to impressive rates of employment growth in China, Eastern Europe, Mexico, and elsewhere, the implications of global production sharing for the volatility of economic activity has only recently attracted scholarly attention. In the case of Mexico, the country's offshoring industries experience fluctuations in economic activity that are twice as volatile as the corresponding industries in the US (Bergin, Feenstra, and Hanson, 2009). In this chapter, we find that fluctuations in offshoring employment in Mexico result in part from adjustment at the extensive margin, as products enter and exit trade between the two countries.

To account for differences in US and Mexican employment variability, we develop a theoretical model in which heterogeneous firms in a high wage country (the US) are free to enter and exit offshoring relationships with firms in a low-wage country (Mexico). Shocks that change US–Mexico relative wages induce US firms to alter which products they offshore to Mexico. Adjustment in the offshoring margin is the main mechanism through which US shocks become amplified in Mexico. Stochastic simulations show that the model matches the empirical regularities observed in US offshoring to Mexico. For Mexico, one consequence of economic integration with the US appears to be greater variability in its manufacturing employment.

Appendix

A.1. *Deriving labor demands in the offshoring sector*

Labor demand in the multinational sector at home is obtained by integrating over the variable labor input requirement $a_{Mt}(z)y_{Mt}(z)$ for those products $z \in [z_t', 1]$:

$$L_t = \int_{z_t'}^{1} a_{Mt}(z)y_{Mt}(z)dz. \tag{A1}$$

Multiply the labor input requirement in the integral by the wage W_t to obtain the expenditure $[C_{Mt} + C_{Mt}^*(1-n)/n]$ on each variety. So the expression inside the integral of (A1) equals $[C_{Mt} + C_{Mt}^*(1-n)/n]W_t$, which is integrated over $z \in [z_t', 1]$ to yield (5).

For foreign labor demand, we integrate the variable labor input requirement $a_{Mt}^*(z)y_t^*(z)$ for $z \in [0, z_t']$:

$$L_t^* = \int_0^{z_t'} a_{Mt}^*(z)y_t^*(z)dz. \tag{A2}$$

Multiplying the labor input requirement $a^*y_t^*(z)$ by the wage W_t^*, we again obtain the expenditure $[C_{Mt} + C_{Mt}^*(1-n)/n]$ on each variety. So the expression inside the integral of (A2) equals $[C_{Mt} + C_{Mt}^*(1-n)/n]/W_t^*$, which is integrated over $z \in [0, z_t']$ to yield (6).

A.2. *Derivation of price index for multinational goods sector*

$$\begin{aligned}
\ln P_{Mt} &= \int_0^{z_t'} \ln(W_t^* a_{M,t}^*(z_t))\, dz + \int_{z_t'}^{1} \ln(W_t a_{M,t}(z_t))\, dz \\
&= \int_0^{z_t'} \ln\left(W_t^*\left(\frac{T^*}{1-z}\right)^{\frac{1}{\theta}}\right) dz + \int_{z_t'}^{1} \ln\left(W_t\left(\frac{T}{z}\right)^{\frac{1}{\theta}}\right) dz
\end{aligned}$$

$$= \int_0^{z'_t} \ln\left(W_t^* T^{*\frac{1}{\theta}}\right) dz - \frac{1}{\theta}\int_0^{z'_t} \ln(1-z)\, dz$$

$$+ \int_{z'_t}^{1} \ln\left(W_t T^{\frac{1}{\theta}}\right) dz - \frac{1}{\theta}\int_{z'_t}^{1} \ln(z)\, dz$$

$$= \ln\left(W_t^* T^{*\frac{1}{\theta}}\right) z\Big|_0^{z'_t} + \frac{1}{\theta}((1-z)\ln(1-z) - (1-z))\Big|_0^{z'_t}$$

$$+ \ln\left(W_t T^{\frac{1}{\theta}}\right) z\Big|_{z'_t}^{1} - \frac{1}{\theta}\left(z\ln z - z\right)\big|_{z'_t}^{1}$$

$$= \ln\left(W_t^* T^{*\frac{1}{\theta}}\right) z'_t + \ln(W_t T^{\frac{1}{\theta}})(1-z'_t) + \frac{1}{\theta}((1-z'_t)\ln(1-z'_t))$$

$$-\frac{1}{\theta}(z'_t \ln z'_t) + \frac{2}{\theta} z'_t + \frac{1}{\theta}$$

A.3. *Deriving comparative statics for offshoring margin*

$$\text{Define } F \equiv \left(\frac{z}{1-z}\right)^{\frac{1}{\theta}\left(1+\frac{1}{\mu}\right)} \left(\frac{\alpha\omega z'_t + (1-\omega)}{\omega(1-\alpha z'_t)}\right)$$

$$-(\zeta)^{\frac{1}{\mu}} \left(\frac{T}{T^*}\right)^{\frac{1}{\theta}\left(1+\frac{1}{\mu}\right)} \left(\frac{1-n}{n}\right)$$

$$\frac{\partial F}{\partial z} = \left(\frac{z}{1-z}\right)^{\frac{1}{\theta}\left(1+\frac{1}{\mu}\right)} \left(\frac{\omega(1-\alpha z'_t)\alpha\omega + (\alpha\omega z'_t + (1-\omega))\alpha\omega}{(\omega(1-\alpha z'_t))^2}\right)$$

$$+ \left(\frac{\alpha\omega z'_t + (1-\omega)}{\omega(1-\alpha z'_t)}\right)\left(\frac{1}{\theta}\left(1+\frac{1}{\mu}\right)\right)\left(\frac{z}{1-z}\right)^{\frac{1}{\theta}\left(1+\frac{1}{\mu}\right)-1}$$

$$\times \left(\frac{1}{(1-z)^2}\right) > 0$$

So we know $\frac{\partial z}{\partial \omega} = -\frac{\partial F}{\partial \omega} / \frac{\partial F}{\partial z} > 0$.

$$\frac{\partial F}{\partial \omega} = \left(\frac{z}{1-z}\right)^{\frac{1}{\theta}\left(1+\frac{1}{\mu}\right)}$$

$$\times \left(\frac{\omega(1-\alpha z'_t)(\alpha z'_t - 1) - (\alpha\omega z'_t + (1-\omega))(1-\alpha z'_t)}{(\omega(1-\alpha z'_t))^2}\right) < 0$$

A.4. *Deriving necessary and sufficient condition (22–23)*

Rearrange (21) as follows

$$\frac{d\ln L_{Mt}}{d\omega_t} = \frac{d\ln L^*_{Mt}}{d\omega_t} - \left(1+\frac{1}{\theta}\right)\frac{1}{(1-z'_t)}\frac{d\ln z'_t}{d\omega_t}$$

and use this to write:

$$\begin{aligned}\mathrm{var}(\ln L_{Mt}) = \mathrm{var}(\ln L^*_{Mt}) + \left(1+\frac{1}{\theta}\right)^2\left(\frac{1}{1-\overline{z}'}\right)^2 \mathrm{var}(\ln z'_t)\\ -2\left(1+\frac{1}{\theta}\right)\left(\frac{1}{1-\overline{z}'}\right)\mathrm{cov}(\ln L^*_{Mt}, \ln z'_t).\end{aligned}$$

Sum this with (22) to write (23).

Acknowledgment

We thank Thomas Chaney, Fabio Ghironi and seminar participants at the NBER Summer Institute 2007, ASSA 2007 meetings in Chicago, UC San Diego, Carnegie Mellon University, Princeton University, University of Colorado, University of Paris, University of Southern California, the International Monetary Fund and Academia Sinica in Taipei for helpful comments.

References

Ambler, S., E. Cardia, and C. Zimmerman. 2002. International transmission of the business cycle in a multi-sectoral model. *European Economic Review*, 46: 273–300.

Amiti, M. and S.-J. Wei. 2006. Service offshoring and productivity: Evidence from the United States. National Bureau of Economic Research Working Paper No. 11926.

Antràs, P. and E. Helpman. 2004. Global sourcing. *Journal of Political Economy*, 112: 552–580.

Bergin, P. R., R. C. Feenstra, and G. H. Hanson. 2007. Offshoring and volatility. NBER Working Paper #13144.

Bergin, P. R., R. C. Feenstra, and G. H. Hanson. 2009. Offshoring and volatility: Evidence from Mexico's maquiladora industry. *American Economic Review*, 99: 1664–1671.

Berman, E., J. Bound, and S. Machin. 1998. Implications of skill-biased technological change: International evidence. *The Quarterly Journal of Economics*, 113(4): 1245–1279.

Bils, M. J. 1987. Real wages over the business cycle: Evidence from panel data. *Journal of Political Economy*, 93(4): 666–689.

Botero, J., S. Djankov, R. La Porta, F. López de Silanes, and A. Schleifer. 2004. The regulation of labor. *Quarterly Journal of Economics*, 119(4): 1339–1382.

Burstein, A., J. Kurz, and L. Tesar. 2008. Trade, production sharing, and the international transmission of business cycles. *Journal of Monetary Economics*, 55(4): 775–795.

Chari, V. V., P. J. Kehoe, and E. R. McGrattan. 2002. Can sticky price models generate volatile and persistent real exchange rates? *Review of Economic Studies*, 69: 533–563.

Comin, D., N. Loayza, F. Pasha, and L. Serven. 2009. Medium term business cycles in developing countries. NBER Working Paper No. 15428.

Devereux, M. B. and C. Engel. 2001. The optimal choice of exchange-rate regime: price-setting rules and internationalized production," in Blomstrom, M. and Goldberg, L., (eds). *Topics in Empirical International Economics: Festschrift in Honor of Robert Lipsey*, NBER and University of Chicago, 163–189.

Dornbusch, R., S. Fischer, and P. A. Samuelson. 1977. Comparative advantage, trade, and payments in a Ricardian model with a continuum of goods. *American Economic Review*, 67(5): 823–839.

Eaton, J. and S. Kortum. 2002. Technology, geography and trade. *Econometrica*, 70(5): 1741–1779.

Ebenstein, A., A. Harrison, M. McMillan, and S. Phillips. 2010. Estimating the impact of trade and offshoring on American workers using the current population surveys. UC Berkeley Mimeo.

Feenstra, R. C. 2009. *Offshoring in the Global Economy*. MIT Press Cambridge, MA.

Feenstra, R. C. and Hanson, G. H. 1999. The impact of outsourcing and high-technology capital on wages: Estimates for the United States, 1979–1990. *The Quarterly Journal of Economics*, 114(3): 907–940.

Glick, R. and K. Rogoff. 1995. Global versus country-specific productivity shocks and the current account. *Journal of Monetary Economics*, 35(1): 159–192.

Grossman, G. and E. Rossi-Hansberg. 2008. A simple theory of offshoring. *American Economic Review*, 98(5): 1978–1997.

Huang, K. X. D., Z. Liu, and L. Phaneuf. 2004. Why does the cyclical behavior of real wages change over time? *American Economic Review*, 94(4): 836–856.

Hummels, D., J. Ishii, and K.-M. Yi. 2001. The nature and growth of vertical specialization in world trade. *Journal of International Economics*, 54: 75–96.

Kose, M. A. and K.-M. Yi. 2001. International trade and business cycles: IS vertical specialization the missing link? *American Economic Review*, 91: 371–375.

Kose, M. A. and K.-M. Yi. 2006. Can the standard real business cycle model explain the relation between trade and comovement? *Journal of International Economics*, 68(2): 267–295.

Krugman, P. R. 2000. Technology, trade and factor prices. *Journal of International Economics*, 50(1): 51–71.

Zlate, A. 2008. Offshore Production and Business Cycle Dynamics with Heterogeneous Firms. Boston College Mimeo: Boston.

CHAPTER 4

Putting the "New Open Economy Macroeconomics" to a Test*

Paul R. Bergin

Department of Economics, University of California at Davis, One Shields Ave., Davis, CA 95616, USA
prbergin@ucdavis.edu

1. Introduction

Recent years have witnessed a shift in the theoretical approach in studying the international aspects of macroeconomics, with the development of a modeling approach that widely has become known as the "New Open Economy Macroeconomics (NOEM)." The unifying feature of this literature is the introduction of nominal rigidities into a dynamic general equilibrium model based on optimizing agents.[1] Typically, monopolistic competition is incorporated to permit the explicit analysis of price-setting decisions. This literature has tended to focus on shocks to money supply, and demonstrates how such shocks can explain fluctuations in the current account and exchange rate. Following the fundamental work of Obstfeld and Rogoff (1995), there has been a proliferation of models extending the theory in varied directions.[2]

*This article originally appeared in *Journal of International Economics* (2003), 60(1), 3–34.

[1]See Lane (2001) for a detailed survey of this literature.

[2]To name just a few, Kollmann (2001) considers a semi-small open economy version, Hau (2000) considers a version with nontraded goods, and Obstfeld and Rogoff (1998) and Devereux and Engel (1998) considered a reformulated version that permits a discussion of risk.

There are a number of debates within this literature. One such debate regards the choice of currency in which prices are sticky. Betts and Devereux (1996, 2000) argue that assuming prices are sticky in the currency of the buyer (local currency pricing) improves the model's ability to explain exchange rate behavior. On the other hand, Obstfeld and Rogoff (2000) argue in favor of prices sticky in the currency of the seller (producer currency pricing). A second theoretical argument regards whether stickiness is better assumed for prices or for wages. While the literature generally has focused on sticky goods prices, Obstfeld and Rogoff (2000) demonstrate the usefulness of wage stickiness.[3]

Resolution of these theoretical debates is hampered by the fact that while the theoretical literature on New Open Economy Macroeconomics has grown rapidly, the empirical literature has lagged behind. While earlier generations of intertemporal international models were evaluated econometrically using present value tests, this approach cannot accommodate the more complex models of the recent generation.[4] Without empirical testing, it is difficult to know which of the many versions considered in the literature is preferable. And more generally, it is impossible to say whether the overall approach of the NOEM is sufficiently accurate as a characterization of reality, that it could be eventually used reliably for policy analysis.

This chapter explores one approach for addressing these issues. A structural general equilibrium model of a semi-small open economy is estimated by maximum likelihood, and the fit of the model is evaluated by comparing the likelihood to that of an unrestricted counterpart.[5] In addition, alternative versions of the structural model are compared to each other in terms of their fit. The model is fit to a data set that includes the nominal exchange rate, the current account, output, money, home and world price

[3]Work by Erceg (1997) shows that this assumption is important for matching persistence in output data.

[4]See Sheffrin and Woo (1990), Ghosh (1995), and Bergin and Sheffrin (2000), for example.

[5]The estimation methodology used here was developed in Leeper and Sims (1994) and extended in Kim (2000), to estimate closed-economy structural models of monetary policy. The present methodology differs in that it is applied also to an unrestricted counterpart that nests the structural model, so as to permit likelihood ratio tests. The methodology is also extended to consider first differences and to allow correlated shocks. Ireland (1997 and 2001) also estimates parameters in a closed economy model by a related maximum likelihood procedure, but utilizes these for different purposes and tests. Ghironi (2000) estimates a New Open Economy model by nonlinear least squares at the single-equation level and by FIML system-wide regressions, but again the tests applied are quite different.

levels, and the world real interest rate. Three small open economies are considered: Australia, Canada, and the United Kingdom. The model considers a range of structural shocks in addition to money supply, including shocks to technology, foreign interest rate, foreign demand, and consumer tastes.

Results show mixed support for a benchmark New Open Economy model. A likelihood ratio test does not reject the benchmark theoretical model in comparison with the unrestricted counterpart model for two of three countries considered. Comparisons with a more standard vector autoregression using the Schwarz criterion favor the structural model for all three countries. However, in forecasting individual variables, the structural model does better for some variables than others. The model has some predictive value for the price level and output, but the model cannot beat a random walk in predicting movements in the exchange rate or the current account for any of the three countries. Price rigidities appear to be a useful element in the model, since a version that assumes no such rigidity is rejected for all three countries. Results are ambiguous regarding the importance of wage stickiness. Also, price stickiness of the local currency variety appears to be more useful than the alternative of stickiness in the currency of the producer, as the latter case generates a somewhat lower likelihood value for all three countries.

The next section will present the structural model, and Section 3 will present the estimation methodology. Section 4 will present results and Section 5 will draw some conclusions.

2. The Model

The benchmark model to be tested will be a small open economy model.[6] This is a simpler starting point than the larger, two-country models more widely used in the theoretical literature.

2.1. *Demand specifications*

Final goods in this economy (Y_t) are produced by aggregating over a continuum of intermediate home goods indexed by $i \in [0, 1]$ along with aggregating over a continuum of imported foreign goods indexed by

[6]Its basic features are based on the model of Kollmann (1997).

$j \in [0, 1]$. The aggregation technology for producing final goods is

$$Y_t = (Y^d_{Ht})^{\theta}(Y^d_{Ft})^{1-\theta}, \quad \text{where} \tag{1}$$

$$Y^d_{Ht} = \left(\int_0^1 y_{Ht}(i)^{\frac{1}{1+\upsilon}} di \right)^{1+\upsilon} \tag{2}$$

$$Y^d_{Ft} = \left(\int_0^1 y_{Ft}(j)^{\frac{1}{1+\upsilon}} dj \right)^{1+\upsilon}. \tag{3}$$

Here Y^d_{Ht} represents an aggregate of the home goods sold in the small open economy, and Y^d_{Ft} is an aggregate of the imported foreign goods, where lower case counterparts represent outputs of the individual firms.

Final goods producers behave competitively, maximizing profit each period:

$$\pi_{1t} = \max \left[P_t Y_t - P_{Ht} Y^d_{Ht} - P_{Ft} Y^d_{Ft} \right], \tag{4}$$

where P_t is the overall price index of the final good, P_{Ht} is the price index of home goods, and P_{Ft} is the price index of foreign goods, all denominated in the home currency. These may be defined:

$$P_t = (1-\theta)^{\theta-1}\theta^{-\theta} P^{\theta}_{Ht} P^{1-\theta}_{Ft}, \quad \text{where} \tag{5}$$

$$P_{Ht} = \left(\int_0^1 p_{Ht}(i)^{-\frac{1}{\upsilon}} di \right)^{-\upsilon} \tag{6}$$

$$P_{Ft} = \left(\int_0^1 p_{ft}(j)^{-\frac{1}{\upsilon}} dj \right)^{-\upsilon}, \tag{7}$$

and where lower case counterparts again represent the prices set by individual firms.

Given the aggregation functions above, demand will be allocated between home and foreign goods according to

$$Y^d_{Ht} = \theta Y_t (P_t / P_{Ht}) \tag{8}$$

$$Y^d_{Ft} = (1-\theta) Y_t (P_t / P_{Ft}) \tag{9}$$

with demands for individual goods:

$$y^d_{Ht}(i) = Y^d_{Ht}(p_{Ht}(i)/P_{Ht})^{-(1+\upsilon)/\upsilon} \tag{10}$$

$$y^d_{Ft}(j) = Y^d_{Ft}(p_{Ft}(j)/P_{Ft})^{-(1+\upsilon)/\upsilon}. \tag{11}$$

Foreign demand and prices will be specified in a way analogous to home demand. Let X_t be a quantity index of exports:

$$X_t = \left(\int_0^1 x_t(i)^{\frac{1}{1+\upsilon}} di \right)^{1+\upsilon}, \tag{12}$$

and let P_{Xt} be an index of export prices denominated in foreign currency:

$$P_{Xt} = \left(\int_0^1 p_{Xt}(i)^{-\frac{1}{\upsilon}} di \right)^{-\upsilon}. \tag{13}$$

It will be assumed that foreign demand for the exports of our small economy is negatively related to the ratio of export prices to the price level in the rest of the world (P_t^*):

$$X_t = \chi (P_{Xt}/P_t^*)^{-(1+\upsilon)/\upsilon}, \tag{14}$$

where χ represents a stochastic shock to overall foreign demand. It is assumed that the export demand function for good i resembles the domestic demand function for that good (10):

$$x_t^d(i) = X_t (p_{Xt}(i)/P_{Xt})^{-(1+\upsilon)/\upsilon}. \tag{15}$$

In addition, home firms produce their goods out of differentiated home labor inputs, indexed by $h \in [0, 1]$. Let $l_t(h, i)$ represent the demand for labor input h by producer i. These differentiated labor inputs are aggregated into the total demand for labor by firm i, $L_t(i)$, according to

$$L_t(i) = \left(\int_0^1 l_t(h, i)^{\frac{1}{1+\eta}} dh \right)^{1+\eta}. \tag{16}$$

Let $w_t(h)$ denote the nominal wage of worker h, and let W_t denote the price index for labor inputs. Cost minimization then implies that this index be

$$W_t = \left(\int_0^1 w_t(h)^{-\frac{1}{\eta}} dh \right)^{-\eta}. \tag{17}$$

Given the aggregation function above, labor demand will be

$$l_t(h, i) = L_t(i) \left(\frac{w_t(h)}{W_t} \right)^{-\frac{1+\eta}{\eta}}. \tag{18}$$

Demand for labor of worker h may be aggregated over producers as follows:

$$l_t(h) = \int_0^1 l_t(h, i)di \tag{19}$$

and overall labor demand as

$$L_t = \int_0^1 L_t(i)di. \tag{20}$$

2.2. *Firm behavior*

There are two types of monopolistically competitive intermediate goods suppliers in the small open economy. The first type produces intermediate goods to sell domestically and to export. The second type of firm imports foreign goods to resell in the domestic markets. Both types of firms are owned by domestic households and maximize discounted profits.

The domestic producing firm (i) rents capital $(K_t(i))$ at the real rental rate r_t, and hires labor $(L_t(i))$ at the nominal wage rate W_t to produce output of home goods $(z_t(i))$. The firm chooses the price for sale of its good in the home market $(p_{Ht}(i))$ and in the foreign market $(p_{Xt}(i))$ to maximize profits $(\pi_{Ht}(i))$, knowing that its choice of price will determine the level of demands for its good $(y^d_{Ht}(i)$ and $x^d_t(i))$. Markets are assumed to be segmented, and the foreign sale price is in terms of the foreign (world) currency. The nominal exchange rate (e_t) is the home currency price of one unit of the world currency. It is assumed that it is costly to reset prices because of quadratic menu costs. The size of costs for adjusting both these prices are assumed to depend upon the same "price adjustment cost parameter," ψ_P.[7] The problem for these firms may be summarized:

$$\max\ E_0 \sum_{t=0}^{\infty} \rho_{t,t+n} \pi_{Ht}(i) \tag{21}$$

where

$$\begin{aligned} \pi_{Ht}(i) = {} & p_{Ht}(i) y^d_{Ht}(i) + e_t p_{Xt}(i) x^d_t(i) - P_t r_{t-1} K_{t-1}(i) \\ & - W_t L_t(i) - P_t AC_{Ht}(i) - e_t P_t AC_{Xt}(i) \end{aligned} \tag{22}$$

[7]It has been demonstrated in Rotemberg (1982) that menu costs of this type, although simple to specify and work with, generate price dynamics identical to those of Calvo random price staggering.

$$\text{s.t.} \quad AC_{Ht}(i) = \frac{\psi_P}{2} \frac{(p_{Ht}(i) - p_{Ht-1}(i))^2}{P_t p_{Ht-1}(i)} y^d_{Ht}(i) \tag{23}$$

$$AC_{Xt}(i) = \frac{\psi_P}{2} \frac{(p_{Xt}(i) - p_{Xt-1}(i))^2}{P_t p_{Xt-1}(i)} y^d_{Xt}(i) \tag{24}$$

$$z_t(i) = A_t K_{t-1}(i)^{\alpha} L_t(i)^{1-\alpha} \tag{25}$$

$$z_t(i) = y^d_{Ht}(i) + y^d_{Xt}(i) \tag{26}$$

and subject to the demand functions for $y^d_{Ht}(i)$ and $y^d_{Xt}(i)$ above. Here A_t represents technology common to all production firms in the country, and it is subject to shocks. Lastly, $\rho_{t,t+n}$ is the pricing kernel used to value random date $t+n$ payoffs. Since firms are assumed to be owned by the representative household, it is assumed that firms value future payoffs according to the household's intertemporal marginal rate of substitution in consumption, so $\rho_{t,t+n} = \beta^n U'_{C,t+n}/U'_{C,t}$, where $U'_{C,t+n}$ is the household's marginal utility of consumption in period $t+n$.

This problem implies an optimal trade-off between capital and labor inputs that depend on the relative cost of each:

$$P_t r_{t-1} K_{t-1}(i) = \frac{\alpha}{1-\alpha} W_t L_t(i). \tag{27}$$

Noting that in equilibrium $p_{Ht}(i) = p_{Ht}$ and $p_{Xt}(i) = p_{Xt}$ for all i, the optimal price setting rules are

$$E_t\left[\frac{\rho_{t,t+i+1}}{\rho_{t,t+i}} \frac{\psi_P}{2}\left(\frac{p^2_{Ht+1}}{p^2_{Ht}} - 1\right)\frac{y^d_{Ht+1}}{y^d_{Ht}}\right] - \psi_P\left(\frac{p_{Ht}}{p_{Ht-1}} - 1\right) + \frac{1+\nu}{\nu} \\ \times\left(\frac{P_t r_{t-1}}{p_{Ht}\alpha A_t\left(L_t(i)/K_{t-1}(i)\right)^{(1-\alpha)}} + \frac{\psi_P}{2}\frac{(p_{Ht} - p_{Ht-1})^2}{p_{Ht}p_{Ht-1}} - 1\right) + 1 = 0 \tag{28}$$

$$E_t\left[\frac{\rho_{t,t+i+1}}{\rho_{t,t+i}} \frac{\psi_P}{2}\left(\frac{p^2_{Xt+1}}{p^2_{Xt}} - 1\right)\frac{e_{t+1}}{e_t}\frac{x^d_{t+1}}{x^d_t}\right] - \psi_P\left(\frac{p_{Xt}}{p_{Xt-1}} - 1\right) + \frac{1+\nu}{\nu} \\ \times\left(\frac{P_t r_{t-1}}{e_t p_{Xt}\alpha A_t\left(L_t(i)/K_{t-1}\right)^{(1-\alpha)}} + \frac{\psi_P}{2}\frac{(p_{Xt} - p_{Xt-1})^2}{p_{Xt}p_{Xt-1}} - 1\right) + 1 = 0. \tag{29}$$

The importing firms choose the resale price $(p_{ft}(j))$ to maximize their profits. They too are subject to quadratic menu costs, which depend upon the same adjustment cost parameter as the goods prices above, ψ_P. Their problem may be summarized:

$$\max E_0 \sum_{t=0}^{\infty} \rho_{t,t+i} \pi_{Ft}(j) \tag{30}$$

where

$$\pi_{Fjt} = (p_{Ft}(j) - e_t P_t^*) y_{Ft}^d(j) - P_t AC_{Ft}(j) \tag{31}$$

and

$$AC_{Ft}(i) = \frac{\psi_P}{2} \frac{(p_{Ft}(i) - p_{Ft-1}(i))^2}{P_t p_{Ft-1}(i)} y_{Ft}^d(j), \tag{32}$$

and subject to the demand functions for $y_{Ft}^d(i)$ above. Noting that in equilibrium $p_{Ft}(j) = p_{Ft}$ for all j, the optimal pricing rule is

$$E_t \left[\frac{\rho_{t,t+i+1}}{\rho_{t,t+i}} \frac{\psi_P}{2} \left(\frac{p_{Ft+1}^2}{p_{Ft}^2} - 1 \right) \frac{y_{Ft+1}^d}{y_{Ft}^d} \right] - \psi_P \left(\frac{p_{Ft}}{p_{Ft-1}} - 1 \right)$$
$$+ \frac{1+\nu}{\nu} \left(e_t \frac{P_t^*}{p_{Ft}} + \frac{\psi_P}{2} \frac{(p_{Ft} - p_{Ft-1})^2}{p_{Ft} p_{Ft-1}} - 1 \right) + 1 = 0. \tag{33}$$

2.3. *Household behavior*

The household/worker h derives utility from consumption $(C_t(h))$, and supplying labor $(L_t(h))$ lowers utility. For simplicity, real money balances $(M_t(h)/P_t)$ are also introduced in the utility function, where P is the overall price level. The household discounts future utility at the rate of time preference β. Preferences are additively separable in these three arguments, and preferences for consumption and money demand are subject to preference shocks. The taste shock for consumption is of a type considered by Stockman and Tesar (1995), in which a rise in τ_C lowers the marginal utility of consumption. The money demand shock is modeled analogously.

Households derive income by selling their labor at the nominal wage rate $(w_t(h))$, renting out capital to firms at the real rental rate (r), receiving real profits from the two types of firms (π_1 and π_2), and from government transfers (T). In addition to money, households can hold a noncontingent real bond (B), measured in terms of the foreign (world) consumption index. This pays an interest rate (R) in terms of the foreign consumption index, which is subject to exogenous shocks. The nominal exchange rate is e and the foreign price level is P^*, so holdings and returns on these bonds may be converted to units of the domestic consumption index by multiplying by $e_t P_t^* / P_t$. Investment ($I_t(h)$) in new capital ($K_t(h)$) involves a quadratic adjustment cost that depends upon the parameter ψ_I, and there is a constant rate of depreciation (δ). Households choose the wage at which they sell their differentiated labor, and there is a cost of changing this wage which depends upon the adjustment cost parameter ψ_W.

The optimization problem faced by the household may be expressed:

$$\max\ E_0 \sum_{t=0}^{\infty} \beta^t U\left(C_t(h), \frac{M_t(h)}{P_t}, L_t(h) \right) \tag{34}$$

$$\begin{aligned} \text{s.t.} \quad & \frac{w_t(h)}{P_t} L_t(h) + r_{t-1} K_{t-1}(h) + \int_0^1 (\pi_{Ht}(j) + \pi_{Ft}(j)) dj + T_t(h) \\ & + \left(\frac{e_t P_t^*}{P_t} \right) R_{t-1} B_{t-1}(h) - C_t(h) - I_t(h) \\ & - \left(\frac{M_t(h) - M_{t-1}(h)}{P_t} \right) - AC_{It}(h) - AC_{Wt}(h) \\ = & \frac{e_t P_t^*}{P_t} (B_t(h) - B_{t-1}(h)) \end{aligned} \tag{35}$$

$$AC_{It}(h) = \frac{\psi_I}{2} \frac{(K_t(h) - K_{t-1}(h))^2}{K_{t-1}(h)} \tag{36}$$

$$AC_{Wt}(h) = \frac{\psi_W}{2} \frac{(w_t(h) - w_{t-1}(h))^2}{P_t w_{t-1}(h)} l_t(h) \tag{37}$$

$$l_t(h) = L_t \left(\frac{w_t(h)}{W_t} \right)^{-\frac{1+\eta}{\eta}} \tag{38}$$

$$U_t(h) = \frac{1}{1-\sigma_1}(\tau_{ct}C_t(h))^{1-\sigma_1} + \frac{1}{1-\sigma_2}\left(\tau_{mt}\frac{M_t(h)}{P_t}\right)^{1-\sigma_2}$$
$$- \frac{\sigma_3}{1+\sigma_3} l_t(h)^{\frac{1+\sigma_3}{\sigma_3}} \tag{39}$$
$$I_t(h) = K_t(h) - (1-\delta)K_{t-1}(h), \tag{40}$$

where $\sigma_i > 0, \sigma_i \neq 1$, for $i = 1 \ldots 3$, $\psi_I \geq 0$.

The household problem implies the following optimality conditions. First, households will smooth consumption across time periods according to

$$\frac{e_t P_t^*}{P_t} U'_{Ct}(h) = \beta(1+R_t)E_t\left[\frac{e_{t+1}P_{t+1}^*}{P_{t+1}} U'_{Ct+1}(h)\right]. \tag{41}$$

Households prefer expected marginal utilities to be constant across time periods, unless a rate of return on saving exceeding their time preference induces them to lower consumption today relative to the future. Second, household money demand will depend on consumption and the interest rate

$$P_t \frac{U'_{Mt}(h)}{U'_{Ct}(h)} = 1 - \left(\frac{1}{1+R_t}\right) E_t\left[\frac{P_t}{P_{t+1}}\right]. \tag{42}$$

Third, noting that in equilibrium $w_t(h) = W_t$ for all h, the optimal wage-setting equation is

$$E_t\left[\frac{\beta U'_{c,t+1}}{U'_{c,t}} \frac{\psi_W}{2}\left(\frac{W_{t+1}^2}{W_t^2} - 1\right)\frac{L_{t+1}}{L_t}\frac{P_t}{P_{t+1}}\right] - \psi_W\left(\frac{W_t}{W_{t-1}} - 1\right)$$
$$+ \frac{1+\eta}{\eta}\left(\frac{L_t^{\sigma_3} C_t^{\sigma_1} \tau_t^{-\sigma_1}}{W_t/P_t} + \frac{\psi_W}{2}\frac{(W_t - W_{t-1})^2}{W_t W_{t-1}} - 1\right) + 1 = 0. \tag{43}$$

Finally, capital accumulation is set to equate the costs and expected benefits:

$$(1+R_t)\left(1 + \frac{\psi_I(K_t(h) - K_{t-1}(h))}{K_{t-1}(h)}\right)$$
$$= r_t + (1-\delta) + \frac{\Psi_I}{2}E_t\left(\frac{K_{t+1}^2(h) - K_t^2(h)}{K_t^2(h)}\right). \tag{44}$$

The cost, on the left side, is the gross return if the funds instead had been used to purchase bonds; and the benefits on the right include the return from rental of the capital plus the resale value after depreciation, and the fact that a larger capital stock lowers the expected adjustment cost of further accumulation in the subsequent period.

2.4. *Equilibrium*

The government uses final goods for a fixed amount of government purchases, G. It also chooses a money supply, M_t, which it distributes by transfers to households. The government budget constraint is

$$\int_0^1 T_t(h)dh + G = \frac{1}{P_t}(M_t - M_{t-1}), \tag{45}$$

and the money market clearing condition is

$$M_t = \int_0^1 M_t(h)dh. \tag{46}$$

The resource constraint for final goods is

$$\begin{aligned} Y_t = &\int_0^1 (C_t(h) + I_t(h) + AC_{It}(h) + AC_{Wt}(h))dh + G \\ &+ \int_0^1 AC_{Xt}(i)di + \int_0^1 AC_{Ft}(j)dj. \end{aligned} \tag{47}$$

The current account may be computed as

$$CA_t = \frac{e_t P_t^*}{P_t} \int_0^1 (B_t(h) - B_{t-1}(h))dh. \tag{48}$$

and the real exchange rate as

$$q_t = \frac{e_t P_t^*}{P_t}. \tag{49}$$

The stochastic shocks in the model are specified to follow:

$$\begin{aligned} (R_t - \overline{R}) &= \rho_R(R_{t-1} - \overline{R}) + \varepsilon_{Rt} \\ (\log P_t^* - \log P_{t-1}^*) &= \rho_{P^*}(\log P_{t-1}^* - \log P_{t-2}^*) + \varepsilon_{P^*t} \\ (\log \chi_t - \log \overline{\chi}) &= \rho_x(\log \chi_{t-1} - \log \overline{\chi}) + \varepsilon_{xt} \\ (\log A_t - \log \overline{A}) &= \rho_A(\log A_{t-1} - \log \overline{A}) + \varepsilon_{At} \end{aligned}$$

$$(\log \tau_{ct} - \log \overline{\tau_c}) = \rho_c(\log \tau_{ct-1} - \log \overline{\tau_c}) + \varepsilon_{ct}$$

$$(\log \tau_{mt} - \log \overline{\tau}_m) = \rho_m(\log \tau_{mt-1} - \log \overline{\tau_m}) + \varepsilon_{mt}$$

$$(\log M_t - \log M_{t-1}) = \rho_M(\log M_{t-1} - \log M_{t-2}) + \varepsilon_{Mt} \tag{50}$$

$$[\varepsilon_{Rt}, \varepsilon_{P^*t}, \varepsilon_{xt}, \varepsilon_{At}, \varepsilon_{ct}, \varepsilon_{mdt}, \varepsilon_{Mt}]'\tilde{}N(0, \Sigma_1).$$

Note that the shocks may be correlated with each other. This was found to be important in improving the fit of the theoretical model and allow it to compete with the unrestricted counterpart, which likewise allows the shocks to be correlated. Recall that the theoretical restrictions to be tested all relate to the autoregressive coefficients of the model. Further, this assumption is arguably well suited to a small open economy, where several of the variables are taken to be determined outside the model.[8] Further, the fact that the shocks to money growth may be correlated with the other shocks may be useful in that it allows us to approximate a money growth rule in which policy makers can respond to economic conditions. Although there are no explicit fiscal shocks, the shock to foreign demand specified here could in principle be viewed as representing a wide variety of exogenous shocks to demand. Note also that since the data to which the model is fit are detrended, this is consistent with the fact that the shock processes above do not try to explain exogenous trends in series like money supply.

The model will be analyzed in a form log-linearized around a deterministic steady state. Equilibrium for this economy includes sequences for 16 endogenous variables: consumption (C), labor (L), home goods production (Z), capital stock (K), bond position (B), home price index (P), price of home goods sold at home (P_H), price of imported goods (P_F), export price of home goods (P_X), domestic demand for home goods (Y_H^d), domestic demand for imported goods (Y_F^d), demand for foreign exports (X), wage (W), real rental rate on capital (r), nominal exchange rate (e), and final goods demand (Y). These variables are matched by 16 equilibrium conditions: the consumption Euler Equation (41), production function (25),

[8]Given that the small open economy model does not explain foreign production, there is no global technology shock here of the type emphasized in Glick and Rogoff (1995). However, correlated shocks to the domestic technology term (A) and the world real interest rate (R) may in practice reflect supply shocks that are global in nature.

definition of home goods production (26), capital accumulation optimality condition (44), the resource constraint (47), price index definition (5), optimal price setting conditions (28, 29, 33), shares of home and imported goods in domestic final output (8, 9), export demand function (14), optimal wage setting condition (43), capital–labor trade-off in production (27), money demand condition (42), and the household budget constraint (35).

In addition, there are three conditions to define related variables that are of interest in the empirical exercise: one to define the current account (48), define investment (40), and define the real exchange rate (49). There are also the seven stochastic equations in (50) defining the role of shocks for the exogenous variables: R, P^*, X, A, τ_c, τ_m, and M. Because the equations above involve expected future values of prices and wages, four equations are used to define these. Finally, because the equations above involve double lags of capital, interest rate, and money, three equations are created to define these variables in the context of the first-order autoregressive structure. Altogether this amounts to a set of 33 variables and 33 linearized equations. A solution for the model equilibrium is found using the method of Blanchard and Kahn (1980).

3. Empirical Methods

3.1. *Data*

Data from three small open economies will be considered: Australia, Canada, and the United Kingdom. The model will be fit to seven series: the current account, nominal exchange rate, domestic price index, foreign price index, output, money supply, and world real interest rate. Because the estimation algorithm is computationally very intensive, it is important to limit the list of variables to the most essential. Given that the New Open Economy literature is primarily interested in explaining real and nominal exchange rates as well as the current account, this mandates the first four variables listed above. To capture the potentially important roles of shifts in technology and policy, output and money supply are included. Finally, the world interest rate provides a simple way to capture explanatory factors arising outside the small open economy. All data are seasonally adjusted quarterly series at annual rates for the period 1973:2 to 1996:4, obtained from International Financial Statistics. Quantities are deflated to real terms using the GDP deflator and put in per capita terms. Series other than the interest rate and the current account are logged. Because the steady state value of the current account in the theoretical model is necessarily zero, this variable cannot be expressed in the model in a form that represents deviations from steady state in log form. Instead the current account is scaled by taking it as a ratio to the mean level of output. The real interest rate is not logged because it can take negative values.

Output (Y) is measured as national GDP, money (M) by $M1$, and the domestic price level (P) by the CPI.[9] A measure of the world real interest rate (r) is computed following the method of Barro and Sala i Martin (1990). I collected short-term nominal interest rates, T-bill rates or the equivalent, on the G-7 economies. Short-term interest rates are used because I wish to adjust for inflation expectations, which are much more reliably forecast over a short-time horizon. Inflation in each country is measured using that country's consumer price index, and expected inflation is forecast using a six-quarter autoregression. The nominal interest rate in each country then is adjusted by inflation expectations to compute an *ex-ante* real interest rate. The aggregate real interest rate is an average over the G-7 countries, excluding the domestic country under consideration. The time-varying weights used in this average are based on each country's share of real GDP in the total.

A measure of the foreign price index is computed in a similar manner to the interest rate. The national CPIs of the G-7 economies, excluding the domestic country under consideration, are averaged using the same GDP weighting scheme. Similarly, the nominal exchange rate is the average of the relative price of the domestic currency to a weighted average of the currencies of the remaining G-7 countries. Given that the data set includes measures of domestic and foreign CPIs as well as the nominal exchange rate, the data set thereby implicitly contains data on the real exchange rate.

As a preliminary step, the data series are tested for unit roots. Table 1 shows the results. The seven series appear to be nonstationary in levels but stationary in first differences. Using the Phillips–Perron test, the presence of a unit root cannot be rejected for any of the data series used here for any of the countries, with one exception. Nonstationarity is rejected only

[9]For the UK the series quasi money, supplied by IFS, is used.

Table 1. Unit root tests

	Australia	Canada	UK
Phillips–Perron Test:			
Output			
Levels	−2.4622	−1.3565	−2.1387
Differences	−10.6771**	−5.4435**	−8.5192**
Current account			
Levels	−3.8756*	−2.1228	−2.1297
Differences	−13.6025**	−10.8494**	−12.5137**
Money			
Levels	0.5865	−1.1555	−1.2471
Differences	−8.8466**	−8.0456**	−9.1453**
Exchange rate			
Levels	−2.6189	−2.4922	−2.4559
Differences	−10.6173**	−9.0604**	−7.5132**
Price level			
Levels	−1.1286	0.4643	−1.3842
Differences	−5.9960**	−5.0791**	−8.7884**
World price level			
Levels	−0.5104	−0.6122	−0.5138
Differences	−5.7204**	−5.8607**	−5.9572**
Interest rate			
Levels	−2.4869	−2.5530	−2.6385
Differences	−12.9088**	−13.1721**	−13.1493**

Notes: **Indicates unit root rejected at 1% significance level; *Indicates rejected at 5% level. Tests run with 3 lags. Range is 1973Q2 to 1996Q4. Critical values: 1% −4.06; 5% −3.46; 10% −3.15.

for the current account in Australia. However, it may be worth noting that the statistics for the current account data in Canada and the UK are near their 10% critical values.[10] As will be explained below, this data will be used in the form of log differences that are demeaned. This follows the standard practice in the related present value test literature. (See Bergin and Sheffrin (2000) for a discussion.)

3.2. *Econometric methods*

The econometric methodology estimates the linear approximation to the structural model, adapting a maximum likelihood algorithm developed in

[10]Results for the Dickey–Fuller test, not shown, are similar.

Leeper and Sims (1994) and Kim (2000). This estimation methodology is extended here to accommodate first differences in the data and to allow for correlations among the shocks. The method is also adapted to estimate an analogous unrestricted model, and the two models are compared on the basis of their likelihood values. Because the linearized structural model is a nested version of the unrestricted model, where the only difference is a set of theoretical restrictions imposed, a likelihood ratio test can be used as a test of these theoretical restrictions.

The linearized and solved structural model discussed in the previous section is a set of seven stochastic equations and 26 deterministic equations. By using model equations to substitute out variables, the linearized model can be written in its most compact first-order autoregressive form as 15 equations involving the seven variables on which we have data, as well as eight other variables. (These additional eight variables are those that appear in lagged form in the equations above, so they cannot be substituted out and still retain the first-order autoregressive form of the model.) Seven of these equations are stochastic and eight deterministic. This model system can be arranged in the following form:

$$y_t = Ay_{t-1} + A\varepsilon_t, \tag{51}$$

$$\varepsilon_t \sim N(0, \Sigma t)\Sigma = \begin{bmatrix} \Sigma_2 & 0 \\ 0 & 0 \end{bmatrix},$$

where y is a 15-element column vector of variables in percent deviations from steady state; A, which appears twice, is a 15×15 matrix, where each cell is a nonlinear function of the structural parameters; ε is a column vector, where the first seven elements are functions of the seven structural disturbances and the remaining eight elements are zeros; and Σ_2 is the 7×7 covariance matrix of the disturbances in ε.

The model will be dealt with in first differences. This is done for several reasons. The first is that the unit root tests discussed in the previous section cannot in general reject a unit root for the data series used here. A second and equally important reason for using first differences is that the structural model implies the presence of a unit root in the linearized system (51). Given that asset markets are assumed to be incomplete, a wide range of transitory shocks will cause domestic households to borrow abroad as they smooth their consumption. This has a permanent effect on the wealth allocation between the small open economy and the rest of the world, and hence also on the endogenous variables which depend on this wealth allocation. This unit root implies that the methods used for estimation here cannot be applied to these variables in levels, because the variance–covariance matrix is not defined for these variables. A third reason is that I hope to relate my results to the preceding papers in the literature, especially Ahmed *et al.* (1993), which worked with the data in first differences. In addition, the differenced data will be demeaned, to remove a linear trend. This is the common practice in the present value tests of intertemporal models, such as Sheffrin and Woo (1990) and Bergin and Sheffrin (2000).

The model system may be rewritten in terms of first differences as follows:

$$y_t^* = Ay_{t-1}^* + A\varepsilon_t - A\varepsilon_{t-1}, \tag{52}$$

where

$$y_t^* = y_t - y_{t-1}.$$

This stochastic model implies a log likelihood function:

$$L(\Pi) = -\cdot 5 \ln |\Omega| - \cdot 5 x'\Omega^{-1} x, \tag{53}$$

where x is the vector of differenced variables to which the model is fit, over all periods and stacked into a single vector. Ω is the theoretical variance–covariance matrix of x. The appendix discusses the details of how Ω is computed as a function of the matrices A and Σ_2. But note that each cell in A is a nonlinear function of the structural parameters from the theoretical model. An algorithm is used to search for values of these structural parameters and for the elements of the symmetric positive-definite covariance matrix Σ_2, which will maximize the likelihood function.

Note that taking first differences should not introduce the classic problem of "overdifferencing" here. The fact that differencing may introduce a moving average term is taken into consideration in Equation (52) and hence the computation of Ω and the likelihood function, so a misspecified model is not being estimated. It is true that the presence of a unit moving average root may mean the moving average is not invertible, so that an approximate likelihood conditional on the initial observations may not be a good approximation to the true unconditional likelihood. In part for this reason, the true likelihood is used here, unconditional on the initial observations. Again details are in the appendix.

The estimated model will be compared to an entirely analogous reduced form model. Like the structural model, the reduced form counterpart also takes the form of (51) and (52), and it involves the same differenced variables. However, the estimation algorithm treats the cells of the matrix A as distinct parameters, rather than as functions of underlying structural parameters. For the covariance matrix, Σ_2, the estimation algorithm is permitted to choose any symmetric positive semidefinite matrix, exactly as with the structural model. The structural model then is a nested version of the reduced form model, with an extra set of restrictions specifying the elements of the A matrix as functions of a common set of structural parameters, and shocks defined to have structural interpretations.

Estimating the reduced form model amounts to searching over values for the cells of A and Σ_2 to maximize the likelihood function, computed in exactly the same way as for the structural model using the unconditional likelihood.[11] Because the reduced form estimation is unhindered by theoretical restrictions, it is certain to generate a higher likelihood value than the restricted model. A likelihood ratio offers a way to compare the two likelihood values, adjusting for the number of restrictions, which will equal the number of cells in A and the lower triangular portion of Σ_2, minus the number of structural parameters that are free to be chosen by the estimation algorithm. This chapter also reports approximate standard errors for the parameter estimates and residuals from a one-step ahead forecast. The appendix describes how these are computed.

A few parameters will not be estimated here, but instead are pinned down ahead of time. This is because the data set omits the relevant series for these parameters, like capital and investment, or because the data set in first differences is not very relevant for parameters pertaining to steady states. As a result, these parameters are pinned down at values common in the Real Business Cycle literature. In particular, the capital share in production (α) is set at 40, the depreciation rate (δ) is set at 10, the share of home

[11] As in the structural model, A is restricted to have roots less than or equal to unity. See the appendix for details.

intermediate goods in the home final goods aggregate (θ) is set at 80, and the discount factor (β) is set at 96.[12]

Some regions of the parameter space do not imply a well defined equilibrium within the model. These regions can be precluded by imposing boundaries on the parameters by functional transformations. For example, the variances of shocks and the intertemporal elasticity are restricted to be positive. The depreciation rate and discount factor must be restricted between zero and unity: Autoregressive coefficients on shock processes are also restricted to be greater than zero and less than unity. Finally, the covariances between shocks must be restricted so that the implied correlations lie between −1 and 1.

Convergence here can be time-consuming and dependent on good starting values. Numerical issues such as rounding error can create problems for convergence. Optimization software developed by Christopher Sims is used which is more robust to these difficulties.

4. Results

4.1. *Benchmark model*

The results of the estimated benchmark model are reported in Table 2, where an overall evaluation of the model can be read from the log likelihood value. First consider a comparison with the unrestricted counterpart model defined in the previous section. Line 4 of Table 2 indicates that a likelihood ratio test fails to reject the restrictions implied by the structural model relative to this counterpart in two of the three cases, Australia and Canada. For the case of the United Kingdom, the model is rejected at the 5% significance level. The structural model can be compared also with an unrestricted model that is more standard and familiar, a simple first-order

---

[12]It is widely understood that when some parameters in a model are calibrated exogenously and some estimated, the estimation should be viewed as conditional on the choice of calibration values. In principal, these calibrated values could be regarded as part of the specification of the particular model that is being tested here, akin to the choice of functional forms. (The choice of a Cobb–Douglas form for the production function implies an elasticity of substitution equal to 1.0.) Future work using this methodology could extend the method to a larger data set, to permit all the structural parameters in the model to be estimated. However, increasing the dimension of the estimation job has the disadvantage of increasing the time for convergence, which already is very long.

Table 2. Benchmark sticky price and wage model

		Australia	Canada	UK
Measures of fit				
Log likelihood value				
Model		2491.73	2629.00	2430.92
Unrestricted		2597.54	2749.26	2556.94
Likelihood ratio		211.60	240.52	252.04
p-value*		0.48	0.08	0.03
Standard VAR		2481.84	2640.91	2427.57
Schwarz (model)		2450.40	2587.66	2389.58
Schwarz (VAR)		2406.05	2565.12	2351.78
RMSE: Structural model/standard VAR				
Current account		1.13	1.03	1.12
Nominal e		1.06	1.07	1.06
Real e		1.06	1.05	1.09
Output		1.05	1.21	1.08
Price level		0.98	1.18	1.09
RMSE: Structural model/random walk				
Current account		1.01	1.01	1.03
Nominal e		1.04	1.04	1.04
Real e		1.03	1.03	1.06
Output		0.99	0.93	0.98
Price level		0.73	0.59	0.80
Main structural parameter estimates				
Consumption elasticity term	σ_1	37.084	18.777	24.599
		(1.697)	(2.522)	(0.549)
Money demand elasticity term	σ_2	4.972	3.822	2.523
		(0.203)	(0.036)	(0.163)
Labor-supply elasticity	σ_3	0.0004	0.0008	0.0002
		(0.0000)	(0.0001)	(0.0000)
Investment adjustment cost	ψ_I	265.418	267.682	439.792
		(77.571)	(47.976)	(60.184)
Price adjustment cost	ψ_P	189.628	68.129	330.483
		(34.284)	(4.243)	(27.529)
Wage adjustment cost	ψ_W	0.077	0.044	0.064
		(0.001)	(0.002)	(0.001)
Demand elastasticity term for goods	ν	1.087	6.102	0.678
		(0.079)	(1.027)	(0.017)

Notes: Values in parentheses indicate standard errors.
*Degress of freedom = 211.

vector autoregression (VAR) of the seven data series. However, the structural model is not nested in such a VAR, which rules out a comparison based on a likelihood ratio test.[13] Lines six and seven of Table 2 present a comparison based on the Schwarz criterion, indicating that the structural model outperforms the standard VAR for all three countries by this measure.[14] These results together offer some statistical support for the benchmark New Open Economy model.

Table 2 also reports the root mean squared errors (RMSE) for one-step ahead forecasts for the five endogenous variables to which the model is fit. As in Meese and Rogoff (1983), these RMSE are reported in comparison with those of a random walk model, indicating whether the theory has any predictive content.[15] As an additional comparison, RMSE are also reported relative to the standard VAR. The structural model appears to perform best for the price level and output, where it beats the random walk model for all three countries. The structural model does less well on the current account, where it fails to beat the random walk. A striking feature here is the very poor performance on exchange rates. The structural model fails to come close to the random walk model for any of the three countries for the nominal or real exchange rate. This is despite the fact that the model is able to replicate the degree of volatility observed in the data: the model implies a standard deviation of the nominal and real exchange rates (as ratios to output) equal to 4.80 and 4.24 respectively, compared to 4.24 and 4.10 in the data. While past studies have found that price stickiness in the currency of the buyer can help a model match the moments of the exchange rate, apparently this is not sufficient to match the actual time path of this variable.

The overall conclusion is one of mixed support. By some criteria of fit, the model performs better than one might have expected for such a highly structural model. Further, the model has some ability in forecasting particular variables like the price level and output. But disappointingly, the model does a poor job in explaining key international variables, especially

[13]Firstly, the structural model requires some state variables to enter the equations lagged more than once, and secondly, its estimation does not condition on the initial observations as does standard VAR estimation.

[14]The Schwarz criterion here is calculated as the log likelihood minus $0.5 \times k \times \log(n)$, where k is the number of free parameters and n is the number of observations.

[15]Unlike Meese and Rogoff (1983), the forecasts here are in sample.

exchange rates. This last conclusion should perhaps not come as a surprise, given the poor performance of structural macroeconomic models on this count documented by Meese and Rogoff (1983) and other researchers.

Table 2 also reports key parameter values implied by the estimation, which are mostly reasonable and statistically significant. For all three countries, the intertemporal elasticity ($1/\sigma_1$) appears to be very small (below 0.1). While these values are smaller than typically are assumed in calibration studies, Hall (1988) and others have found similar results in econometric studies of the intertemporal elasticity. A low elasticity indicates that households are strongly committed to smoothing their consumption across time, and are not willing to adjust consumption in response to the interest rate. The estimate of the labor-supply elasticity (σ_3) is near to zero.[16] The investment adjustment cost is sizable. For Australia, for example, a value of $\psi_I = 265.4$ indicates that if Australia raises investment expenditure 1% above its steady state level, approximately 13.3% of this extra investment expenditure goes toward paying the adjustment cost. The adjustment cost for prices is also sizable. For Australia, the value of $\psi_P = 189.6$ implies that after a shock to money supply, the aggregate price level moves about 9% of the way toward its long run level each quarter, so that it has a half-life of 7.9 quarters. The adjustment cost for wages is much lower than that estimated for prices.

Since there are 35 parameters characterizing the variances, covariances, and persistences of the shocks, these are not reported in the table. But all appear to be reasonable, and the large majority of variances and persistence parameters are statistically different from zero and unity.

Variance decompositions can be used to infer the role of monetary shocks in driving exchange rates and the current account. Given that the shocks are all correlated with each other, they will be orthogonalized here to make the decomposition easier to interpret. Since the structural model provided sufficient theoretical restrictions to identify the shocks without the need to assume orthogonality, it was decided to allow the shocks to be correlated to permit a more fair comparison between the structural

[16]As a check, the model was re-estimated for Australia under the restriction that the labor-supply elasticity takes the more usual value of unity. The maximum likelihood value in this case is 2478.00, much lower than for the benchmark model, and the restriction is rejected even at the 1% significance level.

and unrestricted models. So now a simple Cholesky decomposition will be used to orthogonalize the shocks, similarly to what is common with nonstructural VARs. The ordering of shocks will be as follows: world interest rate, world price level, world demand for home-country exports, home technology shocks, home tastes shocks, home model demand shocks, and home money supply shocks. World shocks are ordered first to reflect the fact they should be exogenous to events within the home small open economy. Money supply shocks are listed last to reflect the possibility that home monetary authorities might respond to other shocks in setting monetary policy.[17]

Table 3 reports the results of variance decompositions for Australia. Results for the other two countries are very similar. Regarding the current account, it appears that money supply shocks account for only a small fraction of the forecast error variance.[18] But in all three countries, the largest share of current account fluctuation is attributed to taste shocks.[19] Regarding output, almost no role is attributed by the model to money supply shocks, with the large share attributed to technology shocks. It is also a fairly common finding in VAR studies that money does not account for a large share of output variations, although the estimate here is even lower than that found in other studies.

However, money supply shocks are assigned a more important role when it comes to exchange rates. Regarding the nominal exchange rate, money supply shocks account for 60–70% of the forecast error in the short run, and for 20–40% in the longer run. Regarding the real exchange rate, money accounts for a similar degree in the short run, and for 40–60% in the long

[17]The estimated correlations between the shocks identified in the model are generally quite low (almost all under 0.10), so that experiments with reordering shocks had only minor impacts on the variance decompositions. The exceptions are taste shocks and foreign demand shocks, which are highly correlated. As a result, it is difficult to distinguish their separate effects, and the ordering of these two variables makes a large difference in variance decompositions.

[18]The role of money supply in current account movements is somewhat larger for Canada than for the other two countries, ranging between 20% and 30%. In related work, Lane (1999) finds using structural VAR techniques that monetary shocks account for between 10% and 50% of current account fluctuations.

[19]As found in Nason and Rogers (2000), models with consumption behavior rooted in the permanent income hypothesis have difficulty explaining observed current account dynamics. Taste shocks provide a way to get away from this type of consumption behavior.

Table 3. Variance decompositions benchmark model, Australia

		Shocks						
	Period	Interest rate	Foreign price	Foreign demand	Technology	Tastes	Money demand	Money supply
Current Account	1	0.011	0.002	0.064	0.014	0.879	0.007	0.024
	2	0.011	0.001	0.036	0.010	0.913	0.006	0.023
	3	0.012	0.001	0.028	0.007	0.926	0.006	0.021
	4	0.014	0.001	0.023	0.006	0.932	0.005	0.020
	5	0.016	0.001	0.020	0.008	0.934	0.005	0.018
	10	0.027	0.001	0.012	0.035	0.910	0.003	0.012
	20	0.050	0.003	0.006	0.093	0.840	0.002	0.007
Nominal *e*	1	0.000	0.026	0.001	0.035	0.005	0.260	0.673
	2	0.000	0.042	0.002	0.026	0.018	0.246	0.666
	3	0.000	0.057	0.004	0.019	0.037	0.232	0.651
	4	0.000	0.072	0.008	0.014	0.062	0.216	0.629
	5	0.000	0.084	0.011	0.012	0.091	0.199	0.602
	10	0.000	0.112	0.033	0.027	0.261	0.123	0.445
	20	0.002	0.087	0.063	0.088	0.496	0.045	0.220
Real *e*	1	0.000	0.005	0.017	0.034	0.001	0.268	0.674
	2	0.000	0.006	0.016	0.029	0.005	0.263	0.681
	3	0.000	0.007	0.015	0.024	0.012	0.258	0.684
	4	0.000	0.008	0.013	0.021	0.022	0.252	0.684
	5	0.000	0.009	0.012	0.018	0.034	0.246	0.681
	10	0.002	0.010	0.008	0.017	0.125	0.208	0.630
	20	0.002	0.007	0.011	0.055	0.324	0.138	0.463
Output	1	0.002	0.041	0.014	0.942	0.001	0.000	0.000
	2	0.003	0.044	0.011	0.941	0.001	0.000	0.000
	3	0.003	0.046	0.009	0.940	0.002	0.000	0.000
	4	0.002	0.048	0.007	0.939	0.004	0.000	0.001
	5	0.002	0.049	0.006	0.936	0.006	0.000	0.001
	10	0.008	0.051	0.008	0.905	0.024	0.000	0.004
	20	0.033	0.044	0.034	0.781	0.099	0.000	0.009

run. The large role for money in driving the real exchange rate probably results from the estimate of a substantial degree of price stickiness. This result is comparable but somewhat larger than that found in past studies. Eichenbaum and Evans (1995) found variance decompositions between 18% and 43% using standard VAR techniques. Rogers (1999) found between 19% and 60%. Faust and Rogers (2000) found estimates ranging from the single digits to around 50% using a structural VAR that considered a wide range of identification assumptions. Ahmed *et al.* (1993) found almost no role for monetary shocks in a structural VAR using long-run identification restrictions.

Finally, impulse responses can confirm that the model implies a reasonable story for the effects of money shocks. Figures 1 and 2 show the impulse

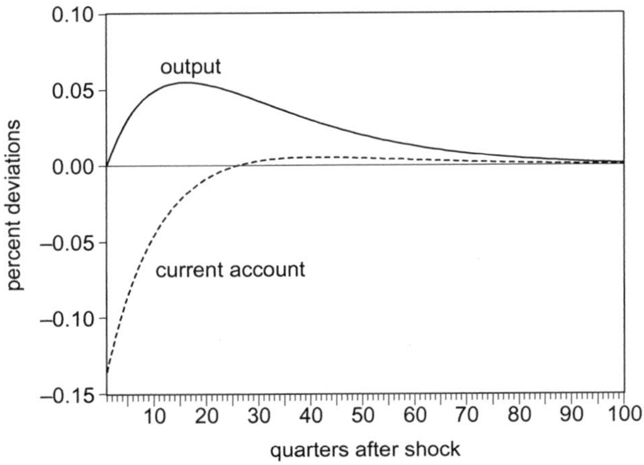

Figure 1. Impulse responses monetary shock, Australia

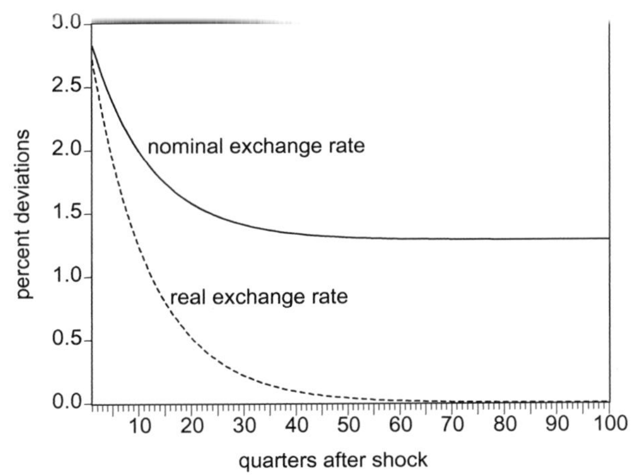

Figure 2. Impulse responses monetary shock, Australia

responses to a 1% shock to the money supply growth rate for Australia. To make interpretation easier, the variables are plotted in percent deviations from the initial steady state rather than in first differences. The model implies a hump shaped response to output, as is often observed in nonstructural VAR studies. It is encouraging that a theoretical model can reproduce this feature. Note also how the real exchange rate moves gradually to its new long run equilibrium. The impulse responses for other countries are very similar.

4.2. *Price and wage flexibility*

Next the model will be used to examine the importance of assuming nominal rigidities. Table 4 reports results for a model in which there is no price or wage stickiness, so the two stickiness parameters ψ_P and ψ_W are set to zero. The likelihood values are much lower than for the reduced form counterpart, and a likelihood ratio test rejects the model for all three countries. The model without stickiness may also be compared to the benchmark model with stickiness from Table 2, since it can be regarded as a restricted version of the benchmark model with two additional restrictions imposed ($\psi_P = \psi_W = 0$). Table 4 reports a likelihood ratio test comparing these two structural models, which specifically rejects the two restrictions of no stickiness. Finally, the Schwarz criterion for all three countries is well below that of the benchmark model.

These rejections are informative, first because they indicate the likelihood ratio testing methodology here is sensitive enough to discriminate between models. In addition, these rejections offer evidence that nominal rigidities are an essential element of the overall success found above for the New Open Economy approach. However, the root mean squared errors reported in the table indicate that nominal rigidities are more important for understanding some variables than others. First, the residuals for price level data are larger for the model without rigidities for Australia and Canada, indicating that stickiness is present and important for understanding how prices move in response to shocks. Regarding output, the residuals are uniformly larger in the case without rigidities. This is surprising, because one may recall that the variance decomposition discussed above indicated that output fluctuations were driven mainly by technology shocks rather than monetary shocks. This offers evidence that stickiness

Table 4. Flexible price and wage model

		Australia	Canada	UK
Measures of fit				
Log likelihood value				
Model		2284.37	2452.31	2256.05
Reduced form		2419.27	2585.63	2397.73
Likelihood ratio		269.79	266.65	283.36
p-value*		0.01	0.01	0.00
Comparison with benchmark model (Table 2)				
Likelihood ratio		71.97	50.28	22.54
p-value**		0.00	0.00	0.00
Schwarz (model)		2245.00	2412.94	2216.68
RMSE: Structural model/VAR:				
Current account		1.12	1.03	1.14
Nominal e		1.03	1.04	1.03
Real e		1.02	1.03	1.04
Output		1.20	1.19	1.07
Price level		1.34	1.37	1.11
RMSE: Structural model/random walk				
Current account		0.99	1.00	1.05
Nominal e		1.00	1.02	1.00
Real e		1.00	1.00	1.01
Output		1.13	0.92	0.98
Price level		1.00	0.70	0.81
Main structural parameter estimates:				
Consumption	σ_1	245.535	3.381	6.921
elasticity term		(171.558)	(0.167)	(0.505)
Money demand	σ_2	16678.881	8.872	5.632
elasticity term		(2752.066)	(0.420)	(0.180)
Labor-supply	σ_3	0.0009	0.0002	0.0002
elasticity		(0.0008)	(0.0000)	(0.0000)
Investment	ψ_I	123456.717	1723.571	527.304
adjustment cost		(124154.819)	(330.331)	(4.161)
Demand elastasticity	ν	0.003	0.711	0.945
term for goods		(0.001)	(0.054)	(0.120)

Notes: *Degrees of freedom = 213; **Degrees of freedom = 2. Standard errors in parentheses.

also has important implications for the effects of real as well as nominal shocks.

The current account residuals are similar under the two cases, indicating that nominal rigidities may not be important for understanding fluctuations in the current account. Finally, the model without nominal rigidities does better explaining the nominal exchange rate than did the benchmark model with rigidities, reflecting the poor performance of the benchmark model described in the previous section.

Now consider the roles of sticky prices and wages separately. This comparison is interesting in that while sticky prices were standard in the early New Open Economy Macro literature, recent additions have proposed sticky wages instead. Some theoretical work argues that sticky wages are important for generating persistence in the real effects of monetary shocks. Table 5 summarizes results for two restricted versions of the model: the top portion shows a version in which goods prices are sticky but wages are flexible, and the bottom portion shows a version in which goods prices are flexible but wages are sticky. For all three countries, we can reject the single restriction that prices are flexible. But the single restriction that wages are flexible is rejected strongly only for one country. While the results are mixed, it appears that price stickiness is generally more important to the model's fit here. It is quite possible that the estimate of the wage adjustment cost

Table 5. Flexible prices or wages

	Australia	Canada	UK
Sticky price, flexible wage			
Log likelihood value			
Model	2491.11	2624.18	2429.70
Unrestricted	2597.54	2749.26	2556.94
Likelihood ratio	212.86	250.16	254.47
p-value*	0.47	0.04	0.02
Comparison with benchmark model (Table 2)			
Likelihood ratio	1.26	9.63	2.43
p-value**	0.26	0.00	0.12
Sticky wage, flexible price			
Log likelihood value			
Model	2471.01	2618.00	2399.38
Unrestricted	2597.54	2749.26	2556.94
Likelihood ratio	253.05	262.51	315.10
p-value*	0.03	0.01	0.00
Comparison with benchmark model (Table 2)			
Likelihood ratio	41.45	21.99	63.06
p-value**	0.00	0.00	0.00

Notes: *Degrees of freedom = 212; **Degrees of freedom = 1.

parameter is influenced by the exclusion of labor market data from the data set. Future work should consider this extension. Nevertheless, the fact that the estimation algorithm had the ability to choose any value of wage stickiness but failed to raise the likelihood value, indicates this was not found to be a particularly useful means in this model of explaining the variables that are in the data set, notably output, current account, and the exchange rate.

4.3. *Producer currency pricing*

A prominent argument in the theoretical literature is whether prices should be regarded as sticky in the currency of the producer or the buyer. The assumption in most of the New Open Economy Macroeconomics has been producer currency pricing. However, Engel (1993, 1999) has presented significant evidence of local currency pricing for a wide range of goods, and this has been incorporated in theoretical models by Betts and Devereux (1996, 2000) and Devereux and Engel (1998). The benchmark model above followed this recent literature by assuming local currency pricing, but now a version of the model will be tested that makes the more traditional assumption of producer currency pricing.

First, if the price set for exported home goods, P_{Xt}, is understood to be denominated in the home currency, the expression P_{Xt} must be replaced with P_{Xt}/e_t in the equation describing foreign demand for these home goods (14). Further, the profits of home exporting firms must be redefined in problem (17) as

$$\begin{aligned}\pi_{Hit} &= p_{Ht}(i)y^{d}_{Ht}(i) + p_{Xt}(i)x^{d}_{t}(i) - P_t r_{t-1}K_{t-1}(i)\\ &\quad - W_t L_t(i) - AC_{Ht}(i) - AC_{Xt}(i),\end{aligned} \tag{54}$$

so the optimal price setting rule for exports (29) is replaced by

$$\begin{aligned}&E_t\left[\frac{\rho_{t,t+i+1}}{\rho_{t,t+i}}\frac{\psi_P}{2}\left(\frac{p^2_{Xt+1}}{p^2_{Xt}}-1\right)\frac{x^d_{t+1}}{x^d_t}\right]\\ &-\psi_P\left(\frac{p_{Xt}(i)}{p_{Xt-1}(i)}-1\right)+\frac{1+\nu}{\nu}\\ &\times\left(\frac{P_t r_{t-1}}{p_{Xt}(i)\alpha A_t(L_t(i)/K_{t-1}(i))^{(1-\alpha)}}+\frac{\psi_P}{2}\frac{(p_{Xt}-p_{Xt-1})^2}{p_{Xt}p_{Xt-1}}-1\right)+1=0.\end{aligned} \tag{55}$$

Similarly, if the price of imported goods, P_{Ft}, is understood to be denominated in the foreign currency, the expression P_{Ft} must be replaced with $e_t P_{Ft}$ in the home demand for imported goods (8) and also the home consumer price index (5). The profits of home importing firms in problem (26) must be redefined:

$$\pi_{Fjt} = (e_t p_{Ft}(j) - e_t P_t^*) y_{Ft}^d(j) - e_t AC_{Ft}(j), \tag{56}$$

so the optimal price setting rule (33) is replaced by

$$E_t \left[\frac{\rho_{t,t+i+1}}{\rho_{t,t+i}} \frac{\psi_P}{2} \left(\frac{p_{ft+1}(i)}{p_{Ft}(i)} - 1 \right)^2 \frac{y_{Ft+1}^d}{y_{Ft}^d} \frac{e_{t+1}}{e_t} \right] - \psi_P \left(\frac{p_{Ft}(i)}{p_{Ft-1}(i)} - 1 \right) + \frac{1+\nu}{\nu} \left(\frac{P_t^*}{p_{Ft}(i)} - 1 \right) + 1 = 0. \tag{57}$$

Results of estimating this model are found in Table 6. While this model cannot be cast as a nested version of the benchmark model with local currency pricing, it still is a nested version of the same unrestricted model used to test this benchmark. Table 6 indicates that the producer currency pricing model is rejected for two of the three countries, Canada and the United Kingdom. Even while the model is not rejected for Australia, the p-value is lower than in the benchmark case. Given that the local currency pricing model was not rejected for two of the three countries, this is taken as generally supportive of the recent trend in the New Open Economy Macroeconomics to assume local currency pricing rather than producer currency pricing.

Looking at the forecast residuals, the PCP model does uniformly less well than the LCP benchmark model for forecasting output and the price level. For the current account, the producer and local currency pricing models are fairly similar. For the exchange rate, the PCP model does better, but it still fails to beat the random walk.

Overall, the results further support the conclusions drawn previously. The local currency pricing benchmark model performs fairly well overall and for particular variables like price level and output. On these counts, the benchmark model also outperforms alternative structural models, like flexible prices and prices sticky in the currency of the producer. But the benchmark model performs poorly in terms of explaining exchange rates,

Table 6. Producer currency pricing model

		Australia	Canada	UK
Measures of fit				
Log likelihood value				
Model		2483.87	2619.66	2428.08
Unrestricted		2597.54	2749.26	2556.94
Likelihood ratio		227.33	259.20	257.71
p-value*		0.21	0.01	0.02
Regular VAR		2481.84	2640.91	2427.57
Schwarz(model)		2442.53	2578.32	2386.74
Schwarz(VAR)		2406.05	2565.12	2351.78
RMSE: Structural model/ VAR				
Current account		1.14	1.02	1.10
Nominal e		1.02	1.04	1.04
Real e		1.03	1.02	1.04
Output		1.13	1.29	1.19
Price level		1.01	1.34	1.09
RMSE: Structural model/ random walk				
Current account		1.01	0.99	1.02
Nominal e		1.00	1.01	1.01
Real e		1.00	1.00	1.01
Output		1.06	1.00	1.09
Price level		0.75	0.67	0.80
Main structural parameter estimates				
Consumption	σ_1	49.268	12.766	48.136
elasticity term		(3.069)	(1.206)	(0.235)
Money demand	σ_2	23.723	99.886	17.268
elasticity term		(1.489)	(11.924)	(0.497)
Labor-supply	σ_3	0.0011	0.0002	0.0010
elasticity		(0.0000)	(0.0000)	(0.0000)
Investment	ψ_I	380.750	16473.796	736.221
adjustment cost		(108.253)	(3650.108)	(39.363)
Price adjustment	ψ_P	46.728	7.704	39.722
cost		(0.249)	(0.689)	(0.496)
Wage adjustment	ψ_W	0.041	0.046	0.099
cost		(0.000)	(0.000)	(0.000)
Demand elastasticity	ν	0.179	0.097	0.138
term for goods		(0.005)	(0.014)	(0.002)

Note: *Degrees of freedom = 211.

relative to reduced form comparison models as well as against alternative structural models.

5. Conclusion

This chapter has explored one promising approach for giving the New Open Economy Macroeconomics an empirical dimension. It has adapted maximum likelihood procedures to estimate and test an intertemporal small open economy model with monetary shocks and sticky prices and wages. The results showed some mixed support for a benchmark model. In comparison with an unrestricted counterpart model, the restrictions of the structural model were not rejected in two of three countries. The structural model fared even better in comparison with a more standard vector autoregression, where the Schwarz criterion favored the structural model for all three countries. However, the model's performance was poorer in terms of forecasting individual variables. While the model has some predictive value for the price level and output, the model cannot beat a random walk in predicting movements in the exchange rate or the current account for any of the three countries.

Price rigidities appear to be a useful element in the model, since a version that assumes no such rigidity is rejected for all three countries. The methodology also tested a version of the model in which prices were assumed to be sticky in the currency of the seller rather than the buyer. Overall, this model performed less well than the benchmark model in terms of likelihood ratios.

Appendix

The estimation strategy applied here is drawn from that developed in Leeper and Sims (1994), although it differs in its handling of first differences, in allowing correlated shocks, and in the fact it is applied also to an unrestricted counterpart model. Given the autoregressive moving average model in (52), the contemporaneous covariances matrix, $R_{y*}(0)$, can be written as follows:

$$R_{y*}(0) \equiv E[y_t^* y_t^{*\prime}] = A\Sigma A' + \sum_{i=0}^{\infty}[BD^i(D-I)B^{-1}]A\Sigma A'[BD^i(D-I)B^{-1}]', \tag{A1}$$

where D is the diagonal matrix of eigenvalues and B the matrix of eigen vectors of A. $R_{y^*}(0)$ can then be computed:

$$R_{y^*}(0) = A\Sigma A' + B[K]B', \tag{A2}$$

where the typical element (i, j) of K is

$$K_{ij} = \begin{cases} \dfrac{(1-d_i)(1-d_j)M_{ij}}{1-d_i d_j} & \text{for } d_i \neq 1 \text{ or } d_j \neq 1, \\ 0 & \text{for } d_i = 1 \text{ and } d_j = 1, \end{cases} \tag{A3}$$

where

$$M = B^{-1}A\Sigma A' B^{-1'}. \tag{A4}$$

and where d_i is the ith diagonal element of the matrix D. It is easily verified that

$$\lim_{d_i \to 1, d_j \to 1} \frac{(1-d_i)(1-d_j)M_{ij}}{1-d_i d_j} = 0. \tag{A5}$$

Once $R_{y^{**}}(0)$ is computed, the covariances across one lag $R_{y^*}(1)$ may be found:

$$R_{y^*}(1) = E\left[y_t^* y_{t-1}^{*\prime}\right] = A\, R_{y^*}(0) - A\Sigma A' \tag{A6}$$

and over lags greater than one:

$$R_{y^*}(k) = E\left[y_t^* y_{t-k}^{*\prime}\right] = A^{k-1}\, R_{y^*}(1) \text{ for } k > 1. \tag{A7}$$

The full covariance matrix, Ω, can be constructed by assembling the blocks for various lags.[20] To reduce numerical problems associated with rounding error, lags of only up to 15 periods are currently used, with covariances assumed to be zero over lags greater than 15 periods. The covariance matrix Ω for the observed variables in vector x then is constructed by selecting only those elements of the full covariance matrix that pertain to these variables. The covariance matrix is a key component in computing the log-likelihood to be maximized:

$$L(\Pi) = -.5 \ln|\Omega| - .5x'\Omega^{-1}x. \tag{A8}$$

Note that the likelihood is computed unconditionally on the initial observations.

[20]An alternative means of computing the likelihood would be to use the Kalman filter.

One difficulty is that some regions of the parameter space are not defined within the model. These regions can be precluded by imposing boundaries on the parameters by functional transformations. For example, the following variables are restricted to be positive: the variances of shocks, the preference parameters $\sigma_1 - \sigma_3$, and $\overline{A}$. The autoregressive coefficients for shocks must be restricted between the values of 0 and 1. Finally, the covariances between shocks must be restricted so that the implied correlations lie between -1 and 1.

The reduced form model used for comparison may also be expressed in the form of Equation (52), and it is estimated in precisely the same manner as the structural model. A likelihood function is computed in the same way as above, as a function of the autoregressive matrix A and the covariance matrix of shocks Σ_2. As with the structural model, this likelihood function is computed unconditionally on the initial observations, and the same search algorithm is used to maximize it. The elements of the matrix Σ_2 for the reduced form model is subject to the identical boundaries as applied to its counterpart in the structural model. In addition, to ensure that the covariance matrix is positive definite, the autoregressive matrix A is required to have roots less than unity in absolute value. This is accomplished by dealing with A in its Jordan decomposition. The free parameters are the roots of the A matrix and all but the last element of each eigen vector.

Optimization is conducted using an algorithm developed by Christopher Sims which is robust to discontinuities. (This algorithm, csminwel.m is available from Christopher Sims as a Matlab.m file.)

A measure of precision can be obtained by looking at the inverse of the Hessian matrix, the diagonal elements of which approximate parameter estimation error variances. The delta method is used to adjust these error variances for the parameter transformations discussed above, used to impose boundaries on the parameter estimates.[21] In addition, a measure of the fit of the model can be obtained by computing residuals from one-step ahead forecasts. Standardized residuals may be computed:

$$v = \varpi^{-1} y^* \tag{A9}$$

[21] In particular, the standard error of the transformed parameter estimate is computed as the standard error of the untransformed estimate multiplied by the derivative of the functional transformation.

where ϖ is the Cholesky decomposition of the overall covariance matrix. Unstandardized residuals may be computed on a period-by-period basis as

$$v_t^* = (\varpi^{-1})_{tt}^{-1} v_t, \tag{A10}$$

where $(w^{-1})_{tt}$ is the t-th diagonal block of the inverse of ϖ.

Acknowledgment

I would like to thank seminar participants at U.C. Berkeley, University of Munich, Institute for Advanced Studies in Vienna, the Federal Reserve Bank of San Francisco, and conference participants at the University of Wisconsin. I acknowledge financial support from the Economics Program of the National Science Foundation.

References

Ahmed, S., B. Ickes, P. Wang, and B. S. Yoo. 1993. International business cycles. *American Economic Review*, 83: 335–339.

Barro, R. J. and X. Sala i Martin. 1990. World real interest rates, in Blanchard, O. J. and Fischer, S. (eds.), *NBER Macroeconomics Annual*, MIT Press: Cambridge, MA, pp. 15–61.

Bergin, P. R. and S. Sheffrin. 2000. Interest rates, exchange rates, and present value models of the current account. *The Economic Journal*, 110: 535–558.

Betts, C. and M. B. Devereux. 1996. The exchange rate in a model of pricing-to-market. *European Economic Review*, 40: 1007–1021.

Betts, C. and M. B. Devereux. 2000. Exchange rate dynamics in a model of pricing-to-market. *Journal of International Economics*, 50: 215–244.

Blanchard, O. and C. Kahn. 1980. The solution of linear difference models under rational expectations. *Econometrica*, 48: 1305–1311.

Devereux, M. B. and C. Engel. 1998. Fixed vs. floating exchange rates: How price setting affects the optimal choice of exchange-rate regime, NBER Working Paper #6867.

Eichenbaum, M. and C. L. Evans. 1995. Some empirical evidence on the effects of shocks to monetary policy on exchange rates. *Quarterly Journal of Economics*, 110: 975–1009.

Engel, C. 1993. Real exchange rates and relative prices: An empirical investigation. *Journal of Monetary Economics*, 32: 35–50.

Engel, C. 1999. Accounting for US real exchange rate changes. *Journal of Political Economy*, 107: 507–538.

Erceg, C. J. 1997. Nominal wage rigidities and the propagation of monetary disturbances. Board of Governors of the Federal Reserve System Working Paper.

Faust, J. and J. H. Rogers. 2000. Monetary policy's role in exchange rate behavior. Board of Governors of the Federal Reserve System Working Paper.

Ghironi, F. 2000. Towards a new open economy macroeconometrics. Boston College Working Paper.

Ghosh, A. R. 1995. International capital mobility among the major industrialised countries: Too little or too much? *Economic Journal*, 105: 107–28.

Glick, R. and K. Rogoff. 1995. Global versus country-specific productivity shocks and the current account, *Journal of Monetary Economics*, 35: 159–192.

Hall, R. E. 1988. Intertemporal substitution in consumption. *Journal of Political Economy*, 96: 339–357.

Hau, H. 2000. Exchange rate determination: the role of factor price rigidities and nontradables. *Journal of International Economics*, 50: 421–447.

Ireland, P. 1997. A small, structural, quarterly model for monetary policy evaluation. *Carnegie-Rochester Conference Series on Public Policy*, 47: 83–108.

Ireland, P. 2001. Sticky-price models of the business cycle: Specification and stability. *Journal of Monetary Economics*, 47: 3–18.

Kim, J. 2000. Constructing and estimating a realistic optimizing model of monetary policy. *Journal of Monetary Economics*, 45: 329–359.

Kollmann, R. 2001. The exchange rate in a dynamic-optimizing current account model with nominal rigidities: A quantitative investigation. *Journal of International Economics*, 55: 243–262.

Lane, P. R. 1999. Money shocks and the current account, Trinity College Dublin Working Paper.

Lane, P. R. 2001. The new open economy macroeconomics: A survey. *Journal of International Economics*, 54: 235–266.

Leeper, E. and C. Sims. 1994. Toward a modern macroeconomic model usable for policy analysis. NBER Macroeconomic Annual, pp. 81–118.

Meese, R. A. and K. Rogoff. 1983. Empirical exchange rate models of the seventies: Do they fit out of sample? *Journal of International Economics*, 14: 3–24.

Nason, J. M. and J. H. Rogers. 2000. The Present Value Model of the Current Account has Been Rejected: Round up the Usual Suspects. Mimeo, University of British Columbia.

Obstfeld, M. and K. Rogoff. 1995. Exchange rate dynamics redux. *Journal of Political Economy*, 103: 624–660.

Obstfeld, M. and K. Rogoff. 1998. Risk and exchange rates. NBER Working Paper #6694.

Obstfeld, M. and K. Rogoff. 2000. New directions for stochastic open economy models. *Journal of International Economics*, 20: 117–153.

Rogers, J. H. 1999. Monetary shocks and real exchange rates. *Journal of International Economics*, 49: 269–288.

Rotemberg, J. 1982. Monopolistic price adjustment and aggregate output. *Review of Economic Studies*, 49: 517–531.

Sheffrin, S. and W. T. Woo. 1990. Present value tests of an intertemporal model of the current account. *Journal of International Economics*, 29: 237–253.

Stockman, A. C. and L. L. Tesar. 1995. Tastes and technology in a two-country model of the business cycle: Explaining international comovements. *American Economic Review*, 85: 168–185.

CHAPTER 5

How Well Can the New Open Economy Macroeconomics Explain the Exchange Rate and Current Account?*

Paul R. Bergin

Department of Economics, University of California at Davis,
One Shields Ave., Davis, CA 95616, USA
prbergin@ucdavis.edu

1. Introduction

International macroeconomists increasingly have come to rely upon a class of models known as New Open Economy Macroeconomics (NOEM), characterized by microeconomic foundations and intertemporal optimization combined with nominal rigidities or other market imperfections. Such models recently have been used to study the effects of monetary policy changes, optimal monetary policy rules, and the benefits of international policy coordination.[1] While theoretical work in the NOEM literature has grown rapidly, there has been relatively little work done on empirical dimensions.[2] This has not been for a lack of interest, as it generally is agreed that if we are to trust these models for policy analysis, we should have some degree

*This article originally appeared in *Journal of International Money and Finance* (2006), 25(5), 675–701.

[1]See Lane (2001) for a survey of this extensive literature.

[2]In open economy work, see Bergin (2003) and Ghironi (2000); in closed economy work, see Ireland (1997 and 2001), Kim (2000), Lubik and Schorfheide (2002), and Smets and Wouters (2002).

of confidence that they accurately reflect basic features of the economy. However, the macroeconomic models developed recently are sufficiently complex that estimating and testing them econometrically is extremely demanding. This paper demonstrates one method that could be useful in filling this gap in empirical work.

The empirical record for earlier classes of macroeconomic models is very mixed. This is especially true with regard to the exchange rate and the current account, key variables for open economy macroeconomics. The current account dynamics of many countries have proved quite difficult to explain in terms of macroeconomic models using present value tests.[3] And in a classic result, Meese and Rogoff (1983) showed that a range of macroeconomic models were unable to beat a random walk in forecasting the nominal exchange rate. Exchange rate movements have proved so problematic, that some recent research has recommended abandoning the attempt of explaining them in terms of macroeconomic models. (See Flood and Rose, 1999.)

As a result, it is becoming a familiar practice in NOEM studies to introduce exchange rate movements in a manner other than macroeconomic fundamentals. This is often done by adding an extra term to the uncovered interest rate parity condition (IRP) in the macro model.[4] Such a term is motivated by well-documented empirical evidence of strong deviations from IRP,[5] and it can be interpreted in a number of different ways: Obstfeld and Rogoff (2001) derive such a term as a currency risk premium which is associated with monetary policy actions; Mark and Wu (1998) and Jeanne and Rose (2002) derive it as a reflection of noise traders and a distribution of exchange rate expectations.

In response to the controversy regarding macro models as explanations for the exchange rate and the current account, this chapter will pay special attention to these two variables. In particular, a maximum likelihood approach is adapted for estimating and evaluating a two country NOEM model. The US is used as one of these countries, and an aggregate of the remaining G-7 is used as the other country. The model is fit to five data

---

[3]For example, see Sheffrin and Woo (1990), Ghosh (1995), and Bergin and Sheffrin (2000).

[4]For examples, see McCallum and Nelson (1999 and 2000), Kollmann (2001 and 2002), and Jeanne and Rose (2002).

[5]For a summary, see Lewis (1995).

series: the exchange rate, current account, output growth, inflation, and interest rate deviations between the two countries. Data is quarterly from 1973:1 to 2000:4.

The model shares many features common in NOEM models, including monopolistically competitive firms, sluggish price setting, capital accumulation subject to adjustment costs, and monetary policy in the form of interest rate setting rules. The procedure will estimate various deep parameters of interest in the theoretical literature. There will be five shocks to the system, including technology, monetary policy, consumption tastes, and the share of home bias in preferences; the fifth shock will be to the interest rate parity condition. The estimation procedure will also estimate the degree of correlation between the four structural shocks and the deviations from IRP.

Results indicate that the model as equipped above is able to explain the exchange rate and current account to some degree, in that it can beat a random walk in one-step ahead in-sample predictions. It is not able to beat a standard vector-autoregression in terms of predictions for the exchange rate and current account, although the overall fit of the model is superior to the vector autoregression (VAR) when the latter is appropriately penalized for its larger set of free parameters.

Parameter estimates are able to help address some current questions in the theoretical NOEM literature. Estimates of the degree of pricing-to-market indicate that a very high degree is needed to successfully explain exchange rate movements. Estimates of the elasticity of substitution between home and foreign goods indicate that the simplifying assumption of a unitary elasticity widely employed in the theoretical literature may not be so bad, with regard to being able to explain the key macroeconomic variables.[6]

Estimates also offer some new insights into the nature of deviations from interest parity. The model indicates that IRP deviations are unrelated to monetary policy actions, as has been proposed in some literature. However, these deviations are very highly correlated with shocks to marginal utility (taste shocks). Surprisingly, it appears that IRP shocks are even more important for explaining movements in the current account than the exchange rate. This may indicate that current account movements are likewise determined by financial shocks, which affect capital account flows,

[6]Note that Bergin (2003) was not equipped to estimate either of these parameters.

and thereby force current account adjustments through the balance of payments identity. This is a theory quite different from the usual NOEM theory of the current account as simply reflecting optimal saving and investment decisions, and it suggests a useful avenue for future research.

The estimated model also gives a window into monetary policy rules. Estimates indicate a strong reaction to inflation and has been exhibited by the countries in the sample, while implying a low response to output. These countries have also exhibited a fairly small systematic response to the bilateral exchange rate with the dollar.

2. The Model

2.1. *Features*

Consider a two-country world, where the countries will be denoted home and foreign, and the population of home is fraction n of the world total. Each country has a representative household and a representative firm, and each country has a distinct continuum of intermediate goods that it produces. Foreign variables will be indicated by an '*', and where necessary also by an F subscript. All variables will be written in per capita terms.

2.2. *Market structure*

Final goods in this economy (Y_t) are produced by aggregating over a continuum of intermediate home goods indexed by $i \in [0, 1]$ along with aggregating over a continuum of imported foreign goods indexed by $j \in [0, 1]$. The aggregation technology for producing final goods is

$$Y_t = \left[\theta_t^{\frac{1}{\mu}} Y_{Ht}^{\frac{\mu-1}{\mu}} + (1-\theta_t)^{\frac{1}{\mu}} Y_{Ft}^{\frac{\mu-1}{\mu}}\right]^{\frac{\mu}{\mu-1}}, \quad \text{where} \tag{1}$$

$$Y_{Ht} = \left(\int_0^1 y_{Ht}(i)^{\frac{1}{1+\nu}} di\right)^{1+\nu} \tag{2}$$

$$Y_{Ft} = \left(\int_0^1 y_{Ft}(j)^{\frac{1}{1+\nu}} dj\right)^{1+\nu}. \tag{3}$$

Here Y_{Ht} represents an aggregate of the home goods sold in the small open economy, and Y_{Ft} is an aggregate of the imported foreign goods, where lower case counterparts with indexes represent outputs of the individual firms. Note that the share parameter, θ_t, is subject to stochastic shocks.

Final goods producers behave competitively, maximizing profit each period:

$$\pi_{1t} = \max \ P_t Y_t - P_{Ht} Y_{Ht} - P_{Ft} Y_{Ft}, \tag{4}$$

where P_t is the overall price index of the final good, P_{Ht} is the price index of home goods, and P_{Ft} is the price index of foreign goods, all denominated in the home currency. It is assumed that fraction s of firms (indexed $i = 0, \ldots s$) exhibit local currency pricing, that is, they set the price of goods in the currency of the buyer. It is assumed that the remaining fraction $1 - s$ of firms (indexed $i = s, \ldots 1$) exhibit producer currency pricing, that is, they set the price of goods in their own currency.

The price indexes may be defined:

$$P_t = \left[\theta_t P_{Ht}^{1-\mu} + (1-\theta_t)\, P_{Ft}^{1-\mu}\right]^{\frac{1}{1-\mu}}, \text{ where} \tag{5}$$

$$P_{Ht} = \left(\int_0^s p_{Ht}(i)^{-\frac{1}{\nu}} di + \int_s^1 p_{Ht}(i)^{-\frac{1}{\nu}} di\right)^{-\nu} \tag{6}$$

$$P_{Ft} = \left(\int_0^s p_{Ft}(j)^{-\frac{1}{\nu}} dj + \int_s^1 e p_{Ft}(j)^{-\frac{1}{\nu}} dj\right)^{-\nu}, \tag{7}$$

and where lower case counterparts again represent the prices set by individual firms. And the price index of home exports may be expressed:

$$P_{Ht}^* = \left(\int_0^s p_{Ht}^*(j)^{-\frac{1}{\nu}} dj + \int_s^1 \frac{1}{e_t} p_{Ht}^*(j)^{-\frac{1}{\nu}} dj\right)^{-\nu}. \tag{8}$$

Given the aggregation functions above, demand will be allocated between home and foreign goods according to

$$Y_{Ht} = \theta_t Y_t \left(P_t / P_{Ht}\right)^{\mu} \tag{9}$$

$$Y_{Ft} = (1-\theta_t)\, Y_t \left(P_t / P_{Ft}\right)^{\mu}, \tag{10}$$

with demands for individual goods:

$$y_{Ht}(i) = Y_{Ht}\left(p_{Ht}(i)/P_{Ht}\right)^{-(1+\nu)/\nu} \tag{11}$$

$$y_{Ft}(j) = Y_{Ft}\left(p_{Ft}(j)/P_{Ft}\right)^{-(1+\nu)/\nu} \quad \text{for } j = 0, \ldots, s \tag{12}$$

$$y_{Ft}(j) = Y_{Ft}\left(e_t p_{Ft}(j)/P_{Ft}\right)^{-(1+\nu)/\nu} \quad \text{for } j = s, \ldots, 1. \tag{13}$$

Analogous conditions apply to the foreign country.

2.3. *Firm behavior*

The firms rent capital (K_t) at the real rental rate r_t, and hire labor (L_t) at the nominal wage rate W_t. The nominal exchange rate (e_t) is the home currency price of one unit of the world currency. It is assumed that it is costly to reset prices because of quadratic menu costs. The problem for the local currency pricing ($i = 0, \ldots s$) firms may be summarized:

$$\max \quad E_0 \sum_{t=0}^{\infty} \rho_{t,t+n} \pi_{Ht}(i) \tag{14}$$

where
$$\pi_{Ht}(i) = p_{Ht}(i) y_{Ht}(i) + e_t p^*_{Ht}(i) \left(\frac{1-n}{n} \right) y^*_{Ht}(i) - P_t r_t K_{t-1}(i) - W_t L_t(i) - P_t AC_{Ht}(i) - e_t P_t AC^*_{Ht}(i) \tag{15}$$

$$\text{s.t.} \quad AC_{Ht}(i) = \frac{\psi_P}{2} \frac{\left(p_{Ht}(i) - p_{Ht-1}(i) \right)^2}{P_t p_{Ht-1}(i)} y_{Ht}(i) \tag{16}$$

$$AC^*_{Ht}(i) = \frac{\psi_P}{2} \frac{\left(p^*_{Ht}(i) - p^*_{Ht-1}(i) \right)^2}{P_t p^*_{Ht-1}(i)} \left(\frac{1-n}{n} \right) y^*_{Ht}(i) \tag{17}$$

$$z_t(i) = A_t K_{t-1}(i)^{\alpha} L_t(i)^{1-\alpha} \tag{18}$$

$$z_t(i) = y_{Ht}(i) + \left(\frac{1-n}{n} \right) y^*_{Ht}(i), \tag{19}$$

and subject to the demand functions for $y_{Ht}(i)$ and $y^*_{Ht}(i)$ above. Here A_t represents technology common to all production firms in the country, and it is subject to shocks. Lastly, $\rho_{t,t+n}$ is the pricing kernel used to value random date $t+n$ payoffs. Since firms are assumed to be owned by the representative household, it is assumed that firms value future payoffs according to the household's intertemporal marginal rate of substitution in consumption, so $\rho_{t,t+n} = \beta^n U'_{C,t+n} / U'_{C,t}$, where $U'_{C,t+n}$ is the household's marginal utility of consumption in period $t+n$. The problem for the producer currency pricing firms ($i = s \ldots 1$) is identical, except that $p^*_{Ht}(i)$ is in units of home currency and Equation (15) is replaced by

$$\pi_{Ht}(i) = p_{Ht}(i) y_{Ht}(i) + p^*_{Ht}(i) \left(\frac{1-n}{n} \right) y^*_{Ht}(i) - P_t r_{t-1} K_{t-1}(i) - W_t L_t(i) - P_t AC_{Ht}(i) - P_t AC^*_{Ht}(i).$$

This problem implies an optimal trade-off between capital and labor inputs that depend on the relative cost of each:

$$P_t r_t K_{t-1}(i) = \frac{\alpha}{1-\alpha} W_t L_t(i). \tag{20}$$

The optimal price setting rule for domestic sales of all home firms ($i = 0, \ldots, 1$) is

$$\begin{aligned}
&\frac{1+\nu}{\nu}\left(\frac{P_t r_t}{P_{Ht}\alpha A_t \left(L_t(i)/K_{t-1}(i)\right)^{(1-\alpha)}} + \frac{\psi_P}{2}\frac{\left(p_{Ht}(i) - p_{Ht-1}(i)\right)^2}{P_{Ht} p_{Ht-1}(i)}\right. \\
&\qquad \left. - \frac{p_{Ht}(i)}{P_{Ht}}\right)\left(\frac{Y_{Ht}}{y_{Ht}(i)}\right)\left(\frac{p_{Ht}(i)}{P_{Ht}}\right)^{-\left(\frac{1+2\nu}{\nu}\right)} \\
&\qquad + \frac{\psi_P}{2} E_t\left[\frac{\rho_{t,t+i+1}}{\rho_{t,t+i}}\left(\frac{p^2_{Ht+1}(i)}{p^2_{Ht}(i)} - 1\right)\frac{y_{Ht+1}(i)}{y_{Ht}(i)}\right] \\
&\qquad - \psi_P\left(\frac{p_{Ht}(i)}{p_{Ht-1}(i)} - 1\right) + 1 = 0.
\end{aligned} \tag{21}$$

The optima price setting rule for exports for local currency pricing firms ($i = 0, \ldots, s$) is

$$\begin{aligned}
&\frac{1+\nu}{\nu}\left(\frac{P_t r_t}{e_t P^*_{Ht}\alpha A_t \left(L_t(i)/K_{t-1}(i)\right)^{(1-\alpha)}} + \frac{\psi_P}{2}\frac{\left(p^*_{Ht}(i) - p^*_{Ht-1}(i)\right)^2}{P^*_{Ht} p^*_{Ht-1}(i)}\right. \\
&\qquad \left. - \frac{p^*_{Ht}(i)}{P^*_{Ht}}\right)\left(\frac{Y^*_{Ht}}{y^*_{Ht}(i)}\right)\left(\frac{p^*_{Ht}(i)}{P^*_{Ht}}\right)^{-\left(\frac{1+2\nu}{\nu}\right)} \\
&\qquad + \frac{\psi_P}{2} E_t\left[\frac{\rho_{t,t+i+1}}{\rho_{t,t+i}}\left(\frac{p^{*2}_{Ht+1}(i)}{p^{*2}_{Ht}(i)} - 1\right)\frac{e_{t+1}}{e_t}\frac{y^*_{Ht+1}(i)}{y^*_{Ht}(i)}\right] \\
&\qquad - \psi_P\left(\frac{p^*_{Ht}(i)}{p^*_{Ht-1}(i)} - 1\right) + 1 = 0,
\end{aligned} \tag{22}$$

and the optimal price for exports by producer currency pricing firms ($i = s, \ldots, 1$) is

$$\begin{aligned}
&\frac{1+\nu}{\nu}\left(\frac{P_t r_{t-1}}{e_t P^*_{Ht}\alpha A_t \left(L_t(i)/K_{t-1}(i)\right)^{(1-\alpha)}} + \frac{\psi_P}{2}\frac{\left(p^*_{Ht}(i) - p^*_{Ht-1}(i)\right)^2}{e_t P^*_{Ht} p^*_{Ht-1}(i)}\right. \\
&\qquad \left. - \frac{p^*_{Ht}(i)}{e_t P^*_{Ht}}\right)\left(\frac{Y^*_{Ht}}{y^*_{Ht}(i)}\right)\left(\frac{p^*_{Ht}(i)}{e_t P^*_{Ht}}\right)^{-\left(\frac{1+2\nu}{\nu}\right)}
\end{aligned}$$

$$+\frac{\psi_P}{2}E_t\left[\frac{\rho_{t,t+i+1}}{\rho_{t,t+i}}\left(\frac{p^{*2}_{Ht+1}(i)}{p^{*2}_{Ht}(i)}-1\right)\frac{y^*_{Ht+1}(i)}{y^*_{Ht}(i)}\right]$$

$$-\psi_P\left(\frac{p^*_{Ht}(i)}{p^*_{Ht-1}(i)}-1\right)+1=0. \tag{23}$$

2.4. *Household behavior*

The household derives utility from consumption (C_t), and supplying labor (L_t) lowers utility. For simplicity, real money balances (M_t/P_t) are also introduced in the utility function, where P_t is the overall price level. The household discounts future utility at the rate of time preference β. Preferences are additively separable in these three arguments, and preferences for consumption are subject to preference shocks (τ_t).

Households derive income by selling their labor at the nominal wage rate (W_t), renting capital to firms at the real rental rate (r_t), receiving real profits from the two types of firms (π_{1t} and π_{2t}), and from government transfers (T_t). In addition to money, households can hold two types of noncontingent bonds, one denominated in home currency (B_t) paying return i_t, and the other denominated in foreign currency ($-B^*_t$) paying return i^*_t. The nominal exchange rate is e_t and the foreign price level is P_t. Investment (I_t) in new capital (K_t) involves a quadratic adjustment cost and a constant rate of depreciation (δ).

The optimization problem faced by the household may be expressed:

$$\max\ E_0\sum_{t=0}^{\infty}\beta^t U\left(C_t,\frac{M_t}{P_t},L_t\right), \tag{24}$$

$$\text{s.t.}\ CA_t=\frac{B_t-B_{t-1}}{P_t}-\frac{e_t(B^*_t-B^*_{t-1})}{P_t}, \tag{25}$$

where

$$CA_t\equiv\frac{W_t}{P_t}L_t+r_tK_{t-1}+\int_0^1\pi_{Ht}(i)di+T_t+\frac{i_{t-1}B_{t-1}}{P_t}+\frac{e_t i^*_{t-1}B^*_{t-1}}{P_t}, \tag{26}$$

$$-C_t-I_t-AC_{It}-\left(\frac{M_t}{P_t}-\frac{M_{t-1}}{P_t}\right), \tag{27}$$

$$U(C_t, L_t) = \frac{\tau_t}{1-\sigma_1}(C_t)^{1-\sigma_1} + \frac{1}{1-\sigma_2}\left(\frac{M_t}{P_t}\right)^{1-\sigma_2} - \frac{\sigma_3}{1+\sigma_3}(L_t)^{\frac{1+\sigma_3}{\sigma_3}}, \tag{28}$$

$$I_t = K_t - (1-\delta)K_{t-1}, \tag{29}$$

$$AC_{It} = \frac{\psi_I}{2}\frac{(K_t - K_{t-1})^2}{K_{t-1}}, \tag{30}$$

where $\sigma_i > 0$ for $i = 1 \ldots 3$, $\psi_I \geq 0$.

The household problem implies the following optimality conditions. First, households will smooth consumption across time periods according to

$$\tau_t C_t^{-\sigma_1} = \beta(1+i_t)E_t\left[\tau_{t+1}C_{t+1}^{-\sigma_1}\left(\frac{P_t}{P_{t+1}}\right)\right]. \tag{31}$$

Households prefer expected marginal utilities to be constant across time periods, unless a rate of return on saving exceeding their time preference induces them to lower consumption today relative to the future. Second, household money demand will be

$$\left(\frac{M_t}{P_t}\right)^{-\sigma_2} = \tau_t C_t^{-\sigma_1}\frac{i_t}{1+i_t}.$$

Third, optimal portfolio choices imply the interest rate parity (IRP) condition:

$$E_t\left[\frac{U'_{Ct+1}}{U'_{Ct}}\frac{e_{t+1}}{e_t}\frac{P_t}{P_{t+1}}(1+i_t^*)\right] = E_t\left[\frac{U'_{Ct+1}}{U'_{Ct}}\frac{P_t}{P_{t+1}}(1+i)_t\right]. \tag{32}$$

Since the model equations will be used only as linear approximations, the IRP condition would appear in the following simplified form:

$$i_t - i_t^* = \frac{1}{1-\beta}(e_{t+1} - e_t). \tag{33}$$

This approximation omits the nonlinear terms involving marginal utilities and prices, which represent risk premium terms and Jensen's inequality. It is well-known that this form of the IRP condition is strongly rejected by the data (Lewis, 1995), so we will generalized this expression by adding a "risk premium term" as follows:

$$RP_t = -\Psi_B \left(\frac{B_t - e_t B_t^*}{P_t Y_t} \right) + \xi_t. \tag{34}$$

One component of this term is a mean-zero disturbance, ξ_t, aimed at capturing time-varying deviations from IRP. Such a term is a common device in macro models (see McCallum and Nelson (1999 and 2000), Kollmann (2001 and 2002), and Jeanne and Rose (2002)). There are a number of ways to interpret this term. McCallum and Nelson (1999 and 2000) interpret it as a representation of the time-varying risk premium omitted by linearization. Obstfeld and Rogoff (2001) show theoretically how this risk premium could vary over time with changes in the properties of monetary policy actions. Mark and Wu (1998) and Jeanne and Rose (2002) derive it as a reflection of noise traders and a distribution of exchange rate expectations. A second component of the RP_t term will be a function of the debt of a country. This can be motivated as a risk premium as well, where lenders demand a higher rate of return on a country with a large debt to compensate for perceived default risk. The primary motivation for including this term here as a device is to remove an element of nonstationarity in the model. Given the incomplete asset markets, shocks can lead to permanent wealth reallocations that would induce nonstationarity and prevent computation of the second moments used in estimation. Introducing the risk premium term as a function of debts forces wealth allocations in the long run to return to their initial distribution. In practice, the parameter Ψ_B will be set at a very low level in applications of the model used for this chapter.

A similar IRP condition is implied by the foreign agent optimization, and these two conditions will be identical when linearized. As a result, a bond allocation rule could be created to solve for B and B^* separately. Instead, we here by solve for $B - B^*$, thereby eliminating the need for the bond allocation rule.

As a fourth optimality condition, households supply labor to the point that the marginal disutility of labor equals its marginal product:

$$L_t^{\frac{1}{\sigma_3}} = \frac{W_t}{P_t} \tau_{ct} C_t^{-\sigma_1}. \tag{35}$$

Finally, capital accumulation is set to equate the costs and expected benefits:

$$\left(1 + \frac{\psi_I\left(K_t - K_{t-1}\right)}{K_{t-1}}\right)$$
$$= \beta E_t\left[\left(\frac{\tau_{t+1}C_{t+1}^{-\sigma_1}}{\tau_t C_t^{-\sigma_1}}\right)\left(r_{t+1} + (1-\delta) + \frac{\Psi_I}{2}\left(\frac{K_{t+1}^2 - K_t^2}{K_t^2}\right)\right)\right]. \tag{36}$$

The cost, on the left side, is the gross return if the funds instead had been used to purchase bonds; and the benefits on the right include the return from rental of the capital plus the resale value after depreciation, and the fact that a larger capital stock lowers the expected adjustment cost of further accumulation in the subsequent period.

Write the resource constraint (define final goods demand):

$$Y_t = C_t + I_t + G_t + AC_{It} + \int_0^1 AC_{Ht}(i)di + \int_0^1 AC_{Ht}^*(i)di. \tag{37}$$

The goods market clearing condition is

$$nY_{Ht} + (1-n)Y_{Ht}^* = nZ_t. \tag{38}$$

Define the trade balance in per capita terms (X):

$$X_t = \left(\frac{1-n}{n}\right)\frac{e_t P_{Ht}^*}{P_t}Y_{Ht}^* - \frac{P_{Ft}}{P_t}Y_{Ft}. \tag{39}$$

To keep the number of state variables to a minimum, we abstract from government issue of debt here. Given that the model has no features to break Ricardian equivalence, this simplification has no impact on the results. The simple government budget constraint is

$$T_t + G = \frac{1}{P_t}\left(M_t - M_{t-1}\right). \tag{40}$$

Combine the budget constraints of the household, firm, and government:

$$P_{Ht}Y_{Ht} + e_t P_{Ht}^*\left(\frac{1-n}{n}\right)Y_{Ht}^* + i_{t-1}B_{t-1} + e_t i_{t-1}^* B_{t-1}^*$$
$$= P_t\left(C_t + I_t + G_t + AC_{Ht} + AC_{Ht}^*\right) + \left(B_t - B_{t-1}\right) - e_t\left(B_t^* - B_{t-1}^*\right).$$

Use the resource constraint above to write this using Y_t, and then rewrite this in terms of home and imported goods:

$$\begin{aligned} &P_{Ht}Y_{Ht} \\ &\quad + \left(\frac{1-n}{n}\right) e_t P^*_{Ht} Y^*_{Ht} - (P_{Ht}Y_{Ht} + P_{Ft}Y_{Ft}) + i_{t-1}B_{t-1} - e_t i^*_{t-1} B^*_{t-1} \\ &= (B_t - B_{t-1}) - e_t \left(B^*_t - B^*_{t-1}\right). \end{aligned}$$

Use the definition of the trade balance to write the balance of payments condition:

$$P_t X_t + i_{t-1}B_{t-1} - e_t i^*_{t-1} B^*_{t-1} = (B_t - B_{t-1}) - e_t \left(B^*_t - B^*_{t-1}\right). \tag{41}$$

The monetary policy will be specified in terms of an interest rate targeting rule:

$$i_t = \bar{i} + a_1 \left(\frac{P_t}{P_{t-1}}\right) - a_2 \left(\frac{Y_t}{\overline{Y}}\right) + a_2 \left(\frac{e_t}{\overline{e}}\right) + \phi_t, \tag{42}$$

where ϕ_t is a monetary policy shock.

The shocks may be specified:

$$\begin{aligned} \phi_t &= \rho_\phi (\phi_{t-1}) + \varepsilon_{\phi t} \\ \left(\log A_t - \log \overline{A}\right) &= \rho_A \left(\log A_{t-1} - \log \overline{A}\right) + \varepsilon_{At} \\ \left(\log \theta_t - \log \overline{\theta}\right) &= \rho_\theta \left(\log \theta_{t-1} - \log \overline{\theta}\right) + \varepsilon_{\theta t} \\ \log \tau_t &= \rho_\tau \left(\log \tau_{t-1}\right) + \varepsilon_{\tau t} \\ \xi_t &= \rho_\xi (\xi_{t-1}) + \varepsilon_{\xi_t t} \end{aligned} \tag{43}$$

$$\left[\varepsilon_{\phi t}, \varepsilon_{At}, \varepsilon_{\theta t}, \varepsilon_{\tau t}, \varepsilon_{\xi t}\right]' \sim N(0, \Sigma_1).$$

The equilibrium conditions all will be used in a form linearized around a deterministic steady state. Further, the variables will be written as country differences, home minus the foreign counterpart. This allows the dimensions of the data set and parameter space to be reduced, which is necessary to make the sizable empirical exercise tractable.[7] Appendix A lists all equilibrium conditions of the model transformed in this way.

3. Empirical Methods

3.1. *Data*

Data for the US will be used for the home country, and an aggregate of the remaining G-7 will be used for the foreign country. The five series used will be the exchange rate and the current account, which are the primary variables of interest here, as well as the interest rate, output, and the price level. The interest rate was included to help identify monetary policy shocks, and output was included to help identify the technology shocks specified in the model. The price level is important for identifying the role of price stickiness in the model, which is an issue of interest in the literature. In addition, these three variables have been a common choice in early tests of how well macroeconomic models can explain exchange rates, as in Meese and Rogoff (1983).

All data are seasonally adjusted quarterly series at annual rates for the period 1973:1 to 2000:4, obtained from International Financial Statistics. The exchange rate for each country is measured as the bilateral rate with the US dollar. The current account is measured as GNP less expenditure on consumption, investment, and government purchases. Output is measured as national GDP, the domestic price level as the CPI, and the interest rate as a treasury bill rate or something similar.[8] Foreign aggregate variables

---

[7]Note that this transformation will require the assumption that many of the deep behavioral parameters are the same for both countries in the model. But this simplification is common in the empirical macroeconomic literature (see Meese and Rogoff, 1983). Given that the foreign country here will represent an aggregate of the G-7 countries less the US, as is common practice, this means that we already are assuming that the parameters of six of the seven countries in the data set are the same. Note that this assumption does not need to be applied to the parameter representing monetary policy responses to the bilateral exchange rate; in this case, the transformation implies that the parameter estimated instead is just the sum of home and foreign parameters. As a result, the model does allow for asymmetric responses by the two countries to the bilateral exchange rate.

[8]The treasury bill rate was used for the US, UK, Canada, and France; the money market rate was used for Italy; and the call money rate was used for Germany and Japan.

Table 1. Unit root tests

	U.S.	Foreign aggregate
Phillips-Perron test:		
Exchange rate		
Levels	−1.8230	—
Differences	−9.4457**	
Current account		
Levels	−0.8041	—
Differences	−9.5258**	
Interest rate		
Levels	−2.2940	−2.4337
Differences	−7.4911**	−5.2423**
Output		
Levels	−1.8986	−1.4111
Differences	−4.1464**	−9.3866**
Price level		
Levels	−1.7126	−3.9689*
Differences	−4.3715**	−9.4550**

Notes: *indicates rejected at 5% level; **indicates unit root rejected at 1% significance level. Tests run with 3 lags, intercept and trend. All variables in logs except current account. Range is 1973Q2 to 2000Q4. Critical values: 1% −4.0444; 5% −3.4512; 10% −3.1507.

are computed as a geometric weighted average, where time-varying weights are based on each country's share of total real GDP. Series other than the current account are logged. Because the steady state value of the current account in the theoretical model is necessarily zero, this variable cannot be expressed in the model in a form that represents deviations from steady state in log form. Instead the current account is scaled by taking it as a ratio to the mean level of output.

As a preliminary step, the data series are tested for unit roots. Table 1 shows the results. The seven series appear to be nonstationary in levels but stationary in first differences. This motivates the decision to fit the model to data in first differences. This is a common practice in the structural VAR studies to which we wish to compare our empirical results.[9] The data will

[9]See Ahmed *et al.* (1993).

also be demeaned and transformed into country differences, home minus the foreign counterpart. The last transformation of course does not apply to the exchange rate or current account, but it means that the last three variables in the data set will be movements in interest rate differentials, differences in output growth rates, and differences in inflation rates.

3.2. *Econometric methods*

The econometric methodology fits the linear approximation to the structural model, adapting a maximum likelihood algorithm developed in Leeper and Sims (1994) and extended in Kim (2000).

The linearized model equations, as derived in the section above and transformed and listed in Appendix A, can be expressed in autoregressive form as

$$y_t = Ay_{t-1} + \varepsilon_t \tag{44}$$
$$\varepsilon_t \tilde{} N(0, \Sigma)$$

where y is the 18-element column vector of variables listed in the Appendix A. A is a 18×18 matrix, where each cell is a nonlinear function of the structural parameters; ε is a column vector, containing the five structural disturbances and where the remaining elements are zeros; and Σ is the covariance matrix of these disturbances.

The model system may be rewritten in terms of first differences as follows:

$$y_t^* = Ay_{t-1}^* + \varepsilon_t - \varepsilon_{t-1} \tag{45}$$

$$\text{where} \quad \begin{aligned} y_t^* &= y_t - y_{t-1} \\ \varepsilon_t^* &= \varepsilon_t - \varepsilon_{t-1}. \end{aligned} \tag{46}$$

This stochastic model implies a log likelihood function:

$$L(\Pi) = -.5 \ln |\Omega| - .5x'\Omega^{-1}x \tag{47}$$

where x is the vector of the five variables on which we have data, over all periods stacked into a single vector, and Ω is the theoretical variance–covariance matrix of the variables in x. The appendix discusses the details of how Ω is computed as a function of the matrices A and Σ. But note that each cell in A is a nonlinear function of the structural parameters from the theoretical model. An algorithm is used to search for values of these structural parameters and for the elements of the symmetric positive-definite covariance matrix Σ, which will maximize the likelihood function. Note that taking first differences should not introduce the classic problem of "overdifferencing" here. The fact that differencing may introduce a moving average term is taken into consideration in Equation (45) and hence the computation of Ω and the likelihood function, so a misspecified model is not being estimated.

A few parameters will not be estimated here, but instead are pinned down ahead of time. This is because the data set omits the relevant series for these parameters, like capital and labor, or because the data set in first differences is not very relevant for parameters pertaining to steady states. As a result, these parameters are pinned down at values common in the Real Business Cycle literature. In particular, the capital share in production (α) is set at 40, the depreciation rate (δ) is set at 10, the labor-supply elasticity ($\frac{1}{\sigma_3}$) is calibrated at unity, the steady state share of home intermediate goods in the home final goods aggregate ($\overline{\theta}$) is set at 0.80, and the discount factor (β) is set at 0.96. The bond cost parameter (Ψ_B) is set at 0.001, which is sufficient to prevent a unit root in the system, but small enough not to noticeably affect the quantitative results.

Some regions of the parameter space do not imply a well defined equilibrium within the model. These regions can be precluded by imposing boundaries on the parameters by functional transformations. For example, the variances of shocks and the intertemporal elasticity are restricted to be positive. The monetary policy reaction to inflation is bounded below to rule out indeterminacy. Autoregressive coefficients on shock processes are also restricted to be greater than zero and less than unity. Finally, the covariances between shocks must be restricted so that the implied correlations lie between -1 and 1.

4. Results

Table 2 shows the basic results from estimating the model. Regarding fit, the table reports the likelihood value as 1797.5, compared to 1823.8 for a standard unidentified VAR of the five variables in the data set. A likelihood ratio test cannot be used to compare the two, since the structural model is

Table 2. Estimation results

Measures of Fit		
Log likelihood value		
Model		1797.55
Standard VAR		1823.78
Schwarz criterion		
Model		1741.14
Standard VAR		1642.81
RMSE: structural model/standard VAR		
Exchange rate		1.013
Current account		1.019
Interest rate		1.104
Output		1.092
Price level		1.171
RMSE: structural model/random walk		
Exchange rate		0.984
Current account		0.986
Interest rate		0.997
Output		1.045
Price level		1.037
Parameter Estimates		
Behavioral parameters		
Consumption elasticity term	σ_1	1.072
		(0.006)
Money demand elasticity term	σ_2	0.253
		(0.003)
Investment adjustment cost	ψ_I	21.523
		(0.512)
Price adjustment cost	ψ_P	31.099
		(2.414)
Bond cost	ψ_B	0.00384
		(0.00010)
Share of local currency pricing	s	0.999
		(0.000)
Elasticity of subst. home-foreign goods	μ	1.130
		(0.062)
Monetary policy rule parameters		
Response to inflation	a_1	0.9891
		(0.0002)
Response to output	a_2	0.0001
		(0.0000)
Response to the exchange rate	a_3	0.1128
		(0.0138)

(Continued)

Table 2. (*Continued*)

Shock autocorrelations	
Technology	0.9671 (0.0003)
Monetary	0.9309 (0.0089)
Tastes	0.9773 (0.0014)
Home bias	0.8908 (0.0046)
IRP deviation	0.9750 (0.0034)
Correlations with IRP shock	
Technology	0.123 (0.035)
Monetary	0.152 (0.029)
Tastes	−0.845 (0.011)
Home bias	−0.427 (0.016)

Note: Values in parentheses indicate standard errors.

not nested in the VAR.[10] However, a comparison can be made in terms of the Schwarz criterion, which penalizes the VAR for the fact it has 40 free parameters compared to the 23 of the structural model. By this comparison, the structural model performs better. The fit of the model can also be evaluated in terms of how well it can forecast the variables one period ahead. The table reports root mean squared errors, indicating that the structural model has larger forecast error for all five variables. It is interesting to note that the model comes closest for the exchange rate and the current account.

Perhaps a more fair comparison, given the VAR's extra parameters is a random walk model. One may recall the classic result of Meese and Rogoff (1983) that no macro model was able to beat a random walk in forecasting the exchange rate out of sample. Table 2 shows that the structural model

[10]Given the unobserved variables in the structural model, it cannot be written as a first-order VAR in just the five observed variables. See Bergin (2003) for details.

here is able to beat a random walk for the exchange rate, as well as for the current account and the interest rate. While these predictions are not out of sample as in Meese–Rogoff, this should not make a large difference here, given that the parameters are intended to be "deep" parameters, and should not be expected to change much over time. Further, conducting out of sample test here is problematic, since these deep parameters as a matter of principle should not be changed period by period.

The model also does quite well in terms of fitting unconditional moments, which is the typical measure of fit used in real business cycle exercises. This is a bit unfair here, given that the maximum likelihood estimation is trying to fit a set of hundreds of moments, not just a handful of arbitrary moments that researchers have in the past chosen to focus upon. Nevertheless, for the data as transformed here (in logged differences and demeaned), the variance of the exchange rate is 0.00290 in the data and 0.00292 in the model, the variance of the current account is 1.44×10^{-5} in the data and 1.51×10^{-5} in the model, and the covariance between the exchange rate and the current account is 6.52×10^{-6} in the data and 5.58×10^{-6} in the model.

The parameter estimates look reasonable and are generally statistically significant. The elasticity of intertemporal substitution ($\frac{1}{\sigma_1}$) is near unity. The interest elasticity of money demand implies an income elasticity of money demand ($\frac{\sigma_1}{\sigma_2}$) which is a bit high, around 4. The investment adjustment cost (Ψ_H) is high but not unreasonable, implying that if investment rises 1% above steady state, about 1.1% of this investment goes toward paying the adjustment cost. The adjustment cost on prices (Ψ_H) is also quite reasonable, indicating that after a money supply shock, the half-life of price-level adjustments is about five quarters.

This model also provides an estimate of the share of firms that engage in local currency pricing. Surprisingly, this estimate presses up closely against the upper boundary of unity. This is best interpreted in light of the particular data set used for estimation, and the fact it is well-known that local currency pricing helps models of this type replicate the high degree of variability of exchange rates (see Betts and Devereux, 1996). This result offers further evidence that a high degree of pricing-to-market is a very useful way of helping macro models of this type capture key aspects of the behavior of exchange rates and the other four variables in this data set. The table also offers another estimated parameter of interest to the literature. Much work in the NOEM has assumed a unitary elasticity of substitution between home and foreign goods as a means to facilitate analytical solution. The estimate of μ here is 1.13, with a standard deviation of 0.09, indicating that the simplifying assumption in common use may not be so bad, inasmuch as a value near unity does not limit the model's ability to explain the macroeconomic variables of interest.

Finally, the model also suggests some interesting estimates of parameters in the monetary policy reaction function. Since the estimate of a_1 is close to its boundary of unity, the monetary response to inflation is close to its lower bound of $(\frac{1}{\beta a_1})$, imposed to ensure a unique equilibrium. This suggests that the model might fit the data better if we permitted it to explore regions of the parameter space that involved indeterminacy, as has been suggested by Lubik and Schorfheide (2002). The response to output (a_2) is near zero, indicating little evidence of active output stabilization. The statistically significant estimate of a_3 indicates some systematic response to stabilize exchange rates by some countries.[11] As will be shown shortly using impulse responses, this does not preclude a fair degree of exchange rate variability in equilibrium.

Table 2 also tells us few things about the nature of the structural shocks. Of particular interest are the correlations at the bottom of the table. The estimated model suggests that the deviations from interest rate parity we observe in the data have little to do with any monetary policy action or with technology shocks. The latter of these two correlations is not statistically different from zero, and while the former is significant, it is rather small in magnitude. However, there is a very high degree of negative correlation with the taste shocks defined in this model (correlation coefficient of -0.86). This result is interesting, as the taste shock (τ) directly affects marginal utility, which is an important element in the risk premium term dropped from the IRP condition due to linearization, as discussed above. Additional interpretation of this relationship between taste shocks and interests rate parity deviations will follow below. Regarding the estimates of shock variances in the table, these do not lend themselves to direct interpretation, but these will be interpreted in the form of variance decompositions

[11]Recall that in the transformed model a_3 is the sum of home and foreign responses to the bilateral exchange rate.

to follow shortly. The shock autocorrelations indicate a fairly high degree of persistence in all the shocks. Fortunately, none presses up against the boundary of unity, required to maintain stationarity of the theoretical system.

Impulse responses can give us a greater sense of what these parameters imply for the dynamics of the economy. Figure 1 shows the impulse responses of the five data variables to a one-standard deviation shock to the monetary policy rule. As the interest rate rises, this induces an immediate fall in output and a gradual fall in the price level. It is encouraging that the model is able to replicate a hump-shaped movement in the interest rate often observed empirically, but it is disappointing that it does not replicate a hump-shaped response in output. The monetary contraction induces a significant exchange rate appreciation, in which the exchange rate overshoots, as discussed in the previous paragraph. It also involves a small degree of worsening in the current account.

Figure 2 is helpful in understanding what is meant by an interest rate parity shock in this model. As the figure shows, such a shock permits the home interest rate to rise relative to the foreign rate and for the value of the domestic currency to depreciate at the same time, as is often observed

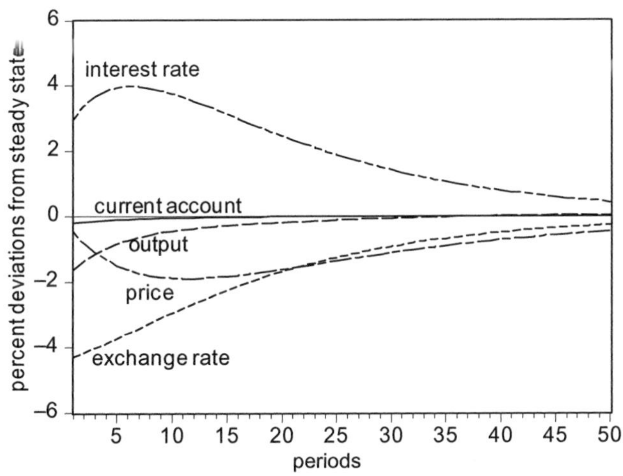

Figure 1. Impulse responses for monetary shock

Note: *Except current account, which is shown as deviation from steady state as a share of steady state output.

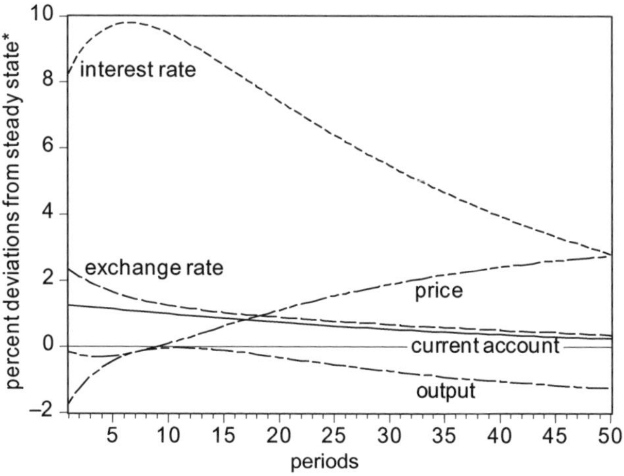

Figure 2. Impulse responses for interest parity shock

Note: *Except current account, which is shown as deviation from steady state as a share of steady state output.

empirically. The shock may be understood as a type of portfolio shift away from home assets, such that a high interest rate and an expected currency appreciation over time both are required to make households willing to hold home bonds in equilibrium. While this shock is often used as a shorthand way of introducing exchange rate fluctuations in a model, it is interesting to note that this shock implies movements in a variety of variables, not just the exchange rate. In particular, the interest rate moves substantially here, but there are also a sizable response in the current account.

Given the apparent relationship between the interest parity shocks and the taste shock, Fig. 3 is included to show the impulse response to a taste shock. It implies a case where the current account moves in very much the same way as in Fig. 2 for an interest parity shock, but the exchange rate moves in the opposite direction. If these taste shocks indeed are highly negatively correlated with IRP shocks, the combination of these two shocks would seem to imply a large change in the exchange rate while an effect on the current account that is substantially canceled out. This observation will be useful in our analysis below.

A natural question to ask here is how important are the interest parity shocks in explaining the exchange rate and other key variables. In

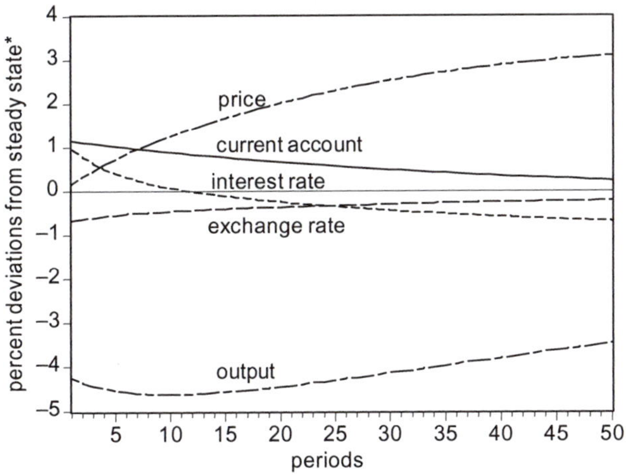

Figure 3. Impulse responses for taste shock

Notes: *Except current account, which is shown as deviation from steady state as a share of steady state output.

particular, is the model able to explain the exchange rate simply because it can invoke the IRP shock to drive the exchange rate as needed to match the data? To address this question, we can consider variance decompositions, which show what fraction of the forecast error variance for each variable is explained by each of the shocks at various time horizons. This analysis is complicated somewhat by the fact that interest rate parity (IRP) deviations are allowed to be correlated here with the four structural shocks. Recall that this choice was made because IRP deviations do not strictly arise from the structural model, and because we wished to gather information that might help us interpret these IRP deviations and offer guidance to future modelers. As a result, if we wish to disentangle the various contributions of these shocks, which must take steps to orthogonalize them in some way. Two ways of doing this are presented below. It might seem that a natural approach would be to re-estimate the model, requiring the shocks to be orthogonal. However, this estimation produced a likelihood value of only 1736.859. This version of the model may be regarded as nested in the benchmark case shown in Table 2, with the addition of four restrictions requiring the correlations between shocks to be zero. As a nested comparison, a likelihood ratio test can be used, where twice the difference of the likelihood values follows a chi-squared distribution with four degrees of freedom. The p-value of such a comparison is zero, indicating we should reject the restrictions. Because the model that assumes orthogonal shocks is strongly rejected by the data, I will continue to utilize the model that permits them to be correlated.

As a result, we must take a stand on how to disentangle the joint contribution of the IRP and other shocks. Table 3 shows variance decompositions which orthogonalize the IRP shock by attributing any contribution shared with another shock to that other shock.[12] The table shows that the independent part of IRP shocks explains only about 1% of exchange rate movements in this model. This suggests that the IRP shock is not being used here to drive the exchange rate and artificially boost the model fit. Instead a bit more than half of the exchange rate movements appear to be driven by monetary policy shocks. This result is comparable but somewhat larger than that found in past studies. Eichenbaum and Evans (1995) found variance decompositions between 18% and 43% using standard VAR techniques. Rogers (1999) found between 19% and 60%. Faust and Rogers (2000) found estimates ranging from the single digits to around 50% using a structural VAR that considered a wide range of identification assumptions. Ahmed *et al.* (1993) found almost no role for monetary shocks in a structural VAR using long-run identification restrictions. In our estimation, taste shocks are also somewhat important, explaining about 25% of exchange rate movements.

In contrast, Table 3 shows that for the current account, a surprisingly large role is played by the IRP shock. Up to two-thirds of current account movements are attributable to these shocks, which raises an interesting possibility. These IRP shocks represent portfolio shifts in the asset market between countries, which naturally affect a country's capital account. These shocks to the capital account then would affect the current account through the balance of payments identity. The model seems to be suggesting that attempts in the New Open Economy literature to explain current account movements in terms of optimal intertemporal saving decisions may be misplaced. Rather, the current account could be driven substantially by financial shocks affecting the capital account side

[12]Mechanically, this is accomplished by a Cholesky decomposition, where the IRP shock is ordered last. Note that the ordering of the other four shocks is inconsequential, since these structural shocks are orthogonal to each other already.

Table 3. Variance decompositions (remove correlated components of interest parity shock)

		Shocks				
	Period	Technology	Monetary policy	Tastes	Home bias	Interest parity
Exchange rate	1	0.11	0.54	0.26	0.07	0.01
	2	0.10	0.57	0.26	0.06	0.01
	3	0.09	0.59	0.25	0.06	0.01
	4	0.08	0.61	0.25	0.06	0.01
	5	0.07	0.62	0.25	0.05	0.01
	10	0.05	0.66	0.24	0.04	0.01
	20	0.04	0.66	0.25	0.04	0.01
Current account	1	0.24	0.00	0.07	0.05	0.64
	2	0.28	0.00	0.06	0.03	0.64
	3	0.30	0.00	0.05	0.02	0.62
	4	0.32	0.01	0.04	0.03	0.60
	5	0.33	0.01	0.04	0.04	0.58
	10	0.35	0.03	0.02	0.14	0.47
	20	0.32	0.05	0.01	0.27	0.36
Interest rate	1	0.48	0.16	0.31	0.01	0.04
	2	0.39	0.19	0.36	0.02	0.04
	3	0.32	0.21	0.39	0.03	0.05
	4	0.27	0.22	0.42	0.04	0.05
	5	0.22	0.23	0.45	0.05	0.05
	10	0.11	0.24	0.51	0.09	0.05
	20	0.06	0.22	0.55	0.11	0.05
Output	1	0.16	0.16	0.37	0.31	0.01
	2	0.22	0.12	0.41	0.24	0.01
	3	0.28	0.10	0.44	0.18	0.00
	4	0.32	0.08	0.46	0.14	0.00
	5	0.35	0.06	0.47	0.11	0.00
	10	0.44	0.03	0.49	0.05	0.00
	20	0.47	0.02	0.49	0.02	0.00
Price level	1	0.50	0.29	0.13	0.07	0.00
	2	0.50	0.30	0.13	0.07	0.00
	3	0.51	0.30	0.13	0.07	0.00
	4	0.51	0.30	0.13	0.06	0.00
	5	0.51	0.30	0.13	0.06	0.00
	10	0.53	0.31	0.13	0.04	0.00
	20	0.56	0.29	0.13	0.02	0.00

of the balance of payments, which then forces adjustment in saving and investment on the current account side. This conjecture warrants further investigation.

For completeness, Table 4 shows variance decompositions with the opposite method of orthogonalization, where comovements in the IRP shock with other shocks is awarded instead to the IRP shock. By this accounting, the role of IRP shocks in driving exchange rates goes up somewhat, but it still explains less than a quarter of exchange rate movements at its maximum. Monetary policy shocks still are the main explanation and explain around half of the forecast error variance. This result suggests that IRP shocks have their greatest usefulness in explaining exchange rate movements not as an independent factor, but as a way of modifying the effect of monetary policy shocks.

The result for the current account in Table 4 suggests a similar conclusion. This time, the effect of IRP shocks essentially disappears and the weight is transferred mainly to taste shocks. This result may be understood by considering again the impulse responses of the two shocks in Figs. 2 and 3 and the fact the two shocks are very strongly negatively correlated. The effects of each of these two shocks on the current account are very similar to each other and are fairly large in magnitude (compared to the effect of the monetary shock in Fig. 1 for example), while their effects on the exchange rate are opposite of each other. If one were to consider the joint effect of an IRP shock combined with the negative of the taste shock, it would be a large exchange rate movement where the effects on the current account would approximately cancel each other out.[13] Again this suggests that the IRP shock has value mainly as a way of modifying the effects of other shocks, in this case, allowing a taste shock to affect the exchange rate without having large effects on the current account or other real quantities. This is one way the model can mimic the exchange rate disconnect puzzle noted by Obstfeld and Rogoff (2001), Duarte and Stockman (2001), and Devereux and Engel (2002).

[13]This helps explain the variance decomposition of Table 4 in the following way: when either the IRP shock or the taste shock is allowed to act independently, it implies large movements in the current account and hence explains a larger portion of the current account forecast error variance.

Table 4. Variance decompositions (remove correlated components of other shocks with interest parity shock)

		Shocks				
	Period	Technology	Monetary policy	Tastes	Home bias	Interest parity
Exchange rate	1	0.08	0.48	0.19	0.00	0.25
	2	0.07	0.49	0.20	0.00	0.24
	3	0.06	0.51	0.20	0.00	0.23
	4	0.05	0.52	0.21	0.00	0.22
	5	0.04	0.53	0.21	0.00	0.21
	10	0.03	0.56	0.22	0.00	0.19
	20	0.02	0.56	0.23	0.00	0.18
Current account	1	0.25	0.17	0.54	0.04	0.00
	2	0.28	0.15	0.55	0.02	0.00
	3	0.30	0.13	0.54	0.02	0.01
	4	0.31	0.11	0.53	0.02	0.03
	5	0.32	0.10	0.52	0.02	0.04
	10	0.31	0.05	0.45	0.08	0.10
	20	0.27	0.03	0.37	0.17	0.15
Interest rate	1	0.58	0.06	0.03	0.04	0.29
	2	0.50	0.07	0.03	0.03	0.37
	3	0.42	0.08	0.03	0.03	0.44
	4	0.36	0.08	0.03	0.02	0.50
	5	0.31	0.09	0.03	0.02	0.55
	10	0.17	0.09	0.03	0.01	0.69
	20	0.10	0.09	0.02	0.01	[illegible]
Output	1	0.14	0.09	0.21	0.51	0.06
	2	0.19	0.07	0.19	0.44	0.11
	3	0.23	0.06	0.17	0.38	0.16
	4	0.27	0.05	0.16	0.33	0.20
	5	0.29	0.04	0.14	0.29	0.24
	10	0.35	0.02	0.10	0.19	0.34
	20	0.38	0.01	0.09	0.13	0.40
Price level	1	0.41	0.20	0.03	0.00	0.36
	2	0.41	0.20	0.03	0.00	0.36
	3	0.41	0.21	0.03	0.00	0.35
	4	0.42	0.21	0.03	0.00	0.35
	5	0.42	0.21	0.03	0.00	0.34
	10	0.44	0.22	0.02	0.00	0.31
	20	0.47	0.23	0.02	0.01	0.27

5. Conclusions

This chapter has explored an empirical method that could be useful for estimating and testing a wide class of complex open economy models. The case here, fit to the US and an aggregate of the remaining G-7, performs reasonably well in that it is able to beat a random walk model for in-sample predictions of the exchange rate and current account, variables of key interest to open economy macroeconomists. The estimated model facilitates empirical answers to a number of interesting questions raised recently in the theoretical literature. For example, it lends additional support to the assumption of local currency pricing by firms, and it suggests that the common simplifying assumption of an unitary elasticity of substitution between home and foreign goods may not be so bad. The exercise indicates that deviations from interest rate parity do not seem to be closely related to monetary policy, as has been suggested in some recent work, but that these deviations do seem to be related to shifts in marginal utilities of consumption. Further, the model indicates that such interest rate parity shocks are not especially helpful as independent explanations for exchange rate movements observed in the data. But on the other hand, these shocks are helpful in explaining movements in the current account. It is hoped that this study may prove helpful for discriminating between alternative theoretical models currently being proposed, and for suggesting productive avenues for future theoretical research.

Appendices

Appendix A: List of equilibrium conditions

These equations are used in linearized form, expressed as differences between the home country variables and foreign country counterparts. The system may be written in the following 18 variables: $c_t - c_t^*$, $l_t - l_t^*$, $y_t - y_t^*$, $p_t - p_t^*$, $w_t - w_t^*$, $p_{Ft} - p_{Ht}^*$, $p_{Ht} - p_{Ft}^*$, $y_{Ht} - y_{Ft}^*$, $y_{Ft} - y_{Ht}^*$, $z_{Ht} - z_{Ht}^*$, $i_t - i_t^*$, $k_t - k_t^*$, $r_t - r_t^*$, $B_t - B_t^*$, $M_t - M_t^*$, e_t, ca_t, x_t. Numbered below are the 18 linearized conditions that determine these sequences.

Linearized home consumption Euler:

$$\sigma_1 c_t - \tau_{ct} = \sigma_1 E_t (c_{t+1}) - E_t (\tau_{ct+1}) + E_t [P_{t+1}] - P_t - (1 - \beta) i_t$$

together with the foreign counterpart:

$$\sigma_1 c_t^* - \tau_{ct}^* = \sigma_1 E_t\left(c_{t+1}^*\right) - E_t\left(\tau_{ct+1}^*\right) + E_t\left[P_{t+1}^*\right] - P_t^* - (1-\beta)i_t^*$$

to form:

$$\begin{aligned}\sigma_1\left(c_t - c_t^*\right) - \left(\tau_{ct} - \tau_{ct}^*\right) \\ &= \sigma_1 E_t\left(c_{t+1} - c_{t+1}^*\right) - E_t\left(\tau_{ct+1} - \tau_{ct+1}^*\right) \\ &\quad + E_t\left[P_{t+1} - P_{t+1}^*\right] - \left(P_t - P_t^*\right) - (1-\beta)\left(i_t - i_t^*\right). \qquad \text{(A1)}\end{aligned}$$

Money demand:

$$\sigma_1 c_t + \sigma_2 p_t - \sigma_2 m_t - \tau_{ct} - \beta i_t = 0$$

combined with foreign:

$$\begin{aligned}&\sigma_1\left(c_t - c_t^*\right) + \sigma_2\left(p_t - p_t^*\right) - \sigma_2\left(m_t - m_t^*\right) \\ &\quad - \left(\tau_{ct} - \tau_{ct}^*\right) - \tfrac{\beta^2}{1-\beta}\left(i_t - i_t^*\right) = 0. \qquad \text{(A2)}\end{aligned}$$

Labor supply:

$$\begin{aligned}\frac{1}{\sigma_3}\left(l_t - l_t^*\right) &= \left(w_t - w_t^*\right) - \sigma_1\left(c_t - c_t^*\right) - \left(p_t - p_t^*\right) \\ &\quad + \left(\tau_{ct} - \tau_{ct}^*\right). \qquad \text{(A3)}\end{aligned}$$

Production function:

$$\left(z_t - z_t^*\right) = \left(a_t - a_t^*\right) + \alpha\left(k_{t-1} - k_{t-1}^*\right) + (1-\alpha)\left(l_t - l_t^*\right). \qquad \text{(A4)}$$

The linearized price setting rule for domestic sales by local currency pricing (lcp) firms is

$$\begin{aligned}&[\nu](y_{Ht}(\text{lcp}) - y_{Ht}) + mc_t - [1+\nu]p_{Ht} + [\nu - (1+\beta)\nu\psi]p_{Ht}(\text{lcp}) \\ &\quad + [\nu\psi]p_{Ht-1}(\text{lcp}) + [\beta\nu\psi]E_t p_{Ht+1}(\text{lcp}) = 0,\end{aligned}$$

where

$$mc_t = p_t + r_t - a_t + (1-\alpha)k_{t-1} - (1-\alpha)l_t.$$

The linearized price setting rule for domestic sales is the same for producer currency pricing (pcp) firms:

$$[v](y_{Ht}(\text{pcp}) - y_{Ht}) + mc_t - [1+v]p_{Ht} + [v - (1+\beta)v\psi]p_{Ht}(\text{pcp}) \\ + [v\psi]p_{Ht-1}(\text{pcp}) + [\beta v\psi]E_t p_{Ht+1}(\text{pcp}) = 0.$$

Given that all lcp firms set the same price as each other, and all pcp firms as each other, we may write the linearized form of the home domestic goods price index as

$$p_{Ht} = sp_{Ht}(\text{lcp}) + (1-s)p_{Ht}(\text{pcp}).$$

Substituting in the price-setting equations above, we find the overall price level of home goods sold at home:

$$mc_t - [1 + (1+\beta)v\psi]p_{Ht} + [v\psi]p_{Ht-1} + [\beta v\psi]E_t p_{Ht+1} = 0.$$

The foreign counterpart is

$$mc_t^* - [1 + (1+\beta)v\psi]p_{Ft}^* + [v\psi]p_{Ft-1}^* + [\beta v\psi]E_t p_{Ft+1}^* = 0$$

where

$$mc_t^* = p_t^* + r_{t-1}^* - a_t^* + (1-\alpha)k_{t-1}^* - (1-\alpha)l_t^*.$$

Similarly, the linearized price setting rule when home lcp firms ($i = 0, \ldots, s$) export is

$$[v]\left(y_{Ht}^*(\text{lcp}) - y_{Ht}^*\right) \\ + mc_t - [1+v]p_{Ht}^* + [v - (1+\beta)v\psi]p_{Ht}^*(\text{lcp}) \\ + [v\psi]p_{Ht-1}^*(\text{lcp}) + [\beta v\psi]E_t p_{Ht+1}^*(\text{lcp}) - e_t = 0.$$

And for pcp firms, this is

$$[v]\left(y_{Ht}^*(\text{pcp}) - y_{Ht}^*\right) + mc_t - [1+v]\,p_{Ht}^* + [v - (1+\beta)v\psi]p_{Ht}^*(\text{pcp}) \\ + [v\psi]p_{Ht-1}^*(\text{pcp}) + [\beta v\psi]E_t p_{Ht+1}^*(\text{pcp}) - [1+v]\,e_t = 0.$$

Since the linearized form of the home export price index implies

$$p_{Ht}^* = sp_{Ht}^*(\text{lcp}) + (1-s)p_{Ht}^*(\text{pcp}) - (1-s)e_t,$$

we can substitute in the pricing equations to write an equation for this export price index as

$$
\begin{aligned}
mc_t &- [1 + (1+\beta)\nu\psi]p^*_{Ht} + [\nu\psi]p^*_{Ht-1} + [\beta\nu\psi]E_t p^*_{Ht+1} \\
&- [(1-s)(1+\beta)\psi\nu + 1]\, e_t + (1-s)\psi\nu e_{t-1} + (1-s)\beta\psi\nu E_t\,[e_{t+1}] \\
&= 0.
\end{aligned}
$$

The counterpart for foreign country exports to the home country is

$$
\begin{aligned}
mc^*_t &- [1 + (1+\beta)\nu\psi]p_{Ft} + [\nu\psi]p_{Ft-1} + [\beta\nu\psi]E_t p_{ft+1} \\
&+ [(1-s)(1+\nu) + 1]\, e_t - (1-s)\psi\nu e_{t-1} - (1-s)\beta\psi\nu E_t\,[e_{t+1}] \\
&= 0.
\end{aligned}
$$

Then combine these four pricing equations to get

$$
\begin{aligned}
&(mc_t - mc^*_t) - [1 + (1+\beta)\nu\psi]\left(p_{Ht} - p^*_{Ft}\right) \\
&\quad + [\nu\psi]\left(p_{Ht-1} - p^*_{Ft-1}\right) + [\beta\nu\psi]E_t\left(p_{Ht+1} - p^*_{Ft+1}\right) = 0 \qquad \text{(A5)}
\end{aligned}
$$

and

$$
\begin{aligned}
&-(mc_t - mc^*_t) - [1 + (1+\beta)\nu\psi](p_{Ft} - p^*_{Ht}) + [\nu\psi](p_{Ft-1} - p^*_{Ht-1}) \\
&\quad + [\beta\nu\psi](E_t(p_{Ft+1}) - E_t\left(p^*_{Ht+1}\right)) - 2\,[(1-s)(1+\beta)\psi\nu + 1]\, e_t \\
&\quad + 2(1-s)\psi\nu e_{t-1} + 2(1-s)\beta\psi\nu E_t\,[e_{t+1}] = 0 \qquad \text{(A6)}
\end{aligned}
$$

Ratio of price indexes:

$$
\begin{aligned}
p_t &= \bar{\theta}p_{Ht} + (1-\bar{\theta})p_{Ft} \\
p^*_t &= (1-\bar{\theta})p^*_{Ht} + \bar{\theta}p^*_{Ft}
\end{aligned}
$$

so

$$
\left(p_t - p^*_t\right) = \left(1-\bar{\theta}\right)\left(p_{Ft} - p^*_{Ht}\right) + \bar{\theta}\left(p_{Ht} - p^*_{Ft}\right). \qquad \text{(A7)}
$$

Demands are

$$
\begin{aligned}
y_{Ht} &= y_t + \mu p_t - \mu p_{Ht} + \theta_t \\
y_{Ft} &= y_t + \mu p_t - \mu p_{Ft} - \left(\frac{\bar{\theta}}{1-\bar{\theta}}\right)
\end{aligned}
$$

$$y^*_{Ft} = y^*_t + \mu p^*_t - \mu p^*_{Ft} + \theta^*_t$$
$$y^*_{Ht} = y^*_t + \mu p^*_t - \mu p^*_{Ht} - \left(\frac{\overline{\theta}}{1-\overline{\theta}}\right)\theta^*_t$$

so

$$(y_{Ht} - y^*_{Ft}) = (y_t - y^*_t) + \mu(p_t - p^*_t) - \mu(p_{Ht} - p^*_{Ft}) + \left(\theta_t - \theta^*_t\right) \quad \text{(A8)}$$
$$(y_{Ft} - y^*_{Ht}) = (y_t - y^*_t) + \mu(p_t - p^*_t) - \mu(p_{Ft} - p^*_{Ht}) - \left(\frac{\overline{\theta}}{1-\overline{\theta}}\right)\left(\theta_t - \theta^*_t\right). \quad \text{(A9)}$$

Capital accumulation:

$$(1+\beta)\psi_I k_t - \beta\psi_I E_t k_{t+1} - \psi_I k_{t-1} - (1-\beta(1-\overline{\delta}))r_{t+1} - \sigma_1 c_t + \sigma_1 E_t c_{t+1} + \tau_{ct} - E_t\left[\tau_{ct+1}\right] = 0$$

combined with foreign:

$$(1+\beta)\psi_I\left(k_t - k^*_t\right) - \beta\psi_I E_t\left(k_{t+1} - k^*_{t+1}\right) - \psi_I\left(k_{t-1} - k^*_{t-1}\right) - (1-\beta(1-\overline{\delta}))\left(r_t - r^*_t\right) - \sigma_1\left(c_t - c^*_t\right) + \sigma_1 E_t\left(c_{t+1} - c^*_{t+1}\right) + \left(\tau_{ct} - \tau^*_{ct}\right) - E_t\left(\tau_{ct+1} - \tau^*_{ct+1}\right) = 0. \quad \text{(A10)}$$

Capital stock transition function:

$$\overline{\delta}\left(i_t - i^*_t\right) = \left(k_t - k^*_t\right) - (1-\delta)\left(k_{t-1} - k^*_{t-1}\right). \quad \text{(A11)}$$

Capital–labor tradeoff:

$$\left(p_t - p^*_t\right) + \left(r_t - r^*_t\right) + \left(k_{t-1} - k^*_{t-1}\right) = \left(w_t - w^*_t\right) + \left(l_t - l^*_t\right). \quad \text{(A12)}$$

Define final goods demand:[14]

$$\left(y_t - y^*_t\right) = \frac{\overline{C}}{\overline{\overline{Y}}}\left(c_t - c^*_t\right) + \frac{\overline{I}}{\overline{\overline{Y}}}\left(i_t - i^*_t\right). \quad \text{(A13)}$$

[14]Given parameter values, $\beta, \delta, \alpha, \sigma_1, \sigma_3, \overline{G}$, I can define the steady state value of A so that the steady state value of I is any desired fraction of $\overline{Y}$, and then the steady state value of C is just $\overline{Y}$–$\overline{I}$–$\overline{G}$.

Goods market clearing conditions are

$$ny_{Ht} + (1-n)y^*_{Ht} = z_t,$$
$$(1-n)y_{Ft} + ny^*_{Ft} = z^*_t,$$

so combining:

$$n(y_{Ht} - y^*_{Ft}) - (1-n)(y_{Ft} - y^*_{Ht}) = (z_t - z^*_t). \tag{A14}$$

Define trade balance (taking X as a share of GDP, Z):

$$\left[\frac{1}{1-\overline{\theta}}\right] x_t = e_t - (p_{Ft} - p^*_{Ht}) - (y_{Ft} - y^*_{Ht}). \tag{A15}$$

Define current account (as share of GDP):

$$ca_t = \left(b_t - \overline{e}b^*_t\right) - \left(b_{t-1} - \overline{e}b^*_{t-1}\right). \tag{A16}$$

Rewrite the balance of payments condition (deviations as shares of GDP):

$$x_t + \frac{1}{\beta}\left(b_{t-1} - \overline{e}b^*_{t-1}\right) - \left(b_t - \overline{e}b^*_t\right). \tag{A17}$$

Linearising the interest rate parity condition, as discussed above:

$$i_t - i^*_t = \frac{1}{1-\beta}(e_{t+1} - e_t) - \Psi_B\left(\frac{B_t - e_t B^*_t}{P_t Y_t}\right) + \xi_t. \tag{A18}$$

Appendix B: Econometric methods

The contemporaneous covariances matrix, $R_{y^*}(0)$, can be written as follows:

$$R_{y^*}(0) \equiv E\left[y^*_t y^{*\prime}_t\right] = \Sigma + \sum_{i=0}^{\infty}[BD^i(D-I)B^{-1}]\Sigma[BD^i(D-I)B^{-1}]', \tag{B1}$$

where D is the diagonal matrix of eigenvalues and B the matrix of eigen vectors of A_1. $R_{y^*}(0)$ can then be computed:

$$R_{y^*}(0) = \Sigma + B\,[K]\,B', \tag{B2}$$

where the typical element (i, j) of K is

$$K_{ij} = \begin{cases} \dfrac{(1-d_i)(1-d_j)M_{ij}}{1-d_id_j} & \text{for } d_i \neq 1 \text{ or } d_j \neq 1 \\ 0 & \text{for } d_i = 1 \text{ and } d_j = 1 \end{cases} \tag{B3}$$

and where

$$M = B^{-1}\Sigma B^{-1'}. \tag{B4}$$

Once $R_{y^*}(0)$ is computed, the covariances across one lag $R_{y^*}(1)$ may be found:

$$R_{y^*}(1) = E\left[y_t^* y_t^{*\prime}\right] = A\, R_{y^*}(0) - \Sigma \tag{B5}$$

and over lags greater than one:

$$R_{y^*}(k) = E\left[y_t^* y_{t-k}^{*\prime}\right] = A^{k-1}\, R_{y^*}(1) \text{ for } k > 1. \tag{B6}$$

The full covariance matrix Ω, then can be constructed by assembling the blocks for various lags. In particular, the only parts of each covariance block used are those relating to the particular data series to be fit, where x_t is the relevant portion of y^* (in percent deviations from the previous period). Further, to reduce numerical problems associated with rounding error, lags of only up to 15 periods are currently used, with covariances assumed to be zero over lags greater than 15 periods.

References

Ahmed, S., B. Ickes, P. Wang, and B. S. Yoo. 1993. International business cycles. *American Economic Review*, 83: 335–339.

Bergin, P., 2003. Putting the new open economy macroeconomics to a test. *Journal of International Economics*, 60, 3–34.

Bergin, P. and S. Sheffrin. 2000. Interest rates, exchange rates, and present value models of the current account. *The Economic Journal*, 110: 535–558.

Betts, C. and M. Devereux. 1996. The exchange rate in a model of pricing-to-market. *European Economic Review*, 40: 1007–1021.

Devereux, M. and C. Engel. 2002. Exchange rate pass-through, exchange rate volatility, and exchange rate disconnect. NBER Working Paper No. 8858.

Duarte, M. and A. Stockman. 2001. Rational speculation and exchange rates. NBER Working Paper No. 8362.

Eichenbaum, M. and C. L. Evans. 1995. Some empirical evidence on the effects of shocks to monetary policy on exchange rates. *Quarterly Journal of Economics*, 110: 975–1009.

Faust, J. and J. H. Rogers. 2000. Monetary policy's role in exchange rate behavior. Board of Governors of the Federal Reserve System Working Paper.

Flood, R. and A. Rose. 1999. Understanding exchange rate volatility without the contrivance of macroeconomics. *Economic Journal*, 109: 660–672.

Ghironi, F. 2000. Towards a new open economy macroeconometrics. Boston College Working Paper.

Ghosh, A. R. 1995. International capital mobility among the major industrialised countries: Too little or too much? *Economic Journal*, 105: 107–128.

Ireland, P. 1997. A small, structural, quarterly model for monetary policy evaluation. *Carnegie-Rochester Conference Series on Public Policy*, 47: 83–108.

Ireland, P. 2001. Sticky-price models of the business cycle: Specification and stability. *Journal of Monetary Economics*, 47: 3–18.

Jeanne, O. and A. Rose. 2002. Noise trading and exchange rate regimes. *Quarterly Journal of Economics*, 117: 537–569.

Kim, J. 2000. Constructing and estimating a realistic optimizing model of monetary policy. *Journal of Monetary Economics*, 45: 329–359.

Kollmann, R. 2001. *Macroeconomic Effects of Nominal Exchange Rates Regimes: New Insights into the Role of Price Dynamics*. University of Bonn mimeo, Bonn.

Kollmann, R. 2002. Monetary policy rules in the open economy: effects on welfare and business cycles. *Journal of Monetary Economics*, 49, 989–1015.

Lane, P. R. 2001. The new open economy macroeconomics: A survey. *Journal of International Economics*, 54: 235–266.

Leeper, E. and C. Sims. 1994. Toward a modern macroeconomic model usable for policy analysis. *NBER Macroeconomic Annual*, 81–118.

Lewis, K. 1995. Puzzles in International Financial Markets, in: Grossman, G. and Rogoff, K. (eds.), *Handbook of International Economics*, Vol. III, Elsevier, Amsterdam, pp. 1913–1971.

Lubik, T. and F. Schorfheide. 2002. *Testing for indeterminacy: An Application to US Monetary Policy*. Johns Hopkins mimeo, Baltimore.

Mark, N. and Y. Wu. 1998. Rethinking deviations from uncovered interest parity: The role of covariance risk and noise. *Economic Journal*, 108: 1686–1706.

McCallum, B. and E. Nelson. 1999. Nominal income targeting in an open-economy optimizing model. *Journal of Monetary Economics*, 43: 553–578.

McCallum, B. and E. Nelson. 2000. Monetary policy for an open economy: An alternative framework with optimizing agents and sticky prices. *Oxford Review of Economic Policy*, 16: 74–91.

Meese, R. A. and K. Rogoff. 1983. Empirical exchange rate models of the seventies: Do they fit out of sample? *Journal of International Economics*, 14: 3–24.

Obstfeld, M. and K. Rogoff. 2000. The six major puzzles in international macroeconomics: Is there a common cause? *NBER Macroeconomics Annual*, 2000: 339–390.

Obstfeld, M. and K. Rogoff. 2001. Risk and exchange rates. U.C. Berkeley mimeo. (Also 1998 NBER Working Paper 6694).

Rogers, J. 1999. Monetary shocks and real exchange rates. *Journal of International Economics*, 49: 269–288.

Sheffrin, S. and W. T. Woo. 1990. Present value tests of an intertemporal model of the current account. *Journal of International Economics*, 29: 237–253.

Smets, F. and R. Wouters. 2002. *Monetary Policy in an Estimated Stochastic Dynamic General Equilibrium Model of the Euro Area*. ECB mimeo, Frankfurt.

Section II

Global Integration of Goods Markets: A Perspective from International Relative Prices

CHAPTER 6

Pricing-to-Market, Staggered Contracts, and Real Exchange Rate Persistence*

Paul R. Bergin[†] and Robert C. Feenstra[‡]

Department of Economics, University of California at Davis, One Shields Ave., Davis, CA 95616, USA
[†]prbergin@ucdavis.edu
[‡]rcfeenstra@ucdavis.edu

1. Introduction

A useful metric of the degree of international integration in goods markets is whether arbitrage has the power to make the prices of goods converge across locations. The theory of purchasing power parity states that, if goods markets are integrated, the ratio of aggregate national price levels in a pair of countries, as summarized in their real exchange, rate should converge to the value of unity. A prominent question in international macroeconomics is why real exchange rates exhibit persistent deviations from purchasing power parity. Table 1 characterizes quarterly data for 1973–1997.[1] Averaging over countries, the one-quarter autocorrelation is about 0.80

*This article originally appeared in *Journal of International Economics* (2001), 54(2), 333–359.

[1]The table closely resembles standard findings in the real business cycle literature: see Backus, Kehoe, and Kydland (1992), Chari, Kehoe, and McGrattan (1998a), and Chang and Devereux (1998).

Table 1. Data

	Serial correlations			Standard dev.	Correlation
	q	q (not filtered)	Output	s.d.(q)/s.d. (output)	cor(s, q)
Canada	0.88	0.95	0.89	2.05	0.94
France	0.78	0.91	0.84	7.57	0.99
Germany	0.74	0.93	0.74	4.35	0.99
Italy	0.79	0.93	0.83	4.26	0.98
Japan	0.81	0.93	0.67	5.87	0.98
United Kingdom	0.79	0.95	0.85	4.79	0.98
Average	0.80	0.93	0.80	4.81	0.98

Notes: All series are quarterly and are Hodrick–Prescott filtered, unless otherwise stated. The real exchange rate (q) is computed as the CPI-adjusted bilateral exchange rate with the US dollar, using quarterly data from International Financial Statistics. The nominal exchange rate is represented in the table by s.

in Hodrick–Prescott filtered data, and about 0.93 in unfiltered data.[2] A related time-series literature concludes that the real exchange rate may be even more persistent.[3] In addition, the table shows the real exchange rate is highly volatile, with a standard deviation between four to five times that of output on average.

Sticky prices are one explanation commonly offered for these real exchange rate movements. Monetary shocks could induce an immediate change in the nominal exchange rate, and this would translate into a change in the real exchange rate if national price levels remain fixed. Intertemporal models presenting this general view include Svensson and van Wijnbergen (1989), Obstfeld and Rogoff (1995), and Kollmann (1996).

A second explanation focuses on pricing-to-market, in which a firm intentionally sets different prices for its good across segmented national markets to compete with the firms serving those markets. This explanation

[2]There is some controversy regarding whether the real exchange rate should be Hodrick–Prescott filtered, so we report results both for filtered and unfiltered versions. All other columns in the table refer to filtered data. The real exchange rate is computed as the CPI-adjusted bilateral exchange rate with the US dollar, using quarterly data from International Financial Statistics.

[3]See Froot and Rogoff (1995) for a summary of the time series literature. Several studies suggest real exchange rate deviations have a half-life of about four to five years. Some studies, such as Engel (2000), cast doubt on whether the real exchange rate is even mean reverting.

is consistent with empirical work by Engel (1993), Knetter (1993), and others, which have documented significant deviations from the law of one price. First developed in a partial equilibrium setting (see Dornbusch (1987), Krugman (1987), Knetter (1989), and Marston (1990)), pricing-to-market has been adapted to general equilibrium settings by Betts and Devereux (1996, 2000), Chang and Devereux (1998), Chari, Kehoe, and McGrattan (1998a), and Devereux and Engel (1998).

Nevertheless, the persistence of real exchange rate movements has posed a significant challenge to theoretical models. Chang and Devereux (1998) find that without price stickiness, a model of pricing-to-market cannot generate adequate persistence. Chari, Kehoe and McGrattan (1998a) find that sticky prices can help replicate persistence in the data, but only if one is willing to accept long-lived price contracts, which set prices for at least three years. It is generally thought that price-setting contracts are shorter than this in practice, and that it would be desirable to have a model in which prices and real exchange rate deviations last longer than the rigidity imposed exogenously by the contract. This is called "endogenous persistence." In principle, overlapping contracts of the type described by Taylor (1980) and Blanchard (1983) should generate such endogenous persistence. However, Chari, Kehoe and McGrattan (1998b) find this is not the case in a general equilibrium setting.

The present chapter will consider an extension of the two-country model of Obstfeld and Rogoff (1995), augmented to allow for pricing-to-market and staggered price contracts. The model incorporates a translog demand structure and a particular production structure proposed by Basu (1995). Kimball (1995) discusses the importance of a demand with a nonconstant elasticity for generating significant real effects of monetary shocks. The translog specification we develop here is a parametric case which exhibits the feature that the elasticity of demand varies with the price a firm sets. It has been argued in Bergin and Feenstra (2000) that a demand structure with a nonconstant elasticity is necessary in a general equilibrium setting to generate the interactions of staggered price setters envisioned by Taylor and Blanchard. The present chapter demonstrates the importance of these interactions for generating endogenous persistence in the real exchange rate.

Furthermore, this chapter demonstrates that these interactions likewise are important if one wishes to consider pricing-to-market behavior. We distinguish pricing-to-market behavior from a related explanation for deviations from the law of one price, suggested by Devereux (1997), in which prices are sticky in the local currency of the buyer. We use the term "local currency pricing" for this, and reserve "pricing-to-market" for a situation where the firm chooses to set different prices for its good across segmented national markets to compete with firms in those markets.

The chapter finds that a translog specification generates greater persistence than the standard CES case. Further, persistence can be increased by assuming a low degree of openness or a large role for intermediate materials in production. However, while certain cases of the model are shown to generate the very high degree of persistence observed in the data, these cases require implausible parameter values. The chapter finds that volatility is an easier target to match in this model than persistence. The model is stable under reasonable parameter values to replicate the degree of volatility observed in real exchange rates.

The next section of the chapter discusses the model framework. Key analytical results are developed in Section 3, and Section 4 conducts model simulations to gauge the model's success quantitatively. Section 5 concludes.

2. The Model

The model considered here has two countries, designated home and foreign. Variables in the foreign country will be denoted by an asterisk, and when necessary for clarity, a subscript h will denote a variable originating in the home country and a subscript f for the foreign country. Each country has a large number of monopolistically competitive firms that produce differentiated varieties of goods, using a particular input–output production structure. Varieties in the home country are indexed by $i = 1, \ldots, N$; varieties in the foreign country are indexed by $j = 1, \ldots, N^*$. A fraction ϕ of all varieties produced in each country are not tradable internationally. In particular, home goods indexed $i = 1, \ldots, \phi N$ are nontradable and goods indexed $i = \phi N + 1, \ldots, N$ are tradable, with foreign goods indexed analogously. This implies that there are $\widetilde{N} = N + (1 - \phi)N^*$ varieties consumed at home and $\widetilde{N^*} = N^* + (1 - \phi)N$ consumed abroad. The markets for internationally traded goods are segmented by country, so that firms have the ability to set distinct prices in each national market. The firms are divided into multiple groups, which must preset the nominal prices of their goods in staggered contracts.

The firms are owned by households, which derive income from firm profits and from labor supplied to firms in the labor market. The analysis will assume complete asset markets.[4] We follow Obstfeld and Rogoff (1995) in abstracting from capital accumulation in the model.[5] One unusual feature of the model is that household preferences over the differentiated goods follow a translog functional form, which does not restrict the elasticity of substitution between goods to be constant. This implies that the demand curve faced by the firms has an elasticity that depends on their price-setting decision. The discussion below will highlight how this demand structure influences the firms' price-setting decisions, and thereby the adjustment of the model to a monetary shock.

2.1. *Preferences and technology*

Household preferences in the home country are represented by the instantaneous utility function

$$U_t = \begin{cases} \left[\dfrac{1}{(1-\sigma_1)} C_t^{1-\sigma_1} + \dfrac{1}{(1-\sigma_2)} \left(\dfrac{M_t}{P_t} \right)^{1-\sigma_2} - \dfrac{L_t^{1+\sigma_3}}{1+\sigma_3} \right] \\ \quad \text{for } \sigma_1 \neq 1, \sigma_2 \neq 1 \\ \left[\ln C_t + \ln \left(\dfrac{M_t}{P_t} \right) - \dfrac{L_t^{1+\sigma_3}}{1+\sigma_3} \right] \\ \quad \text{for } \sigma_1 = 1, \sigma_2 = 1, \end{cases} \tag{1}$$

where C_t is an aggregator over varieties of goods, M_t is nominal money balances, P_t is the home price index, and L_t is labor. The common approach in this literature is to define C_t as a CES consumption index and then derive the associated price index. As in Bergin and Feenstra (2000), we will instead begin by defining the price index as the dual expenditure function,

[4]The authors also performed analysis on a version of the model with only risk-free bonds, but found results to be little changed.

[5]In Bergin and Feenstra (2000), it is demonstrated that capital accumulation has only very small effects on persistence generated by the mechanisms of the type used in this chapter. We do not discuss this issue in detail here, because the focus of the present chapter is exchange rate determination rather than business cycles.

which is assumed to have a translog form. This unit-expenditure function is defined by

$$\ln P_t \equiv \sum_{i=1}^{\widetilde{N}} \alpha_i \ln P_{it} + \frac{1}{2}\sum_{i=1}^{\widetilde{N}}\sum_{j=1}^{\widetilde{N}} \gamma_{ij} \ln P_{it} \ln P_{jt}, \tag{2}$$

where P_{it} is the home-currency price of good i and where $\gamma_{ij} = \gamma_{ji}$. In order for this function to be homogeneous of degree one, we must impose the conditions

$$\sum_{i=1}^{\widetilde{N}} \alpha_i = 1 \text{ and } \sum_{i=1}^{\widetilde{N}} \gamma_{ij} = \sum_{j=1}^{\widetilde{N}} \gamma_{ij} = 0. \tag{3}$$

The unit-expenditure function in Equation (2) may be differentiated to obtain the expenditure shares, ψ_{it}

$$\psi_{it} = \partial \ln P_t / \partial \ln P_{it} = \alpha_i + \sum_{j=1}^{\widetilde{N}} \gamma_{ij} \ln P_{jt}. \tag{4}$$

The home-country demand for each good then may be written

$$X_{it} = \psi_{it} \frac{P_t C_t}{P_{it}}. \tag{5}$$

The (positive) elasticity of demand for each differentiated product in the home country is computed as $\eta_{it} = 1 - \frac{\partial \ln \psi_{it}}{\partial \ln P_{it}} = 1 - \frac{\gamma_{ii}}{\psi_{it}}$, where $\gamma_{ii} < 0$ is needed to ensure that demand is elastic.

While the equations above are the general case of the translog function, we can consider a special case where all goods enter symmetrically. In that case, the parameters become

$$\alpha_i = \frac{1}{\widetilde{N}}, \quad \gamma_{ii} = -\frac{\gamma}{\widetilde{N}}, \quad \text{and} \quad \gamma_{ij} = \frac{\gamma}{\widetilde{N}(\widetilde{N}-1)} \quad \text{for } j \neq i. \tag{6}$$

This choice of parameters satisfies the homogeneity conditions (3), and expressing the parameters as a ratio to $\widetilde{N}$ ensures that the elasticity of demand remains bounded above even as $\widetilde{N}$ becomes large, as we wish to consider in this chapter.[6] For example, if prices are all equal so the shares are $\psi_{it} = 1/\widetilde{N}$, then the elasticity becomes $\eta_{it} = 1 - \frac{\gamma_{ii}}{\psi_{it}} = 1 + \gamma$.

[6]Note that we do not allow $\widetilde{N}$ to vary endogenously. Allowing $\widetilde{N}$ to approach infinity is just a simplifying device.

The production technology follows Basu (1995) by requiring firms to use the aggregated output of all other firms as materials in their own production process. In particular, each home differentiated variety is produced using the following Cobb–Douglas production function

$$Y_{it} = AZ_t^{\theta} L_t^{1-\theta}, \tag{7}$$

where Z_t is a translog aggregate of the home and foreign product varieties. The aggregator used for the materials has the same translog functional form as the expenditure function introduced above. Thus, the elasticity of demand for each good as an intermediate (Z_{it}) will be identical to the elasticity of demand for consumption purposes (X_{it}), as given by $\eta_{it} = 1 - \frac{\gamma_{ii}}{\psi_{it}}$, and the share of each (final or intermediate) variety is given by (4).

Denote the marginal cost of producing in the home country by MC_t. Given the Cobb–Douglas production function in Equation (7), the marginal costs are $MC_t = P_t^{\theta} W_t^{1-\theta}$, where W_t is the nominal wage.[7] Nominal home firm profits then may be defined as

$$\begin{aligned} \Pi_{it} &= (P_{it} - MC_t)(X_{it} + Z_{it}) \quad \text{for } i = 1, \ldots, \phi N \\ &= (P_{it} - MC_t)(X_{it} + Z_{it}) + (\mathcal{E}_t P_{it}^* - MC_t)(X_{it}^* + Z_{it}^*) \\ &\qquad \text{for } i = \phi N + 1, \ldots, N, \end{aligned} \tag{8}$$

where P_{it}^* is the foreign-currency price of a home good sold abroad, and $\mathcal{E}_t$ is the nominal exchange rate. Analogous conditions of course hold for the foreign country. We will suppose that prices are set for T periods, so that a fraction $1/T$ of goods have their prices "renewed" each period, and these are then fixed for T periods.

2.2. *Optimality conditions*

Before writing the budget constraint, we need to be more explicit about uncertainty and the states of nature. In each period t, the economy experiences one of finitely many events s_t. We denote by $s^t = (s_0, \ldots, s_t)$ the history of events up through and including period t. All variables referred to so far are implicitly functions of the states of nature in period t: $C_t \equiv C(s^t)$,

[7] This is the expression for marginal costs for suitable choice of A in Equation (7).

$M_t \equiv M(s^t)$, $L_t \equiv L(s^t)$, and so forth. We will be assuming a case of complete contingent markets, as discussed more fully in Chari, Kehoe, and McGrattan (1998a). In period t, consumers in either country purchase state-contingent assets in the home currency, denoted by $B_{t+1} \equiv B(s^{t+1})$, which bear a return of exactly one unit of the home currency in period $t+1$ if state s^{t+1} occurs. They purchase these assets at the prices $V(s^{t+1}|s^t)$, which denotes the price of one unit of local currency at s^{t+1} in units of home currency at state s^t. The budget constraint facing the home consumer in period t is therefore

$$P_t C_t + M_t + \sum_{s^{t+1}} V(s^{t+1}|s^t) B(s^{t+1}) = W_t L_t + M_{t-1} + B_t + \Pi_t + G_t, \qquad (9)$$

where $B_t \equiv B(s^t)$ refers to assets received in period t contingent on state s^t, G_t represents government transfers and $\Pi_t = \sum_{i=1}^{N} \Pi_{it}$ is profit of home firms. It should be stressed that all variables subscripted by t appearing in Equation (9) are functions of the state of nature s^t in period t, while the money supply $M_{t-1} \equiv M(s^{t-1})$ is carried over from the previous period. There is a separate budget constraint for each of the states of nature s^t, with a distinct Lagrange multiplier.

Households maximize the expected discounted sum of current and future instantaneous utilities represented by Equation (1), using the discount factor β, subject to the budget constraints (9). Letting E_t denote the expectations operator,[8] the first-order conditions for this problem imply a money demand condition

$$\left(\frac{M_t}{P_t}\right)^{-\sigma_2} = \frac{C_t^{-\sigma_1}}{P_t} - \beta E_t \left[\frac{C_{t+1}^{-\sigma_1}}{P_{t+1}}\right] \qquad (10)$$

and a labor-supply condition

$$L_t^{\sigma_3} = \frac{W_t}{P_t} C_t^{-\sigma_1}. \qquad (11)$$

[8] The expectation operator, E_t used over variables dated $t+1$, represents the expected value over all states s^{t+1}, using a set of probabilities for these states conditional on the current state s^t.

Because we are assuming complete markets between home and foreign households, we also obtain a standard risk-sharing condition

$$\left(\frac{C_t^*}{C_t}\right)^{-\sigma_1} = \frac{\mathcal{E}_t P_t^*}{P_t} \equiv Q_t. \tag{12}$$

Efficient risk sharing between home and foreign households requires that the ratio of their marginal utilities is proportional to the ratio of their national price indexes, which is the real exchange rate, Q_t.[9]

Because the production function faced by firms is Cobb–Douglas, it implies constant expenditure shares on the two inputs, labor and the composite intermediate good

$$\frac{P_t Z_t}{W_t L_t} = \frac{\theta}{1-\theta}. \tag{13}$$

Product prices for those goods having their prices renewed are chosen after observing the money shock for the first period of the contract, but before observing the subsequent shocks. The optimality condition for choosing the price of a home good in the home country P_{it}, equal over the following T periods, is[10]

$$E_t \sum_{\tau=t}^{t+T-1} \lambda_\tau \left(\frac{\partial \Pi_{i\tau}}{\partial P_{it}}\right) = 0, \quad \text{for } i = 1, \ldots, N, \tag{14}$$

where λ_τ is the Lagrange multiplier associated with the budget constraint (9) in period τ.[11] For those goods traded internationally, the optimality

[9]For convenience, we ignore a factor of proportionality that should appear in (12), which will not affect our later results. A complete derivation of (12) is provided in Chari, Kehoe and McGrattan (1998a, Eq. 12). Briefly, this equation is obtained because the budget constraint for the foreign consumer is written with the same nominal asset $B(s^{t+1})$ that is used at home. Optimizing with respect to this asset at home and abroad, we obtain two difference equations in the Lagrange multipliers for the budget constraints of each country. Because these difference equations are identical, the solutions for the Lagrange multipliers at home and abroad must be proportional, from which (12) then follows.

[10]Since the profits from home and foreign sales are independent, the choice of home prices is not affected by whether that good is traded or not.

[11]We assume that firms evaluate intertemporal trade-offs in the same way as households, so the Lagrange multiplier is $\lambda_\tau = \beta^\tau \frac{C_\tau^{-\sigma_1}}{P_\tau}$. We make use of this below to obtain (23) and (24).

condition for choosing the price of the home good in the foreign country P^*_{it}, equal over the following T periods, is

$$E_t \sum_{\tau=t}^{t+T-1} \lambda_\tau \left(\frac{\partial \Pi_{i\tau}}{\partial P^*_{it}} \right) = 0, \quad \text{for } i = \phi N + 1, \ldots, N. \tag{15}$$

Making use of the definition of profits in (8), together with demand elasticity defined previously, and the expenditure shares $\psi_{i\tau}$ satisfying (5) with the analogous equation for intermediates inputs, then (14) and (15) can be rewritten as

$$E_t \sum_{\tau=t}^{t+T-1} \lambda_\tau P_\tau (C_\tau + Z_\tau) \left[\left(1 - \frac{\psi_{i\tau}}{\gamma_{ii}} \right) \left(\frac{MC_\tau}{P_{it}} \right) - 1 \right] = 0,$$
$$\text{for } i = 1, \ldots, N \tag{16}$$

and

$$E_t \sum_{\tau=t}^{t+T-1} \lambda_\tau \mathcal{E}_\tau P^*_\tau (C^*_\tau + Z^*_\tau) \left[\left(1 - \frac{\psi^*_{i\tau}}{\gamma_{ii}} \right) \frac{MC_\tau}{\mathcal{E}_\tau P^*_{it}} - 1 \right] = 0,$$
$$\text{for } i = \phi N + 1, \ldots, N. \tag{17}$$

While these are rather complex expressions, they will simplify greatly when we approximate around the steady state, as is done below. Analogous conditions apply to the foreign country.

2.3. *Equilibrium conditions*

Home goods market clearing requires

$$X_{it} + Z_{it} = Y_{it} \quad \text{for } i = 1, \ldots, \phi N$$
$$X_{it} + X^*_{it} + Z_{it} + Z^*_{it} = Y_{it} \quad \text{for } i = \phi N + 1, \ldots, N. \tag{18}$$

Home money is introduced by the government as a lump-sum transfer, defined as

$$G_t = M_t - M_{t-1}. \tag{19}$$

It is assumed that money supply is exogenously determined.

Equilibrium for this economy is a collection of sequences (C_t, Y_t, L_t, W_t, P_t, X_{it}, Z_{it}, P_{it}, P^*_{it}, G_t, M_t, their foreign counterparts, and $\mathcal{E}_t$) satisfying a set of equilibrium conditions. These include the pricing conditions (16), (17), the definition of the price index (2), the demand Equations (5), household optimality conditions (10), (11), (12), the production functions (7), the allocation between intermediates and labor (13), four demand equations for intermediates analogous to those for consumption, the market clearing conditions (18), government budget constraint (19), and the foreign counterparts for each of these.

3. Analytical Results

3.1. *Pricing-to-market and preferences*

To solve the model, we will linearize the equilibrium conditions around steady state. To facilitate an analytical solution, we initially choose convenient values for parameters in the utility function. In particular, we consider a benchmark case where $\sigma_1 = \sigma_2 = 1$ and $\sigma_3 = 0$.[12,13] Under the assumption of $\sigma_1 = \sigma_2 = 1$, the linearized form of (10) implies[14]

$$E_t[p_{t+1} + c_{t+1}] = \frac{1}{\beta}[p_t + c_t] - \frac{1-\beta}{\beta} m_t, \tag{20}$$

where we use lower case letters to represent percent deviations from the deterministic steady state of upper case counterparts. This is a difference equation in nominal expenditure ($p_t + c_t$), with the stable solution

$$p_t + c_t = m_t. \tag{21}$$

This implies that a permanent 1% increase in money supply translates into an equal permanent 1% increase in nominal final expenditure. In an analogous manner, the same can be shown for foreign real final output, c^*_t.

---

[12]This has the implication of an infinite labor-supply elasticity. But this assumption will be relaxed in simulations to follow.

[13]These simplifying assumptions produce essentially the same utility formulation as that used for analytical results in Chapter 10 of Obstfeld and Rogoff (1996). Note that while these authors include output in their utility function rather than labor, they illustrate the equivalence of this by using a production function with an exponent on labor of one-half.

[14]Linearization of the model is not necessary for all the conclusions that follow.

The linearized risk-sharing condition (12) states

$$e_t = (p_t + c_t) - (p_t^* + c_t^*), \tag{22}$$

where e_t represents percent deviations in the nominal exchange rate. Condition (21), its foreign counterpart, and condition (22) together indicate that a permanent 1% increase in money supply translates into an equal permanent 1% depreciation in the nominal exchange rate.

Consider now the behavior of prices. To simplify the pricing equations (16 and 17), suppose that the contracts are only two periods in length. We again take a log-linear approximation around the deterministic steady state.[15,16] The expenditure shares $\psi_{i\tau}$ can be substituted from (4), and then (16 and 17) can be solved for the optimal prices, in terms of marginal cost and the prices of competitors. Also imposing the symmetry conditions (6), the first-order conditions become

$$p_{it} = \frac{1}{2}(1+\beta)^{-1} E_t \sum_{\tau=t}^{t+1} \beta^{\tau-t} \left[mc_\tau + \sum_{j=1(j\neq i)}^{\tilde{N}} \frac{1}{\tilde{N}-1} p_{j\tau} \right], \quad \text{for } i = 1, \ldots, N \tag{23}$$

and

$$p_{it}^* = \frac{1}{2}(1+\beta)^{-1} E_t \sum_{\tau=t}^{t+1} \beta^{\tau-t} \left[mc_\tau - e_\tau + \sum_{j=1(j\neq i)}^{\tilde{N}} \frac{1}{\tilde{N}-1} p_{j\tau}^* \right], \quad \text{for } i = \phi N + 1, \ldots, N. \tag{24}$$

Notice that a 1% permanent depreciation in (24) will reduce the price charged in the foreign country by 0.5%, holding all other prices fixed. This "pass through" coefficient of one-half is a feature of the translog demand system. Empirically, this is a very reasonable value for the

---

[15]We make use of the approximation $\left[\left(1 - \frac{\psi_{i\tau}}{\gamma_{ii}}\right)\frac{MC_\tau}{P_{it}} - 1\right] \approx \ln\left[\left(1 - \frac{\psi_{i\tau}}{\gamma_{ii}}\right)\frac{MC_\tau}{P_{it}}\right] \approx \left(\frac{-\psi_{i\tau}}{\gamma_{ii}}\right) + \ln\left(\frac{MC_\tau}{P_{it}}\right)$, which is valid for $\psi_{i\tau}$ small and P_{it} close to MC_τ.

[16]The steady state value of $P_\tau(C_\tau + Z_\tau)$ is constant, so it cancels out, and terms involving the change in $P_\tau(C_\tau + Z_\tau)$ also drop out because the derivative of profits with respect to price equals zero each and every period in the steady state.

response of price to a change in costs, while holding competitors' prices constant.[17]

To further simplify these pricing equations, we focus on the case of two equally-sized groups of firms in each country, $N = N^*$. The total number of products consumed in either country is then $\widetilde{N} = (2-\phi)N$, where ϕ is the fraction of varieties produced in each country that are not traded internationally. Home firms in group one choose their prices for the home and foreign markets in period t, where t is an odd number, and these prices are then fixed for periods t and $t+1$. Let us denote these prices by p_{h1t} and p^*_{h1t}, which are assumed to be the same across all firms in group one. As a group, these firms then represent a fraction $\frac{1}{2}$ of home-produced goods, or $\frac{1}{2(2-\phi)}$ of the goods available at home, and a fraction $\frac{1-\phi}{2(2-\phi)}$ of goods available in the foreign market. Similarly, the firms in group two choose their prices p_{h2t} and p^*_{h2t} in even periods t, which are then fixed for t and $t+1$. The same applies to two groups of firms in the foreign country, setting prices p_{f1t}, p^*_{f1t}, p_{f2t}, and p^*_{f2t} in staggered fashion. We make use of this notation for prices in (23) and (24), where terms like $\frac{1}{2(2-\phi)}$ and $\frac{1-\phi}{2(2-\phi)}$ tell us how many of each particular price appear in the summations on the right (assuming that $\widetilde{N}$ is large).

Then the price-setting Equations (23) and (24) can be used to find the optimal price of home goods in group one for sale at home and abroad, when t is odd and group one resets its prices

$$p_{h1t} = \frac{2(2-\phi)}{(1+\beta)(7-4\phi)} E_t \left[mc_t + \beta mc_{t+1} + \frac{1}{2(2-\phi)}(p_{h2t} + \beta p_{h2t+1}) + (1+\beta)\frac{(1-\phi)}{2(2-\phi)} p_{f1t} + \frac{1-\phi}{2(2-\phi)}(p_{f2t} + \beta p_{f2t+1}) \right] \tag{25}$$

$$p^*_{h1t} = \frac{2(2-\phi)}{(1+\beta)(7-3\phi)} E_t \left[mc_t + \beta mc_{t+1} + \frac{1-\phi}{2(2-\phi)}(p^*_{h2t} + \beta p^*_{h2t+1}) + \frac{1+\beta}{2(2-\phi)} p^*_{f1t} + \frac{1}{2(2-\phi)}(p^*_{f2t} + \beta p^*_{f2t+1}) - e_t - \beta e_{t+1} \right]. \tag{26}$$

[17] See Moffett (1989) for a summary of studies with pass-through elasticities around 0.5. In the regressions used to obtain these elasticities, it is common to include regressors reflecting competitors' prices and marginal costs, as appear on the right of Equations (23) and (24). Then the "pass-through" elasticity is defined holding these other variables constant.

Analogous expressions apply to the remaining prices. In addition, the overall home price index (Equation (2)) may be simplified to[18]

$$p_t = \frac{1}{2(2-\phi)}p_{h1t} + \frac{1}{2(2-\phi)}p_{h2t} + \frac{1-\phi}{2(2-\phi)}p_{f1t} + \frac{1-\phi}{2(2-\phi)}p_{f2t}. \tag{27}$$

To interpret these price setting rules, note that for values of ϕ ranging from unity to zero, the terms appearing outside the brackets on the right of (26) range from $1/2(1+\beta)$ to $4/7(1+\beta)$. The current and future exchange rates appear with the coefficient $(1+\beta)$ on the right, so a permanent 1% exchange rate depreciation induces the home firm to lower its price on a product sold in the foreign country between 0.5% and 4/7%, holding all else constant. The pass through elasticity is exactly 0.5 if only one product is being exported ($\phi \approx 1$). As ϕ becomes lower, so that more goods are traded internationally, this will increase the degree of pass through because firms will optimally follow what their competitors (resetting their prices at the same time) are doing.

These price setting rules also give insight into pricing-to-market in this model. Marston (1990) defines pricing-to-market as the tendency for firms to choose to set different prices in different national markets because of differing market conditions. A useful measure of pricing-to-market for home firms resetting their prices in the current period would be the ratio of the price set by a firm for sale abroad relative to the price set for sale at home, converted to a common currency[19]

$$ptm_t = e_t + p^*_{h1t} - p_{h1t}. \tag{28}$$

This definition applies to periods when t is odd and firms in group one are resetting their prices. A complete analytical solution for pricing-to-market is not tractable here, but we can gain insight by applying the same strategy as above, considering the pricing rules for (25) and (26) where we hold

[18]Note that the cross terms of the translog functional form drop out under linearization around steady state.

[19]Note that the price terms used in this equation refer to firms in group one, which have observed any change in money supply for the current period, before they need to set their own contract price. This means that "local currency pricing" here will not erroneously be picked up in this measure of pricing-to-market.

all other prices constant. In the presence of a one-time permanent rise in home money supply, pricing-to-market will approximately equal as shown below:

$$ptm_t^{\text{TLOG}} \approx \frac{3-\phi}{7-3\phi}e_t - \frac{2\phi(2-\phi)}{(7-4\phi)(7-3\phi)}E_t\left[\frac{mc_t+\beta mc_{t+1}}{1+\beta}\right]. \quad (29)$$

Because the pass through of the exchange rate to p^*_{h1t} is incomplete, pricing-to-market will arise in this model, i.e. (29) is nonzero. A permanent depreciation in the nominal exchange rate will result in a *rise* in the price ratio defined in (28), though movements in domestic marginal costs may partly offset this effect. Simulations later will confirm this result, solving for pricing-to-market without need for the simplifying assumption that competitors' prices are held constant.

It is instructive to contrast this with the more typical constant elasticity of substitution (CES) case, where prices are set by firms as a constant markup over marginal cost.[20] Bergin and Feenstra (2000) argue that such pricing rules prevent staggered contracts from generating the endogenous persistence envisioned in Taylor (1980) and Blanchard (1983). We further argue here that such pricing rules prevent the occurrence of pricing-to-market. The linearized price-setting functions for the CES case are simply

$$p_{h1t}^{\text{CES}} = \frac{1}{1+\beta}E_t\left[mc_t+\beta mc_{t+1}\right] \text{ and} \quad (30)$$

$$p_{h1t}^{\text{CES}*} = \frac{1}{1+\beta}E_t\left[mc_t+\beta mc_{t+1} - e_t - \beta e_{t+1}\right]. \quad (31)$$

Equation (31) implies that exchange rate pass through is complete. A permanent currency depreciation by 1% will result in a 1% fall in the foreign currency price set for the home good. This implies that the pricing-to-market measure (28) takes on a value of zero for the CES case

$$ptm_t^{\text{CES}} = e_t + p_{h1t}^{\text{CES}*} - p_{h1t}^{\text{CES}} = 0. \quad (32)$$

This measure may be computed exactly here, because under CES we need not worry about changes in competitors' prices.

[20]In the CES case, the consumption aggregator is $C_t = \left[\sum_{i=1}^{\widetilde{N}} X_{it}^{\frac{\gamma}{1+\gamma}}\right]^{\frac{1+\gamma}{\gamma}}$, where $1+\gamma$ is the elasticity of demand.

So the usual CES assumption for preferences here has the implication of ruling out the possibility of pricing-to-market. Firms will not choose to set prices differently in two national markets. This should not be surprising, given that demands with a nonconstant elasticity were assumed in the development of pricing-to-market theories in Dornbusch (1987), Krugman (1987), Knetter (1989), and Marston (1990). It is true that so long as prices are pre-set in the currency of the buyer, then even under a CES demand structure a movement in the exchange rate that is unanticipated will drive a temporary wedge between the home and foreign price, as discussed in Devereux (1997).[21] Although this phenomenon has sometimes of late been characterized as pricing-to-market, it is distinct from the definition given above, in that price setters do not choose to set different prices. Rather than "pricing-to-market," this phenomenon may be better termed "local-currency-pricing."

3.2. *Dynamics*

We now consider the issue of persistence. Recall that conditions (21) and (22) indicate that a permanent 1% increase in money supply translates into an immediate and permanent 1% increase in both nominal expenditure and the nominal exchange rate. The degree to which the impacts on these nominal variables translate into their real counterparts depends, of course, on how the national price levels adjust to the shock. In particular, the persistence in the real level of output and the real exchange rate depends on the persistence in the national price levels (27), and hence on the price-setting rules (25) and (26).

Several analytical results may be demonstrated, regarding these dynamics. First, under the assumption that $\sigma_3 = 0$ the linearized form of the labor-supply condition (11) implies in combination with (21) that

$$w_t = p_t + c_t = m_t. \tag{33}$$

As a result, the marginal cost term in the pricing equations, mc_t, may be expressed in terms of the goods prices themselves and the exogenous

[21] Friberg (1998) has explored conditions under which it is optimal for firms to invoice in the currency of the importer, as we assume. He likewise finds that a sufficient condition for firms to exhibit such invoicing behavior is that the demand have less convexity than the CES case.

money shock

$$mc_t = (1 - \theta)\, w_t + \theta p_t = (1 - \theta)\, m_t + \theta p_t. \tag{34}$$

Condition (22) implies that the nominal exchange rate likewise can be expressed in terms of the money supply shocks

$$e_t = (c_t + p_t) - (c_t^* + p_t^*) = m_t - m_t^*. \tag{35}$$

The pricing equations (25) and (26) and their two foreign counterparts then may be expressed as a system of four equations in four endogenous price variables and the exogenous money shocks.

We wish to consider the model's response to a domestic money shock. While it is not feasible to solve analytically for the dynamics of each price individually, we can solve for the dynamics of two useful linear combinations of these prices. Define the sum of national prices, π_{1t}, and the difference of national prices, π_{2t}:

$$\pi_{1t} = \left[\frac{1}{2-\phi} p_{h1t} + \frac{1-\phi}{2-\phi} p_{f1t}\right] + \left[\frac{1}{2-\phi} p_{f1t}^* + \frac{1-\phi}{2-\phi} p_{h1t}^*\right] \tag{36}$$

$$\pi_{2t} = \left[\frac{1}{2-\phi} p_{h1t} + \frac{1-\phi}{2-\phi} p_{f1t}\right] - \left[\frac{1}{2-\phi} p_{f1t}^* + \frac{1-\phi}{2-\phi} p_{h1t}^*\right]. \tag{37}$$

The appendix uses standard methods to show that the dynamics of these may be written as

$$\pi_{1,t} = a_1 \pi_{1,t-1} + (1 - a_1) m_t \tag{38}$$

and

$$\pi_{2,t} = a_2 \pi_{2,t-1} + (1 - a_2) m_t, \tag{39}$$

where

$$a_1^{\mathrm{TLOG}} = \frac{\sqrt{2} - \sqrt{1-\theta}}{\sqrt{2} + \sqrt{1-\theta}} \tag{40}$$

and

$$a_2^{\mathrm{TLOG}} = \left(\frac{6 - \phi(3+\theta)}{2 - \phi\,(1-\theta)}\right) - \left(\left(\frac{6 - \phi(3+\theta)}{2 - \phi(1-\theta)}\right)^2 - 1\right)^{\frac{1}{2}} \tag{41}$$

The term a_1 is the same autoregressive term found for the case of a single closed economy in Bergin and Feenstra (2000). It has a useful interpretation as a measure of persistence in total world output. To simplify expressions, we will assume that $\beta \approx 1$. Writing the world price index as $p_t^w = \frac{1}{4}(\pi_{1,t} + \pi_{1,t-1})$, its dynamics are

$$p_t^w = a_1 p_{t-1}^w + \frac{1}{4}(1 - a_1)(m_t + m_{t-1}). \tag{42}$$

World final output may be written in percent deviations as

$$c_t^w = \frac{1}{2}(p_t c_t + p_t^* c_t^*) - p_t^w. \tag{43}$$

Since the percent deviation in world nominal expenditure was shown to be equal to the deviation in nominal money, output deviations may be written as the following autoregression

$$c_t^w = a_1 c_{t-1}^w + \frac{1}{4}(1 + a_1)(m_t - m_{t-1}). \tag{44}$$

The term a_1 indicates what fraction of the impact effect on output persists one period later, once all price setters have had a chance to reset their price. As such, it indicates the portion of persistence that is endogenous. In addition, if monetary shocks follow a random walk, then a_1 is interpretable as the first-order serial correlation of output implied by this model.

The term a_2 has an analogous interpretation as the persistence of the real exchange rate. In percent deviations, the real exchange rate may be written as

$$q_t = e_t - \frac{1}{2}(\pi_{2,t} + \pi_{2,t-1}), \tag{45}$$

so that

$$q_t = a_2 q_{t-1} + \frac{1}{2}(1 + a_2)(m_t - m_{t-1}). \tag{46}$$

The term a_2 is the theoretical serial correlation of the real exchange rate implied by this model.

Note that both persistence terms rise with rising θ; persistence rises if materials comprises a larger share of marginal costs. The reason is that materials prices are sticky, so marginal costs rise slower and reduce the incentive for a firm to raise its own price. Note also that real exchange rate persistence rises as ϕ, the share of produced goods that are nontraded, rises. Openness appears to limit persistence in the real exchange rate. As a result, persistence in the real exchange rate is less than that in output, and it is only in cases of complete autarchy ($\phi = 1$) that $a_2^{\text{TLOG}} = a_1^{\text{TLOG}}$. In the extreme case where $\phi = 1$ and $\theta = 1$, then $a_2^{\text{TLOG}} = a_1^{\text{TLOG}} = 1$. This means there is perfect persistence, a serial correlation of unity, for both output and the real exchange rate. Note that at the other extreme where $\phi = 0$ and $\theta = 0$, so that all goods are traded and there are no material inputs, then we still have $a_1^{\text{TLOG}}, a_2^{\text{TLOG}} > 0$, so some persistence in output and the real exchange rate remains.

The role of openness may be understood in more intuitive terms. The pricing equations ((25), (26), and foreign counterparts) indicate that these components of the national price indexes will respond more strongly to a nominal devaluation if there is a greater degree of openness. For example, Equation (26) indicates that home producers will lower the foreign-currency price they charge in the foreign country when the home currency depreciates. If home goods play a larger role in the foreign consumption basket, the overall foreign price index will be lower. In addition, if home goods represent a larger fraction of competitors in the foreign market, foreign producers will tend to lower their prices in response. This will further lower the foreign price index, offsetting the impact on the real exchange rate.[22]

It is instructive to compare the results above with those for the standard CES case. Solving the system in an analogous manner to that outlined in the appendix for the translog case, the theoretical serial correlations are

$$a_1^{\text{CES}} = \frac{1 - \sqrt{1-\theta}}{1 + \sqrt{1-\theta}} \tag{47}$$

and

$$a_2^{\text{CES}} = \left(\frac{4 - \phi(2+\theta)}{\phi\theta}\right) - \left(\left(\frac{4 - \phi(2+\theta)}{\phi\theta}\right)^2 - 1\right)^{\frac{1}{2}}. \tag{48}$$

As in the translog case, persistence rises with the materials share and falls with openness. Unlike the translog case, the serial correlations for output and the real exchange rate in the CES case both approach zero in the

[22]This result does not affect persistence in world output, because this involves the sum of national price indexes, which are affected in an offsetting manner.

extreme as $\phi = 0$ and $\theta = 0$, so the nontraded share and materials share both approach zero. Further, it is a relatively simple algebraic exercise to demonstrate that $a_1^{\text{CES}} < a_1^{TL}$ and $a_2^{\text{CES}} < a_2^{TL}$ for all permissible values of ϕ and θ: persistence in both output and the real exchange rate are always higher under the translog specification than under the standard CES specification.

4. Model Simulations

The preceding analytical results indicate that persistence is enhanced by a translog demand structure. The analysis also indicates that the degree of openness and the share of materials in marginal costs are important for persistence in this model, and that for certain values of these parameters, it is possible to generate arbitrarily high levels of persistence. We will now use model simulations to check whether the model can generate adequate persistence under reasonable values for parameters.

What are reasonable values for the key parameters controlling openness and materials share? Empirical investigations have found that nontraded goods make up about half of the consumption basket in the US[23] This would imply a value of $\phi = 0.67$ in the our model. We will use this value as a benchmark. Second, Basu (1995) recommends a value for θ between 0.8 and 0.9. This is based on work by Jorgenson, Gollop, and Fraumeri (1987) estimating that the share of intermediates in total sales is 50% or more. Basu (1995) transforms this ratio in terms of sales into a ratio in terms of marginal cost using an estimate of the markup of 1.6 by Domowitz Hubbard, and Petersen (1988). Our model does not have a constant markup, but in steady state this markup will be $\frac{1+\gamma}{\gamma}$. By setting $\gamma = 2$, the model implies a markup of 1.5, making our framework comparable to that used by Basu. We will choose a value in the middle of the range suggested by Basu, $\theta = 0.85$.[24]

The analytical solution in the previous section required that the interest elasticity of real money balances $(1/\sigma_2)$ be unity. Empirical studies find a

[23] See Stockman and Tesar (1995).

[24] Recent research has suggested lower values of the markup. Our work below will also consider the case of $\theta = 0.5$, which would be the value implied by Basu's findings in the lower boundary case of a markup equal to 1.0.

wide range of estimates: from 0.39 in Chari, Kehoe and McGrattan (1998a) to 0.05 in Mankiw and Summers (1986). We choose an intermediate value of 0.25 ($\sigma_2 = 4$). Empirical studies estimate that the income elasticity of real money demand (σ_1/σ_2) here is about unity, so we also set $\sigma_1 = 4$ as well. While the analytical solution required $\sigma_3 = 0$, a more standard value would be unity. A unitary labor-supply elasticity is consistent with the fact that per capita labor supply has changed little while real wages have risen in recent decades. Our calibration of $\gamma = 2.0$ implies a demand elasticity in steady state of $1 + \gamma = 3$, which is not unreasonable.[25] We will calibrate $\beta = 0.99$, and interpret a period in the model as one quarter. The model is analyzed in linearized form, in percent deviations from steady state. The steady state affects this linearization only through the goods market clearing condition, which depends on the steady-state share of intermediates in total production. This may be computed as

$$\frac{\overline{Z}}{\overline{Y}} = \theta \frac{\gamma}{1+\gamma}. \tag{49}$$

First, consider the impulse responses of our model to the shock considered in the analytical solution, a permanent 1% increase in home money supply. As in the analytical section, it will be assumed at first that there are two contracting groups, each setting a contract for two periods, and that contracts in the current period are set after observing the shock. Figure 1 plots the impulse response of pricing-to-market ($e_t + p^*_{h1t} - p_{h1t}$) for the CES and translog cases. As predicted in the analytical section, the CES cases produces virtually no pricing-to-market, whereas the translog case leads firms to set different prices across national markets. Figure 2 plots the real exchange rate in the two cases. The impact effect is somewhat higher in the translog case, and more importantly, persistence is higher. One year after the shock, once all price setters have had a chance to reset price, 28% of the initial impact still persists in the translog case, compared to only 10% in the CES case. Figure 3 plots the impulse response of home real output. Again the degree of endogenous persistence is higher. One year after the shock, 46% of the initial impact persists under the translog case, compared to 32% under CES.

[25]See Bergin and Feenstra (2000) for a detailed discussion of this point.

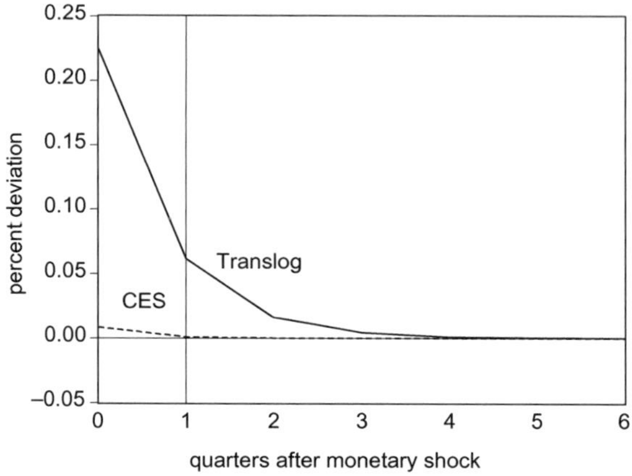

Figure 1. Pricing-to-market

Note: Contracts last two periods, and the contract in the first period is set after the shock is observed. Parameter values: beta = 0.99, gamma = 2, phi = 0.67, theta = 0.85, sigma1 = sigma2 = 4, and sigma3 = 1.

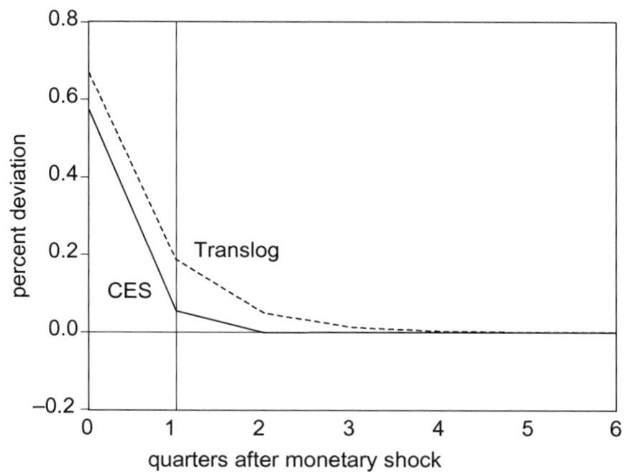

Figure 2. Real exchange rate

Note: Contracts last two periods, and the contract in the first period is set after the shock is observed. Parameter values: beta = 0.99, gamma = 2, phi = 0.67, theta = 0.85, sigma1 = sigma2 = 4, and sigma3 = 1.

Next consider stochastic simulations of the model. A simple rule is assumed for the growth rate of money in each country, μ:

$$\ln \mu_t = \rho_\mu \ln \mu_{t-1} + (1 - \rho_\mu) \ln \overline{\mu} + \epsilon_t,$$

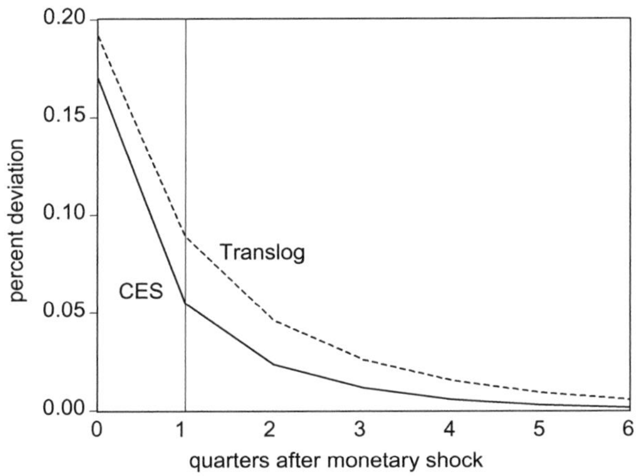

Figure 3. Home output

Note: Contracts last two periods, and the contract in the first period is set after the shock is observed. Parameter values: beta = 0.99, gamma = 2, phi = 0.67, theta = 0.85, sigma1 = sigma2 = 4, and sigma3 = 1.

where ϵ_t is a normally distributed mean zero shock with a standard deviation of σ_μ. We follow Chari, Kehoe, and McGrattan (1998a) in calibrating $\rho_\mu = 0.57$, $\sigma_\mu = 0.0092$, and $\overline{\mu} = 1.105$. The shocks are assumed to be independent across countries.[26] Because there is some question regarding whether the real exchange rate should be Hodrick–Prescott filtered, the tables report this variable both ways.

The first line of Table 2 shows the case of two-period contracts, as considered in the impulse responses above. As predicted by the analytical solution, the serial correlation for the real exchange rate in the CES case, is close to zero. In the translog case, the serial correlation is significantly higher. While the translog case is able to generate a larger amount of persistence, the degree still falls well short of that observed in the data. This is also true for movements in home real final output. This leads us to consider longer contract periods. These do produce larger degrees of persistence, but they still do not match the data. In addition, note that as the contract length grows, the CES and translog cases become more similar. This is because "exogenous" persistence becomes a more important portion of

[26]Results are reported for 100 simulations of 100 periods for each of the cases considered.

Table 2. Simulation results: Contract length and number of overlapping groups

	Serial correlations			Standard dev.	Correlation
	q	q (no filter)	Output	s.d.(q)/s.d.(output)	cor(s, q)
CES					
2 quarters	0.013	0.091	0.255	4.470	0.409
4 quarters	0.493	0.588	0.572	4.894	0.636
6 quarters	0.633	0.736	0.658	5.237	0.765
8 quarters	0.677	0.793	0.695	5.155	0.833
12 quarters	0.716	0.853	0.703	5.524	0.922
Translog					
2 quarters	0.173	0.269	0.357	4.647	0.482
4 quarters	0.559	0.675	0.619	4.963	0.717
6 quarters	0.655	0.775	0.675	5.251	0.837
8 quarters	0.688	0.819	0.680	5.416	0.893
12 quarters	0.711	0.868	0.704	5.284	0.957

Notes: All series are Hodrick–Prescott filtered, unless otherwise stated. The real exchange rate (q) is computed as the CPI-adjusted bilateral exchange rate with the US dollar, using quarterly data from International Financial Statistics. The nominal exchange rate is represented in the table by s.
Simulations are based on 100 iterations of 100 periods. Contracts are set after the shock is observed for the current period. Parameter values: $\beta = 0.99$, $\gamma = 2$, $\phi = 0.67$, $\theta = 0.85$, $\sigma_1 = \sigma_2 = 4$, and $\sigma_3 = 1$.

total persistence, and this benefits CES and translog alike. What is a reasonable length to assume for these contracts? A number of empirical studies have found industrial contracts tend to set prices for approximately one year. For simulations below, the benchmark case will assume four period contracts.

Note that while the model has some difficulty with persistence, it seems to be surprisingly easy to match the volatility of the real exchange rate observed in the data. Under the benchmark parameters, all contract lengths in Table 1 generate a standard deviation of the real exchange rate that is about 4 to 5 times that of real output. While volatility has been a difficult issue in past studies focusing on technology shocks, this does not seem to be a significant obstacle if one considers monetary shocks.

Table 3 shows the effects of varying the degree of openness and materials share, which the analytical section found were important for persistence. Confirming those earlier results, the table indicates that persistence is always

Table 3. Simulation results: Role of openness and materials

		Serial correlations			Standard dev.	Correlation
		q	q (not filtered)	Output	s.d.(q)/s.d.(output)	cor(s, q)
CES						
$\phi = 0.0$	$\theta = 0.0$	0.463	0.552	0.456	5.782	0.5836
	$\theta = 0.5$	0.457	0.548	0.498	5.311	0.5868
	$\theta = 0.85$	0.457	0.548	0.569	4.648	0.5868
	$\theta \to 1.0$	0.453	0.546	0.679	1.371	0.5859
$\phi = 0.67$	$\theta = 0.0$	0.454	0.543	0.448	5.803	0.591
	$\theta = 0.5$	0.472	0.565	0.494	5.459	0.604
	$\theta = 0.85$	0.493	0.588	0.572	4.894	0.636
	$\theta \to 1.0$	0.515	0.611	0.684	1.520	0.672
$\phi \to 1.0$	$\theta = 0.0$	0.465	0.551	0.462	5.624	0.586
	$\theta = 0.5$	0.482	0.569	0.508	5.521	0.615
	$\theta = 0.85$	0.534	0.633	0.587	5.168	0.667
	$\theta \to 1.0$	0.685	0.929	0.695	5.663	1.000
Translog						
$\phi = 0.0$	$\theta = 0.0$	0.518	0.620	0.511	5.863	0.667
	$\theta = 0.5$	0.515	0.618	0.541	5.466	0.666
	$\theta = 0.85$	0.511	0.613	0.592	4.779	0.667
	$\theta \to 1.0$	0.522	0.619	0.672	1.539	0.667
$\phi = 0.67$	$\theta = 0.0$	0.507	0.613	0.507	5.692	0.673
	$\theta = 0.5$	0.527	0.635	0.535	5.571	0.686
	$\theta = 0.85$	0.557	0.675	0.619	4.963	0.717
	$\theta \to 1.0$	0.571	0.685	0.685	1.684	0.753
$\phi \to 1$	$\theta = 0.0$	0.507	0.615	0.492	5.750	0.660
	$\theta = 0.5$	0.542	0.645	0.534	5.541	0.702
	$\theta = 0.85$	0.593	0.711	0.620	5.333	0.782
	$\theta \to 1.0$	0.687	0.935	0.686	5.775	1.000

Notes: In the above table, 'ϕ' is the share of all varieties produced in each country that are not tradable internationally; 'θ' is the share of material inputs in marginal costs. All series are Hodrick–Prescott filtered, unless otherwise stated. The real exchange rate (q) is computed as the CPI-adjusted bilateral exchange rate with the US dollar, using quarterly data from International Financial Statistics. The nominal exchange rate is represented in the table by s. Simulations are based on 100 iterations of 100 periods. Contracts last four periods, and are set after the shock is observed for the current period. Parameter values: $\beta = 0.99$, $\gamma = 2$, $\sigma_1 = \sigma_2 = 4$, and $\sigma_3 = 1$.

higher for the translog case than for CES, but in both cases a smaller degree of openness (large ϕ) and a larger role for materials (large θ) improve persistence. In further confirmation of the analytical results, it is found that in the extreme case of $(\phi \to 1, \theta \to 1)$ the model can generate real

Table 4. Simulation results: Further sensitivity analysis

	Serial correlations			Standard dev.	Correlation
	q	q (not filtered)	Output	s.d.(q)/ s.d.(output)	cor(s, q)
Demand elasticity					
$(1+\gamma) =$					
0.1	0.560	0.683	0.624	4.919	0.732
1	0.559	0.671	0.622	4.928	0.732
3	0.559	0.675	0.619	4.963	0.717
10	0.547	0.647	0.602	5.002	0.696
100	0.526	0.627	0.588	4.984	0.670
Money demand Elasticity:					
$(1/\sigma_2)^* =$					
0.10	0.558	0.665	0.619	11.775	0.727
0.25	0.559	0.675	0.619	4.963	0.717
1	0.557	0.668	0.590	1.339	0.703
2	0.555	0.670	0.589	0.673	0.698
10	0.553	0.661	0.535	0.147	0.695

Notes: $^*\sigma_1$ is adjusted with σ_2 ($\sigma_1 = \sigma_2$) to keep the income elasticity of money demand constant at unity.
All series are Hodrick–Prescott filtered, unless otherwise stated. The real exchange rate (q) is computed as the CPI-adjusted bilateral exchange rate with the US dollar, using quarterly data from International Financial Statistics. The nominal exchange rate is represented in the table by s. Simulations are based on 100 iterations of 100 periods. Contracts last four quarters, and are set after the shock is observed for the current period. Benchmark settings: $\beta = 0.99, \gamma = 2, \phi = 0.67, \theta = 0.85, \sigma_1 = \sigma_2 = 4$, and $\sigma_3 = 1$.

exchange rate persistence that more than matches with that present in the data, if the series are not Hodrick–Prescott filtered. This is not true if the series are filtered.[27]

Finally, Table 4 reports additional sensitivity analysis. If the level of steady state demand elasticity is altered $(1+\gamma)$, this appears to only have very small effects on persistence. This should not be surprising, as the steady state demand elasticity does not directly enter any of the price-setting rules. The next part of the table considers various levels of money demand elasticity $(1/\sigma_2)$, while keeping the income elasticity of money

[27] It is not clear why filtering has such a deleterious effect on the type of persistence generated here, whereas it does not have so strong an effect on actual data.

demand constant ($\sigma_1 = \sigma_2$), so the intertemporal elasticity ($1/\sigma_1$) varies along with ($1/\sigma_2$). This again has only very small effects on persistence; however it does strongly affect the degree of volatility. A low degree of money elasticity increases exchange rate volatility by inducing overshooting, while a low intertemporal elasticity dampens the volatility of output. Taken together, this has a large impact on the volatility of the exchange rate relative to output. Evidently, to obtain the empirically plausible value of 4 or 5 for this ratio, then our benchmark value of $\sigma_1 = \sigma_2 = 4$ is the best choice.

5. Conclusion

This chapter has explored a potential explanation for the high degree of persistence observed in the real exchange rate. It is found that staggered price contracts combined with pricing-to-market are able to generate significant endogenous persistence beyond the exogenously imposed rigidity. Translog preferences are important for amplifying the effects of both these mechanisms. In fact, pricing-to-market will not arise under the usual case of CES preferences. Nevertheless, the theoretical model is not able to reproduce the degree of persistence observed in the data, at least not under reasonable parameter values. The model is more successful in generating volatility in the real exchange rate, and is able to reproduce the level observed in real exchange rate data.

The differences between the translog and CES demand systems show up most prominently for pricing contracts that are relatively short: 2 or 4 quarters in length. With this length of contract, the model cannot reproduce the degree of persistence in the data (without using extreme parameter values). Longer contracts (2 or 3 years) do better at matching the persistence in the data, but this is really due to "exogenous" rather than "endogenous" persistence. In other words, the original insights of Taylor (1980) and Blanchard (1983) that overlapping contracts might lead to persistence exceeding the contract length, are valid in this model with translog preferences, but not to the extent that actual persistence can be replicated. Is this a reason to be discouraged with the results? We think not, for two reasons.

First, we do not expect a single explanation for output and exchange rate persistence, such as the overlapping contracts considered here, to necessarily be sufficient to replicate all features of the data. Surely, other complementary explanations (such as technology shocks, possibly combined with more sophisticated money supply rules) could be considered. Second, while we have treated the contract length as exogenous, this should more properly be modeled as a choice variable of the firm. In contrasting the CES and translog cases, the question then arises as to whether firms would have an incentive to change prices *less* frequently under one system or the other, with the longer contracting length resulting in more persistence. We think that this incentive might be created under the translog system, precisely because firms care about the prices of their competitors, and these are changing more slowly than marginal costs. If so, then this would be an added reason for the translog system to generate more persistence in prices, and therefore output and the real exchange rate, than under the CES case.

Appendix

The dynamics of the system of price-setting Equations ((25), (26), and their two foreign counterparts) may be characterized as follows. Defining the terms

$$\pi_t = \frac{1}{2-\phi} p_{h1t} + \frac{1-\phi}{2-\phi} p_{f1t} \tag{A1}$$

and

$$\pi_t^* = \frac{1}{2-\phi} p_{f1t}^* + \frac{1-\phi}{2-\phi} p_{h1t}^*, \tag{A2}$$

the four price-setting equations may be combined and written as

$$\begin{bmatrix} \pi_t \\ \pi_t^* \end{bmatrix} = F\left\{\begin{bmatrix} \pi_{t-1} \\ \pi_{t-1}^* \end{bmatrix} + 2\begin{bmatrix} \pi_t \\ \pi_t^* \end{bmatrix} + E_t\begin{bmatrix} \pi_{t+1} \\ \pi_{t+1}^* \end{bmatrix}\right\} + GE_t\,(m_{t+1} + m_{t+2}), \tag{A3}$$

where

$$F = \frac{1}{8(2-\phi)}\begin{bmatrix} 2+\theta-\phi & \theta\,(1-\phi) \\ \theta(1-\phi) & 2+\theta-\phi \end{bmatrix} \tag{A4}$$

and

$$G = \frac{1}{4(2-\phi)}\begin{bmatrix} 2-\theta-\phi \\ -(1-\phi)\theta \end{bmatrix}. \tag{A5}$$

Using standard methods, the solution to this matrix difference equation is

$$\begin{bmatrix} \pi_t \\ \pi_t^* \end{bmatrix} = H \begin{bmatrix} \pi_{t-1} \\ \pi_{t-1}^* \end{bmatrix} + H(I - HL)^{-1}F^{-1}GE_t(m_{t+1} + m_{t+2}), \qquad \text{(A6)}$$

where L is the *lead* operator, and H is the matrix

$$H = \frac{1}{2}(F^{-1} - 2I) \pm \frac{1}{2}[(F^{-1} - 2I)^2 - 4I]^{1/2}. \qquad \text{(A7)}$$

Assuming that the money supply follows a random walk, then this solution is simplified as

$$\begin{bmatrix} \pi_t \\ \pi_t^* \end{bmatrix} = H \begin{bmatrix} \pi_{t-1} \\ \pi_{t-1}^* \end{bmatrix} + 2H(I - H)^{-1}F^{-1}Gm_t. \qquad \text{(A8)}$$

In order to convert this two-variable system to a univariate equation, we pre-multiply by the eigenvectors of H, which are the same as the eigenvectors of F. By inspection, these are the vectors $v_1 = (1, -1)$ and $v_2 = (1, 1)$. Pre-multiplying the system above by v_1 yields

$$\pi_{1,t} = a_1\pi_{1,t-1} + (1 - a_1)m_t, \qquad \text{(A9)}$$

while pre-multiplying by v_2 yields

$$\pi_{2,t} = a_2\pi_{2,t-1} + (1 - a_2)m_t, \qquad \text{(A10)}$$

where $\pi_{1,t} = \pi_t + \pi_t^*$, $\pi_{2,t} = \pi_t - \pi_t^*$, and $a_1$and a_2 are the respective eigenvalues of H.

Here a_1 is the solution to the equation

$$a_1^2 - \left(\left(\frac{8}{1+\theta}\right) - 2\right) a_1 + 1 = 0, \qquad \text{(A11)}$$

which is (40). Similarly, a_2 is the solution to the equation

$$a_2^2 - \left(\left(\frac{8\,(2-\phi)}{2-\phi\,(1-\theta)}\right) - 2\right) a_2 + 1 = 0, \qquad \text{(A12)}$$

which is (41).

Acknowledgment

Special thanks go to Charles Engel and Patrick Asea for detailed comments. We also thank the participants in the NBER summer institute on International Finance and Money and seminar participants at the University of Washington, and two anonymous referees.

References

Backus, D., P. Kehoe, and F. Kydland. 1992. International real business cycles. *Journal of Political Economy*, 100: 745–775.

Basu, S. 1995. Intermediate goods and business cycles: Implications for productivity and welfare. *American Economic Review*, 85: 512–531.

Bergin, P. and R. Feenstra. 2000. Staggered price setting, translog preferences, and endogenous persistence. Forthcoming in *Journal of Monetary Economics.*

Betts, C. and M. Devereux. 1996. The exchange rate in a model of pricing-to-market. *European Economic Review*, 40: 1007–1021.

Betts, C. and M. Devereux. 2000. Exchange rate dynamics in a model of pricing-to-market. *Journal of International Economics*, 50: 215–244.

Blanchard, O. J. 1983. Price asynchronization and price level inertia, in Dornbusch, R. and Simonsen, M.H. (eds.), *Inflation, Debt, and Indexation*, MIT Press, Cambridge, pp. 3–24.

Chang, R. and M. Devereux. 1998. *Dynamic Collusion, Pricing-to-Market, and Real Exchange Rates.* University of British Columbia mimeo.

Chari, V. V., P. Kehoe, and E. McGrattan. 1998a. Can sticky price models generate volatile and persistent real exchange rates? Federal Reserve Bank of Minneapolis staff report 223.

Chari, V. V., P. Kehoe, and E. McGrattan. 1998b. Sticky price models of the business cycle: can the contract multiplier solve the persistence problem? Federal Reserve Bank of Minneapolis staff report 217.

Devereux, M. 1997. Real exchange rates and macroeconomics: Evidence and theory. *Canadian Journal of Economics*, 30: 773–808.

Devereux, M. and C. Engel. 1998. Fixed vs. floating exchange rates: How price setting affects the optimal choice of exchange-rate regime. NBER Working Paper 6867.

Domowitz, I., R. Hubbard, and B. Petersen. 1988. Market structure and cyclical fluctuations in U.S. manufacturing. *Review of Economics and Statistics*, 70: 55–66.

Dornbusch, R. 1987. Exchange rates and prices. *American Economic Review*, 77: 93–106.

Engel, C. 1993. Real exchange rates and relative prices: An empirical investigation. *Journal of Monetary Economics*, 32: 35–50.

Engel, C. 2000. Long run PPP might not hold after all. *Journal of International Economics*, 57: 243–273.

Friberg, R. 1998. In which currency should an exporter set his price? *Journal of International Economics*, 45: 59–76.

Froot, K. and K. Rogoff. 1995. Perspectives on PPP and long-run real exchange rates, in: Grossman, G. and Rogoff, K. (eds.), *Handbook of International Economics*, Vol. 3, North-Holland, Amsterdam, pp. 1647–1688.

Jorgenson, D., F. Gollop, and B. Fraumeni. 1987. *Productivity and U.S. Economic Growth*, Harvard University Press, Cambridge.

Kimball, M. 1995. The quantitative analytics of the basic neomonetarist model. *Journal of Money, Credit, and Banking*, 27: 1241–1277.

Knetter, M. 1989. Price discrimination by U.S. and German exporters. *American Economic Review*, 79: 198–210.

Knetter, M. 1993. International comparisons of price-to-market behavior. *American Economic Review*, 83: 473–486.

Kollmann, R. 1996. The exchange rate in a dynamic optimizing current account model with nominal rigidities: A quantitative investigation, University of Montreal Working Paper.

Krugman, P. 1987. Pricing-to-market when the exchange rate changes, in: Arndt S. W. and Richardson, J. D. (eds.), *Real Financial Linkages Among Open Economies*, (MIT Press, Cambridge), pp. 49–70.

Mankiw, N. G. and L. Summers. 1986. Money demand and the effects of fiscal policies. *Journal of Money, Credit and Banking*, 18: 415–429.

Marston, R. 1990. Pricing-to-market in Japanese manufacturing. *Journal of International Economics*, 29: 217–236.

Moffett, M. 1989. The J-curve revisted: an empirical examination for the United States. *Journal of International Money and Finance*, 8: 425–444.

Obstfeld, M. and K. Rogoff. 1995. Exchange rate dynamics redux. *Journal of Political Economy*, 103: 624–660.

Obstfeld, M. and K. Rogoff. 1996. *Foundations of International Macroeconomics*, MIT Press, Cambridge.

Stockman, A. and L. Tesar. 1995. Tastes and technology in a two-country model of the business cycle: Explaining international comovements. *American Economic Review*, 85: 168–185.

Svensson, L. and S. van Wijnbergen. 1989. Excess capacity, monopolistic competition, and international transmission of monetary disturbances. *Economic Journal*, 99: 785–805.

Taylor, J. 1980. Aggregate dynamics and staggered contracts. *Journal of Political Economy*, 88: 1–23.

CHAPTER 7

Endogenous Tradability and Some Macroeconomic Implications*

Paul R. Bergin[†,§] and Reuven Glick[‡,¶]

[†] *Department of Economics, University of California at Davis, One Shields Ave., Davis, CA 95616, USA*

[‡] *Economic Research Department, Federal Reserve Bank of San Francisco, San Francisco, CA 96105, USA*

[§] *prbergin@ucdavis.edu*

[¶] *reuven.glick@sf.frb.org*

1. Introduction

Open economy macroeconomics has long found it useful to assume that some goods are not tradable, reflecting an inherent limitation in the degree of international goods market integration. Positing the existence of a non-traded goods sector lies behind some classic results in the literature, such as the behavior of real exchange rates in Balassa (1964) and Samuelson (1964), and current account adjustment in Dornbusch (1983). But this assumption implies stark and counterfactual behavior for the relative price of nontraded to traded goods. The domestic prices of goods that are freely traded internationally are subject to international arbitrage and pinned to world prices, while the prices of nontraded goods are free to move

*This article originally appeared in *Journal of Monetary Economics* (2009), 56, 1086–1095.

independently of world prices. These models imply that real exchange rate movements are attributable primarily to movements in the relative price of nontraded goods.

Recent empirical work has demonstrated this to be far from the truth: nontraded prices tend to move with traded prices, and only a small fraction of real exchange rate movements are due to movement in the relative price of nontraded to traded goods. This chapter argues that this counterfactual implication in the macro literature is the result of viewing tradedness as an exogenous characteristic of a good, and it can be resolved by recognizing that the status of a good as nontraded is an endogenous response to explicit trade costs that vary heterogeneously across goods.

Betts and Kehoe (2006) document the empirical puzzle, studying the properties of the real exchange rate and the relative price of nontraded goods between the US and five trading partners with annual data for the period 1980–2000. Their preferred measure computes the relative price of nontraded goods as the ratio of the gross output deflator for manufacturing, agriculture, and mining to the gross output deflator for all sectors. For the case of Canada, the standard deviation of nontraded relative prices to that of the overall real exchange rate varies from 0.40 to 0.47, depending on the method of detrending. For other countries, the ratio is even lower: varying from 0.13 to 0.20 for Germany, all at 0.12 for Japan, 0.18 to 0.23 for Korea, and 0.25 to 0.38 for Mexico. Earlier work by Engel (1999) suggests the relative volatility of nontraded prices can be yet lower, below 0.10. As an additional stylized fact, Betts and Kehoe (2006) note that the volatility ratio is systematically related to the strength of the trading relationship: those countries that trade more with the US have more volatility in nontraded prices.

This chapter argues that the difficulty in explaining the low volatility in the relative price of nontraded goods may stem from a rigid and artificial dichotomy, where some goods exogenously are labeled as tradable and others as nontradable. Recent advances in trade theory provide insight regarding the endogenous nature of tradedness. Consider all goods as parts of a single continuum, where the iceberg costs of trade vary by good. Whether a good is tradable or not depends on whether the costs of trading that good make trade profitable or not. On the margin, there is a good whose seller is indifferent between selling his good domestically only, or branching out into the international market. As a result, this marginal nontraded good forms a link between the prices of goods that are traded and other similar goods that are nontraded.

To explain this point and illustrate its usefulness in a transparent manner, this chapter builds on the two-period small open economy model with trade costs used in Obstfeld and Rogoff (2000). When the small open economy is subjected to demand shocks, the degree to which the relative price of nontraded goods moves depends on the degree of heterogeneity of the trade cost distribution. A calibration exercise shows that this model generates the low volatility in nontraded prices found in the empirical literature.

While our model endogenizes the tradedness of goods by building upon recent developments in the trade literature, it differs in focusing upon heterogeneity in trade costs among goods rather than upon heterogeneity in productivity among firms. In contrast to the latter convention, we think that when the issue of primary interest is tradedness, it makes more sense to focus on the variation of trade costs among goods. For example, the reason that services comprise a disproportionate share of nontraded goods is because most services are particularly costly to trade across borders. Further, the usual convention does not account for the empirical observations that there is a great deal of heterogeneity among goods in terms of their deviations from the law of one price across countries, nor that these deviations systematically tend to be greater for nontraded goods than for traded goods (Crucini, Telmer, and Zachariadis, 2005).

This chapter is also related to recent research in Ghironi and Melitz (2005), Bergin, Glick, and Taylor (2006), and Naknoi (2008) which incorporate trade features in a macro model with a continuum of heterogeneous firms. One significant difference is that these papers follow the trade literature in specifying heterogeneity in terms of firm productivity. Betts and Kehoe (2001) allow heterogeneous trade costs, but we differ in that we have a share of goods that are fully nontraded, which is what allows us to examine shifts of the nontraded extensive margin.

2. Empirical Motivation

Because the argument in this chapter relies upon two new ideas, a time-varying share of nontraded goods and heterogeneity in trade costs over goods, this section provides some empirical support for these features. Canada's trade with the United States is chosen as a case that generally

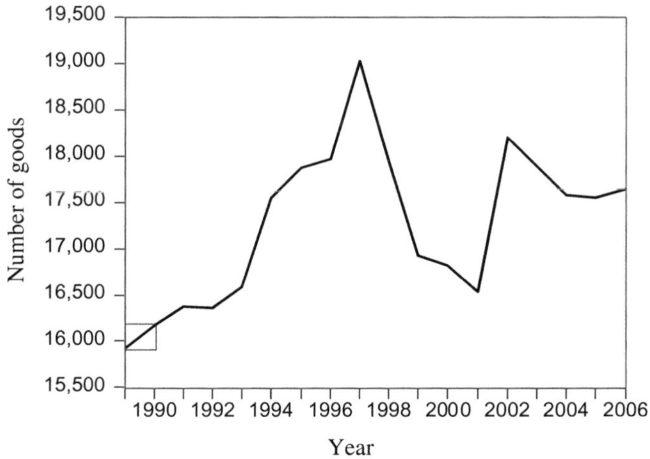

Figure 1. Number of canadian goods exported to the United States

Note: The figure reports the number of HS 10-digit goods exported from Canada to the United States each year during 1989–2007.

Source: NBER-UN trade database.

suits the small open economy assumption. First, consider movements in the share of nontraded goods. The NBER-UN trade database reports the value of US imports from Canada in the harmonized system 10 digit industries (HS-10).[1] These data reveal that there are many goods categories with zero trade in any given year, and that there is significant variation over time in the total number of goods traded. Figure 1 plots the number of HS-10 goods classifications traded at some point during a given year, starting from 1989 when the CUSFTA trade agreement was implemented between Canada and the United States. Note that there is significant variation in the number of traded goods both upward and downward over time, with a standard deviation of 3.4% in the HP-filtered annual data. Further, it appears that this variation is related to business cycle movements, as low points coincide with economic downturns in Canada or the US in the early 1990s and 2000s. This provides supportive evidence that the shares of traded and nontraded goods are time-varying and should be treated as endogenous.

[1]This analysis parallels that in Bergin *et al.* (2008) for Mexican trade with the US associated with offshoring.

Next, consider heterogeneity in trade costs among goods. There is some appreciation of this point in the existing trade literature. Empirical work by Hummels (2001a, 2001b) describes how freight costs alone can range from more than 30 % of value for raw materials and mineral fuels down to 4 % for some manufactures. Depending on factors such as weight, distance, and the time sensitivity of demand, trade costs can be high and variable for many manufactured goods as well. Bernard *et al.* (2006), reports a detailed measure of trade costs including tariff rates for 20 US industries at the 2-digit level. They observe that there is significant variation in trade costs, ranging from 4.9% to 23.2%.

In their review of the literature on trade costs, Anderson and van Wincoop (2004) note that the most common method of measuring trade costs in macroeconomics is in terms of their implications for prices, that is, deviations from the law of one price across countries. Here we can provide some original evidence well suited for the theoretical analysis to follow. Denoted by τ_i, the iceberg trade cost for a good i, which is the fraction of a good that disappears in transshipment. If this good is exported by the home country to a foreign market, then arbitrage implies that the wedge between home and foreign price (the latter indicated by a *) will be $p_i/p_i^* = 1 - \tau_i$. Price wedges are an appropriate measure of trade costs here, first, because it is iceberg trade costs that are the type of trade cost that the theoretical model will deal with, and second, because it ultimately consists of puzzles involving such international relative prices that the model is trying to explain.

The Economist Intelligence Unit collects retail price data on a range of consumer goods in cities around the world, such as 100-count aspirin bottles and a pair of 60 watt light bulbs. The analysis will focus on US and Canada in 2007, and on the 101 goods classified as traded by Engel and Rogers (2004) when they used this data set. Average relative prices wedges will be computed for each good by averaging over the 64 Canadian–US city pairs with available data. One immediate conclusion is that there is a great deal of heterogeneity in price dispersion: relative prices range from 62.4% cheaper in Canada to 62.2% more expensive, and the cross-sectional standard deviation of the price-wedge observations is 39%. Interestingly, the average level of price dispersion is 0.1%, with about as many goods overpriced as underpriced. Figure 2 plots the values of price wedges for half of the sample with values less than unity, where goods are cheaper

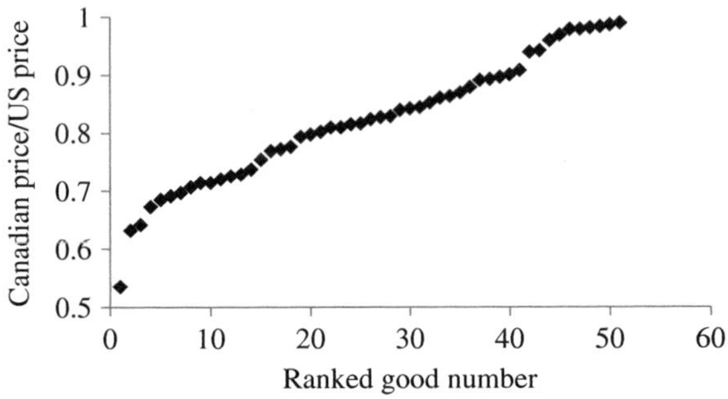

Figure 2. Price wedges for Canada–US goods

Note: Figure shows the ratio of the Canadian price to the US price for 50 selected traded goods in 2007. They are ordered in increasing order of the price ratio.

Source: Economist Intelligence Unit.

in Canada, ranked in order of decreasing price wedge. (A symmetric set of goods are greater than unity.) Price wedges in principle can also reflect other differences between countries such as exchange rate fluctuations and Balassa–Samuelson effects on the real exchange rate. But the fact that these factors should affect all goods suggests that they can in part be removed by demeaning the price wedges by their cross-good average. The fact that this average value is so near zero in the Canada-US 2007 sample suggests it is not a large issue in this particular sample.

Figure 2 suggests that the distribution of trade costs across goods is fairly uniform, with a steady progression of rising trade costs as one moves from right to left. This is very different from the distribution of productivity heterogeneity across firms, which has been the focus in trade literature. The standard assumption in recent trade models is that productivity heterogeneity follows a Pareto distribution, arguing that this fits the highly skewed distribution of firm size, where there is a large number of small firms and a very small number of very large firms. The model developed below will propose a distribution better suited to capturing the particular features of trade cost heterogeneity. For corroboration, Fig. 3 plots the trade costs reported in Bernard *et al.* (2006) for their sample of 20 2-digit industries. Their numbers for $\tau_i$are plotted in the form of $1 - \tau_i$ to be comparable to Fig. 2. Again the distribution of trade costs appears quite linear.

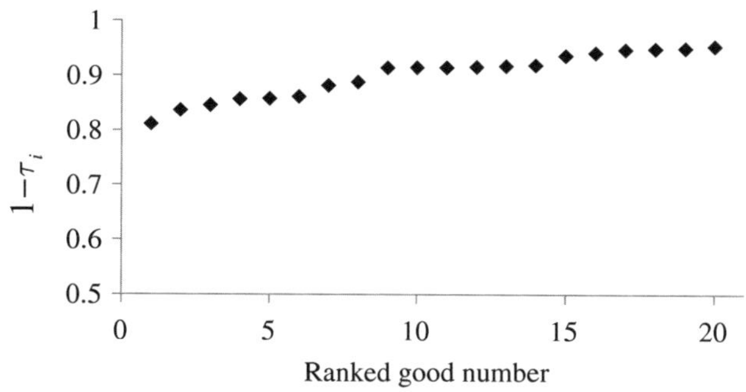

Figure 3. Distribution of trade costs for 2-digit US industries

Note: The figure plots the range of trade costs for 20 2-digit industries reported in Bernard *et al.* (2006), covering tariffs plus transportation costs, 1988–1992. The trade cost is reported here as $1-\tau_i$, where τ_i is the fractional trade cost taken from Table 1 of Bernard *et al.* (2006).

3. Model and Analytical Results

To facilitate tractability and transparency, the chapter follows Obstfeld and Rogoff (2000) in studying a simple small open endowment economy.[2] The discussion begins with a static version, helpful in understanding the determination of tradedness. It then extends the model to a second period, to study dynamics in relative prices.

3.1. *Static model*

The country is endowed with a continuum of goods indexed by i on the unit interval, where y_i represents the level of endowment, c_i is the level of consumption, and p_i is the domestic price level of this good. All of these home goods have the potential of being exported, but some endogenously determined fraction of the goods, n, will be nontraded in equilibrium. For each traded home good, there is a prevailing world price p_i^* that may differ from the home price because of trade costs. The small open economy may also import foreign goods for consumption purposes, with consumption level c_F and price level p_F. For simplicity, assume that the endowments and

[2]Bergin and Glick (2003, revised 2007) demonstrate that the results are robust to including production in the model.

world price levels of all home goods are uniform, implying $y_i = y, p_i^* = p^*$ for all i.

The aggregate consumption index is specified as

$$c = \frac{c_H^{\theta} c_F^{1-\theta}}{\theta^{\theta}(1-\theta)^{1-\theta}}. \tag{1}$$

Here c_H is an index of home goods consumption:

$$\begin{aligned} c_H^{(\phi-1)/\phi} &= \int_0^n (c_i)^{(\phi-1)/\phi} di + \int_n^1 (c_i)^{(\phi-1)/\phi} di \\ &= n\left(\frac{c_N}{n}\right)^{(\phi-1)/\phi} + (1-n)\left(\frac{c_T}{1-n}\right)^{(\phi-1)/\phi} \end{aligned} \tag{2}$$

where $c_N \equiv n\left(\frac{1}{n}\int_0^n c_i^{(\phi-1)/\phi} di\right)^{\phi/(\phi-1)}$ and $c_T \equiv (1-n)\left(\frac{1}{1-n}\int_n^1 c_i^{(\phi-1)/\phi} di\right)^{\phi/(\phi-1)}$ are consumption indexes of nontraded and traded goods, respectively, and n is the share of goods on the continuum {0,1} that are nontraded. Price indexes are defined as usual for each category of goods, in correspondence to the consumption indexes above:

$$p = p_H^{\theta} p_F^{1-\theta} \tag{3}$$

$$p_H^{1-\phi} = \int_0^n (p_i)^{1-\phi} di + \int_n^1 (p_i)^{1-\phi} di = np_N^{1-\phi} + (1-n)p_T^{1-\phi} \tag{4}$$

where p is the aggregate price level, p_H is the price index of all home goods, and the price index of home nontraded goods, p_N and the price index of home traded goods, p_T are defined as

$$p_N \equiv \left(\frac{1}{n}\int_0^n p_i^{1-\phi} di\right)^{1/(1-\phi)}$$

and

$$p_T \equiv \left(\frac{1}{1-n}\int_n^1 p_i^{(1-\phi)/\phi} di\right)^{1//(1-\phi)}.$$

Note that if world prices are normalized to unity, i.e. $p^* = 1$ and $p_F = 1$, then p may be interpreted as the reciprocal of the real exchange rate for this small open economy.

The home goods are distinguished from each other by heterogeneous iceberg costs (τ_i), where a certain fraction of the good disappears in transport. As discussed above, arbitrage requires that the domestic price will be $p_i = p^*(1 - \tau_i)$ if the country exports good i. These trade costs are defined to follow the specification: $\tau_i = 1 - (i^\beta/\alpha); \alpha \geq 1, \beta \geq 0, i \in [0, 1]$, which implies the following distribution of export prices

$$\frac{p_i}{p_i^*} = \frac{i^\beta}{\alpha}. \tag{5}$$

This implies that the trade cost and price ratio vary between 0 and 1 (for $\alpha = 1$) as the goods index varies over the unit interval. The parameter β controls the curvature of the distribution, while α scales the level. This specification is easy to integrate over, as is the Pareto distribution commonly used in the trade literature to characterize productivity heterogeneity. But the present specification is better suited to the case of trade costs in two respects. First, the support for iceberg trade costs needs to be the interval from 0 to 1, whereas that for a Pareto distribution is from some positive lower bound (usually taken to be unity) to infinity. While such an assumption is well suited for a firm's productivity level, it is not well suited for a fractional trade cost. Second, a Pareto distribution famously implies a high degree of concentration of firms near the lower bound, whereas Figs. 2 and 3 suggested a more uniform distribution of trade costs over goods.[3] This need not be the case for our specification, depending on the choice of curvature parameter β.

In the endowment economy, the decision of whether to export a good is determined solely on the basis of whether the export price (i.e. the world price) less iceberg costs, exceeds the domestic price. If the export price is higher, then the good is exported, if it is lower, then it is not traded.

Given the cutoff between traded and nontraded goods at index n, it is straightforward to compute the price index for traded goods from the price distribution of exported varieties:

$$\begin{aligned} p_T &= \left(\left(\frac{1}{1-n}\right)\left[\int_n^1 \left(\frac{p^* i^\beta}{\alpha}\right)^{1-\phi} di\right]\right)^{1/(1-\phi)} \\ &= \left(\frac{p^*}{\alpha}\right)\left(\left(\frac{1}{1-n}\right)\left(\frac{1}{\omega}\right)\left\{\left(\frac{1}{n}\right)^{\omega} - 1\right\}\right)^{1/(1-\phi)} \end{aligned} \tag{6}$$

[3]As discussed in Ghironi and Melitz (2005), the curvature parameter in the Pareto distribution needs to be higher than the elasticity of substitution; this restriction does not apply here.

where $\omega \equiv \beta(\phi - 1) - 1$. Equation (6) expresses the price of traded goods as a function of the share of nontraded goods n, the elasticity of substitution across domestic goods ϕ, and the trade cost parameters, β and α. It is straightforward to establish that $\partial p_T / \partial n > 0$; i.e. the price of traded goods increases with the share of nontraded goods. The reason is that, as the proportion of home goods that are nontraded rises, it is no longer profitable to export goods with marginally higher trade costs; as these goods are withdrawn from export markets, the average price of the remaining export goods rises.[4]

The price index of nontraded goods is even easier to determine. As usual, intratemporal optimization implies relative demands for each pair of home goods i and j: $c_i/c_j = (p_i/p_j)^{-\phi}$. Since consumption must equal the endowment of nontraded goods, and endowments are uniform for all goods here (i.e. $y_i = y$ for all i), then for any pair of nontraded goods it will be true that $c_i/c_j = y_i/y_j = 1$, and so $p_i/p_j = 1$. In other words, the price of each nontraded good will be identical, because they each are by definition not affected by the trade costs which vary by good. This logic applies equally well to the home good that is just on the margin between being traded and nontraded ($i = n$). The marginal trader decides to export solely on the basis of whether the world price less iceberg costs exceeds the domestic price. But because this good is on the margin of being traded, the domestic price must be the same as that as if it were sold in the world market: $p_n = (p^*/\alpha)n^\beta$. As a result, the price index of nontraded goods is pinned down as the price of the marginal traded good by the following marginal tradability condition:

$$\begin{aligned} p_N &\equiv \left(\left(\frac{1}{n}\right) \left[\int_0^n (p_i)^{1-\phi} di \right] \right)^{1/(1-\phi)} \\ &= \left(\left(\frac{1}{n}\right) \left[\int_0^n (p_n)^{1-\phi} \, di \right] \right)^{1/(1-\phi)} = p_n = \left(\frac{p^*}{\alpha}\right) n^\beta. \qquad (7) \end{aligned}$$

[4]This conclusion is robust to the particular definition of the price index. If a naïve statistician did not know the set of traded goods had changed, but collected price data on all goods that previously had been traded, this average price level would still rise. However, the reason would be that the average includes newly nontraded goods, whose individual prices have risen, rather than the fact that an average is being taken over a subset of goods where the lower price items have been removed.

This implies that the price of nontraded goods rises with the share of nontraded goods with elasticity β.

The tradability condition (7) provides intuition for why the model will imply a low degree of volatility in the relative price of nontraded to traded goods. The price indexes of nontraded and traded goods are linked together through this condition, and therefore tend to move together. In particular, the condition states that the nontraded price index equals the price of the marginal traded good, and in turn, the price of this marginal traded good is linked to all other traded goods in the traded price index by the distribution of trade costs that determine all traded prices. In a standard small open economy model, a shock raises the price of nontraded goods dramatically without any change in the price of traded goods which are pinned at world prices. In our model, the movement in nontraded prices is dampened by the linkage to traded prices. And the prices of traded goods differ from the world price by varying amounts depending on the size of heterogeneous trade costs. As the set of traded goods changes, the set of trade costs that enter the price index changes.

As additional equilibrium conditions, intratemporal optimization implies the demand functions:

$$c_N = n\left(\frac{p_N}{p_H}\right)^{-\phi} c_H, \quad c_T = (1-n)\left(\frac{p_T}{p_H}\right)^{-\phi} c_H,$$

$$c_H = \theta\left(\frac{p_H}{p}\right)^{1} c, \quad \text{and} \quad c_F = (1-\theta)\left(\frac{p_F}{p}\right)^{1} c. \tag{8–11}$$

It is assumed that residents of the small open economy must pay the cost of transport for imports of foreign goods. The price of imported foreign goods is normalized to unity in the world market, so its domestic price is set exogenously as $p_F = 1/(1-\tau_F) \equiv \alpha_F$ for some given τ_F representing iceberg trade costs for imported goods.

Market clearing for nontraded goods requires

$$p_N c_N = \int_0^n p_i y_i di \quad \text{or} \quad c_N = ny \tag{12}$$

since (7) implies $p_N = p_i$ for all $i \leq n$ with uniform endowments $y_i = y$ for all i. The static model is closed by assuming balanced trade:

$$p_H y_H - pc = 0. \tag{13}$$

3.2. *Implications for the share of nontraded Goods*

Viewing tradedness as endogenous offers some new insights into what drives the degree of openness of a country's goods markets. The equilibrium conditions above can be solved together to yield the following expression for the equilibrium trade balance (surplus) Z:

$$Z \equiv \frac{1 + n^{\beta+1}\beta}{1+\beta} - \frac{1}{\omega\theta}[n^{\beta+1}(\omega + 1) - n^{\beta\phi}] = 0. \tag{14}$$

See the supplementary material in the appendix for derivation of this condition and the proofs of the conclusions that follow in this section. The trade balance Z falls as n increases. Intuitively, increasing n implies trade in fewer varieties of goods and lowers the trade surplus. Condition (14) implies that the balanced trade condition determines the steady-state share of nontraded goods, $\overline{n}$. It is easily verified that this solution is the unique solution that lies within the permissible range of 0 to 1. It is clear that if n were 0 and all goods were traded, then the trade balance is positive. For some $n > 0$, the trade balance will fall to 0.

Condition (14) provides a number of new insights into factors that determine the endogenous share of nontraded goods. One such factor is the curvature in the distribution of trade costs, β. Implicit differentiation of (14) indicates that $\partial\overline{n}/\partial\beta > 0$, as shown in the appendix. The nontraded share rises as the curvature of the trade cost distribution rises. Intuitively, if trade costs rise very quickly as more classes of goods are exported, it is optimal to export a smaller number of classes of goods. A country should then concentrate its exports in those commodities for which international trade is so much less costly.[5]

Another determinant of tradedness is the elasticity of substitution between home goods, ϕ. Implicit differentiation of (14) indicates that $\partial\overline{n}/\partial\phi > 0$, as shown in the appendix. The intuition is that if home goods are highly substitutable in consumption, one can conserve on trade costs by concentrating one's exports in the goods that are easiest to trade. This means there will be a smaller quantity of these particular classes of goods to consume, but under a high elasticity, it is easy to compensate by consuming a greater quantity of other types of goods.

[5]The level parameter of trade costs (α) does not appear under the Cobb–Douglas preferences assumed. It does appear if preferences are generalized to a CES case, as shown in Bergin and Glick (2003, revised 2007).

3.3. *Two-period model*

To study the dynamics of relative prices, the goods market described above will be analyzed in the context of a two-period model with a representative consumer. Variable time periods will be indicated by subscript. The equilibrium conditions developed above apply in both periods 1 and 2. In addition, the consumer maximizes two-period utility

$$\delta U(c_1) + U(c_2),$$

subject to the intertemporal budget constraint

$$\left(\frac{p_{H2}}{p_2} y_{H2} - c_2\right) = -\left(\frac{p_1}{p_2}\right)(1+r)\left(\frac{p_{H1}}{p_1} y_{H1} - c_1\right). \qquad (15)$$

Here r is the world interest rate on debt in world currency units. The term δ is an exogenous discount factor that can change, thereby allowing us to consider shifts in demand from one period to the next. Intertemporal optimization implies the usual intertemporal Euler equation:

$$U'_{c1} = \frac{1}{\delta}\left(\frac{p_1}{p_2}\right)(1+r)U'_{c2}. \qquad (16)$$

Equilibrium here determines values each period for the variables c_t, c_{Ht}, c_{Tt}, c_{Nt}, c_{Ft}, p_t, p_{Ht}, p_{Ft}, p_{Nt}, n_t, satisfying Equations (3)–(4) and (6)–(12) for each period as well as the intertemporal budget constraint (15) and the intertemporal consumption Euler equation (16); see the appendix. This is the model simulated in the following section. Note that the static model specified in Section 3.1 represents the steady state of the dynamic model, defined when the disturbance δ is set to zero, so that consumption and all other variables are constant across the two periods. According to the intertemporal budget constraint, the value of domestic production equals the value of domestic consumption in this steady state, and the trade balance is zero: $p_{H1}y_{H1} - p_1c_1 = p_{H2}y_{H2} - p_2c_2 = 0$, as was assumed in the specification of the static model.

4. Calibration Exercise

Because the two-period model cannot be solved analytically, a calibration experiment is used to study its implications for relative price movements.

4.1. *Calibration*

The model is calibrated to Canadian data, as representative of the small open economy case. First, to calibrate the distribution of trade costs, distribution (5) is fit to the US–Canadian price data used to create Fig. 2. In particular, the price wedges are ordered for the goods between a Canadian and US city pair in 2007, and the log of this is regressed on the log of the good index. Because the goods are all traded goods, the index is rescaled to run from $\overline{n}$ to 1 rather than from 0 to 1. A value for $\overline{n}$ is computed by collecting data on Canadian GDP in the categories of manufacturing, mining, and agriculture; as a share of overall GDP this averages 0.24 in annual data over 1981–2000, the period for which data was available. This implies a share for nontraded goods of 0.76. Regressing the log of the price gap on the log of the index for each of the goods adjusted by $\overline{n}$, the average estimate of β over the goods is 3.1. Foreign trade costs are calibrated at $\tau_F = 0.1$, following Obstfeld and Rogoff (2000). We retain the normalization that $p^*/\alpha = 1$.

The home bias preference parameter, θ, is calibrated at 0.73 as the share of domestic goods in the consumption bundle of Canada in 2007. The standard calibration in macroeconomic models for our parameter ϕ, the elasticity of substitution between home goods is 6 (see Rotemberg and Woodford, 1992, as well as Ghironi and Melitz, 2005).

We employ the usual assumption that the steady state value of the exogenous discounting factor δ equals the reciprocal of the gross world interest rate $(1 + r)$, which then cancel out each other. The calibration experiment will take 1,000 independent random draws for δ and feed them into the two-period model. Standard deviations are computed over the logged values of variables in period 1 of the model. Shocks to δ are log-normally distributed, and calibrated to imply that the consumption level has a standard deviations of 0.95%, which is the standard deviation in annual Canadian real consumption data during 1980–2000.

4.2. *Implications for nontraded prices*

Simulation results for the benchmark calibration are reported in the first row of Table 1. Of key interest is the volatility ratio for relative nontraded prices, reported in column (4). The benchmark calibration, based on Canadian data, generates a price volatility ratio of 0.38. This compares well

Table 1. Simulation results

			Endogenous n				Exogenous n[1]
(1) β	(2) ϕ	(3) $\overline{n}$	(4) $\frac{\text{sdev}(p_N/p_T)}{\text{sdev}(1/p)}$	(5) sdev$(1-n)$	(6) sdev(p_N)	(7) sdev(p_T)	(8) $\frac{\text{sdev}(p_N/p_T)}{\text{sdev}(1/p)}$
3.1	6	0.772	0.381	0.0169	0.0155	0.0115	1.460
0.1	6	0.275	2.536	0.0090	0.0024	0.0008	3.842
1	6	0.660	0.661	0.0147	0.0076	0.0045	1.645
10	6	0.858	0.197	0.0154	0.0254	0.0218	1.397
3.1	2	0.720	0.797	0.0130	0.0157	0.0083	1.694
3.1	10	0.783	0.233	0.0178	0.0153	0.0128	1.418
10	10	0.860	0.110	0.0150	0.0244	0.0224	1.385

Notes: Standard deviations are of logged variables.
Benchmark parameter values: $p*/\alpha = 1, \theta = 0.73, \tau_F = 0.1$.
[1]Computed for the corresponding level of $\overline{n}$, to facilitate comparison with the endogenous n case.
Simulations of 1,000 draws of the intertemporal preference δ, under alternative assumptions for the trade cost distribution parameter, β, and the elasticity of substitution between goods, ϕ. p_N is the price of nontraded goods, p_T is the price of traded goods, and p is the consumer price index, the reciprocal of which here equals the real exchange rate; n is the share of nontraded goods.

with the range of values estimated by Betts and Kehoe (2006) for Canada, ranging from 0.40 to 0.48, and shows that our model can succeed in generating low degrees of volatility in the relative price of nontraded goods.[6]

In contrast, column (8) of Table 1 shows that a low price volatility ratio is not possible in a small open economy model where the share of nontraded goods is given as exogenous. The model is identical to the one reported in the earlier columns, except that the marginal tradability condition (Equation (7)) is dropped. To maintain comparability with the earlier columns of the table, the exogenous value of the nontraded share, n, is set at the level

[6]The traded goods included in the aggregate price index include only home traded goods and exclude imported foreign goods. This is in part a matter of technical necessity: the model is designed to avoid an *a priori* demarcation between different types of home goods, so there is no clear way to define a price index combining imported foreign goods together with a subset of goods in the home goods CES index, while excluding other goods in this CES index. Fortunately, the stylized fact which the model is trying to replicate is defined in precisely the same manner.

of $\overline{n}$ found for the corresponding endogenous nontraded model reported in the preceding columns. The price volatility ratio in this case rises to 1.46. It is easy to demonstrate that the ratio of volatilities reported in column (8) must always be greater than unity when n is exogenous. Since the aggregate price level p is a weighted average of nontraded prices (p_N), traded home goods prices (p_T), and import prices (p_F), where the latter two are fixed by the integrated world market at world levels, the percentage movement in the first component must always be larger than the movement in the overall average that it induces.

This explains why classic small open economy models of nontraded goods are incapable of reproducing the low volatility in relative nontraded prices. Intuitively, when nontraded goods are exogenously determined, a rise in home demand requires a rise in the relative price of nontraded goods, to convince households to take their extra consumption in the form of additional imports of tradable goods, given that the consumption of nontraded goods is limited to the domestic supply of such goods. But when nontraded goods are endogenously determined, some traded goods sellers on the margin will respond to the rising price of nontraded goods and find it profitable to sell more in the home market, to the point of abandoning attempts to market their good abroad where they need to deal with costs of trade. This endogenous rise in the share of nontraded goods allows the supply of nontraded goods to increase, despite the fact that the endowment of each individual good is fixed. This increase in supply reduces the pressure for the relative price of nontraded goods to rise in the face of the higher demand.

The mechanism described above does not require an implausibly high degree of movement in the endogenous nontraded share. As reported in column (5) of the table, the percentage change in the share of traded goods is a modest 1.7%. It was noted previously that the standard deviation in the number of traded goods for Canadian data plotted in Fig. 1 was 3.4%. So the model's volatility in the margin of tradability is easily justifiable, and even modest, by the standards of Canadian data.

The remaining rows of Table 1 report sensitivity to alternative calibrations. First, higher values for the curvature parameter β reduce the relative volatility ratio. From the marginal tradability condition (Equation 7), it is clear that β reflects the elasticity of the nontraded price index with respect to changes in n. It is at high values of β where the demand shock induces a small change in n and a large change in the price of nontraded goods. But this also requires a larger change in the price index of traded goods, so the overall price index changes more. Second, a higher elasticity of substitution between home goods ϕ also lowers the relative price volatility ratio. Intuitively, if the last nontraded good and the marginal traded good are highly substitutable, this makes the link between their two prices stronger. This in turn strengthens the linkages between the price indexes of traded and nontraded goods. The table shows that for sufficiently high values of β or ϕ, it is possible to explain very low degrees of volatility in the price of nontraded goods, similar to those described by Betts and Kehoe (2006) for non-Canadian countries in their sample. Our estimates for β for Japan, Korea, and Germany, applying the same methodology as for Canada, are higher than those for Canada, ranging from 3.8 to 4.2. Higher estimates of ϕ at 10 are suggested by empirical work in Basu (1996).

Lastly, higher values of β and ϕ imply a higher steady state share of nontraded goods, along with the lower relative price volatility. Taking the nontraded share as a measure of a country's lack of openness to trade, we can conclude that our model offers an explanation for the finding in Betts and Kehoe (2006) that volatility in the relative price of nontraded goods is positively related to the degree of trade between countries.

4.3. *Implications for real exchange rates and current account adjustment*

Finally, we follow Obstfeld and Rogoff (2000) in using our two-period model to study how trade costs affect current account dynamics. The current account in period 1 equals the constant endowment less consumption, so a rise in the consumption ratio c_1/c_2 indicates a rising current account deficit. The Euler equation (16) indicates that the consumption based real interest rate used by agents to decide intertemporal consumption allocations is $(p_1/p_2)(1 + r)$, as the world interest rate r needs to be converted to domestic consumption units. Obstfeld and Rogoff (2000) demonstrated that a progressively greater rise in current consumption induces a temporary rise in the real exchange rate, which raises the cost of borrowing abroad to finance current consumption. We can simulate a range of shocks to δ in our model, and Fig. 4 plots how the log of the intertemporal price, p_1/p_2,

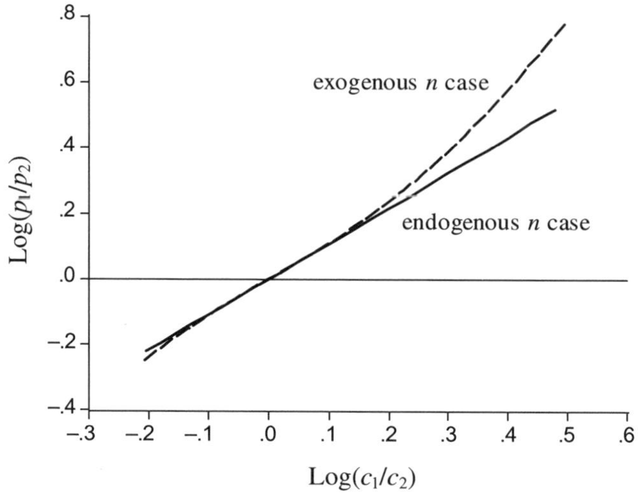

Plotted for $\beta = 3.1, \alpha = 1, \phi = 6, \theta = 0.73, \tau_F = 0.1$

Figure 4. Intertemporal price

Note: The figure plots the intertemporal price, log of p_1/p_2, associated with a range of consumption and current account imbalances, measured as the log of c_1/c_2. A relative increase in current consumption generates a rise in the current price index relative to the future, implying a rise in the cost of borrowing abroad to finance a current account deficit.

rises with the log of c_1/c_2. The solid line represents the benchmark model with endogenous tradability and the dashed line the exogenous nontraded case defined above. The exogenous share of nontraded goods for this case is calibrated to equal the share of the endogenous model in steady state.

One conclusion is that the intertemporal price rises smoothly with progressively rising consumption in both cases. This contrasts with Obstfeld and Rogoff (2000), where there is a discrete jump in p_1/p_2 when the single home good in their model switches from being exported to nontraded. Our result indicates that there is no nonlinear cost that switches on to strongly discourage particularly large current account deficits.

A second conclusion is that the intertemporal price rises less steeply when tradedness is endogenous rather than exogenous. When consumption rises in period 1 and falls in period 2, the share of nontraded goods rises in period 1 to free up more domestic goods for home consumption, and the share of nontraded goods falls in period 2 as the country needs to export more goods to repay its debt. In each case, the endogenous movement in the quantity of nontraded goods insulates the price of nontraded goods and thereby the real exchange rates. This is a further reason that real exchange rate adjustments are dampened by endogenous tradability, and respond less to discourage current account imbalances.

5. Conclusions

This chapter models tradedness as endogenous response to heterogeneous good-specific trading costs. The model offers an explanation for a prominent puzzle in the empirical literature: the relative price of nontraded goods tends to move with much less volatility than the real exchange rate. This fact stands in contrast to standard theoretical models such as Balassa–Samuelson, which rely almost entirely on such relative price movements. Endogenous tradability also is found to limit the ability of real exchange rates to dampen current account fluctuations. The mechanism developed here is sufficiently simple that it has the potential for being applied to a wide variety of macro models to analyze a range of macroeconomic issues.

Appendix

A.1. *Derivation of trade balance condition (14) and static model equilibrium*

Combine (8) and (12) to solve out for c_N:

$$c_H = y(p_N/p_H)^{\phi}. \tag{A1}$$

Substitute in (A1) for p_N with (7):

$$p_H c_H = (p^*/\alpha)^{\phi} y n^{\beta\phi} p_H^{1-\phi}. \tag{A2}$$

Substitute in (4) for p_T with (6) and for p_N with (7):

$$p_H^{1-\phi} = \left(\frac{p^*}{\alpha}\right)^{1-\phi} \frac{1}{\omega}[n^{-\omega}(1+\omega) - 1] \tag{A3}$$

where $\omega \equiv \beta(\phi - 1) - 1$. Combine (A3) with (A2) to obtain

$$p_H c_H = \frac{p^* y}{\alpha}\left(\frac{n^{\beta\phi}}{\omega}\right)[n^{-\omega}(1+\omega) - 1]. \tag{A4}$$

Note next that the domestic value of aggregate home production can be derived as

$$p_H y_H = \int_0^n p_i y_i di + \int_n^1 p_i y_i di = \int_0^n p_N y di + \int_n^1 p_i y di$$
$$= (p^*/\alpha)(n^\beta)ny + y\int_n^1 \left(\frac{p^* i^\beta}{\alpha}\right) di$$
$$= \frac{p^* y}{\alpha} n^{\beta+1} + \frac{p^* y}{\alpha}\left(\frac{1}{\beta+1}\right)(1-n^{\beta+1})$$

implying

$$p_H y_H = \frac{p^* y}{\alpha}\left[\frac{1+n^{\beta+1}\beta}{1+\beta}\right]. \tag{A5}$$

With balanced trade, $p_H y_H = pc$. Noting that (10) implies $p_H c_H = \theta pc$ and combining this with the balanced trade condition gives

$$p_H y_H = \left(\frac{1}{\theta}\right) p_H c_H. \tag{A6}$$

Substituting in (A6) on the left-hand side for $p_H y_H$ with (A5) and on the right-hand side for $p_H c_H$ with (A4):

$$\left(\frac{p^* y}{\alpha}\right)\left[\frac{1+n^{\beta+1}\beta}{1+\beta}\right] = \frac{p^* y}{\theta\alpha}\left(\frac{n^{\beta\phi}}{\omega}\right)[n^{-\omega}(1+\omega)-1].$$

Canceling $p^* y/\alpha$ from both sides, recalling $\omega \equiv \beta(\phi - 1) - 1$, and rearranging gives Equation (14) in the text, the equilibrium condition for n in the case of a zero trade balance surplus Z:

$$Z \equiv \frac{1+n^{\beta+1}\beta}{1+\beta} - \frac{1}{\omega\theta}[n^{\beta+1}(\omega+1) - n^{\beta\phi}] = 0. \tag{14}$$

Given the level of n that implicitly solves condition (14), it is straightforward to solve for the other endogenous variables: first the prices, p_T and p_N through (6) and (7), p_H through (A3), p through (3); and then the quantities, c_N and c_T through (8) and (9), c_H and c_F through (10) and (11), and c through (1).

A.2. *Demonstrating unique solution for condition (14)*

It is straightforward to see that for $n = 0$, $Z = 1/(1+\beta) > 0$, and for $n = 1$, $Z = -(1-\theta)/\theta < 0$. Showing that $\partial Z/\partial n < 0$ implies that Z crosses the 0 axis only once and is sufficient to establish the existence of a unique solution for n. Accordingly, it can be proven that

$$\begin{aligned}\frac{\partial Z}{\partial n} &= \frac{(\beta+1)n^{\beta}\beta}{1+\beta} - \frac{1}{\omega\theta}[(\beta+1)n^{\beta}(\omega+1) - \beta\phi n^{\beta\phi-1}] \\ &= \frac{\theta-1}{\theta}n^{\beta}\beta - \left(\frac{1-n^{\omega}}{\omega}\right)\frac{1}{\theta}n^{\beta}\beta\phi < 0\end{aligned}$$

since $\theta < 1$ and $\frac{1-n^{\omega}}{\omega} > 0$ for $0 < n < 1$.

A.3. *Response of equilibrium $\overline{n}$ to β and ϕ*

First consider $\frac{\partial n}{\partial \beta} = -\frac{\partial Z}{\partial \beta} / \frac{\partial Z}{\partial n}$

From Section A.2, we know that $\partial Z/\partial n < 0$.

Differentiation of (14) with respect to β:

$$\begin{aligned}\frac{\partial Z}{\partial \beta} &= -\frac{1}{(1+\beta)^2} + \frac{\beta}{1+\beta}\exp\left((\beta+1)\ln(n)\right)\ln(n) \\ &\quad + \exp\left((\beta+1)\ln(n)\right)\frac{(1+\beta)-\beta}{(1+\beta)^2} \\ &\quad - \frac{\beta(\phi-1)}{(\beta(\phi-1)-1)\theta}\exp\left((\beta+1)\ln(n)\right)\ln(n) - \exp\left((\beta+1)\ln(n)\right) \\ &\quad \times \left(\frac{(\beta(\phi-1)-1)\theta(\phi-1) - \beta(\phi-1)(\phi-1)\theta}{(\beta(\phi-1)-1)^2\theta^2}\right) \\ &\quad + \frac{(\beta(\phi-1)-1)\theta\exp(\beta\phi\ln(n))\phi\ln(n) - \exp(\beta\phi\ln(n))(\phi-1)\theta}{((\beta(\phi-1)-1)\theta)^2}.\end{aligned}$$

Rearranging and using the equilibrium condition (14)

$$\begin{aligned}\frac{\partial Z}{\partial \beta} &= -\frac{1}{(1+\beta)^2} + \frac{\beta}{1+\beta}n^{\beta+1}\ln(n) + \frac{1}{(1+\beta)^2}n^{\beta+1} \\ &\quad - \frac{\beta(\phi-1)}{\omega\theta}n^{\beta+1}\ln(n) + \left(\frac{\phi-1}{\omega^2\theta}\right)n^{\beta+1} \\ &\quad + \frac{\omega\phi\ln(n)}{\omega^2\theta}n^{\beta\phi} - \frac{(\phi-1)}{\omega^2\theta}n^{\beta\phi}.\end{aligned}$$

Rearranging further:

$$\frac{\partial Z}{\partial \beta} = \frac{1}{(1+\beta)^2}(n^{\beta+1} - 1 - \ln(n^{1+\beta})) + \frac{\phi - 1}{\omega^2\theta} n^{\beta\phi}(n^{-\omega} - 1 - \ln(n^{-\omega})) + \frac{1}{(1+\beta)^2} n^{\beta+1}.$$

All three terms in the expression above are positive for any $0 < n < 1$. The first two terms can be signed because for any value of $x \in (0,1)$ it is true that $x > 1 + \ln(x)$, where x is taken here to be $n^{\beta+1}$ and $n^{-\omega}$ in turn. So we conclude $\frac{\partial n}{\partial \beta} = -\frac{\partial Z}{\partial \beta}/\frac{\partial Z}{\partial n} > 0$.

Next consider $\frac{\partial n}{\partial \phi} = -\frac{\partial Z}{\partial \phi}/\frac{\partial Z}{\partial n}$.

$$\begin{aligned}\frac{\partial Z}{\partial \phi} &= -n^{\beta+1}\frac{(\beta(\phi-1)-1)\theta\beta - \beta(\phi-1)\beta\theta}{(\beta(\phi-1)-1)^2\theta^2} \\ &\quad + \frac{(\beta(\phi-1)-1)\theta n^{\beta\phi}\beta\ln(n) - n^{\beta\phi}\beta\theta}{(\beta(\phi-1)-1)^2\theta^2} \\ &= \left\{\frac{\theta\beta}{\omega^2\theta^2}\right\} n^{\beta\phi}\left\{n^{-\omega} - 1 - \ln(n^{-\omega})\right\}.\end{aligned}$$

This is positive for $0 < n < 1$, where the last term in braces is signed the same way as the second term in the expression for $\partial Z/\partial \beta$ above. So we conclude $\frac{\partial n}{\partial \phi} = -\frac{\partial Z}{\partial \phi}/\frac{\partial Z}{\partial n} > 0$.

A.4. *Derivation of two-period equilibrium*

For the two-period case, we introduce time subscripts and solve out for c_{Ht} with (A2) and (10) together to get

$$\frac{y_t}{\alpha^\phi} n_t^{\beta\phi} p_{Ht}^{1-\phi} = \theta p_t c_t. \tag{A7}$$

Substitute in (3) for p_{Ht} with (A3) to get

$$p_t = \frac{1}{\alpha^\theta}\left\{\frac{1}{\omega}[n_t^{-\omega}(1+\omega) - 1]\right\}^{\theta/(1-\phi)} p_{Ft}^{1-\theta}. \tag{A8}$$

Substitute in (A7) for p_{Ht} with (A3) and for p_t with (A8):

$$\frac{y_t}{\alpha} n_t^{\beta\phi}\frac{1}{\omega}[n_t^{-\omega}(1+\omega) - 1] = \theta\frac{1}{\alpha^\theta}\left\{\frac{1}{\omega}[n_t^{-\omega}(1+\omega) - 1]\right\}^{\theta/(1-\phi)} p_{Ft}^{1-\theta} c_t. \tag{A9}$$

Rearranging gives Equation (A10) that express the intratemporal consumption allocation relation between c_t and n_t that holds for each period $t = 1, 2$:

$$y_t n_t^{\beta\phi} \left\{ \frac{1}{\omega} [n_t^{-\omega}(1+\omega) - 1] \right\}^{\frac{1-\phi-\theta}{1-\phi}} = \theta\alpha^{1-\theta} p_{Ft}^{1-\theta} c_t. \tag{A10}$$

Lastly, we rearrange the intertemporal budget constraint (15) to get

$$c_2 = [(1+r)(p_{H1}y_{H1} - p_1 c_1) + p_{H2}y_{H2}]/p_2. \tag{A11}$$

Substituting in (A11) for $p_{Ht}y_{Ht}$ with (A5) and for p_t with (A8), $t = 1, 2$ gives (A12):

$$c_2 = \left[(1+r) \left(\frac{y_1[1 + n_1^{\beta+1}\beta]}{\beta+1} - \left(\left\{ \left[n_1^{-\omega} \left(\frac{1+\omega}{\omega} \right) - \frac{1}{\omega} \right]^{\frac{1}{1-\phi}} \right\}^{\theta} \times (\alpha p_{F1})^{1-\theta} c_1 \right) \right) + \frac{y_2[1 + n_2^{\beta+1}\beta]}{\beta+1} \right] \cdot \left\{ \left[n_2^{-\omega} \left(\frac{1+\omega}{\omega} \right) - \frac{1}{\omega} \right]^{\frac{-\theta}{1-\phi}} \right\}^{-\theta} (\alpha p_{F2})^{\theta-1}. \tag{A12}$$

The system of three equations – (A10) for t = 1, 2 and (A12) — can be solved numerically for n_1, n_2, and c_2 given a value of c_1. The Euler equation (16) completes the system.

References

Anderson, J. and E. van Wincoop. 2004. Trade costs. *Journal of Economic Literature*, 42: 691–751.

Balassa, B. 1964. The purchasing power parity doctrine: A reappraisal. *Journal of Political Economy*, 72: 584–596.

Basu, S. 1996. Procyclical productivity: Increasing returns or cyclical utilization? *Quarterly Journal of Economics*, 111: 719–751.

Bergin, P. R., R. C. Feenstra, and G. H. Hanson. 2008. Volatility due to offshoring: Theory and evidence, U.C. Davis mimeo.

Bergin, P. R. and R. Glick. 2003. revised 2007. Endogenous nontradability and macroeconomic implications. NBER Working Paper No. 9739.

Bergin, P. R., R. Glick, and A. M. Taylor. 2006. Productivity, tradability, and the long run price puzzle. *Journal of Monetary Economics*, 53: 2041–2066.

Bernard, A., J. B. Jensen, and P. K. Schott. 2006. Trade costs, rirms and productivity. *Journal of Monetary Economics*, 53: 917–937.

Betts, C. and T. Kehoe. 2001. Tradability of goods and real exchange rate fluctuations. Federal Reserve Bank of Minneapolis Staff Report.

Betts, C. and T. Kehoe. 2006. U.S. real exchange rate fluctuations and relative price fluctuations. *Journal of Monetary Economics*, 53: 1297–1326.

Crucini, M. J., C. I. C Telmer, and M. Zachariadis. 2005. Understanding european real exchange rates. *American Economic Review*, 95: 724–738.

Dornbusch, R. 1983. Real interest rates, home goods and optimal external borrowing. *Journal of Political Economy*, 91: 141–153.

Engel, C. 1999. Accounting for real exchange rate changes. *Journal of Political Economy*, 107: 507–538.

Engel, C. and J. H. Rogers. 2004. European product market integration after the Euro. *Economic Policy*, 39: 347–383.

Ghironi, F. and M. Melitz. 2005. International trade and macroeconomic dynamics with heterogeneous firms. *The Quarterly Journal of Economics*, 120: 865–915.

Hummels, D. 2001a. Toward a geography of trade costs. Purdue University Working Paper.

Hummels, D. 2001b. Time as a trade barrier. Purdue University Working Paper.

Naknoi, K. 2008. Real exchange rate fluctuations, endogenous tradability, and exchange rate regimes. *Journal of Monetary Economics*, 55: 645–663.

Obstfeld, M. and K. Rogoff. 2000. The six major puzzles in international macroeconomics: Is there a common cause? in Bernanke, B. and Rogoff, K. (eds.), *NBER Macroeconomics Annual*. MIT Press, Cambridge, pp. 339–390.

Rotemberg, J. J. and J. Woodford. 1992. Oligopolistic pricing and the effects of aggregate demand on economic activity. *Journal of Political Economy*, 100: 1153–1207.

Samuelson, P. A. 1964. Theoretical notes on trade problems. *Review of Economics and Statistics*, 46: 145–154.

CHAPTER 8

Productivity, Tradability, and the Long-Run Price Puzzle*

Paul R. Bergin,[†,§] Reuven Glick[‡,¶] and Alan M. Taylor[†,||]

[†] *Department of Economics, University of California at Davis, One Shields Ave., Davis, CA 95616, USA*

[‡] *University of California, San Diego, 9500 Gilman Dr., MC: 0519 La Jolla, CA 92093-0519, USA*

[§] *prbergin@ucdavis.edu*

[¶] *rcfeenstra@ucdavis.edu*

[||] *amtaylor@ucdavis.edu*

1. Introduction and Conventional Wisdom

One of the ways that the real exchange rate deviates from the purchasing power parity paradigm of perfect arbitrage and goods market integration is the generally accepted empirical regularity that richer countries tend to have higher price levels than poorer countries. Figure 1 illustrates this idea, displaying the association of 1995 log price levels and log per capita incomes based on Penn World Table (PWT) data. That this is the consensus view is clear since similar charts appear in most textbook discussions of these phenomena (e.g. Krugman and Obstfeld, 2003, Figure 15.4). While a number of potential explanations have been proposed, the standard story appeals to the Balassa–Samuelson (BS) theory, based on the divergence

*This article originally appeared in *Journal of Monetary Economics* (2006), 53(8), 2041–2066.

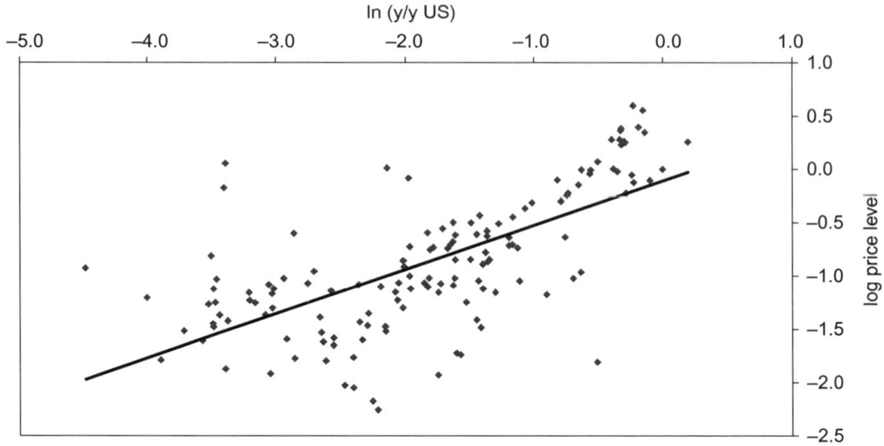

Figure 1. Log price level versus log per capita income, 1995 US = 0, PWT sample ($N = 142$)

of productivity levels in a world of traded and nontraded goods. Having languished from time to time, these ideas are now enjoying a renaissance and are being incorporated into many new open-economy macroeconomic models.

Of course, the apparent robustness of this story has proved to be of considerable relevance for many derivative conclusions in the theoretical and empirical literature. From work on sophisticated mathematical models of real exchange rates to the serious applied problem of judging differences in international living standards, the presumed correlation has had important economic and political ramifications. Since many of our PPP-based real income estimates, past and present, often rely on extrapolations from the PWT based on this kind of relationship, and since such estimates are then used for such diverse tasks as evaluating long-run growth performance or allocating foreign aid, it is important that the patterns in the data be judged stable and predictable.

This chapter raises some challenges to this comfortable consensus on the sources of covariance in international prices and incomes. The first challenge is empirical. Whilst correlations such as those seen in Fig. 1 are indisputably present in today's data, one need only to look back into the past to find evidence of weak or zero correlations between national price levels and incomes per capita. After examining postwar data in detail, we conclude that the price–income correlation was not really very strong until the last three or four decades. The search to explain this empirical finding leads us to propose a new model of real exchange rates that poses a theoretical challenge to a building block of the traditional BS model, the exogenous distinction between traded and nontraded sectors. In particular, while standard BS theory must assume that productivity gains are concentrated by coincidence in the existing traded goods sector, our model accounts for how productivity gains in the production of particular goods can in turn lead to those goods becoming traded endogenously. It therefore offers insight into how the trading pattern underlying the BS relationship can evolve over time.

The finding that the BS coefficient has emerged gradually in the data has a number of implications. While it reaffirms the potential for macroeconomic fundamentals to play a role in driving the real exchange rate in the long run, it also warns that the relationships modelers need to capture may be subtle and changing over time. And it suggests that empirical work on real exchange rates and deviations from PPP likewise should consider allowing for these relationships to change in the time series (Taylor and Taylor, 2004).

Our focus on the BS theory reflects a recently renewed appreciation of the role nontraded good prices play in helping drive real exchange rates (see Burstein, Eichenbaum, and Rebelo, 2005; Betts and Kehoe, 2005). Our theoretical approach to incorporate trade costs to understand real exchange rates is related to recent work by Ghironi and Melitz (2004) and Fitzgerald (2003). In contrast to Fitzgerald, our shipping technology has fixed costs while hers are iceberg only. Instead, her fixed costs appear in production, leading to intra-industry trade and endogenous specialization through a scale-related mechanism *à la* Krugman. Her paper is not directly related to the BS channel, which is the focus of our work. Ghironi and Melitz (2004), like us, propose a theory of an "endogenous BS effect." However the mechanism at work in their model is very different in spirit from that proposed by Balassa and Samuelson, as it arises out of entry of new firms into domestic production, and it is not dependent upon productivity differences between traded and nontraded goods. In contrast, this chapter may be viewed as an update and defense of the original BS logic, where we extend the basic theory with some new trade features to understand how and why the empirical effect has emerged over time.

2. Stylized "Facts" and a Simple Model

In theories of the real exchange rate built around tradable and nontradable goods, the central stylized fact to be "explained" is the effect noted by many scholars over the years, but highlighted by Balassa and Samuelson in their seminal papers from the year 1964: the tendency for poorer countries to have lower overall price levels than rich countries.[1] Figure 1(a) shows a scatter plot of log relative price levels versus log relative income per capita for a cross-section of 142 countries for the year 1995. We performed an OLS regression on these data, of the form

$$\ln (P_i/P_{US}) = \alpha + \beta \ln (y_i/y_{US}) + \varepsilon_i, \qquad (1)$$

and the fitted values are shown as a straight line in the figure.[2] We follow standard terminology and use the term *Balassa–Samuelson effect*, or BS effect, as shorthand for a positive (and statistically significant) slope estimate β. In our example, the slope is 0.41 with a standard error of 0.04.

The theory that Balassa and Samuelson constructed to explain this phenomenon is also now a textbook material, and the simplest version runs as follows.[3] Consider two countries, home and foreign, where foreign variables are denoted with an asterisk (*). Let there be two goods, traded (T) and nontraded (N), produced competitively in each country using only homogeneous labor as an input, with wages W and W^* in each country. Let the labor productivity in each sector be A_T and A_N at home, and A_T^* and A_N^*

---

[1] In Samuelson's (1994) paper, it is so central as to be labeled the "BASIC FACT" (uppercase in the original). In that paper, it is also explained, as we shall see, why "explained" might belong in quotes.

[2] Note that in our diagrams the abscissa is measured in PPP-adjusted *real* international dollars and so too is the independent variable in the econometrics that follow. The BS effect could, equivalently, be measured by the slope of a plot of relative prices on the ordinate versus *nominal* incomes converted at exchange rates on the abscissa (e.g. Balassa, 1964, Figure 1). In this case, the slope would be slightly different (lower) and equal to $\beta/(1+\beta)$. This nonlinear transformation of the coefficient, naturally, should make no material difference to the analysis, but in small samples, or with noisy PPP estimates, the effect might be to blur a borderline slope, which might explain the conflicting results of Clague and Tanzi (1972) using actual versus PPP exchange rates. Officer (1982) considers PPP-adjusted exchange rates the correct choice (p. 216).

[3] A two-factor variant with internationally mobile capital is presented by Froot and Rogoff (1995). The results are similar.

in the foreign country. Trade is costless for the traded goods, so their prices are equalized in the two countries and this pins down the relative wage levels in the two countries, since $W/A_T = P_T = P_T^* = W^*/A_T^*$. The wage levels, in turn, pin down the nontraded goods prices with $W/A_N = P_N$ and $W^*/A_N^* = P_N^*$. With an arbitrary choice of numéraire, say $P_T^* = 1$, one can easily solve the six equations in the six unknowns for four prices and two wage levels. Now construct a simple price index, say, Cobb–Douglas, where the share of nontraded goods in consumption is θ in both countries. Then the relationship between the price levels of the two countries is given by

$$\frac{P}{P^*} = \frac{(P_N)^\theta (P_T)^{1-\theta}}{(P_N^*)^\theta (P_T^*)^{1-\theta}} = \left(\frac{P_N}{P_N^*}\right)^\theta = \left(\frac{A_T/A_N}{A_T^*/A_N^*}\right)^\theta. \tag{2}$$

The relevance of Equation (2) for explaining the typical pattern in regression (1) depends on the assumed sources of economic growth. Though rarely tested directly, the conventional auxiliary assumption asserts that differential modern economic growth has been achieved as a result of the rapid productivity advance (in rich countries) of traded goods industries (for example, textiles, manufacturing, and hi-tech). In the meantime, the nontraded goods sectors are assumed to have been relatively quiescent, and their productivities to have changed relatively little (the well worn example is the haircut). For notational convenience, let $A_T = ab$, $A_N = a$, $A_T^* = a^*b^*$, and $A_N^* = a^*$. The a and a^* terms capture *balanced productivity growth*, which affects both sectors, and the b and b^* terms capture *biased growth* (or "BS growth") that only affects traded goods. Equation (2) can then be rewritten

$$\frac{P}{P^*} = \left(\frac{b}{b^*}\right)^\theta. \tag{3}$$

This expression is independent of a and a^* because *balanced productivity growth does not affect any relative prices.* We can also find a simple expression for real national income, which is given by real wage income, hence

$$\frac{W/P}{W^*/P^*} = \left(\frac{A_T P_T}{A_T^* P_T^*}\right) \Big/ \left(\frac{P_N}{P_N^*}\right)^\theta = \left(\frac{a}{a^*}\right)\left(\frac{b}{b^*}\right)^{1-\theta}. \tag{4}$$

Thus, *assuming* fixed a and a^* but varying b and b^*, the BS effect is present and the elasticity of the relative price level with respect to real income would be $\theta/(1-\theta)$. This elasticity will be zero when the range of nontraded goods vanishes, but is otherwise positive and can be arbitrarily large when the nontraded share approaches unity.

However, it is also clear from the above that the BS effect is *not* guaranteed to exist. The BS effect will be zero if the sources of growth are spread across the two sectors evenly, as when a/a^* changes but b/b^* does not. And, since $\theta > 0$, it is only biased technological change favoring the traded sector that can generate the BS effect. And there is even the possibility of an anti-BS effect: if technological change were biased toward nontraded goods (here equivalent to a rise in a and a fall in b such that ab remains constant), then the price level could *fall* as a country got richer.

3. A Puzzle

Returning to the long-run data, Fig. 2 shows that in the 1950 PWT data for 53 countries the BS effect was much weaker, with a slope of only 0.08 and a standard error of 0.07. Table 1 confirms that, in a sequence of annual PWT cross-sections every fifth year from 1950 to 1995, the BS effect has gradually

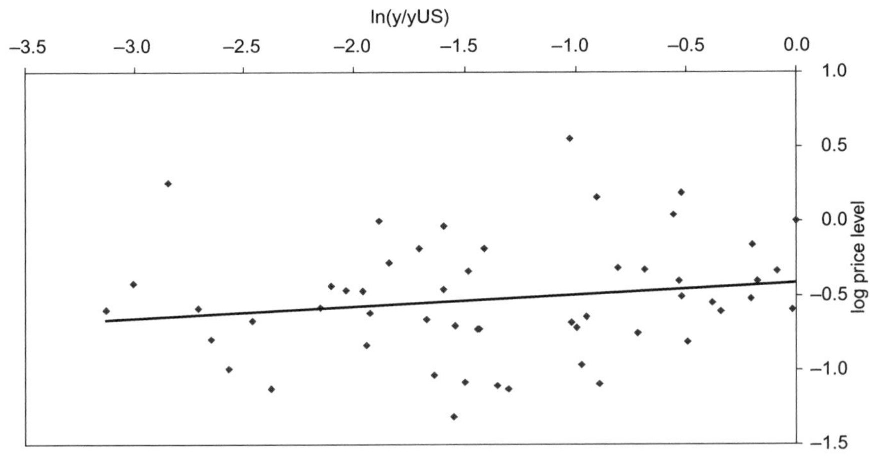

Figure 2. Log price level versus log per capita income, 1950 US = 0, PWT sample ($N = 53$)

Note: Scatter plots of log price level versus log per capita income. Various samples.

Source: Penn World Table.

Table 1. The BS effect 1950–1995 in cross-section OLS regression of the log relative price level on log relative real income per capita

Year	N	β	s.e.
1950	53	0.08	(0.07)
1955	69	0.11	(0.07)
1960	108	0.19	(0.05)***
1965	109	0.20	(0.05)***
1970	111	0.20	(0.05)***
1975	112	0.20	(0.05)***
1980	118	0.20	(0.05)***
1985	118	0.27	(0.04)***
1990	128	0.36	(0.04)***
1995	142	0.41	(0.04)***

Note: Significance levels: * 10%, ** 5%, *** 1%.
Source: Penn World Table 6.

strengthened, with the slope estimate roughly quadrupling in size over half a century. In their 1964 contribution, Balassa and Samuelson were certainly very timely, if not quite ahead of their time, since the 1960 cross-section supports their hypothesis, but from a statistical standpoint there was not much evidence when they wrote, and the overwhelming support in large samples has accumulated ever since.

We have examined the data in other ways to check the robustness of our finding. Running a cross-section regression on these data in *every year* produced the slope estimates (and 95% confidence intervals) shown in Fig. 3. Figure 4 shows that the PWT result is not an artifact of changing sample size, since the effect is just as large when we restrict attention to a balanced panel of 53 countries from 1950 to 1998. Thus, even outside the benchmark dates in Table 1, our basic story is reinforced. The PWT data show an almost monotonic upward trend in the slope estimate.

Our evidence hints at a new stylized fact: perhaps the BS effect has *not* been a universal feature of modern economic development. If indeed the BS effect has strengthened markedly in the last 50 years, this could reconcile the mixed findings in a wider literature that has from time to time examined the BS effect in postwar data. Older studies that focused on the 1950s and 1960s

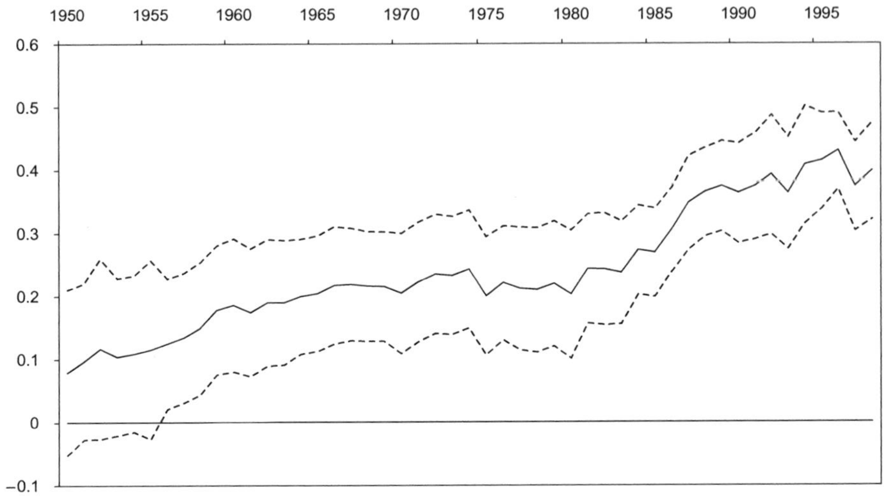

Figure 3. The BS effect in cross-sections PWT data 1950–1998, full sample (53^2N^2165)

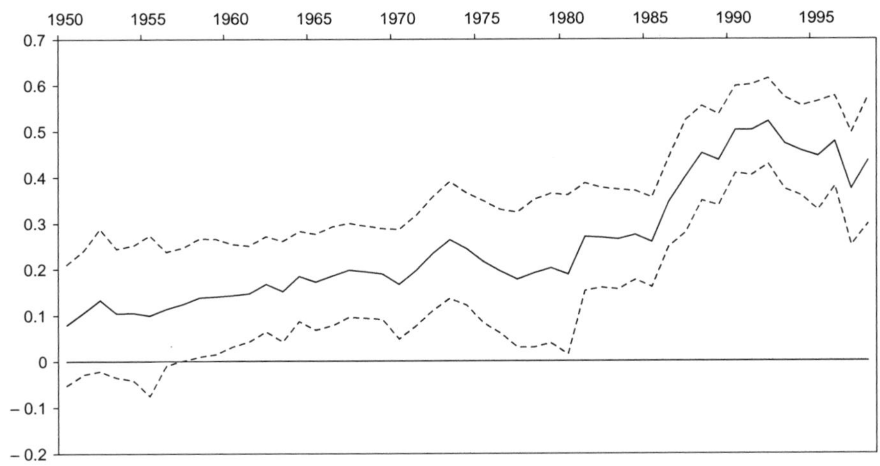

Figure 4. The BS effect in cross-sections PWT data 1950–1998, 1950 sample of countries ($N = 53$)

Note: Coefficient from cross-country regression of log price level on log per capita income (solid line) with 95% confidence interval (dashed lines).

Source: Author computations.

tended to find weak evidence, such as Officer (1982).[4] More recent studies have sometimes found stronger results, but, according to a recent survey, "[o]verall, the empirical evidence on the Harrod–Balassa–Samuelson effect is quite mixed" (Sarno and Taylor 2002, 82).[5]

The data seem to be sending a consistent message. The BS effect has not always been a fact of economic life, and appears to be a phenomenon of only the postwar period, growing in strength steadily over time. This new stylized fact raises interesting questions: Which models can most plausibly explain such an historical pattern in the data? And what do the theory and the empirics tell us about the mechanics of economic development?

4. A More General Model

The simple model presented above potentially could be rigged to produce the actual historical changes seen, essentially by imposing convenient changes in exogenous variables. There are two ways for the BS result to emerge over time in that model. Either the biasedness of productivity growth would have to increase, meaning more growth via b than via a; or, the nontraded share θ would have to rise over time to steepen the slope for a given b.

But addressing the puzzle in terms of such purely exogenous changes in the parameters of the model is not a very satisfying explanation, and it

[4]Our slope coefficients can be compared with those of Officer (1982, Chapter 16, especially Table 2). He examined the OECD economies in successive annual cross-sections from 1950 to 1973 and found no BS effect in (1). The slope was often close to zero in the 1950s and 1960s, though rising to around 0.25 circa 1970. Our results are in broad agreement: we find that most of the BS action has arrived in the years since Officer's analysis ended, although even in the 1960s, a small effect *was* there, but was only detectable in a large sample that included more low income countries. Thus, Officer's weak results might be explained by a small sample ($N = 15$ at most). Alternatively, a focus on countries at similar levels of development might rob the regression of variance or introduce countervailing effects (Bhagwati, 1984; Fitzgerald, 2003).

[5]See, *inter alia*, Hsieh (1982); Marston (1990); Micossi and Milesi-Ferreti (1994); De Gregorio, Giovannini, and Wolf (1994); De Gregorio and Wolf (1994); Chinn and Johnston (1996); Ito, Isard, and Symansky (1999); Chinn (2000); Lothian and Taylor (2004). The newer studies and their estimates are not directly comparable to ours, since they address some of the internal workings of the BS hypothesis, e.g. using manufacturing and/or services employment attempted to pin down the underlying sectoral productivity shocks.

offers little to no insight into the underlying causes of the phenomenon or the mechanisms that propagate it. However, this particular shortcoming of the simple BS model can be addressed readily by extending it with recent advances in trade theory.

4.1. *Model motivation*

Recent theories in trade offer some interesting suggestions for why the result above might arise endogenously. It has been documented in recent work on trade that there is a good deal of heterogeneity in terms of productivity among firms, even within the same sector. It is only a relatively small number of firms that participate in international trade, and these firms systematically tend to be large and have high levels of productivity. Trade theory has offered models to replicate this pattern, by assuming a continuum of firms with heterogeneous draws from a productivity distribution, who must pay a fixed cost to engage in international trade (Melitz, 2003). The result is that only those firms with the highest productivity draws find it profitable to engage in trade.

The purpose of this section is to adapt this logic to help explain the macroeconomic stylized fact of rising relative prices over time. First, this logic offers a clear way to endogenize the BS precondition that productivity shocks be biased toward traded goods. This coincidence need not be by chance; firms or industries endogenously become traded in direct response to the fact they happen to benefit from a positive sequence of productivity shocks. Further, one might hope that a model where the BS effect arises endogenously would be better equipped to explain why this effect could continue to grow over time. As productivity shocks accumulate over time, they could become a more dominant determinant of what goods are traded, so that the correlation of productivity and tradability rises over time as well.

Is there any empirical motivation for thinking that the set of traded goods can actually change and evolve much over time, as the story above would suggest? Again the trade literature is helpful. Using a panel of US manufacturing plants from 1987 to 1997, Bernard and Jensen (2001) find that there is significant movement of firms between traded and nontraded status on a year-to-year basis: on average 13.9% of nonexporters begin to export in any given year during the sample, and 12.6% of exporters stop. In addition, trade literature has noted that a fair fraction of the growth in

Table 2. Correlations between productivity and tradability in US manufacturing data

SIC industry level	Spearman rank correlations		Level correlations (in logs)	
	1958	1994	1958	1994
2-digit	0.34	0.53	0.21	0.35
3-digit	0.29	0.47	0.25	0.45
4-digit	0.31	0.40	0.27	0.38

Source: Productivity data from the NBER-CES manufacturing industry database, export data from the NBER database on "U.S. Trade by 1972-SIC Category."

trade observed over time has been at the extensive margin, with the entry of goods previously nontraded.[6]

To see if there is any evidence at the macro level for our story, we obtained data on real productivity for US industries at 2, 3, and 4-digit industry levels for 1958 to 1994, and corresponding data on the share each sector represents in US exports. The productivity data were drawn from the NBER–CES manufacturing industry database. Nominal productivity was defined as value-added per employee (Vadd divided by emp) based on 1972 SIC codes; the industry shipments price deflator (Piship) was used for the conversion to real terms.[7] The export data were drawn from the NBER database on "U.S. Trade by 1972-SIC Category." When the industries were ranked in terms of productivity and tradability, we found that there was a fairly large increase in the Spearman correlation between productivity ranking and tradability ranking at all levels of disaggregation. At the 2-digit industry level, the correlation rose from 0.34 in 1958 to 0.53 in 1994; at the 3-digit level, the increase is from 0.29 to 0.47, and at the 4-digit level from 0.31 to 0.40. An increase in correlations is also apparent when we compute "raw" correlations of the actual (log) levels of exports and productivity. See Table 2 for full results.

The US export data above can also be used to see if there was any obvious change in the concentration of trade over time. While there was not a clear pattern at more aggregated levels, there is evidence of increasing concentration at the 4-digit SIC level for US manufactures. Figure 5 shows

[6] See Kehoe and Ruhl (2002) for a discussion.

[7] For further information, see Bartelsman and Gray (1996). Both databases are at http://www.nber.org/data/.

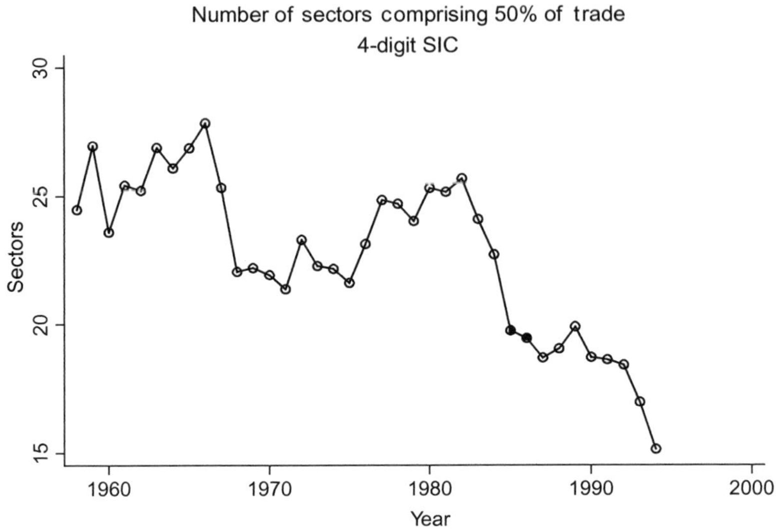

Figure 5. Concentration of trade in US manufacturing

the number of 4-digit industries (out of a total of 450) needed to account for 50% of US manufacturing exports for each year from 1958 to 1994. (The data are converted into real terms using the shipments price deflator.) There was a decline over the period from 25 industries to 15, mainly in the latter half of the time period. This indicates, first, that there is a pretty high degree of concentration of trade in a small share of goods categories, with the majority of trade accounted for by around only 5% of industry categories. But it also offers suggestive evidence that this degree of concentration may have risen over time.

This evidence offers some guidance for our theoretical research. It is noteworthy that the basic precondition for the BS theory finds support in the disaggregated data: high productivity levels do seem to be more concentrated in more tradable goods. This indicates that the basic mechanism of the BS theory may be a useful approach to maintain in our current analysis.[8] Further, we find some support for the BS-based explanation,

[8]This contrasts with the theory of Ghironi and Melitz (2004), which does not rely upon the usual BS precondition; instead it generates the relative price effect mainly on the basis of new firm entrants into the domestic market driving up the demand for labor and hence the wage.

as presented in Section 2 above, for the finding that the relative price effect has risen over time. If the precondition for the simple BS model to explain this fact is that productivity shocks have become progressively more skewed toward the tradable goods sector, the counterpart for a world of many goods with varying degrees of tradability would be that the correlation between productivity and tradability has increased over time. The model developed below will show one way of incorporating these recent advances in trade theory into a macro context, as a way of extending the BS model.

4.2. *Model specification*

The model here differs from the simple model of Section 2 in several key respects. It specifies a continuum of goods that differ in terms of their productivity levels, rather than just two sectors with differing productivity levels. Tradability of each good is endogenized as the decision of a firm, which must pay a fixed cost to trade its good. Firms are here monopolistically competitive and pay the fixed cost out of their resulting profits.

In the model, there are two countries, home and foreign (the latter denoted *), and each country's output consists of a distinct continuum of differentiated goods (labels H and F will be used here).[9] Each country's goods are indexed on the unit interval, and for each classification of goods there is a continuum of brands.[10] These are produced by monopolistically competitive firms using labor as the sole input in a linear (constant returns

[9]Note that by assuming different goods in each country, the LOP basis of PPP is essentially discarded. This model can generalize simply to an N-country world with a distinct range of goods in each country. A different approach to the Ricardian model is to allow a common set of goods to be potentially produced in all countries, and then have only the lowest-cost supplier actually export the good to each market, as in the probabilistic model of Eaton and Kortum (2002). An interesting avenue for future research would be to explore the implications of endogenous tradability and the BS effect in that type of setting.

[10]The only reason to refer here to brands of goods is to allow a separate elasticity in the markup decision of the firms from that used by consumers when substituting between home and foreign goods. We wished to avoid implausibly high markups, despite evidence of low substitutability between broader classes of goods.

to scale) technology. In principle, any good can be exported but there are fixed costs of exporting f_X for any good, which are borne by the exporting firm.[11] Traded sector aggregates are labeled T and nontraded N. Agents preferences are standard CES and apply to home goods and importables. Key assumptions are that each country specializes in a range of goods that are unique to that country (albeit goods from different countries are substitutes) and that the continua of goods are exogenously given.

Details of the model are laid out in the appendix, but the essential building blocks are as follows. Home and foreign residents consume CES aggregates (C, C^*) of their own goods (C_H, C_F^*) and the other country's traded (export) goods (C_{FT}, C_{HT}^*). Let n and n^* denote the (endogenous) share of nontraded goods in each country, where goods are ordered such that $[0, n]$ and $[0, n^*]$ are the nontraded goods. Then the top-level aggregations are

$$C = \left((\theta[n^*])^{\frac{1}{\phi}}(C_H)^{\frac{\phi-1}{\phi}} + (1-\theta[n^*])^{\frac{1}{\phi}}(C_{FT})^{\frac{\phi-1}{\phi}}\right)^{\frac{\phi}{\phi-1}},$$

$$C^* = \left((\theta[n])^{\frac{1}{\phi}}(C_F^*)^{\frac{\phi-1}{\phi}} + (1-\theta[n])^{\frac{1}{\phi}}(C_{HT}^*)^{\frac{\phi-1}{\phi}}\right)^{\frac{\phi}{\phi-1}}, \tag{5}$$

where $\phi > 1$ is the elasticity of substitution between domestic and foreign goods aggregates, and $\theta[n^*]$ is the domestic residents' own-goods bias coefficient that depends (endogenously) on the number of imported varieties. As n^* rises and fewer varieties are imported by domestic residents, the relative weight in the consumption basket placed on home goods rises and on imported goods falls, i.e. $\theta' > 0$. The own-bias coefficient for foreign residents, $\theta[n]$, is interpreted analogously.[12] The indices for domestically

[11] Bergin and Glick (2003, 2004) consider variable (iceberg) trade costs also. The general intuition developed in this paper would generalize to this case, although the computational difficulty would, in general, be greater (for reasons to be explained later). To facilitate intuition, we study the fixed cost case where the greater range of closed-form solutions obtain. It suffices to note that the model studied here does include the case of uniform iceberg costs on all traded goods. Problems arise when the iceberg cost varies by good, as noted below.

[12] In the appendix, we show formally that the bias weights on own goods $\theta[n^*], \theta[n]$ depends on the mass of own goods (normalized to 1 in each country) relative to the total mass of (own plus imported) varieties available for own consumption ($1 + 1 - n^*$ in the domestic country and $1 + 1 - n$ in the foreign country).

produced goods, and their subindices, are in turn defined by

$$
\begin{aligned}
(C_H)^{(\phi-1)/\phi} &= \int_0^n (c_{Hi})^{(\phi-1)/\phi} di + \int_n^1 (c_{Hi})^{(\phi-1)/\phi} di \\
&= n\left(\frac{C_{HN}}{n}\right)^{(\phi-1)/\phi} + (1-n)\left(\frac{C_{HT}}{1-n}\right)^{(\phi-1)/\phi}, \\
(C_F^*)^{(\phi-1)/\phi} &= \int_0^{n*} (c_{Fi}^*)^{(\phi-1)/\phi} di + \int_{n^*}^1 (c_{Fi}^*)^{(\phi-1)/\phi} di \\
&= n^*\left(\frac{C_{FN}^*}{n^*}\right)^{(\phi-1)/\phi} + (1-n^*)\left(\frac{C_{FT}^*}{1-n^*}\right)^{(\phi-1)/\phi}, \qquad (6)
\end{aligned}
$$

where the elasticity of substitution among home goods and among foreign goods is also assumed equal to ϕ. At home, the HN goods occupy $[0, n]$ and HT goods $[n, 1]$; on a separate foreign interval, the FN goods occupy $[0, n^*]$ and FT goods $[n^*, 1]$. Using duality, and noting symmetry, it is equivalent to proceed using the corresponding price indices for all of the above aggregates: $P, P^*, P_{HN}, P_{HT}, P_{FT}, P_{FN}^*, P_{FT}^*$, and P_{HT}^*.

The production side is simple. Each home firm employs l_{Hi} workers and pays them the wage W, and similarly for the foreign firms. On each interval, the output of good i is given by

$$
y_{Hi} = A_i l_{Hi}, \quad y_{Fi} = A_i^* l_{Fi}, \qquad (7)
$$

where A_i, A_i^* are productivity coefficients for each individual good i. Profit maximization by the monopolists leads to the standard cost-markup pricing. In the presence of iceberg shipping costs, pricing would differ across markets; but this is not crucial for intuition and is omitted in the case considered here[13]:

$$
p_{Hi} = p_{Hi}^* = \frac{\varphi}{\varphi-1}\frac{W}{A_i}, \quad p_{Fi} = p_{Fi}^* = \frac{\varphi}{\varphi-1}\frac{W^*}{A_i^*}, \qquad (8)
$$

[13]The introduction of good-specific iceberg costs trade costs creates a gap between the domestic and foreign sales price: $p_{Hi}^* = p_{Hi}/(1-\tau_i)$, where τ_i denotes the fraction of good i that disappears in transport. Bergin and Glick (2004) show that the extension to good-specific iceberg shipping costs introduces similar terms to these in the markup calculation, but that the derivation of equilibrium is analogous once export goods' productivities are adjusted for the iceberg loss.

where $\varphi/(1-\varphi)$, the markup factor, is assumed to depend on an elasticity of substitution parameter φ that differs from that across varieties of goods ϕ.[14]

The crux of the model is the distribution of productivities across goods in each country. Firms in the domestic (foreign) country have a distribution of productivity levels $F[A_i](F[A_i^*])$. Among these firms, $1-n = F[A_n](1-n^* = F[A_n^*])$ are exporters. We define weighted productivity averages for home goods $\tilde{A}$, nontraded home goods $\tilde{A}_N$, traded home goods $\tilde{A}_T$, and their foreign analogues

$$
\begin{aligned}
(\tilde{A})^{\phi-1} &\equiv \int_0^1 A_i^{\phi-1} di, \quad (\tilde{A}^*)^{\phi-1} \equiv \int_0^1 (A_i^*)^{\phi-1} di, \\
(\tilde{A}_N[n])^{\phi-1} &\equiv \frac{1}{n}\int_0^n (A_i)^{\phi-1} di, \quad (\tilde{A}_N^*[n^*])^{\phi-1} \\
&\equiv \left(\frac{1}{n^*}\right)\int_0^{n^*} (A_i^*)^{\phi-1} di, \\
(\tilde{A}_T[n])^{\phi-1} &\equiv \left(\frac{1}{1-n}\right)\int_n^1 A_i^{\phi-1} di, \quad (\tilde{A}_T^*[n^*])^{\phi-1} \\
&\equiv \left(\frac{1}{1-n^*}\right)\int_{n^*}^1 (A_i^*)^{\phi-1} di. \qquad (9)
\end{aligned}
$$

While $\tilde{A}$ is independent of n, $\tilde{A}_N$ and $\tilde{A}_T$ are not. If goods are ordered with increasing productivity, then $\partial\tilde{A}_T/\partial n > 0$, $\partial\tilde{A}_N/\partial n < 0$, i.e. average productivity rises (falls) in the traded sector (nontraded) sector with increasing n. Intuitively, as the share of nontraded goods in the economy rises, goods at the low productivity end of the traded goods sector become nontraded, and the average level of productivity of all remaining traded goods rises.[15]

---

[14]In our simulations, we assume that $\phi < \varphi$ on the presumption that the elasticity of substitution among firms in a given industry (e.g. between Honda and Toyota) is greater than that across industries (e.g. between autos and food).

[15]We will show that the solution to our model can be simply expressed as a function of the weighted productivities. Setting aside the endogeneity of n, the relationship of our model to the basic, textbook BS model is then clear, since the model depends only on "average" productivity levels in the traded and nontraded parts of the economy each viewed as a whole. A similar result has been derived independently in another model of endogenous tradability by Melitz (2003).

4.3. *Solving for tradedness and relative prices*

The model solves conditionally as follows. Given n and n^*, consider the set of 24 endogenous variables, consisting of C, C_H, C_{HN}, C_{HT}, C_{FT}, P, P_H, P_{HN}, P_{HT}, P_{FT}, and W, plus the foreign counterpart variables (denoted *). Production markups link prices to wages. Standard CES demand conditions link prices to consumption quantities and, hence, via technology, to derived labor demand. Market clearing (plus balanced trade) and a numéraire choice complete the solution.

It is possible to derive an equilibrium for trade, given n and n^*, as shown in the appendix. But what determines these nontraded shares? On the margin, the producers of the borderline traded–nontraded good must be indifferent between home and foreign sales, and, given the fixed costs of shipping, this entails two simple extra conditions that pin down n and n^* in equilibrium:

$$\left(p^*_{Hn} - \frac{W}{A_n}\right)\left(\frac{1}{P}\right)c^*_{Hn} = \left(\frac{W}{P}\right)f_X,$$
$$\left(p_{Fn} - \frac{W^*}{A^*_n}\right)\left(\frac{1}{P^*}\right)c_{Fn} = \left(\frac{W^*}{P^*}\right)f^*_X. \quad (10)$$

Consider the first of these equations. The left-hand side represents the real profit per unit of home good sold in the foreign market multiplied by sales volume; the right-hand side is the fixed cost of exporting, where W/P represents the effective real wage rate of the labor employed to cover these costs. For the borderline good n the two sides are equal, and profits from export are zero. The same is true in the foreign country. Taking sales as given, the profit term (like the A term) is increasing in n, so all goods on the interval to the left of n are nontraded and all to the right are traded, confirming the maintained assumption.

In this framework, endogenous tradability arises naturally, because only goods with high enough productivity are able to surmount the export cost barrier.[16] Moreover, goods which are *a priori* nontraded ($i < n$)

[16]This insight has been more extensively developed in the trade and policy literature and is not well-known in the macroeconomics literature. See for example, Richardson and Rindal (1996) and Bernard and Jensen (1999). For a related equilibrium analysis, see especially Helpman, Melitz, and Yeaple (2004).

but experience productivity gains relative to other goods may become traded over time as their operating profits exceed the fixed costs of exporting. Correspondingly, goods which are initially traded may subsequently become nontraded as their profits are reduced below export costs by the wage increases generated by the goods with more rapid productivity growth.

The equilibrium conditions can be combined to gain some analytical results and insights into the effects of productivity on the tradability of goods and on relative aggregate price levels, i.e. the real exchange rate. We can also show that an increase in the dispersion of productivities across goods will tend to concentrate trade in a smaller number of goods. As derived in the appendix, the export profitability conditions can be rearranged to obtain:

$$\frac{1}{\varphi-1}\left(\frac{A_n}{\tilde{A}_T[n]}\right)^{\phi}\frac{C^*_{HT}}{1-n}=f_X,\quad \frac{1}{\varphi-1}\left(\frac{A^*_n}{\tilde{A}^*_T[n^*]}\right)^{\phi-1}\frac{C_{FT}}{1-n^*}=f^*_X. \tag{11}$$

Observe that in this form, export profits depend on the productivity of the marginally traded nth good A_n, relative to the average productivity of all exported goods, $\tilde{A}_T[n]$. For given aggregate exports C^*_{HT}, a productivity shock biased towards traded goods will lower the productivity of the initially marginal traded good relative to the average, since the productivity of all intramarginally traded goods is higher. The resulting decline in $A_n/\tilde{A}_T[n]$ implies export operating profits fall below the fixed costs of exporting, inducing some firms to cease exporting. As the equilibrium n rises and trade becomes concentrated in a smaller set of firms, the profitability of the marginal exported good rises as its share of aggregate exports $(C^*_{HT}/(1-n))$ rises until these profits increase to just cover the fixed costs of entering into the foreign export market. Note that a balanced change in productivity for all home goods, leaving $A_n/\tilde{A}_T$ unchanged, does not affect the marginal profitability of exports. So if technology accumulates in a progressively more skewed distribution across goods, this tends to raise the equilibrium value of n and concentrate trade in a smaller set of goods over time.

As also derived in the appendix, the relative national price level may be written

$$\left(\frac{P}{P^*}\right)^{\phi-1} = \left(\frac{\theta[n]\left(\frac{W/\tilde{A}}{W^*/\tilde{A}^*}\right)^{\phi-1} + (1-\theta[n])\left(\frac{\tilde{A}_T[n]}{\tilde{A}}\right)^{\phi-1}}{\theta[n^*] + (1-\theta[n^*])\left(\frac{\tilde{A}^*_T[n^*]}{\tilde{A}^*}\cdot\frac{W/\tilde{A}}{W^*/\tilde{A}^*}\right)^{\phi-1}}\right), \qquad (12)$$

where the notation indicates the dependence of $\theta, \tilde{A}_T, \tilde{A}^*_T$ on n^*, n. Observe that the domestic country experiences a real appreciation (P/P^* rises) in response to: (i) a *ceteris paribus* increase in the relative cross-country domestic wage rate, adjusted by economy-wide average productivity levels $((W/\tilde{A})/(W^*/\tilde{A}^*))$; or (ii) a *ceteris paribus* increase in home productivity biased towards tradables $(\tilde{A}_T/\tilde{A})$.[17] These effects are analogous to those of the standard BS model.[18] Clearly, the fact that the set of traded goods is determined endogenously in this model raises the likelihood of generating BS effects on prices. If large productivity shocks accumulate in a good, regardless of which good this happens to be, the good will tend to become traded and hence it will raise the $\tilde{A}_T/\tilde{A}$ term in the relative price expression (12).

However, expression (12) also indicates additional effects on relative prices operating through endogenous changes in n(or n^*) associated with the changing tradability of goods. These effects operate through two channels: (i) an effect on the relative productivity of tradables, $\tilde{A}_T/\tilde{A}$, and (ii) an effect through the home bias weight θ. With the first channel, if the share of nontraded goods in the economy n rises, goods at the low productivity end of the traded goods sector become nontraded, and the average level of productivity of all remaining traded goods rises. This amplifies the rise in $\tilde{A}_T/\tilde{A}$ and increase in relative prices. With the second channel, if fewer home varieties are traded, the weight placed on imported goods in the foreign price index falls, i.e. $1-\theta$ falls and θ rises. Inspection of (12) indicates

[17] The first result presumes own goods bias in each country: $\theta[n] \geq 1/2, \theta[n^*] \geq 1/2$.

[18] In the special case of no export costs at all: $f_X = f^*_X = 0$, implying all goods are traded ($n = n^* = 0$), then $\theta = 1/2, \tilde{A} = \tilde{A}_T, \tilde{A}^* = \tilde{A}^*_T$, so that $\left(\frac{P}{P^*}\right)^{\phi-1} = \frac{(\tilde{A}^*/W^*)^{\phi-1} + (\tilde{A}/W)^{\phi-1}}{(\tilde{A}/W)^{\phi-1} + (\tilde{A}^*/W^*)^{\phi-1}} = 1$, i.e. consumption price levels are equalized across countries.

that this raises the impact of the relative cross-country domestic wage rate $((W/\tilde{A})/(W^*/\tilde{A}^*))$, but lowers the impact of relative productivity in the traded sector $(\tilde{A}_T/\tilde{A})$. Given these multiple and potentially offsetting channels, it is not immediately obvious on the basis of analytical results whether the endogenous movement in the share n will make BS effects more or less likely. Simulations will address this ambiguity.

5. Numerical Simulations

The purpose of this section is to provide an illustration of how the model can generate a BS effect on national relative prices that arises endogenously and grows over time. Although we view the exercise mainly as an illustration of principles rather than a formal quantitative investigation, we nonetheless connect model and distribution parameters with data where possible to enhance the relevance of the experiment. To implement the model numerically, the continuum of goods is made discrete, with ten industries. The experiment allows the productivity of the ten industries in the home country, which we interpret as the US, to grow in response to a sequence of random productivity shocks that differ by industry, and it allows the tradability of the industries to respond as productivity accumulates in this heterogeneous manner. This experiment is run 1,000 times, and the range of paths traced by the implied BS coefficient β among the runs is summarized (where, in the two-country experiment, β is simply the log price ratio divided by the log income ratio, as in previous sections).

For the starting cross-sectional distribution of productivity among these ten industries at the beginning of each experiment run, we simply take the distribution for the first year of the US productivity data set used in Section 4 above. Thus, the levels of the ten industries in the home country are set equal to the ten decile levels of productivity in the US data for 1958. For each of the 1,000 runs, a sequence of 40 random productivity shocks is drawn for each industry from a given Pareto probability distribution, representing 40 years of technological advancement. In any period, each firm uses its best draw to date; in this setting there is no technological regress (as with Gaussian shocks to productivity). The Pareto distribution was chosen here following the convention in the trade literature, which largely comes from the fact this distribution seems to characterize the highly skewed cross-sectional distribution of productivities and sizes among firms.

We also follow the literature in taking the draws to represent a change in the set of new ideas available to the industry. With each new draw, the sector has the choice of using the new productivity level or keeping the old one, whichever is higher.[19] The goal is to have a distribution for the home country at the end of 40 years of random draws that on average resembles the distribution for the last complete year in our data on the US productivity distribution, 1994. In particular, the data show a large number of industries with low levels of productivity gain, with a small number of industries with very high productivity gains. With suitably chosen parameters, the stochastic specification here is well-suited to reflect this feature.[20]

Figure 6 shows that this specification of stochastic productivity accumulation does lead to a cross-sectional distribution of productivity levels that resembles what we see in the data. The figure superimposes the distribution for the actual 1994 US productivity data (over 448 industries), and the 5–95% confidence band for the 1,000 draws of the terminal home productivity distribution in our benchmark simulation (over the 10 industry deciles). Regarding the foreign country, the initial productivity distribution is taken to be the same as for the home country, and it is simply held constant at this level throughout the experiment. So the experiment focuses on how the relative national price level evolves as the productivity distribution of the home country shifts up relative to that of the foreign country.

---

[19]This "extreme value" approach has convenient properties, such as converging in the limit to a Frechet distribution, which likewise seems to characterize the highly skewed shape of the cross-sectional distribution of productivities across firms.

[20]Here we provide further detail regarding the mechanics of the stochastic draws. For each period, random draws are taken for 1,000 industries, and the deciles of this distribution are assigned in random order to the 10 industries of the model. We do this rather than simply taking random draws in isolation for each of the 10 industries, since in this case there tended to be an occasional very extreme draws occurring somewhere in the experiment which prevented model solution. This problem is prevented by taking deciles from a larger set of draws. The idea is to reflect what an experiment would be like if we had 1,000 distinct industries rather than just 10. We should note that the tenth decile is actually the 9.8 decile of the distribution, to further limit the likelihood of very extreme draws that prevent model solution. To compensate for this truncation of the upper tail, we use more extreme Pareto distribution parameter values. The Pareto "scale" parameter is 0.001 and the "shape" parameter is 0.8. The 40 years of accumulated productivity in the experiment is combined additively with the initial productivity distribution.

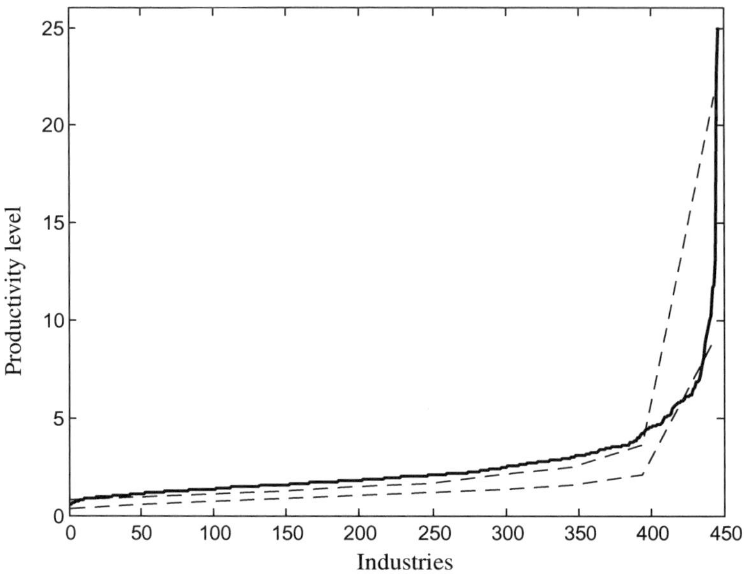

Figure 6. Final productivity distribution in data and simulations

Note: Distribution for actual 1994 data (solid line) and the 5–95% coverage band after 40 years of stochastic draws for the 10 deciles used for the endogenous n case (exogenous n case is similar).

Model parameters are calibrated as follows. The elasticity of substitution between different industries (ϕ) is 2, and the elasticity between brands within an industry (φ) is 6. The markup is derived from the latter value, and follows Rotemberg and Woodford (1992) and the convention in the open economy macro literature in implying a price markup of 20% over marginal cost.[21] The fixed cost (f_X) is calibrated at 0.10, so that the number of nontraded industries (n) for the initial distribution of productivity is 5 out of the 10 industries.

Table 3 reports the mean values for various summary statistics over the 1,000 runs after 10, 20, 30, and 40 years of technological accumulation. Note that the relative income of the home country rises over time, as does the relative price level, though the latter accelerates relative to the income level. The key result is that the BS coefficient indeed rises over time. This

[21]Since exports involve a fixed cost, the markup of export prices over average cost will be lower.

Table 3. Simulation results: Endogenous set of nontraded goods

Simulated year	Income ratio (y/y^*)	Price ratio (p/p^*)	BS coefficient $\left(\frac{\log(p/p^*)}{\log(y/y^*)}\right)$	Home nontraded share[1]	Foreign nontraded share[1]
0	1.00	1.00	—	0.50	0.50
10	1.11	1.00	0.024	0.59	0.50
20	1.28	1.04	0.147	0.71	0.48
30	1.44	1.08	0.213	0.78	0.43
40	1.61	1.12	0.233	0.84	0.40

Notes: Values reported are means over 1,000 stochastic simulations with calibration: $\phi = 2$, $\varphi = 6$, $f_X = 0.10$, Pareto shape parameter $= 0.8$, and Pareto scale parameter $= 0.001$.
[1]Nontraded share is the fraction of the ten industries not engaging in trade ($n/10$ or $n^*/10$).

is confirmed in Fig. 7, which plots the 5% and 95% bands for the BS coefficient among the 1,000 runs. Note that the bands for the initial period are wide and centered around zero, but that they narrow and rise over time. By the end of the 40 years, both bands are above the zero line, indicating that by the end of the period almost all of the 1,000 random experiments predicted a positive BS effect.[22]

A more detailed comparison of the time paths of the BS coefficients shows more nuance. Both the simulation and the empirical estimation indicate initial values for the BS coefficient that are insignificantly different from zero, and from each other. While both show a rise in the BS coefficient over time, the rate of increase in the simulation falls progressively in later periods, while that in the historical estimation is more irregular, with an acceleration at the end of the sample. Finally, the terminal value of the simulated BS coefficient is definitely below that observed in the historical estimation, with the confidence bands for each not quite intersecting with each other. We conclude that while the model can generate the general

[22]There is a debate as to whether it is reasonable to allow the definition of the price index to reflect changes in spending patterns implied by models of endogenous trade. Given the long time horizon, we consider in the present experiment, updating of the price index weights is not unreasonable. Nonetheless, it is worth noting that the result derived here does not rely upon such updating. If we hold constant the weighting of foreign and home goods in the price index, we still find that the BS effect rises over time and is strongly positive. In particular, the BS coefficients corresponding to those reported for our first experiment for years 10 through 40 are: 0.31, 0.75, 1.09, and 1.31.

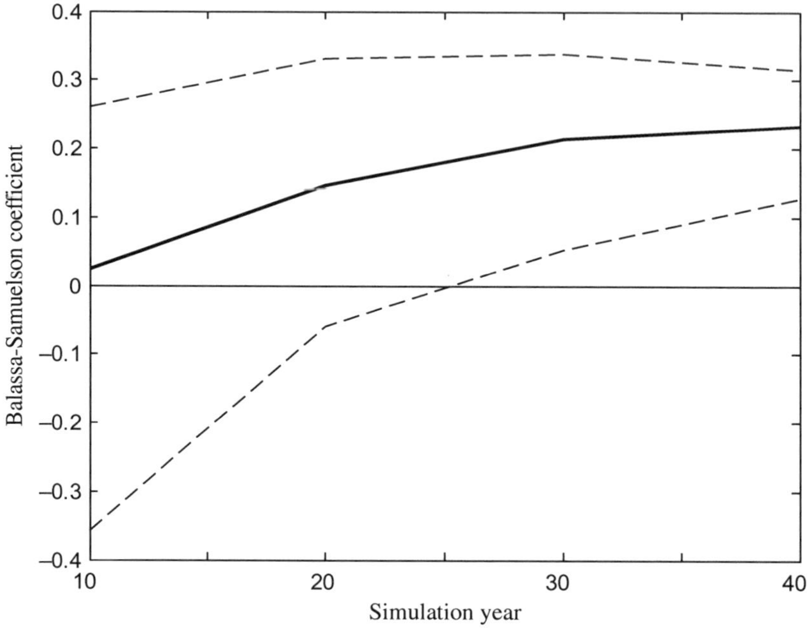

Figure 7. BS coefficient for stochastic simulation with endogenous nontraded goods
Note: Ratio of log price level over log income (solid line) with 5–95% coverage band (dashed lines).

upward trend observed in the BS coefficient, it remains too stylized to replicate some of the more detailed features of the time path.

Which feature of the model is most responsible for generating this rising BS coefficient in the simulation? Of distinct importance is the fact that the ordering of the industries in terms of their tradability evolved over the 40 years of the experiment. Consider one set of draws, where productivity gains happen to be concentrated in the industries that had low starting productivity levels and hence were the *a priori* nontraded industries. As productivity accumulates in these industries, this raises the relative productivity of the nontraded sector to be more similar to that of the traded, which generates a strong negative BS coefficient. But over time, these industries one by one surpass some of the *a priori* traded goods in terms of productivity and thereby become traded. The rise in wages generated by the productivity gains in these industries makes some of the *a priori* traded goods unprofitable enough so as not to cover the fixed cost of exporting, and these previously-traded industries then become nontraded. As a result, productivity ends up accumulating among industries that are traded ex post, which means the precondition for a positive BS effect is satisfied endogenously.

Table 3 also indicates a second effect at work generating the large positive BS coefficient. The last two columns show that in addition to changes in the relative tradability of industries, a progressively larger set of home industries are becoming nontraded over time. This again results from the fact that when the highly skewed Pareto distribution asserts itself over time, the small number of highly productive firms at the upper end of the distribution generates a significant rise in home wages. This forces out from trade a number of marginal industries. By the end of the 40 years, only 1 or 2 of the 10 industries engage in trade. This does not mean that the volume of trade is small, but just that the trade is highly concentrated in the most productive firms. As discussed in Section 4.3, this rise in the share of nontraded goods can amplify the positive BS effect.

To demonstrate the role of endogenous tradability in generating the rising BS effect, the next experiment closes off this effect. The set of industries that are permitted to trade is exogenously held constant throughout the experiment, rather than being allowed to evolve in response to the incidence of productivity gains. Table 4 and Fig. 8 show that a positive BS coefficient does not emerge here and does not grow over time. The mean BS coefficient is strongly negative and the 5–95% bands are wide, including

Table 4. Simulation results: Exogenous set of nontraded goods

Simulated year	Income ratio (y/y^*)	Price ratio (p/p^*)	BS coefficient $\left(\frac{\log(p/p^*)}{\log(y/y^*)}\right)$	Home nontraded share[1]	Foreign nontraded share[1]
0	1.00	1.00	—	0.50	0.50
10	1.11	0.95	−0.695	0.50	0.50
20	1.27	0.90	−0.686	0.50	0.50
30	1.42	0.86	−0.674	0.50	0.50
40	1.57	0.83	−0.659	0.50	0.50

Notes: Values reported are means over 1,000 stochastic simulations with calibration: $\phi = 2$, $\varphi = 6$, $f_X = 0.10$, Pareto shape parameter $= 0.8$, and Pareto scale parameter $= 0.001$.
[1]Nontraded share is the fraction of the ten industries not engaging in trade ($n/10$ or $n^*/10$).

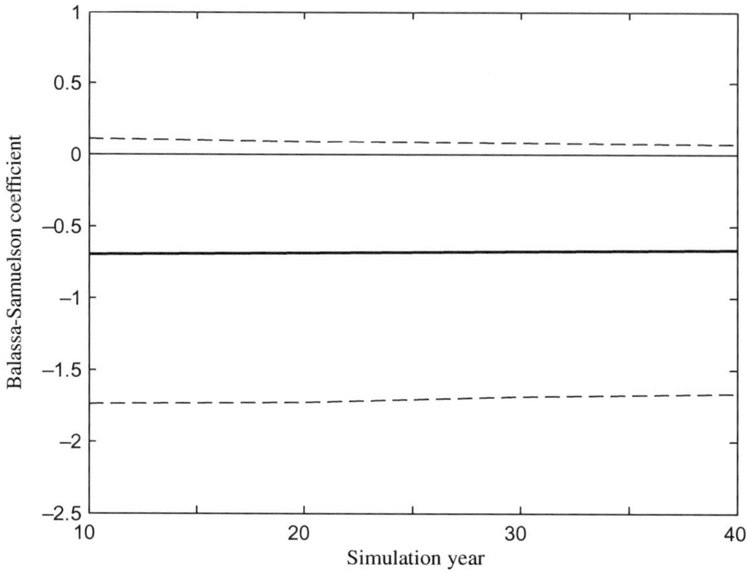

Figure 8. BS coefficient for stochastic simulation with exogenous set of nontraded goods
Note: Ratio of log price level over log income (solid line) with 5–95% coverage band (dashed lines).

a zero BS effect for all periods. Thus, endogenous tradability is necessary for our result.

Recall that there are two features of endogenous tradability at work to generate the BS effect in the benchmark experiment: the endogenous ranking of tradability and the endogenous share of nontraded goods. To distinguish the separate contributions of these two features, the final experiment here allows for the former but not the latter. The total number of traded industries is fixed exogenously, but the identity of the particular traded industries is determined endogenously in the model. More precisely, the ranking in terms of tradability of the 10 industries evolves endogenously in response to shocks, but only the 5 most tradable industries are allowed to trade in each period. Table 5 and Fig. 9 show that this case does generate a rising BS coefficient, but it is limited in how high a positive value it can achieve. The mean value of the 1,000 runs is only 0.04, much smaller than the benchmark experiment, but the 5–95% band does clear the 0 line by the end of the 40 years, indicating the positive sign of the coefficient, though

Table 5. Simulation results: Fixed share of nontraded goods ($n = n^* = 5$)

Simulated year	Income ratio (y/y^*)	Price ratio (p/p^*)	BS coefficient $\left(\frac{\log(p/p^*)}{\log(y/y^*)}\right)$	Home nontraded share[1]	Foreign nontraded share[1]
0	1.00	1.00	—	0.50	0.50
10	1.14	1.00	−0.031	0.50	0.50
20	1.35	1.01	0.028	0.50	0.50
30	1.55	1.02	0.040	0.50	0.50
40	1.75	1.02	0.043	0.50	0.50

Notes: Values reported are means over 1,000 stochastic simulations with calibration: $\phi = 2$, $\varphi = 6$, $f_X = 0.10$, Pareto shape parameter = 0.8, and Pareto scale parameter = 0.001.
[1]Nontraded share is the fraction of the ten industries not engaging in trade ($n/10$ or $n^*/10$).

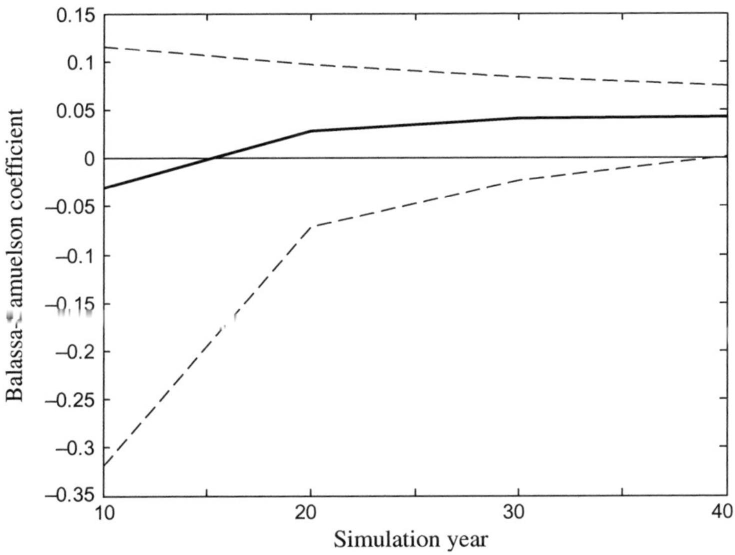

Figure 9. BS coefficient for stochastic simulation with fixed nontraded share, n

Note: Ratio of log price level over log income (solid line) with 5–95% coverage band (dashed lines).

small, is meaningful. The conclusion arising from these three experiments is that both the endogenous ordering of tradability and the endogenous concentration of traded goods are important contributors in replicating a rising BS coefficient.

6. Conclusion

This chapter has investigated the empirical basis of, and theoretical rationale for, the venerable BS effect over the very long run. The first surprise is that there is little to no support for this effect as of the mid 20th century, contrary to general conception. The second surprise is that this effect has grown steadily over time to rather large values in the most recent years. These observations invite new thinking, with implications for international economists, macroeconomists, and economic historians.

We present a new model that supplies a set of tools for thinking about these results and we think it will be of interest to theoreticians in various fields. International economists will find here a new application of endogenous tradability that is complementary to several new directions in the literature. Macroeconomists and economic historians interested in long-run growth in more than one sector will discover not only an important set of stylized facts but also some conjectures on how these should be modeled in terms of sectoral growth behavior.

The picture offered by our theoretical model is that the BS effect may be the product of a gradual evolutionary process in a growing economy. Productivity shocks that are heterogeneous among goods not only induce a response in relative prices, as usually conceived in a standard BS model, but they can also induce a response in the relative tradability of these goods as well. The new insight offered by the endogenous trade approach here, is that the BS effect need not be viewed as the chance outcome of shocks that happen to be biased toward an *a priori* traded sector, but rather it can be viewed as the natural, even likely, outcome of an evolutionary process that does not need to depend on the incidence of the shocks. But while the BS effect may be a likely outcome, this story implies that it can take time for the structure of the economy to adapt in response to the shocks and gradually express the BS effect.

We remain agnostic as to whether the most significant reordering of tradability occurs at the firm level or more aggregated industry level. Trade literature recently has provided evidence that significant shifts in tradability take place at the individual firm level. In this chapter, we have offered some suggestive evidence that reordering also has taken place at a more aggregated level between industries. But endogenous tradability at either level could usefully contribute to the mechanisms identified in our model which generate an endogenous and growing BS effect.

The finding here also has implications for the future of the BS theory. It has been observed that productivity gains in the service sector have been important for recent growth in many developed countries. Since services are commonly classified as part of the nontraded sector, this might be thought to imply a period of limited real exchange rate appreciations and shrinking BS coefficients. However, our research indicates that this need not be the case if the dividing line between traded and nontraded sectors evolves in response to these technological developments. Indeed, it appears that some service industries are becoming increasingly traded internationally, leading some commentators to argue that the world is becoming "flatter" (Friedman, 2005). This rise in tradability likely is not alone a response to a rise in productivity in these industries, but also a response to lower trade costs for services like telecommunications. Nonetheless, it underscores the importance of allowing for evolution in the traded–nontraded distinction when we endeavor to interpret the long-run behavior of the real exchange rate.

Appendix

A.1. Consumption

Our model consists of two countries, with each specializing in a range of goods that are uniquely produced in that country, denoted by H and F, respectively. Residents in each country consume a CES-weighted basket of locally-produced goods and tradable goods imported from the other country. The continuum of goods produced in each country is indexed by i on the interval $[0, 1]$. Let n and n^* denote the (endogenous) share of goods in each country that are nontraded, where goods are ordered such that $i \in [0, n], [0, n^*]$ are nontraded and $i \in [n, 1], [n^*, 1]$ are traded in the home and foreign country, respectively.

To derive expression (5) in the text for aggregate consumption by domestic residents C as a CES index of domestic consumption (C_H) and imports of the foreign country's traded (export) good (C_{FT}), we denote consumption by domestic residents of the individual varieties i of the home good and foreign goods as $c_{Hi}, i \in [0,1]$, and $c_{FTi}, i \in [0, 1-n^*]$, respectively. Indexing all goods available for consumption in the domestic country by j on the interval $[0, 2-n^*]$ and ordering consumption as $c_j = c_{Hi}$ for $j = i \in [0,1]$, and $c_j = c_{Fi}$ for $j = i+1, j \in [1, 2-n^*]$ implies[23]

$$
\begin{aligned}
C^{\frac{\phi-1}{\phi}} &= \left(\frac{1}{2-n^*}\right)^{\frac{1}{\phi}} \left[\int_0^1 (c_j)^{\frac{\phi-1}{\phi}} dj + \int_1^{2-n^*} (c_j)^{\frac{\phi-1}{\phi}} dj\right] \\
&= \left(\frac{1}{2-n^*}\right)^{\frac{1}{\phi}} \left(\frac{1}{1}\right)^{\frac{1}{\phi}} \int_0^1 (c_j)^{\frac{\phi-1}{\phi}} dj \\
&\quad + \left(\frac{1-n^*}{2-n^*}\right)^{\frac{1}{\phi}} \left(\frac{1}{1-n^*}\right)^{\frac{1}{\phi}} \int_1^{2-n^*} (c_j)^{\frac{\phi-1}{\phi}} dj \\
&= \left(\frac{1}{2-n^*}\right)^{\frac{1}{\phi}} (C_H)^{\frac{\phi-1}{\phi}} + \left(\frac{1-n^*}{2-n^*}\right)^{\frac{1}{\phi}} (C_{FT})^{\frac{\phi-1}{\phi}} \\
&= (\theta[n^*])^{\frac{1}{\phi}} (C_H)^{\frac{\phi-1}{\phi}} + (1-\theta[n^*])^{\frac{1}{\phi}} (C_{FT})^{\frac{\phi-1}{\phi}}
\end{aligned}
$$

where

$$
(C_H)^{\frac{\phi-1}{\phi}} \equiv \int_0^1 (c_{Hi})^{\frac{\phi-1}{\phi}}, \quad C_{FT} \equiv \left[\left(\frac{1}{1-n^*}\right)^{\frac{1}{\phi}} \int_{n^*}^1 (c_{Fi})^{\frac{\phi-1}{\phi}} di\right]^{\frac{\phi}{\phi-1}}, \tag{A1}
$$

$\phi > 1$ is the elasticity of substitution between all varieties, and $\theta[n^*]$ is the own-goods bias coefficient that depends (endogenously) on the number of varieties produced locally relative to the total number of varieties available to the domestic country:

$$
\theta[n^*] \equiv \frac{1}{2-n^*}, \quad 1-\theta[n^*] \equiv \frac{1-n^*}{2-n^*}, \quad 0 \le \theta[n^*] \le 1.
$$

[23]With the total mass of goods produced in each country normalized to $1, 1-n$, and $1-n^*$ also represent the number of goods in each country that are traded. Consequently, the total mass of varieties of goods available for consumption in the home country is the sum of the mass of domestic varieties and of the goods exported by the foreign country, i.e. $1 + (1 - n^*) = 2 - n^*$; analogously, the total mass of goods available in the foreign country is $2 - n$.

The derivation of the foreign consumption aggregate C^* is analogous. Observe that if $n = n^* = 0$ and all home and foreign varieties are traded, then there is no goods bias, i.e. $\theta[n] = \theta[n^*] = 1/2$. As n, n^* rise and fewer varieties are imported by each country, the relative weight placed on own goods rises and on imported goods falls, i.e. $\theta' > 0$.[24]

Consumption of each country's own-good (C_H, C_F^*) is in turn defined as a CES consumption index of its nontraded (C_{HN}, C_{FN}^*) and traded own goods (C_{HT}, C_{FT}^*), as given by (6) in the text, where

$$C_{HN} \equiv \left[\left(\frac{1}{n}\right)^{\frac{1}{\phi}} \int_0^n (c_{Hi})^{\frac{\phi-1}{\phi}} di\right]^{\frac{\phi}{\phi-1}},$$

$$C_{HT} \equiv \left[\left(\frac{1}{1-n}\right)^{\frac{1}{\phi}} \int_n^1 (c_{Hi})^{\frac{\phi-1}{\phi}} di\right]^{\frac{\phi}{\phi-1}} \tag{A2}$$

$$C_{FN}^* \equiv \left[\left(\frac{1}{n^*}\right)^{\frac{1}{\phi}} \int_0^{n^*} (c_{Fi}^*)^{\frac{\phi-1}{\phi}} di\right]^{\frac{\phi}{\phi-1}},$$

$$C_{FT}^* \equiv \left[\left(\frac{1}{1-n^*}\right)^{\frac{1}{\phi}} \int_{n^*}^1 (c_{Fi}^*)^{\frac{\phi-1}{\phi}} di\right]^{\frac{\phi}{\phi-1}} \tag{A3}$$

Note that the elasticity of substitution ϕ is assumed constant within and across countries.[25]

A.2. *Prices and relative demands*

Price indexes are defined as usual for each category of goods, in correspondence to the consumption indexes above:

$$P = (\theta[n^*](P_H)^{1-\phi} + (1-\theta[n^*])(P_{FT})^{1-\phi})^{\frac{1}{1-\phi}} \tag{A4}$$

[24]Since the mass of home (foreign) goods is normalized to 1, the bias coefficient of domestic (foreign) residents depends on n^* (n), the number of varieties of the foreign (domestic) good that are imported.

[25]That is, $c_{Hi}/c_{Hj} = (p_{Hi}/p_{Hj})^{-\phi}$ and $c_{Fi}^*/c_{Fj}^* = (p_{Fi}^*/p_{Fj}^*)^{-\phi}$ for any two goods i and j.

where

$$P_H^{1-\phi} = \int_0^n (p_{Hi})^{1-\phi} di + \int_n^1 (p_{Hi})^{1-\phi} di$$

$$= n(P_{HN})^{1-\phi} + (1-n)(P_{HT})^{1-\phi} \quad \text{(A5)}$$

$$P_{HN} \equiv \left(\left(\frac{1}{n}\right)\int_0^n p_{Hi}^{1-\phi} di\right)^{\frac{1}{1-\phi}}, \quad P_{HT} \equiv \left(\left(\frac{1}{1-n}\right)\int_n^1 p_{Hi}^{1-\phi} di\right)^{\frac{1}{1-\phi}} \quad \text{(A6)}$$

$$P_{FT} \equiv \left(\left(\frac{1}{1-n^*}\right)\int_{n^*}^1 p_{Fi}^{1-\phi} di\right)^{\frac{1}{1-\phi}} \quad \text{(A7)}$$

with P denoting the aggregate price level, P_H the price index of all home goods, P_{HN} the price index of nontraded home goods, P_{HT} the price index of traded home goods, and P_{FT} the price (to domestic residents) of imported foreign goods. The price indices for foreign goods and imported home goods (by foreign residents) are analogous.

Note that the consumption and price indices imply the following relative demand functions for domestic residents[26]:

$$C_H/C = (\theta[n^*])(P_H/P)^{-\phi}, \quad C_{FT}/C = (1-\theta[n^*])(P_{FT}/P)^{-\phi} \quad \text{(A8)}$$

$$C_{HN}/C_H = n(P_{HN}/P_H)^{-\phi}, \quad C_{HT}/C_H = (1-n)(P_{HT}/P_H)^{-\phi}. \quad \text{(A9)}$$

Again, the conditions for foreign residents are analogous.

A.3. *Production and productivity*

The production sector in each country consists of constant-returns-to-scale technologies for the output of each differentiated good, as given by (7) in the text. Profit maximization under monopolistic competition implies pricing is determined by the standard cost markup rules, given by (8) in the text.

[26]Also note that the CES specification implies for individual goods variety i

$$c_{Hi}/C_H = (p_{Hi}/P_H)^{-\phi}, \quad c_{Hi}/C_{HT} = (1-n)^{-1}(p_{Hi}/P_{HT})^{-\phi},$$
$$c_{Fi}/C_{FT} = (1-n^*)^{-1}(p_{Fi}/P_{FT})^{-\phi}$$

and $c_{Fi}^*/C_F^* = (p_{Fi}^*/P_F^*)^{-\phi}, \quad c_{Fi}^*/C_{FT}^* = (1-n^*)^{-1}(p_{Fi}^*/P_{FT}^*)^{-\phi},$

$$c_{Hi}^*/C_{HT}^* = (1-n)^{-1}(p_{Hi}^*/P_{HT}^*)^{-\phi}$$

It is straightforward to express the price index for nontraded and traded home goods in terms of the productivity averages by using (8) to substitute for p_{Hi}, p^*_{Hi} and (9) in turn to substitute with $\tilde{A}, \tilde{A}_T, \tilde{A}_N$ in (A6):

$$\begin{aligned} P_{HN} &= \left(\left(\frac{1}{n}\right)\left[\int_0^n \left(\frac{\varphi}{\varphi-1}\frac{W}{A_i}\right)^{1-\phi} di\right]\right)^{\frac{1}{1-\phi}} \\ &= \frac{\varphi}{\varphi-1}\left(\frac{W}{\tilde{A}_N[n]}\right) \qquad \text{(A10)} \\ P_{HT} &= P^*_{HT} \\ &= \left(\left(\frac{1}{1-n}\right)\left[\int_n^1 \left(\frac{\varphi}{\varphi-1}\frac{W}{A_i}\right)^{1-\phi} di\right]\right)^{\frac{1}{1-\phi}} \\ &= \left(\frac{\varphi}{\varphi-1}\right)\frac{W}{\tilde{A}_T[n]} \qquad \text{(A11)} \end{aligned}$$

with (A5) implying

$$P_H = \frac{\varphi}{\varphi-1}\frac{W}{\tilde{A}}. \qquad \text{(A12)}$$

Observe nontraded and traded goods depend on the share of nontraded goods n, which itself is an endogenous variable that will be solved as part of the general equilibrium system. Since $\tilde{A}$ is independent of n, the nontraded vs. traded goods composition of the economy affects P_H only through its effect on the average wage level in the economy.[27] The foreign counterparts are analogous.

A.4. *Marginal trading condition*

The equilibrium shares of nontraded goods n, n^* are determined by the condition that at the margin the (real) operating profits from exporting the nth home good equals the (real) fixed cost of exporting f_X, given by (10).

[27] In the absence of any transport costs at all, all goods are traded ($n = 0$), implying $\tilde{A} = \tilde{A}_T$, and $P_H = P_{HT} = P^*_{HT}$.

A.5. *Labor market equilibrium*

Labor market equilibrium in the domestic country requires that labor employed in the production of nontraded and traded home goods *plus* labor employed to cover the fixed costs of exporting equal the (exogenous) domestic labor supply L_H:

$$\int_0^n l_{Hi}di + \int_n^1 l_{Hi}di + (1-n)f_X = L_H. \tag{A13}$$

Substituting for l_{Hi} with the production function (7):

$$\int_0^n \frac{y_{Hi}}{A_i}di + \int_n^1 \frac{y_{Hi}}{A_i}di + (1-n)f_X = L_H \quad \text{or}$$

$$\int_0^n \frac{c_{Hi}}{A_i}di + \int_n^1 \frac{c_{Hi}+c^*_{Hi}}{A_i}di + (1-n)f_X = L_H$$

since $y_{Hi} = c_{Hi}$ for $i \in [0,n]$, $y_{Hi} = c_{Hi} + c^*_{Hi}$ for $i \in [n,1]$. Substituting with $c_{Hi}/C_H = (p_{Hi}/P_H)^{-\phi}$ and $c^*_{Hi}/C^*_{HT} = (1-n)^{-1}(p^*_{Hi}/P^*_{HT})^{-\phi}$ gives

$$\int_0^n \frac{C_H}{A_i}\left(\frac{p_{Hi}}{P_H}\right)^{-\phi} di + \int_n^1 \left(\frac{1}{A_i}\right)\left[C_H\left(\frac{p_{Hi}}{P_H}\right)^{-\phi} + \left(\frac{1}{1-n}\right)C^*_{HT}\left(\frac{p^*_{Hi}}{P^*_{HT}}\right)^{-\phi}\right]di + (1-n)f_X = L_H.$$

Using (8) to substitute for p_{Hi}, p^*_{Hi} and (9) to substitute with $\tilde{A}, \tilde{A}_T[n]$ gives

$$W = (L_H - (1-n)f_X)^{-1/\phi}\left(\frac{\varphi-1}{\varphi}\right) \times \left[\left(\frac{P_H C_H}{(P_H)^{1-\phi}}\right)(\tilde{A})^{\phi-1} + \left(\frac{P^*_{HT}C^*_{HT}}{(P^*_{HT})^{1-\phi}}\right)(\tilde{A}_T[n])^{\phi-1}\right]^{\frac{1}{\phi}}.$$

Substituting for P_H, P^*_{HT} with (A11), and (A12) and canceling terms gives

$$WL_H - (1-n)f_X W = \left(\frac{\varphi-1}{\varphi}\right)[P_H C_H + P^*_{HT}C^*_{HT}] \tag{A14}$$

i.e. the domestic wage bill — net of wages paid for workers employed in covering fixed costs, $W(1-n)f_X$ — is proportional to the value of home goods consumed domestically or exported, with the proportionality constant equal to 1 minus the profit rate $1/\varphi$. The foreign counterpart expression is analogous.

A.6. *Closing the model*

We close the model with the balanced trade condition that the value of exports equals the value of imports

$$P^*_{HT} C^*_{HT} = P_{FT} C_{FT} \tag{A15}$$

and the normalization condition

$$P^* = 1. \tag{A16}$$

Equilibrium determines the 24 variables $C, C_H, C_{HN}, C_{HT}, C_{FT} P, P_H, P_{HN}, P_{HT}, P_{FT}, W$, and n and their foreign counterparts (denoted by *) by solving the system of 24 equations (5), (6), (A1)–(A5), (A10)–(A11), (11), and (A14) plus their foreign counterparts, together with (A15) and (A16).

A.7. *Tradability condition and the real exchange rate*

Further insights may be obtained by developing the marginal export condition and a relative price expression in terms of productivity averages. Since the condition $c^*_{Hi}/C^*_{HT} = (1-n)^{-1}(p^*_{Hi}/P^*_{HT})^{-\phi}$ holds for all goods i in the range $[n, 1]$ (see footnote 27), it can be used to substitute for c^*_{Hn} in (10). Canceling the variable P from both sides, substituting for p^*_{Hn} with (8), multiplying and dividing by P^*_{HT}, and lastly substituting with (A11) for P^*_{HT} in the denominator on the left-hand side gives (11). Expression (12) for the real exchange rate is obtained by using (A11) and (A12), and their foreign analogues to substitute for $P_H, P^*_{HT}, P^*_F, P_{FT}$, respectively, in the definitions of P, P^* given by (A4) and its foreign counterpart.

Acknowledgment

Taylor gratefully acknowledges the support of the Chancellor's Fellowship at the University of California, Davis. We thank David Jacks, Alyson Ma, Sandra Naylor, and Janine Wilson for excellent research assistance. For helpful comments we thank Stephen Broadberry, Nicholas Crafts, Robert

Feenstra, Maurice Obstfeld, Mark Taylor, Marianne Ward, and seminar participants at Australian National University; University of Adelaide; Claremont McKenna College; Columbia University; New York University; University of California, Berkeley; University of California, Davis; University of Southern California; University of Texas; the NBER International Trade and Investment program meeting (Palo Alto, 2003); the European Summer Symposium in International Macroeconomics (Limassol, Cyprus, 2005); and the European Economic Association meetings (Amsterdam, 2005). The views expressed below do not represent those of the Federal Reserve Bank of San Francisco or the Board of Governors of the Federal Reserve System. All errors are ours.

References

Balassa, B. 1964. The purchasing-power parity doctrine: A reappraisal, *Journal of Political Economy*, 72: 584–596.

Bartelsman, E. and W. Gray. 1996. The NBER manufacturing productivity database, Technical Working Paper No. 205, National Bureau of Economic Research.

Bergin, P. R. and R. Glick. 2003. Endogenous nontradability and macroeconomic implications, Working Paper Series No. 9739, National Bureau of Economic Research.

Bergin, P. R. and R. Glick. 2004. *Tradability, Productivity, and Understanding International Integration*, University of California at Davis mimeo.

Bernard, A. and J. B. Jensen. 1999. Exporting and productivity, Working Paper Series No. 7135, National Bureau of Economic Research.

Betts, C. and T. Kehoe. 2005. U.S. real exchange rate fluctuations and relative price fluctuations, forthcoming in *Journal of Monetary Economics*.

Bhagwati, J. N. 1984. Why are services cheaper in the poor countries? *Economic Journal*, 94: 279–286.

Burstein, A., M. Eichenbaum and S. Rebelo. 2005. Large devaluations and the real exchange rate, forthcoming in *Journal of Political Economy*, 113: 742–784.

Chinn, M. D. 2000. The usual suspects? Productivity and demand shocks and Asia-Pacific real exchange rates. *Review of International Economics*, 8: 20–43.

Chinn, M. D. and L. Johnston. 1996. Real exchange rate levels, productivity and demand shocks. Working Paper Series No. 5709, National Bureau of Economic Research.

Clague, C. and V. Tanzi. 1972. Human capital, natural resources and the purchasing-power parity doctrine: Some empirical results. *Economia Internazionale*, 25: 3–18.

De Gregorio, J., A. Giovannini, and H. C. Wolf. 1994. International evidence on tradable and nontradables inflation. *European Economic Review*, 38: 1225–1244.

De Gregorio, J. and H. C. Wolf. 1994. Terms of trade, productivity, and the real exchange rate. Working Paper Series No. 4807, *National Bureau of Economic Research.*

Eaton, J. and S. Kortum. 2002. Technology, geography, and trade. *Econometrica*, 70: 1741–1779.

Fitzgerald, D. 2003. *Terms-of-Trade Effects, Interdependence and Cross-country Differences in Price Levels*, Photocopy, Harvard University.

Friedman, T. L. 2005. *The World is Flat: A Brief History of the Twenty-first Century.* Farrar Straus & Giroux, New York.

Froot, K. A. and K. Rogoff. 1995. Perspectives on PPP and long-run real exchange rates, in: G. Grossman and K. Rogoff, (eds.), *Handbook of International Economics*, Vol. 3, North-Holland, Amsterdam, pp. 1647–1688.

Ghironi, F. and M. J. Melitz. 2004. International trade and macroeconomic dynamics with heterogeneous firms, Working Paper Series No. 10540, *National Bureau of Economic Research.*

Helpman, E., M. J. Melitz, and S. R. Yeaple. 2004. Export versus FDI with heterogeneous firms. *American Economic Review*, 94: 300–316.

Hsieh, D. 1982. The determination of the real exchange rate: the productivity approach. *Journal of International Economics*, 12: 355–362.

Ito, T., P. Isard and S. Symansky. 1999. Economic growth and real exchange rate: An overview of the Balassa–Samuelson hypothesis in Asia, in Ito, T. and Krueger, A. O. (eds.), *Changes in Exchange Rates in Rapidly Developing Countries: Theory, Practice and Policy Issues*, University of Chicago Press, Chicago, pp. 109–128.

Kehoe, T. J. and K. J. Ruhl. 2002. How Important is the New Goods Margin in International Trade? Working paper, University of Minnesota.

Krugman, P. and M. Obstfeld, 2003. *International Economics: Theory and Policy.* 6th edition, Addison-Wesley, Reading, Mass.

Lothian, J. R. and M. P. Taylor. 2004. *Real Exchange Rates Over the Past Two Centuries: How Important is the Harrod–Balassa–Samuelson effect?* Fordham University. Photocopy.

Marston, R. C. 1990. Systematic movements in real exchange rates in the G-5: Evidence on the integration of internal and external markets, *Journal of Banking and Finance*, 14: 1023–1044.

Melitz, M. 2003. The impact of trade on intra-industry reallocations and aggregate industry productivity, *Econometrica*, 71: 1695–1726.

Micossi, S. and G. M. Milesi-Ferretti, 1994. Real exchange rates and the prices of nontradable goods. Working Papers No. 94/19, International Monetary Fund.

Officer, L. H. 1982. *Purchasing Power Parity and Exchange Rates: Theory, Evidence and Relevance*, JAI Press, Greenwich, Connecticut.

Richardson, J. D. and K. Rindal. 1996. *Why Exports Matter: More*! Institute for International Economics, Washington, D.C.

Rotemberg, J. J. and M. Woodford. 1992. Oligopolistic pricing and the effects of aggregate demand on economic activity. *Journal of Political Economy*, 100: 1153–1207.

Samuelson, P. A. 1964. Theoretical notes on trade problems. *Review of Economics and Statistics*, 46: 145–154.

Sarno, L. and M. P. Taylor. 2002. *The Economics of Exchange Rates*. Cambridge University Press, Cambridge.

Taylor, M. P., and A. M. Taylor. 2004. The purchasing power parity debate, *Journal of Economic Perspectives*, 8: 135–158.

CHAPTER 9

Tradability, Productivity, and International Economic Integration*

Paul R. Bergin[†,§] and Reuven Glick[‡,¶]

[†] *Department of Economics, University of California at Davis, One Shields Ave., Davis, CA 95616, USA*

[‡] *Economic Research Department, Federal Reserve Bank of San Francisco*

[§] *prbergin@ucdavis.edu*

[¶] *reuven.glick@sf.frb.org*

1. Introduction

This chapter studies the implications of international goods market integration for price dispersion by developing a theoretical model where goods are endogenously tradable and heterogeneous. Empirical studies of recent episodes of international goods market integration in Europe and North America have produced a richer picture of how market integration affects cross-border trade and price differences. This picture has pointed out limitations in existing open economy macro models.

One empirical finding relates to quantities, in particular, the fact that trade integration works in part through increases at the extensive margin of goods not previously traded. For example, consider the set of "least traded goods" prior to the North American Free Trade Agreement (NAFTA), defined as the set of 4-digit SITC industries ordered

*This article originally appeared in *Journal of International Economics* (2007), 73(1), 128–151.

Table 1. Trade response to integration

Exporting country	Importing country or region	Least traded goods, as share of total exports		Total exports (mil$)		Increase in least traded goods exports/increase in total exports
		1990	2000	1990	2000	
Sweden	EU	0.10	0.17	40,959	44,862	2.02
Italy	EU	0.10	0.14	111,485	124,438	1.44
Portugal	EU	0.10	0.19	13,607	17,727	0.86
France	EU	0.10	0.13	116,917	190,043	0.35
UK	EU	0.10	0.14	88,793	153,943	0.34
Spain	EU	0.10	0.16	40,629	71,384	0.25
		1989	1999	1989	1999	
Canada	Mexico	0.10	0.42	525	953	0.99
Mexico	Canada	0.10	0.28	1,578	5,825	0.41
Mexico	US	0.10	0.17	27,590	101,842	0.25
US	Mexico	0.10	0.16	24,969	80,342	0.24

Note: Increase in least traded goods exports relative to increase in total exports defined as col5 = [col2 × col4 − (col1) × (col3)]/[col4 − col3].

Sources: Exports of least traded goods accounting for 10% or less of total trade in 1989 or 1990, from Kehoe and Ruhl (2002); total trade figures from *Direction of Trade* Yearbooks 1996, 2003, 1999, and 2000 figures deflated by US GDP goods deflator.

in terms of trade shares, from that with the lowest trade share up to the point that they collectively account for 10% of trade between the US, Canada, and Mexico. During the 1990s, these least traded goods accounted for roughly 25% of increased Mexican exports to the US, 40% of increased Mexican exports to Canada, and almost 100% of increased Canadian exports to Mexico. (See Table 1, showing calculations based on data from Kehoe and Ruhl (2002)). In the case of the European Union's implementation of the Single Market Program in the early 1990s, least traded goods accounted for more than 100% of the increased trade of Sweden and Italy and almost 90% of that of Portugal with the rest of Europe.

A second empirical finding relates to the price effects of market integration. The top panel of Table 2 extends the analysis of Engel and Rogers (2004) with more recent Economist Intelligence Unit (EIU) data on price dispersion across European countries. It shows that the implications of

Table 2. Price dispersion response to integration

Country pairs or region	Change in price dispersion			
	1990–1994	1994–1998	1998–2004	
Euro zone, all country pairs	−8.70	−0.14	3.02	
Core–core pairs	−4.49	0.40	4.14	
Peripheral–core pairs	−11.11	−0.54	2.44	
Peripheral–peripheral pairs	−24.34	−1.70	−0.91	
	1990–1994	1994–2001	1990–1993	1996–2001
North America, all country pairs	−9.11	7.49	−9.38	7.69
Mexico–Canada	−31.95	21.78	−33.00	17.51
Mexico–US	−27.95	16.86	−27.71	8.08
US–Canada	−2.46	3.95	−2.79	6.76

Notes: Positive values imply price divergence; negative values imply price convergence. Peripheral countries in the Eurozone are Finland, Ireland, Portugal, and Spain; core countries are Austria, Belgium, France, Germany, Italy, Luxemburg, and Netherlands. Calculations based on mean squared error of product price differences across cities. Since some countries are represented by more than one city, the reported dispersion figures for all country pairs differ from the average of figures for the subset pairs.

Sources: EIU Citybase data and authors' calculations. See Engel and Rogers (2004) for the cities used and the product items included.

market integration for price convergence can vary widely: there was significant price convergence in the early 1990s with the Single Market Program, but little to no convergence after the European Monetary Union (EMU) was established in 1999. The bottom panel of Table 2 shows a similar result for North America: Price dispersion declined considerably in the early 1990s, but appeared to increase after 1994 at the time of the adoption of NAFTA.[1]

Standard open economy macro models are ill-suited for studying such dynamics of economic integration, since they tend to posit by assumption that a good is either tradable or nontradable by nature, and that a firm is either able to price to market or not by assumption. Recent advances have been made in modeling the costs of trade, and how they determine the decision of firms to export and the export price that is set (see Melitz, 2003; Ghironi and Melitz, 2005; Kehoe and Ruhl, 2002; Ruhl, 2003). This chapter

[1]This result is unaffected if the peso crisis years of 1994 and 1995 are excluded.

builds upon this endogenous trade approach, to study how extensive margin movements interact with firm heterogeneity to influence price convergence. Of special importance is how new entrants differ in systematic ways from incumbent traders.

The model considers the possibility of two types of heterogeneity that might be at work. In addition to the productivity heterogeneity common in the trade literature, we also consider the possibility of heterogeneity in terms of trade costs. Hummels (1999, 2001) and Anderson and van Wincoop (2004) have emphasized that trade costs vary widely over different types of goods, depending on factors such as weight, distance, and the time sensitivity of demand. Further, models without trade cost heterogeneity have difficulty explaining recent findings regarding price deviations in Crucini, Telmer, and Zachariadis (2005): Firstly, international price wedges vary widely, and secondly, higher price wedges are associated with less traded goods.[2] While trade cost heterogeneity is most readily apparent at the goods level, it potentially may also operate at the firm level, due to variation in firm characteristics, such as their geographic location or size.[3] Although this model is among the first to explore theoretically the implications of heterogeneity in per-unit trade costs, our results are in no way dependent on this. In fact, one of our findings is that heterogeneity in this dimension is isomorphic to the more familiar productivity heterogeneity, in terms of their implications for the extensive margin and the resulting changes in price dispersion.

This chapter formulates a two-country two-good macro model where each country specializes in the production of a single good. Each good is available in a continuum of distinct varieties produced by monopolistically

[2]For example, the classic model of Dornbusch, Fisher, and Samuelson (1977) ranks goods by their productivities, while the size of trade costs are assumed to be uniform. Those goods with the greatest comparative advantage in one country or the other are traded, while those goods with small gains from trading relative to the uniform trade costs remain nontraded. This implies that international price wedges are smallest for nontraded goods.

[3]The model of Chaney (2006) also allows for heterogeneity in trade costs, though this is at the sectoral level, rather than the firm level where extensive margin movements take place. The possibility of trade cost heterogeneity at the firm level might be understood to reflect differences in the distribution of firms geographically, where firms with a shorter distance to travel to a border or port have lower transportation costs. This heterogeneity might also reflect a spillover from heterogeneity among firms in terms of size or productivity, if some portion of the distribution service needed for trade is produced within the firm.

competitive firms, which must choose whether to sell in the domestic market alone or also export to the foreign market. This decision is affected by two types of real trade frictions: One in the form of per-unit iceberg trade costs which can vary by variety, and the other a fixed cost of international trade which does not depend upon the quantity traded and does not vary by variety. The first type of cost is motivated by tariffs and transportation costs, as discussed above; the second type reflects establishment costs or the cost of learning to deal with a foreign language or legal system.[4]

The model shows that the implications of market integration policies depend greatly on whether the policy works through reductions in tariffs or fixed costs of trade. A general implication is that when trade integration works more through the extensive margin entry of previously nontraded varieties, the degree of price convergence will be weakest. Part of the intuition is that reductions in the fixed costs of trade are associated with greater extensive margin shifts, but less price adjustment. While tariff reductions have large direct effects on the price setting behavior of monopolistically competitive firms through their marginal costs, this is not so for fixed costs. A second part of the intuition is that if the decision by firms to trade is endogenous, then new entrants will differ systematically from incumbent traders. Under productivity heterogeneity, new entrants will be less productive; under trade cost heterogeneity they will have higher trade costs. In either case, new entrants will charge higher prices than incumbent traders, which will tend to worsen the average international price wedge for a country's exports. Depending on the strength of these two effects, trade integration can have a wide range of implications for international price deviations.

The final section of the chapter studies cross-sectional regressions for European data on price dispersion and extensive margins. These are found to support the prediction of the model. In particular, we find consistently across periods that a greater movement at the extensive margin has a negative effect on the degree of price convergence.

[4]The distribution services in the models of Corsetti and Dedola (2005) and Burstein, Neves, and Rebelo (2003) are related in spirit to our trade costs, in that they also generate international price wedges. However, they differ from trade costs by typically involving the use of a nontraded service produced in the destination country.

2. Model Specification

The model consists of two countries, home and foreign, each of which produces a distinct country-specific good, labeled H and F, respectively. Each country's good is available in a continuum of differentiated varieties, produced by monopolistically competitive firms using labor as the sole input.

In principle, any good can be exported, but there are variable costs τ and fixed costs of exporting f_X for any good, which are borne by the exporting firm. Consequently, an endogenously determined fraction will be nontraded in equilibrium. Nontraded goods are labeled N and traded goods T. Home and foreign agents consume constant elasticity of substitution (CES) aggregates of their own domestic good and the other country's traded (export) good varieties. Quantities and prevailing prices for the goods varieties consumed in the foreign country are denoted by *. (Below we present consumption and price expressions for the home country only; corresponding foreign expressions are analogous.)[5]

2.1. *Consumption and prices*

The varieties in each country are indexed by i on the unit interval [0, 1]. Let n denote the endogenous share of these varieties in the home country that are nontraded, where varieties are ordered such that $i \in [0, n]$ are nontraded and $i \in [n, 1]$ are traded. (Analogously, n^* represents the share of foreign nontraded goods.) Residents consume a basket of locally-produced varieties and tradable good varieties imported from the other country. Consequently, the total mass of varieties of goods available for consumption in the home country is the sum of the mass of domestic varieties and of the good varieties exported by the foreign country, i.e. $1 + (1 - n^*) = 2 - n^*$.

Accordingly, aggregate consumption (C) is defined as a CES aggregate of consumption of the home country's own good (C_H) and imports of the foreign country's traded good varieties (C_{FT}):

$$C = \left((\theta[n^*])^{\frac{1}{\phi}}(C_H)^{\frac{\phi-1}{\phi}} + (1 - \theta[n^*])^{\frac{1}{\phi}}(C_{FT})^{\frac{\phi-1}{\phi}}\right)^{\frac{\phi}{\phi-1}}, \qquad (1)$$

[5]Bergin, Glick, and Taylor (forthcoming) formulate a similar model without iceberg costs in order to investigate the effects of productivity growth on the real exchange rate and the range of goods traded.

where $\phi > 1$ is the elasticity of substitution between home and foreign goods, and $\theta[n^*]$ is the own-good bias coefficient that depends endogenously on the number of imported varieties (see the appendix for the derivation):

$$\theta[n^*] \equiv \frac{1}{2-n^*}, \quad 1-\theta[n^*] \equiv \frac{1-n^*}{2-n^*}, \quad 0 \leq \theta[n^*] \leq 1.$$

As n^* rises and fewer varieties are imported by domestic residents, the relative weight in the consumption basket placed on the home good rises, i.e. $\theta' > 0$.

Consumption of the home country's own-good is in turn defined as a CES consumption index of its nontraded (C_{HN}) and traded own varieties (C_{HT}):

$$\begin{aligned}(C_H)^{\frac{\phi-1}{\phi}} &= \int_0^n (c_{Hi})^{\frac{\phi-1}{\phi}} + \int_n^1 (c_{Hi})^{\frac{\phi-1}{\phi}} di \\ &= \left(\frac{C_{HN}}{n}\right)^{\frac{\phi-1}{\phi}} + (1-n)\left(\frac{C_{HT}}{1-n}\right)^{\frac{\phi-1}{\phi}}, \end{aligned} \tag{2}$$

where

$$C_{HN} = \left[\left(\frac{1}{n}\right)^{\frac{1}{\phi}} \int_0^n (c_{Hi})^{\frac{\phi-1}{\phi}} di\right]^{\frac{\phi}{\phi-1}}, \tag{3}$$

$$C_{HT} \equiv \left[\left(\frac{1}{1-n}\right)^{\frac{1}{\phi}} \int_n^1 (c_{Hi})^{\frac{\phi-1}{\phi}} di\right]^{\frac{\phi}{\phi-1}} \tag{4}$$

and lower cases are used to denote consumption of individual varieties i of each differentiated good.[6] The elasticity of substitution among individual

[6]Our specification follows the tradition of standard open economy macro models by defining consumption aggregates as the sum of consumptions of individual varieties. This rules out the "love of variety" effect characteristic of Dixit–Stiglitz specifications which imply that utility rises nonlinearly with the number of varieties consumed. Benassy (1996) formulates a general specification of aggregate consumption with a parameter that nests "no love of variety" and "Dixit–Stiglitz love" as special cases; our specification corresponds to the case that exhibits no love of variety.

varieties of the home good and the foreign good is also assumed equal to ϕ.[7] At home, the HN varieties occupy $[0, n]$ and the HT varieties $[n, 1]$.

Analogously, the consumption index of the foreign good varieties imported by domestic residents C_{FT} is defined as

$$C_{FT} \equiv \left[\left(\frac{1}{1-n^*} \right)^{\frac{1}{\phi}} \int_{n^*}^{1} (c_{Fi})^{\frac{\phi-1}{\phi}} di \right]^{\frac{\phi}{\phi-1}}. \tag{5}$$

Price indexes are defined as usual for each range of varieties, in correspondence to the consumption indices above:

$$P = (\theta[n^*](P_H)^{1-\phi} + (1-\theta[n^*])(P_{FT})^{1-\phi})^{\frac{1}{1-\phi}} \tag{6}$$

where

$$\begin{aligned} P_H^{1-\phi} &= \int_0^n (p_{Hi})^{1-\phi} di + \int_n^1 (p_{Hi})^{1-\phi} di \\ &= n(P_{HN})^{1-\phi} + (1-n)(P_{HT})^{1-\phi}, \end{aligned} \tag{7}$$

$$P_{HN} \equiv \left(\left(\frac{1}{n} \right) \int_0^n p_{Hi}^{1-\phi} di \right)^{\frac{1}{1-\phi}}, \tag{8}$$

$$P_{HT} \equiv \left(\left(\frac{1}{1-n} \right) \int_n^1 p_{Hi}^{1-\phi} di \right)^{\frac{1}{1-\phi}}, \tag{9}$$

$$P_{FT} \equiv \left(\left(\frac{1}{1-n^*} \right) \int_{n^*}^1 p_{Fi}^{1-\phi} di \right)^{\frac{1}{1-\phi}}, \tag{10}$$

where P is the aggregate domestic country price level, P_H is the price index of the home good, P_{HN} is the price index of nontraded home varieties, P_{HT} is the price index of traded home varieties, and P_{FT} is the price (to domestic residents) of the imported foreign good.

[7]In our specification with endogenous home bias weights, the elasticity between the home and foreign goods must be the same as that among individual varieties of home (and foreign) goods. With exogenous home bias weights, this constraint can be dropped and different elasticities can be posited.

These imply relative demand functions for domestic residents:[8]

$$C_H/C = (\theta[n^*])(P_H/P)^{-\phi}, \quad C_{FT}/C = (1-\theta[n^*])(P_{FT}/P)^{-\phi} \tag{11}$$

$$C_{HN}/C_H = n(P_{HN}/P_H)^{-\phi}, \quad C_{HT}/C_H = (1-n)(P_{HT}/P_H)^{-\phi}. \tag{12}$$

2.2. *Production and productivity*

The production sector in each country consists of constant-returns-to-scale technologies for the output of each differentiated good:

$$y_{Hi} = A_i l_{Hi}, \tag{13}$$

where y_{Hi} represents the level of home output, l_{Hi} denote workers employed in production, and A_i is the home productivity coefficient for each individual variety i. Labor is mobile across sectors within each economy, but immobile across countries.

Profit maximization under monopolistic competition implies pricing is determined by the standard cost markup rule. For domestic sales of all home varieties, either traded or nontraded:

$$p_{Hi} = \frac{\phi}{\phi-1}\frac{W}{A_i}, \quad i \in [0,1], \tag{14}$$

where W denotes the home wage rate, and $\phi/(1-\phi)$ is the markup. For export sales of traded varieties,

$$p^*_{Hi} = \frac{\phi}{\phi-1}\frac{W}{A_i}\frac{1}{1-\tau_i}, \quad i \in [n,1], \tag{15}$$

$$p_{Fi} = \frac{\phi}{\phi-1}\frac{W}{A_i}\frac{1}{1-\tau^*_i}, \quad i \in [n^*,1] \tag{16}$$

where $\tau_i (0 < 1-\tau_i < 1)$ is the fraction of each variety i lost during shipment and it is assumed that consumers fully absorb these iceberg costs of shipping. Thus for each traded varieties the foreign sales price exceeds

---

[8] Also note that the CES specification implies for individual good variety i $c_{Hi}/C_H = (p_{Hi}/P_H)^{-\phi}$, $c_{Hi}/C_{HT} = (1-n)^{-1}(p_{Hi}/P_{HT})^{-\phi}$, and $c_{Fi}/C_{FT} = (1-n^*)^{-1}(p_{Fi}/P_{FT})^{-\phi}$.

the domestic price by the proportion $1/(1-\tau_i) > 1$:

$$p^*_{Hi} = p_{Hi}\frac{1}{1-\tau_i}, \quad p_{Fi} = p^*_{Fi}\frac{1}{1-\tau^*_i}.$$

An important feature of the model is the distribution of productivities across each country. Firms in the domestic country have a distribution of productivity levels given by $F[A_i]$. Among these firms, $n = 1 - F[A_n]$ are nontraders and $1 - n = F[A_n]$ are exporters.

We define special weighted productivity averages for home varieties $\tilde{A}$, nontraded home varieties $\tilde{A}_N$, and traded home varieties $\tilde{A}_T$:[9]

$$(\tilde{A})^{\phi-1} \equiv \int_0^1 A_i^{\phi-1}\, di, \tag{17}$$

$$(\tilde{A}_N[n])^{\phi-1} \equiv \frac{1}{n}\int_0^n (A_i)^{\phi-1}\, di, \tag{18}$$

$$(\tilde{A}_T[n])^{\phi-1} \equiv \left(\frac{1}{1-n}\right)\int_n^1 A_i^{\phi-1}\, di. \tag{19}$$

If varieties are ordered with increasing productivity, then $\partial\tilde{A}_T/\partial n > 0$, $\partial\tilde{A}_N/\partial n < 0$, i.e. average productivity rises (falls) in the traded sector (nontraded) sector with increasing n. Intuitively, as the share of nontraded varieties in the economy rises, varieties at the low productivity end of the traded varieties sector become nontraded, and the average level of productivity of all remaining traded varieties rises.

Trade costs may also vary heterogeneously across varieties. We define the "effective" productivity of home good exports as $A_i(1-\tau_i)$, i.e. productivity adjusted by the trade costs of varieties exported abroad, since higher τ effectively lowers the productivity of these varieties relative to the same varieties sold domestically.

We define the *average* effective productivity of home exports $\tilde{A}_{(1-\tau)T}$ as

$$(\tilde{A}_{(1-\tau)T}[n])^{\phi-1} \equiv \left(\frac{1}{1-n}\right)\int_n^1 ((1-\tau_i)A_i)^{\phi-1}\, di \tag{20}$$

where the "T" in the subscript indicates that these averages are computed over the range of varieties that are traded. It is straightforward to express

[9]As pointed out by Melitz (2003), weighting by the elasticity parameter ϕ, makes the weights proportional to the relative output shares of firms.

the price index for nontraded and traded home good varieties in terms of these productivity averages by using (14) to substitute for p_{Hi} in (8) and (9):

$$P_{HN} = \frac{\phi}{\phi - 1}\left(\frac{W}{\tilde{A}_N[n]}\right), \tag{21}$$

$$P_{HT} = \left(\frac{\phi}{\phi - 1}\right)\frac{W}{\tilde{A}_T[n]} \tag{22}$$

with (7) implying

$$P_H = \frac{\phi}{\phi - 1}\frac{W}{\tilde{A}}. \tag{23}$$

Correspondingly, the price of home varieties exported to foreign residents is

$$P^*_{HT} = \left(\frac{\phi}{\phi - 1}\right)\frac{W}{\tilde{A}_{(1-\tau)T}[n]}. \tag{24}$$

Observe that these prices are increasing in the wage rate and decreasing in average productivity.

2.3. *Marginal trading condition*

The additional profit to a home firm i of exporting to the foreign market may be written:

$$\pi^*_{Hi} = \left(p^*_{Hi} - \frac{W}{A_i}\frac{1}{1-\tau_i}\right)c^*_{Hi} - Wf_X \tag{25a}$$

where the operating profits are defined as the export price minus marginal cost, *times* the volume of sales to foreign residents. We follow Ghironi and Melitz (2005) in assuming that firms employ domestic workers to cover the fixed costs. With f_X measured in units of effective domestic labor and W as the wage rate of this labor, labor costs are expressed as Wf_X. If this additional profit is positive, the firm will choose to export; if negative, the firm will not. This provides the condition that pins down the index of the marginal trading firm and hence the share of nontraded goods. For firm index $i = n$, the profit from exporting is exactly zero, so

$$\left(p_{Hn}^{*} - \frac{W}{A_n}\frac{1}{1-\tau_n}\right) c_{Hn}^{*} = Wf_X. \tag{25b}$$

2.4. *Closing and solving the model*

Labor market equilibrium in each country requires that labor employed in production of nontraded and traded home varieties *plus* labor employed to cover the fixed costs of exporting equal the exogenous domestic labor supply L_H. In the appendix, we show that this condition implies the following relation for the home country:

$$WL_H - (1-n)f_X W = \left(\frac{\phi - 1}{\phi}\right)[P_H C_H + P_{HT}^{*} C_{HT}^{*}] \tag{26}$$

i.e. the domestic wage bill — net of wages paid for workers employed in covering fixed costs, $W(1-n)f_X$ — is proportional to the value of the home good consumed domestically or exported, with the proportionality constant equal to 1 minus the profit rate $1/\phi$.

Close the model with the balanced trade condition, equating the values of exports and imports

$$P_{HT}^{*} C_{HT}^{*} = P_{FT} C_{FT} \tag{27}$$

and the normalization condition

$$P^{*} = 1. \tag{28}$$

Equilibrium determines the 24 variables $C, C_H, C_{HN}, C_{HT}, C_{FT}, P, P_H, P_{HN}, P_{HT}, P_{FT}, W$, and n and their foreign counterparts (denoted by *) by solving the system of 24 equations (1)–(7), (21)–(22), (25b), and (26) plus their foreign counterparts, together with (27) and (28).

3. Analytical Results and Discussion

3.1. *Preliminaries: Decomposition into homogenous and heterogeneous components*

The model permits heterogeneity in two different dimensions: in terms of productivity and in terms of iceberg trade costs. In the following discussion, it will prove useful to decompose productivity and iceberg trade costs for varieties i into homogenous (α) and heterogeneous (β) components. We will address two polar cases: (i) heterogeneity in productivity only, and (ii) heterogeneity in iceberg costs only. (We report only home country expressions; the foreign country counterparts are analogous):

In the case of heterogeneity in productivity only, we may write the distributions as

$$A_i = \alpha_A \beta_A[i], \quad i \in [0,1],\ 0 < \alpha_A, \beta_A$$
$$1 - \tau_i = \alpha_{1-\tau}, \quad i \in [0,1],\ 0 \leq \alpha_{1-\tau} \leq 1$$

implying effective productivity can be expressed as $A_i(1 - \tau_i) = (\alpha_A \beta_A[i])\alpha_{1-\tau}$. Changes in $\alpha_A, \alpha_{1-\tau}$ represent balanced changes in productivity and trade costs affecting all varieties equally. Note a rise in $\alpha_{1-\tau}$ implies a *decline* in iceberg costs. Home productivity averages can be expressed:

$$\tilde{A} = \alpha_A \left[\int_0^1 (\beta_A[i])^{\phi-1} di \right]^{\frac{1}{\phi-1}} \equiv \alpha_A(\tilde{\beta}_A) \tag{29a}$$

$$\tilde{A}_T[n] = \alpha_A \left[\frac{1}{1-n} \int_n^1 (\beta_A[i])^{\phi-1} di \right]^{\frac{1}{\phi-1}} \equiv \alpha_A(\tilde{\beta}_{AT}[n]) \tag{30a}$$

$$\tilde{A}_{(1-\tau)T}[n] = \alpha_A \alpha_{1-\tau} \left[\frac{1}{1-n} \int_n^1 (\beta_A[i])^{\phi-1} di \right]^{\frac{1}{\phi-1}}$$
$$= \alpha_A \alpha_{1-\tau}(\tilde{\beta}_{AT}[n]), \tag{31a}$$

Assuming that varieties are ordered with increasing productivity, i.e. $\partial\tilde{\beta}_A/\partial i > 0$, then $\partial\tilde{\beta}_{AT}/\partial n > 0$, $\partial\tilde{A}_T/\partial n > 0$. That is, average productivity in the traded sector rises as n increases and the traded good share declines.

In the alternative case of heterogeneity in trade costs only, we write the distributions

$$A_i = \alpha_A, \quad i \in [0,1],\ 0 < \alpha_A$$
$$1 - \tau_i = \alpha_{1-\tau}\beta_{1-\tau}[i], \quad i \in [0,1],\ 0 \leq \alpha_{1-\tau}, \beta_{1-\tau} \leq 1$$

implying effective productivity is $A_i(1 - \tau_i) = \alpha_A(\alpha_{1-\tau}\beta_{1-\tau}[i])$. The corresponding averages are

$$\tilde{A} = \alpha_A \tag{29b}$$

$$\tilde{A}_T[n] = \alpha_A \tag{30b}$$

$$\tilde{A}_{(1-\tau)T}[n] = \alpha_A \alpha_{1-\tau} \left[\frac{1}{1-n} \int_n^1 (\beta_{1-\tau}[i])^{\phi-1} di \right]^{\frac{1}{\phi-1}}$$
$$\equiv \alpha_A \alpha_{1-\tau} (\tilde{\beta}_{(1-\tau)T}[n]). \tag{31b}$$

Assuming that varieties are ordered with *decreasing* iceberg costs, i.e. $\partial\beta_{1-\tau}/\partial i > 0$, then $\partial\tilde{\beta}_{(1-\tau)T}/\partial n > 0$, $\partial\tilde{A}_{(1-\tau)T}/\partial n > 0$, i.e. average heterogeneity and transportability rise in the traded sector with increasing n.

3.2. *Tradability*

One immediate conclusion is the equivalence between the two types of heterogeneity in terms of their effects on tradability. This may be seen by considering the trading condition for firm i (25a), substituting out all firm-specific endogenous variables and making some additional simplifying substitutions. Use the price setting conditions (15) and (24) to substitute for p^*_{Hi} and P^*_{HT} and the relative demand condition $c^*_{Hi}/C^*_{HT} = (1-n)^{-1}(p^*_{Hi}/P^*_{HT})^{-\phi}$ for c^*_{Hi} to find:

$$(A_i(1-\tau_i))^{\phi} \left(\frac{(\tilde{A}_{(1-\tau)T}[n])^{-\phi} C^*_{HT}}{(\phi-1)(1-n)} \right) = f_X.$$

In this equation, the variety-specific trade cost term and that for technology appear only as a product, $A_i(1-\tau_i)$, so it is only the net effect of the two terms that matters for the relative ranking of varieties in terms of their tradability. For example, even if a variety i is more costly to trade than a variety j, $\tau_i > \tau_j$, variety i nevertheless can be more tradable if it has a sufficiently high level of productivity so that $A_i(1-\tau_i) > A_j(1-\tau_j)$. Conversely, there also may be some highly productive varieties that nevertheless will probably never be traded, because they have particularly high trade costs. Varieties can in principle be ranked in terms of tradability using this composite metric.

We next obtain some insight into the extensive margin of trade by considering the trading condition for the marginal variety (25b). Using the price setting condition (15) for p^*_{Hn} and noting that the relative demand condition $c^*_{Hi}/C^*_{HT} = (1-n)^{-1}(p^*_{Hi}/P^*_{HT})^{-\phi}$ holds for all varieties i in $[n, 1]$:

$$\left\{ \frac{1}{\phi-1} \left(\frac{1}{A_n(1-\tau_n)} \right) \right\} \left\{ \left(\frac{p^*_{Hn}}{P^*_{HT}} \right)^{-\phi} \frac{C^*_{HT}}{1-n} \right\} = f_X. \tag{32}$$

In this form, we can infer that the nth firm's variable profits depend on two factors. The first is per unit export profits, the term in the first set of curlicue brackets on the left hand side (LHS), expressed as a proportion $1/(\phi - 1)$ of marginal costs. The second factor is the quantity of exports sold, in the second set of curlicue brackets. This in turn can be decomposed into the relative price effect on demand for the nth firm's exports, $(p^*_{Hn}/P^*_{HT})^{-\phi}$, and its share of the aggregate level of exports sold abroad, $C^*_{HT}/(1-n)$.

When variable export profits exceed the fixed costs of exporting — either because per unit profits or the volume of exports are high — varieties with effective productivity lower than that of the initial nth variety will become traded (since even though $A_i(1-\tau_i) < A_n(1-\tau_n)$ for these varieties, it has become profitable to export them). The resulting decline in n and rise in the share of tradable varieties $1-n$ raises the marginal cost and price of the marginally traded variety and reduces its share of aggregate exports. These effects cause both per unit profits and the export volume to fall. In equilibrium, profits are reduced to just cover the fixed costs of the nth firm entering the export market.

Equation (32) can be used to understand the effects of trade policies on the pattern of trade. Consider first a balanced cut in per unit (iceberg) costs, i.e. a rise in $\alpha_{1-\tau}$, $\alpha^*_{1-\tau}$. This policy will have offsetting effects on the components of the marginal firm's variable profits. Per-unit profits fall, since monopolistically competitive firms pass on the decline in tariffs into lower sales price, multiplied by the markup. But export sales rise since the lower relative price of exports boosts foreign demand. Under elastic demand the rise in sales will tend to dominate, so that variable profits exceed fixed export costs for the nth firm and induce entry into trading.[10] Since this

[10]To see this, combine Equations (29)–(32) with the foreign counterpart to Equation (12) and assume for simplicity that productivity heterogeneity is described by the distribution $A_i = \alpha_A(1+i)^{\beta_A}$, $i \in [0,1]$, $0 < \alpha_A, \beta_A$, implying

$$\frac{(1+n)^{\beta(\phi-1)}}{2-n}\left\{\frac{1}{\phi-1}\left(\frac{\phi}{\phi-1}\right)^{-\phi}(\alpha_A)^{\phi-1}\right\}\{W^{-\phi}P^{*\phi}C^*\} = f_X\left(\frac{1}{\alpha_{1-\tau}}\right)^{\phi-1}.$$

Provided that demand is elastic ($\phi > 1$), it can be seen that a cut in per unit trade costs that raises $\alpha_{1-\tau}$ reduces the right-hand side of this expression, which should lead to extensive margin entry (fall in n). This abstracts from possible changes in aggregate wages, foreign prices, or foreign consumption, which are endogenous and prevent full analytical solution. But simulations in Section 4 confirm that endogenous movements in these aggregates do not overturn the prediction.

reduction in trade costs affects the pricing decisions of incumbent exporters as well as potential exporters, lowering their prices and raising their share of the foreign market, this policy will also have an effect on trade through the intensive margin.[11] So the intensive and extensive margins both will be operative. In contrast, a reduction in fixed costs (f_X, f_X^*) will have no impact on the prices of incumbent firms and hence no intensive margin effect. Yet it will have a direct effect of encouraging the entry of new firms, lowering n. Combining these observations, we conclude that the share of any rise in total exports due to the extensive margin is larger after a fixed cost reduction than after a per-unit cost reduction. A closed-form solution verifying this claim is not possible in this model, but the claim is verified for a reasonable calibration of parameters in the numerical simulations presented in Section 4.

3.3. *Law of one price and price divergence*

We next examine the circumstances under which deviations from the law of one price (LOP) may emerge in our model. At the level of individual varieties i, conditions (14) and (15) make clear that the export price exceeds the domestic price of goods variety i by a wedge associated with trade costs:

$$\frac{p_{Hi}^*}{p_{Hi}} = \frac{1}{1-\tau_i} = \frac{1}{\alpha_{1-\tau}\beta_{1-\tau}[i]} > 1, \quad i \in [n, 1].$$

With homogeneous trade costs, the degree of price divergence is constant across varieties. However, if $\beta_{1-\tau}[i]$ and $1-\tau_i$ vary with i, the degree of price divergence varies with i as well. Thus, variations across varieties in the degree of LOP deviations depend on the presence of heterogeneous trade costs. Note that heterogeneous productivity will not have this effect.

We will summarize results for price dispersion as the ratio of the *average* price of the home good in the foreign country to the *average* price of this good at home. This measure is related to that used in empirical work to

[11]Chaney (2006) solves a similar model analytically to find that as the elasticity of substitution rises (ϕ), the intensive margin effect is amplified and the extensive margin effect gets dampened.

follow. Expressions (22) and (24) together with (17) and (19) imply

$$\frac{P^*_{HT}}{P_H} = \frac{\tilde{A}}{\tilde{A}_{(1-\tau)T}[n]}, \tag{33}$$

i.e. the average price to foreign residents of the exported home good relative to the average price of the home good depends inversely on the average *effective* productivity of home tradable varieties (i.e. including trade costs) relative to the average productivity at home. Note that the average effective productivity of tradables and hence the foreign price of the home good depends on how many varieties are traded. Note also that whether the average foreign export price is higher or not than the average domestic price depends on the combination of the distribution and level of productivity and trade costs. In the cases studied below, we assume trade costs are sufficiently high to ensure that the price of the home good is higher in the foreign country than at home, $P^*_{HT}/P_H > 1$.[12]

How does economic integration affect these price deviations? The answer depends on two sets of distinctions. First, is the trade policy reducing per-unit costs of trade or fixed costs? Second, are new entrants distinguished by heterogeneity in terms of trade costs or productivity? These two sets of distinctions imply a total of four cases, which will be studied in turn below.

First, consider a decline in iceberg costs ($\alpha_{1-\tau}, \alpha^*_{1-\tau}$ rise) under the assumption of productivity heterogeneity. In this case, (30a) and (31a) imply (33) reduces to

$$\frac{P^*_{HT}}{P_H} = \left(\frac{1}{\alpha_{1-\tau}}\right)\left(\frac{\tilde{\beta}_A}{\tilde{\beta}_{AT}[n]}\right), \tag{34a}$$

indicating that deviations from LOP at the aggregate level depend on the homogenous trade cost parameter $\alpha_{1-\tau}$, as well as overall productivity $\tilde{\beta}_A$

[12]An alternative metric of price dispersion based on pricing-to-market comparison is the price of the traded home good abroad relative to the price of the same set of varieties in the domestic marketP^*_{HT}/P_{HT}. Expressions (22) and (24) together with (19) and (20) imply $P^*_{HT}/P_{HT} = \tilde{A}_T[n]/\tilde{A}_{(1-\tau)T}[n]$, which always exceeds unity in value because the presence of transport costs implies $\tilde{A}_T > \tilde{A}_{(1-\tau)T}$, i.e. the average productivity of tradable varieties is less than the average effective productivity of those varieties after being exported abroad.

relative to the average productivity of traded varieties of the home $\tilde{\beta}_{AT}$.[13] An increase in $\alpha_{1-\tau}$, i.e. balanced decrease in trade costs, has the direct effect of lowering P^*_{HT}/P_H and reducing the average deviation from LOP.[14] In addition, there is an indirect effect through the endogenous change in tradability on the heterogeneous component of productivity. Specifically, a decrease in n, implying an increase in the number of tradable varieties, implies that productivity is averaged over varieties with lower productivity, i.e. lower A_i. The resulting fall in $\tilde{\beta}_{AT}[n]$ (since $\partial\tilde{\beta}_{AT}[n]/\partial n > 0$) raises P^*_{HT}/P_H. In this case, the indirect channel works to raise the degree of price divergence. The relative size of these two offsetting effects will be evaluated by numerical simulation in the following section.

Second, consider how this policy changes under trade cost heterogeneity. In this case (33) reduces to

$$\frac{P^*_{HT}}{P_H} = \left(\frac{1}{\alpha_{1-\tau}}\right)\left(\frac{1}{\tilde{\beta}_{(1-\tau)T}[n]}\right) > 1 \qquad (34b)$$

and deviations from LOP at the aggregate level depend on the relative heterogeneity of trade costs ($\tilde{\beta}_{(1-\tau)T}$) as well as on the homogeneous trade cost component ($\alpha_{1-\tau}$).[15] Note that in the absence of any productivity heterogeneity, trade costs imply that the average price of the home good to foreigners always exceeds its average home price. The direct effect of a homogenous cut in costs (i.e. increase in $\alpha_{1-\tau}$) is to reduce price divergence. But there is also a potentially offsetting effect to consider through the endogenous changes in tradability on the heterogeneous component of

[13] The pricing-to-market (PTM) measure of price dispersion with productivity heterogeneity is $P^*_{HT}/P_{HT} = 1/\alpha_{1-\tau} > 1$.

[14] The direct effects and indirect effects of lower transport costs are reversed if initially trade costs are low enough (i.e. $\alpha_{1-\tau}$ is high enough) so that P^*_{HT} is less than P_H. In this case, the increase in $\alpha_{1-\tau}$ will lower the ratio P^*_{HT}/P_H further below unity, implying greater price dispersion, while the decrease in $\tilde{\beta}_{AT}[n]$ will raise the ratio, implying less price dispersion. In addition, note that with productivity heterogeneity alone, lower transport costs (i.e. an increase in $\alpha_{1-\tau}$) only have the direct effect of lowering the PTM measure of price dispersion $P^*_{HT}/P_{HT} = 1/\alpha_{1-\tau}$; there is no indirect effect on this measure since price differences for individual tradable varieties do not depend on productivity and hence on new entrants.

[15] With trade cost heterogeneity only, (34b) also defines the PTM measure of price dispersion, implying that the dispersion measures P^*_{HT}/P_H and P^*_{HT}/P_{HT} always move together.

trade costs. Specifically, a decrease in n, implying an increase in the number of tradable varieties, implies that trade costs are averaged over varieties with higher costs, i.e. lower $1 - \tau_i$. The resulting fall in $\tilde{\beta}_{(1-\tau)T}[n]$ (since $\partial\tilde{\beta}_{(1-\tau)T}[n]/\partial n > 0$) raises the degree of price divergence.

Now consider the type of policy that cuts fixed costs (f_X, f_X^* fall). Fixed costs do not affect deviations from LOP at the individual firm level, but they can affect deviations at the aggregate level to the extent they affect n. In the case of productivity heterogeneity, the relation (34a) applies, and the degree of price divergence depends on the heterogeneity of productivity ($\tilde{\beta}_{AT}$) as well as homogeneous trade costs ($\alpha_{1-\tau}$). In this case, a decline in fixed costs that fosters decreased n and increased tradability, reduces $\tilde{\beta}_{AT}[n]$ and reduces the average export price of tradables to foreign residents. In words, if the source of heterogeneity is in terms of productivity, then the newly tradable varieties systematically will be those varieties with lower productivity. Given the lower fixed costs, it now becomes profitable to trade these varieties, despite the higher per unit costs. Given that price setting responds to these costs, the newly traded varieties will tend to have a higher price in the foreign market. Assuming there initially is a positive price wedge between the foreign price of home tradables and the domestic country price of the home good, the size of the price wedge will increase, i.e. the average foreign price of traded varieties will rise relative to the overall home good price level.

Finally, in the presence of trade cost heterogeneity, (34b) holds and deviations from LOP then depend on the heterogeneity of trade costs ($\tilde{\beta}_{(1-\tau)T}$). In this case, a decline in fixed costs that fosters decreased n and increased tradability, reduces $\tilde{\beta}_{(1-\tau)T}[n]$ and raises price disparity. If the source of heterogeneity is in terms of iceberg costs, then the newly tradable varieties systematically will be those varieties with higher per unit costs. Given the lower fixed costs, it now becomes profitable to trade these varieties, despite the higher per unit costs. Given that price setting responds to these costs, the newly traded varieties will tend to have a greater price wedge between national markets, so that average price dispersion of traded varieties will increase unambiguously.

To sum up, iceberg costs play an important role in the model in explaining market segmentation as measured in terms of price deviations, because fixed costs have no impact on the pricing behavior of monopolistically competitive firms. Cuts in iceberg costs reduce price disparities across markets.

Moreover, only heterogeneity in iceberg costs can explain heterogeneity of LOP deviations. In contrast, fixed trade cost reductions in the presence of either productivity or trade cost heterogeneity has the potential to explain why price divergence may actually increase when account is taken of endogenous changes in the tradability of varieties.

One can also use the model to trace the effects of policies on a third important variable, the total volume of trade. We find there are several offsetting effects which obscure analytical conclusions. So we instead present results for this variable in the numerical simulations below, and refer the reader interested in the analytical discussion to the appendix.[16]

4. Numerical Results

4.1. *Calibrations*

In several of the cases discussed above, trade liberalization had ambiguous implications due to multiple offsetting effects. Numerical simulations are helpful to resolve these ambiguities.

The elasticity of substitution between any two varieties, ϕ, is calibrated at the value six. This implies a price markup of 20% over cost, which is a common value in the literature (Obstfeld and Rogoff, 2000).[17] Simulations require that particular distributions be specified for the heterogeneous elements. Productivity will follow the distribution:

$$A_i = \alpha_A(1+i)^{\beta_A}, \quad i \in [0,1], \; 0 < \alpha_A$$

and iceberg costs follow the distribution:

$$1 - \tau_i = \alpha_{1-\tau}(1+i)^{\beta_{1-\tau}}, \quad i \in [0,1], \; 0 \leq \alpha_{1-\tau}$$

where α_A and $\alpha_{1-\tau}$ are scale parameters representing level effects common to all varieties, while β_A and $\beta_{1-\tau}$ are parameters indicating the degree of heterogeneity over firms along the continuum indexed by i.

[16] Implications for price may differ from the analysis above if strategic interactions between firms make price markups vary with extensive margin entry. See Bergin and Glick (2005) for analysis of this case.

[17] Note that this parameter also doubles as the elasticity between home and foreign goods. An alternative specification with two different elasticities will be considered at the end of this section.

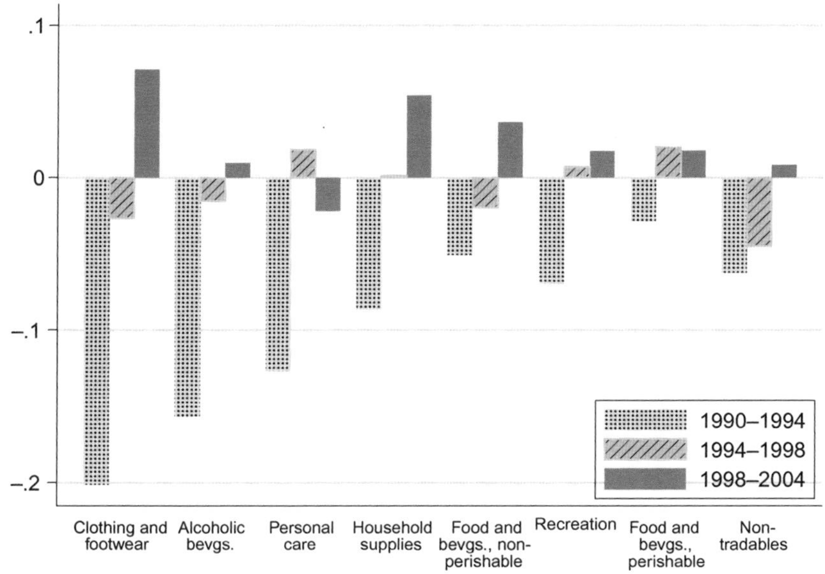

Figure 1. Change in price dispersion in the Euro-11

Note: Positive values imply price divergence; negative values imply price convergence over the period.

Source: EIU Citybase data and authors' calculations. See Engel and Rogers (2004) for the cities used and the product items included in each goods category.

4.2. *Per unit cost reductions*

The first simulation will consider the case where the source of heterogeneity is productivity, with distribution parameters set at $\alpha_A = 1$, $\beta_A = 1$, and $\alpha_{1-\tau} = 0.8$, $\beta_{1-\tau} = 0$. This implies a constant per-unit trade cost near 20% for all firms, similar to that assumed in Obstfeld and Rogoff (2000). Figure 2 illustrates the distributions for technology and iceberg costs over the continuum of home good varieties. This calibration implies that the foreign price of tradables is greater than the domestic price of the home good in the initial steady state, implying that a rise (decline) in the ratio P^*_{HT}/P_H corresponds to a greater price dispersion (convergence). The experiment will consider a symmetric rise in $\alpha_{1-\tau}$ of 1% for both countries, which lifts the $1 - \tau_i$ line for all varieties. This could be viewed as a 5% scaled reduction in the tariff rate. To ensure a share of nontraded varieties of 50%, the fixed cost f_X is calibrated at 0.0365. The foreign country is exactly symmetric.

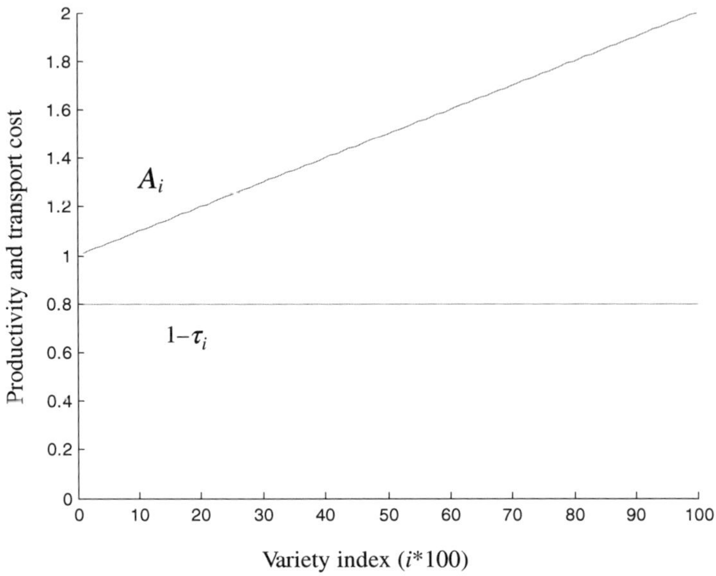

Figure 2. Distribution in simulation with productivity heterogeneity only

Table 3a. Simulation results: Cut in per unit trade costs

	Steady state	% Change (endogenous n)	% Change (exogenous n)
Nontraded share (n)	0.50	−2.20	0.00
Export share[1]	0.21	4.75	4.00
Extensive share[2]	—	0.20	0.00
Price gap ratio[3]	1.13	−0.75	−1.00

Notes: [1]Export share: value of exports as ratio to GDP.
[2]Extensive share: fraction of new import value due to new entrants.
[3]Price gap ratio: P^*_{HT}/P_H; Calibration: $\beta_A = 1, \alpha_A = 1, \beta_{1-\tau} = 0, \alpha_{1-\tau} = 0.8$, $\phi = 6$, and $f_X = 0.0365$.

The results of this experiment are shown in Table 3a, where column (1) reports initial values before the tariff reduction. The export share of less than one half indicates some degree of home bias in consumption, arising from the presence of trade costs that make imported varieties more expensive than domestic goods. Column (2) reports the percentage change from steady state values after the tariff reduction. Recall that one ambiguity in the analytical solution of Section 3 is the degree of entry and increase in trade share. While the fall in export prices raises foreign demand for home exports, thereby increasing the profitability of paying the fixed cost of exporting, any new entrants will have systematically lower productivity and hence higher prices than the average among previous entrants. Line 1 of the table shows that there indeed is entry of new exporters, as the share of nontraded goods (n) falls. Line 2 shows that new entry amplifies the increase in trade volume, compared to the case where there is no entry, shown in the last column. But line 3 shows that the contribution of this extensive margin shift is relatively modest, accounting for 20% of the increased trade.

There was also an ambiguity in the analytical solution for price dispersion, which depended on the relative size of a direct and indirect effect of a tariff reduction. The direct effect of a 1% increase in $\alpha_{1-\tau}$ is a 1% reduction in the international price gap ratio, which can be seen at the bottom of column (3), which isolates the direct effect by holding fixed the extensive margin. But any entry of new firms with lower productivity will tend to raise the average price of the home good in the foreign market, raising it yet further above the price in the home market and worsening price dispersion. As can be seen in line 4 of the table, the fact that the extensive margin shifts only a modest amount in this case implies that the secondary effect of new entrants on price deviation is likewise small. So the direct effect dominates, and there is significant price convergence.

Next, we explore the effects of assuming heterogeneity in terms of per-unit trade costs instead of productivities. The distributions are parameterized by: $\alpha_A = 1$, $\beta_A = 0$, $\alpha_{1-\tau} = 0.5$, and $\beta_{1-\tau} = 1$, and depicted in Fig. 3. The fixed cost is again calibrated at 0.0365. Again consider an experiment where $\alpha_{1-\tau}$ rises 1%, representing a tariff cut that raises the $1 - \tau_i$ line for all varieties. For this calibration of trade cost heterogeneity, the experiment generates identical values as those shown in Table 3a for the case of productivity heterogeneity. Again there is a small secondary effect limiting price convergence somewhat, which arises from the extensive margin shift and entry of new firms. The reasoning is different, however, in that now the new entrants are distinguished from incumbent traders by having larger per-unit trade costs, which raises the average price wedge among varieties of the home good available in the foreign country. The isomorphism of the two types of heterogeneity arises from the fact that both distributions are calibrated to vary in the same way over varieties: $\beta_{1-\tau} = \beta_A$. If

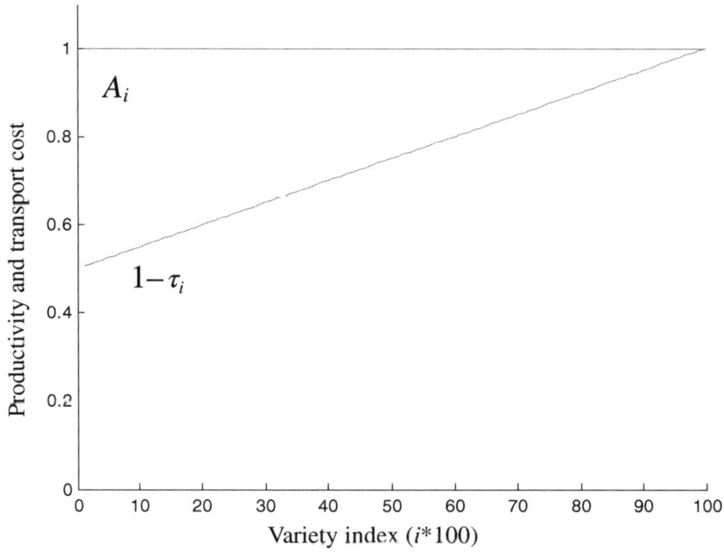

Figure 3. Distribution in simulation with transport cost heterogeneity only

heterogeneity of one type is thought to vary more steeply over varieties, this case will tend to generate the weaker degree of price convergence.[18]

4.3. *Fixed cost reduction*

Consider next experiments that instead reduce the fixed cost of trade. The two cases will use the same pair of distributions graphed in the previous section, and this will imply that the starting equilibrium values for variables likewise will be the same as in the previous section. The experiment will be a reduction in the term f_X by 10%.

Table 3b reports the result for the case of productivity heterogeneity, which confirms the conjecture from the analytical section that there should

[18]It should be noted that the two types of heterogeneity are not isomorphic in the effects of lower tariff costs on the PTM measure of price dispersion p^*_{HT}/p_{HT}. With productivity heterogeneity alone, there is no indirect effect through new entrants and p^*_{HT}/p_{HT} falls by the full 1% decline in tariff costs. This contrasts with the case of trade heterogeneity where the PTM measure and the measure reported in Table 3a coincide (i.e. $p^*_{HT}/p_{HT} = p^*_{HT}/p_H$) and new entry dampens the decline in dispersion, so that the price gap ratio falls only 0.75%.

Table 3b. Simulation results: Cut in fixed cost of trade

	Steady state	% Change (endogenous n)	% Change (exogenous n)
Nontraded share (n)	0.50	−6.00	0.00
Export share[1]	0.21	1.93	0.00
Extensive share[2]	—	1.51	0.00
Price gap ratio[3]	1.13	0.68	0.00

Notes: [1]Export share: value of exports as ratio to GDP.
[2]Extensive share: fraction of new import value due to new entrants.
[3]Price gap ratio: P^*_{HT}/P_H; Calibration: $\beta_A = 1, \alpha_A = 1, \beta_{1-\tau} = 0, \alpha_{1-\tau} = 0.8$, $\phi = 6$, and $f_X = 0.0365$.

be much more entry into exporting. However, despite this greater extensive margin growth, the overall export share in gross domestic product (GDP) rises less. This is because as new firms enter the market, firms previously trading experience an actual decline in their share of the export market. This implies the intensive margin growth is smaller, so that the share of new trade due to the extensive margin exceeds 100%. The large extensive margin shift also implies that the indirect effect on foreign prices will be large. The last line of the table shows that this indirect effect dominates the direct effect, and there is greater price divergence on net.

When this experiment is run for the case of trade cost heterogeneity, it generates values identical to those in Table 3b for productivity heterogeneity.[19] So both types of heterogeneity can offer explanations for cases where trade integration appears to raise international price dispersion.[20]

[19]As in the case of tariff cuts, the effects of a fixed trade cost reduction on a PTM measure of price dispersion differ according to the underlying type of heterogeneity. Specifically, with productivity heterogeneity the price ratio p^*_{HT}/p_{HT} is unaffected by a fixed cost cut, while with transport cost heterogeneity it rises by 0.68%, the same as the measure p^*_{HT}/p_H reported in Table 3b.

[20]We also simulated a version of the model where the elasticity of substitution between home and foreign goods was calibrated at 1.5, a value lower than the elasticity of six assumed between varieties of the same good. While such a case proved problematic for analytical solution because the home bias coefficient θ no longer can be viewed as endogenous, simulations showed that our results are robust. Calibrating the value of θ to 0.776 replicates the initial steady state of the simulations above. The only significant change in results is that trade volume and the extensive margin responded less to tariff reductions. Price convergence is stronger under tariff reductions, with a percent change in the price

5. Empirical Implications

A key testable implication of the theory above is that growth in trade along the extensive margin is negatively related to price convergence. We investigate the prediction with a regression of the change in European price dispersion on the change in the extensive trade margin across country pairs.

Our measure of price dispersion is based on price level data drawn from the EIU for about 100 traded as well as 38 nontraded goods, as described in Table 2. These data cover 18 cities within the Eurozone for the period 1990–2004. The metric used for dispersion is the mean squared error of (the relative logs of) product item prices across cities in the Eurozone, averaged over goods categories. This measure of price dispersion is closely related to expression (33) for the relative price ratio derived in our theoretical analysis in Section 4. The EIU instructs its data collectors to obtain the price of a representative item in each city for each of its goods categories, where the item conforms to an international standard. A simple way to model this data collection process is as a random draw from the population of varieties available for sale in a given market. The expected value of this price draw then would equal the average price level over the range of varieties available, with weights equal to the volume of sales of each variety. As with the CES price indexes in our model, changes in the set of varieties available in the market will affect this market average. In fact, the EIU notes in its literature that its price measures could be affected by such shifts in the extensive margin: "As governments welcome foreign investment and open up their markets to international companies, so the variety and availability of imported products improves."[21]

---

gap ratio of −0.98. Price divergence remains strong under a fixed cost reduction, with a percentage change in the price gap ratio of 0.56.

[21]Other assumptions must be made to draw a correspondence between the two country model and our multicountry data set. The model assumes that each country produces a country-specific home good, implying each good is exported by one country and imported by the other. Our dataset includes more than two goods, of course. We assume each good can be categorized as being either an H or F good and construct our empirical price dispersion measure as an average of the price wedges across all of these goods. Another subtle difference is the fact that our empirical measure of price dispersion is constructed from price deviations that are squared to prevent positive deviations for some goods from canceling negative deviations for other goods. The model-based measure of price dispersion

Figure 1 shows the changes in price dispersion for different subperiods and eight different product groups. It indicates that for all eight groups of goods there was a fall in price dispersion in the early 1990s, and this was followed by a period of stasis or even worsening price dispersion after 1998. The top line of Table 2 confirms the observation for the average over all goods, that there were periods with strikingly different degrees of price convergence.[22] Other recent papers support this general conclusion (See the European Commission (2004), Baye *et al.* (2002) and Lutz (2002)).[23]

The extensive trade margin is measured using the metric of Kehoe and Ruhl (2002), as the share of trade represented at the end of the period by the set of least traded goods that initially represented 10% of trade in the base year of 1992 (or in 1993 in some cases depending on data availability). We construct these measures from OECD data on International Trade by Commodity Statistics (ITCS), disaggregated at the four-digit SITC product level. The regressions also include geographic distance between countries as a control variable, as is common in gravity regressions.

We consider two time periods: first 1992–1998, corresponding to the period of implementation of the Single Market Program in the early 1990s but prior to monetary union, and second 1998–2002, corresponding to the period after formation of the Monetary Union. The first period begins in

---

does not need to square deviations because the country specialization structure of the model implies all home good exports are more expensive in the importing country than at home. Thus, there is a monotonic relationship between the two measures. Note that our price indexes by definition are free of love of variety effects, which certainly would not be present in the EIU price data.

[22]The fact that this finding continues to hold in our extended data set through 2004 suggests it likely is not just a temporary byproduct of transition to new currency units at the onset of the monetary union.

[23]This result is consistent with the findings of the European Union's "Internal Market Scoreboard" (available at http://ec.europa.eu/internal_market/scoreboard/) that price differences persist across Europe for general grocery and household items. However, some micro-level studies do find convergence to the LOP in particular industries for narrowly defined goods, such as particular brands of autos and televisions (see Imbs *et al.*, 2004; Goldberg and Verboven, 2005). Our finding of greater price dispersion in recent years is a distinct issue from the evident lack of convergence in European national inflation rates: for example, divergent inflation rates may still be associated with convergence in price levels if the higher rates of change are in countries that initially had low price levels.

Table 4. OLS estimates: Change in bilateral price dispersion in Euro area

	1992–1998 period		1998–2002 period	
	(1)	(2)	(3)	(4)
ExtMargin	0.514***	0.697***	0.130*	0.448***
	(0.154)	(0.213)	(0.065)	(0.101)
ExtMargin*Dum_CP		−0.081		−0.271***
		(0.146)		(0.090)
ExtMargin*Dum_PP		−0.211		−0.418***
		(0.180)		(0.103)
Distance	−77.3***	−64.0**	21.9	19.1
	(22.1)	(27.7)	(18.4)	(19.5)
Constant	−0.050*	−0.075**	0.012	−0.039*
	(0.026)	(0.034)	(0.016)	(0.019)
R-squared	0.290	0.317	0.091	0.358
No. of country pairs	45	45	45	45

Notes: OLS estimation, where the dependent variable is the change in bilateral price dispersion over each period across (45) individual country pairs in the Eurozone. ExtMargin, the extensive margin variable for each country pair, is defined as the share of total bilateral trade in 1998 or 2002 of the ("least traded") goods that accounted for 10% of this trade in 1992 or 1993, depending on data availability. Dum_CP and Dum_PP are dummies for core–peripheral or peripheral–peripheral country pairs, respectively; see notes to Table 2. Standard errors in parentheses. Variables significant at 10%, 5%, and 1% indicated by *, **, and ***, respectively.

Sources: price dispersion figures based on EIU citybase data. Extensive margin figures based on bilateral trade data from OECD International Trade by Commodity Statistics, SITC rev. 3, disaggregated to the four-digit level.

1992 and the second period ends in 2002 because of the absence of bilateral product-disaggregated trade data for most countries before and after these years.[24]

Results are reported in Table 4, where columns (1) and (2) pertain to the early time period, and columns (3) and (4) pertain to the later period. Recall from Table 1 that the early period was characterized by significant price convergence on average, whereas the second period was characterized by price divergence on average. Nonetheless, in each of the periods, the

[24]The EIU price data are not available before 1990.

estimate for the effect of the extensive margin is significantly positive, with a p-value less than 1% in the early sample and 5.2% in the latter sample. This indicates that our model's prediction regarding the relationship between the two variables finds empirical support throughout the sample, robust to the fact that the outcomes for price convergence were different between the two periods.

If prices nonetheless converged during the pre-EMU period, it must be that something different was happening during this period. We get some clue regarding this issue, since the coefficient on distance is negative and highly significant in the first period, but it is insignificant (and with a positive point estimate) in the later period. Distance is often included in gravity regressions to reflect iceberg transport costs, which are isomorphic in our model to the per unit costs τ_i.The negative coefficient could indicate a reduction in trade costs due to improved shipping technology or the reduction in some other trade cost related to distance. This result itself is new to the literature.[25]

An additional finding in the regressions is that the result for the extensive margin above works mainly through a particular subset of countries. Columns (2) and (4) of the table introduce dummies to distinguish "core" and "periphery" countries in the bilateral observations, where Finland, Ireland, Portugal, and Spain as peripheral countries, and Austria, Belgium, France, Germany, Italy, Luxemburg, and the Netherlands as the core countries. This distinction makes sense based on both geography and the extent to which lowered trade barriers have had time to foster stronger cross-country trade links. The former countries are located in the outer areas of Europe. Moreover, Ireland joined in 1973, Portugal and Spain in 1986, and Finland in 1995, well after the core members formed the European Union in 1957.[26] Table 1 shows that price divergence during the latter period was greatest among the core countries. In fact, for these countries the increase in price dispersion since 1998 has almost fully offset the decline in price

[25]The European Commission (2004) estimates that the elimination of border controls and reduced transit times in the transition towards a Single European Market significantly reduced the freight costs of cross-border transit. Air transportation costs also fell with liberalization allowing greater access to foreign carriers and new startups.

[26]Austria did not join the European Union until 1995, but is treated as a core country because of its long-standing trade links with Germany and its central geographic position within Europe.

dispersion experienced in the early 1990s. In contrast, the peripheral countries experienced a much greater decline in price dispersion in the early 1990s and a much weaker increase in dispersion with core countries since adoption of the Euro. Further, the regressions in Table 4 show that the extensive margin effect on price dispersion is significant only for the case of core countries trading with other core countries. The degree of significance of this relationship is very high for both time periods.

6. Conclusion

Empirical evidence arising from recent experiences in Europe and North America suggest that international price convergence and trade volume expansion, two common measures for the integration of goods markets across countries, need not coincide. This chapter proposes a model of economic integration which can explain a range of varied relationships between price and quantities. Firstly, the model highlights the distinction between trade policies that focus on reducing fixed costs of trade and those that focus on per unit costs of trade like tariffs. Secondly, as an alternative to heterogeneity in productivity, the model allows for heterogeneity in terms of iceberg trade costs, where the reason some goods are not traded is that these goods tend to have higher costs of trade. The main prediction of the theoretical model is that cases where trade integration works more heavily through the extensive margin of goods not previously traded are the cases where price convergence is likely to be the weakest. Empirical work supports this theoretical relationship, and indicates this way of thinking about integration could be useful in understanding the recent experiences of integration in Europe and elsewhere.

Our theoretical research also raises a basic question regarding the appropriate metric for gauging international integration policies, analogous to that discussed in Feenstra (1994) for computing import price indexes. Past research has tended to prefer price-based measures, since quantity-based alternatives are affected by factor endowments and opportunities for scale economies. But our model indicates that standard price metrics might also be problematic, if integration takes place at the extensive margin and if new goods are different from those previously traded. This indicates the need for research to find appropriate metrics of international economic integration.

Appendix

A.1. *Derivation of consumption aggregate expression (1) with endogenous bias weights*

To derive (1), define consumption by domestic residents of the home good and foreign traded good as c_{Hi}, $i \in [0,1]$, and c_{FTi}, $i \in [0, 1-n^*]$, respectively. We index all varieties available for consumption in the domestic country by j on the interval $[0, 2-n^*]$, and order consumption as $c_j = c_{Hi}$ for $j = i \in [0,1]$, and $c_j = c_{Fi}$ for $j = i+1, j \in [1, 2-n^*]$, $i \in [0, 1-n^*]$. Accordingly, assuming the elasticity of substitution between all varieties, domestic or foreign, is the constant ϕ, we define aggregate consumption as

$$\begin{aligned}
C^{\frac{\phi-1}{\phi}} &= \left(\frac{1}{2-n^*}\right)^{\frac{1}{\phi}} \left[\int_0^1 (c_i)^{\frac{\phi-1}{\phi}} di + \int_1^{2-n^*} (c_i)^{\frac{\phi-1}{\phi}} di\right] \\
&= \left(\frac{1}{2-n^*}\right)^{\frac{1}{\phi}} \left(\frac{1}{1}\right)^{\frac{1}{\phi}} \int_0^1 (c_i)^{\frac{\phi-1}{\phi}} di \\
&\quad + \left(\frac{1-n^*}{2-n^*}\right)^{\frac{1}{\phi}} \left(\frac{1}{1-n^*}\right)^{\frac{1}{\phi}} \int_1^{2-n^*} (c_i)^{\frac{\phi-1}{\phi}} di \\
&= \left(\frac{1}{2-n^*}\right)^{\frac{1}{\phi}} (C_H)^{\frac{\phi-1}{\phi}} + \left(\frac{1-n^*}{2-n^*}\right)^{\frac{1}{\phi}} (C_{FT})^{\frac{\phi-1}{\phi}} \\
&= (\theta[n^*])^{\frac{1}{\phi}} (C_H)^{\frac{\phi-1}{\phi}} + (1-\theta[n^*])^{\frac{1}{\phi}} (C_{FT})^{\frac{\phi-1}{\phi}}
\end{aligned}$$

where $\theta[n^*] \equiv \frac{1}{2-n^*}$, $1-\theta[n^*] \equiv \frac{1-n^*}{2-n^*}$, $0 \le \theta[n^*] \le 1$.

A.2. *Derivation of labor market equilibrium condition (26)*

Labor market equilibrium in the domestic country requires that labor employed in production of nontraded and traded home varieties *plus* labor employed to cover the fixed costs of exporting equal the (exogenous) domestic labor supply L_H:[27]

$$\int_0^n l_{Hi} di + \int_n^1 l_{Hi} di + (1-n) f_X = L_H.$$

[27]When all home goods are nontraded, i.e. $n = 1$, then no labor is employed to cover fixed costs of exporting.

Substituting for l_{Hi} with the production function (13):

$$\int_0^n \frac{y_{Hi}}{A_i} di + \int_n^1 \frac{y_{Hi}}{A_i} di + (1-n)f_X = L_H$$

or

$$\int_0^n \frac{c_{Hi}}{A_i} di + \int_n^1 \frac{c_{Hi} + \frac{c^*_{Hi}}{1-\tau_i}}{A_i} di + (1-n)f_X = L_H$$

since $y_{Hi} = c_{Hi}$ for $i \in [0, n]$, $y_{Hi} = c_{Hi} + \frac{c^*_{Hi}}{1-\tau_i}$ for $i \in [n, 1]$. Substituting with $c_{Hi}/C_H = (p_{Hi}/P_H)^{-\phi}$ and $c^*_{Hi}/C^*_{HT} = (1-n)^{-1}(p^*_{Hi}/P^*_{HT})^{-\phi}$ gives

$$\begin{aligned}
&\int_0^n \frac{C_H}{A_i}\left(\frac{p_{Hi}}{P_H}\right)^{-\phi} di \\
&\quad + \int_n^1 \left(\frac{1}{A_i}\right)\left[C_H\left(\frac{p_{Hi}}{P_H}\right)^{-\phi} + \frac{1}{1-\tau_i}\left(\frac{1}{1-n}\right)C^*_{HT}\left(\frac{p^*_{Hi}}{P^*_{HT}}\right)^{-\phi}\right] di \\
&\quad + (1-n)f_X = L_H.
\end{aligned}$$

Using (14) and (15) in turn to substitute for p_{Hi}, p^*_{Hi} and (17) and (20) to substitute for the definitions of $\tilde{A}$, $\tilde{A}_{(1-\tau)T}[n]$ gives

$$\begin{aligned}
W &= (L_H - (1-n)f_X)^{-1/\phi}\left(\frac{\phi-1}{\phi}\right) \\
&\quad \times \left[\left(\frac{P_H C_H}{(P_H)^{1-\phi}}\right)(\tilde{A})^{\phi-1} + \left(\frac{P^*_{HT} C^*_{HT}}{(P^*_{HT})^{1-\phi}}\right)(\tilde{A}_{(1-\tau)T}[n])^{\phi-1}\right]^{\frac{1}{\phi}}.
\end{aligned}$$

Substituting for P_H, P^*_{HT} with (23), (24) and canceling terms gives

$$\begin{aligned}
W &= (L_H - (1-n)f_X)^{-1/\phi}\left(\frac{\phi-1}{\phi}\right)\left[\left(\frac{P_H C_H}{\left(\frac{\phi}{\phi-1}\frac{W}{\tilde{A}}\right)^{1-\phi}}\right)(\tilde{A})^{\phi-1}\right. \\
&\quad \left. + \left(\frac{P^*_{HT} C^*_{HT}}{\left(\frac{\phi}{\phi-1}\frac{W}{\tilde{A}_{(1-\tau)T}[n]}\right)^{1-\phi}}\right)(\tilde{A}_{(1-\tau)T}[n])^{\phi-1}\right]^{\frac{1}{\phi}}
\end{aligned}$$

which reduces to (26).

A.3. *Model implications for trade volume*

Balanced trade (see (27)) implies that exports and imports as ratios of total aggregate consumption are equal:

$$\frac{P^*_{HT}C^*_{HT}}{PC} = \frac{P_{FT}C_{FT}}{PC}.$$

Relative demand conditions imply:

$$\frac{P^*_{HT}C^*_{HT}}{PC} = (1-\theta^*[n])\left(\frac{P^*_{HT}}{P^*}\right)^{1-\phi},$$

$$\frac{P_{FT}C_{FT}}{PC} = (1-\theta[n^*])\left(\frac{P_{FT}}{P}\right)^{1-\phi}$$

implying that exports relative to consumption — which equals GDP in our single period model — depends on two factors: The relative import price for foreign residents P^*_{HT}/P^* and (ii) the foreign bias coefficient for imported home varieties $1-\theta^*[n]$. A decrease in the relative price of imports and/or an increase in bias towards imports raises the home country's exports.

How does trade liberalization affect exports? We proceed by considering first a reduction in iceberg costs and then a reduction in fixed costs. We assume a symmetric steady state which, because the foreign aggregate price level is normalized to unity, implies $P = P^* = 1$. We also assume that changes are symmetric across countries and lead to equal declines in n, n^* and hence increases the number of tradable varieties. Because of the symmetric nature of the experiment, relative aggregate prices remain constant and equal to unity as well. Hence, we may infer the change in relative prices solely from the change in P^*_{HT} given by (24):

$$P^*_{HT} = \left(\frac{\phi}{\phi-1}\right)\frac{W}{\tilde{A}_{(1-\tau)T}[n]}.$$

For reference, we express this price in terms of the relevant productivity averages when productivity is heterogeneous

$$P^*_{HT} = \frac{\phi}{\phi-1}\left(\frac{W}{\alpha_{1-\tau}\alpha_A\tilde{\beta}_{AT}[n]}\right),$$

and when transport costs are heterogeneous

$$P^*_{HT} = \frac{\phi}{\phi - 1}\left(\frac{W}{\alpha_{1-\tau}\alpha_A\tilde{\beta}_{(1-\tau)T}[n]}\right).$$

A fall in iceberg costs (increase in $\alpha_{1-\tau}$) directly reduces the price of goods exported to foreign residents, increases demand, and raises the home country's level of exports. But there is an opposing effect, as falling n and increased trade at the extensive margin imply varieties with either lower effective productivity or higher transport costs become traded, raising the average price of imported varieties.[28] Wages W rise as well because of increased demand for labor to produce the greater export volume. The effect on θ^* tends also to raise exports: as more varieties become traded, the weight placed on the imported good in the foreign price index increases, and the relative demand by foreign residents for the imported good in their consumption basket rises.[29]

With a fixed cost reduction, there is no direct effect on the relative price of exports to foreigners. But the decline in n also implies good with lower effective productivity or higher transport costs become traded, raising the average price of the exported good.[30] In addition, W falls in this case since less labor is needed to cover the fixed costs of exporting. The effect on θ^* works in the direction of raising home exports, as the increase in imported varieties raises the demand by foreigners for home country exports.

The theoretical ambiguities of the effects of trade liberalization on trade volume shares are resolved in the simulation analysis reported in Section 4.

References

Anderson, J. E. and E. van Wincoop. 2004. Trade costs. *Journal of Economic Literature*, 42: 691–751.

[28] Mathematically, since $\partial\tilde{\beta}_{AT}/\partial n > 0$, $\partial\tilde{\beta}_{(1-\tau)T}/\partial n > 0$, the fall in n implies that $\tilde{\beta}_{AT}[n]$, $\tilde{\beta}_{(1-\tau)T}[n]$ both decline.

[29] Since $\partial\theta^*/\partial n > 0$ (recall $\theta^*[n] = 1/(2-n)$), a decrease in n, i.e. an increase in tradables varieties, decreases θ^* and raises $1-\theta^*$.

[30] Mathematically, since $\partial\tilde{\beta}_{AT}/\partial n > 0$, $\partial\tilde{\beta}^*_{(1-\tau)T}/\partial n > 0$, the fall in n implies the terms in the denominator $\tilde{\beta}_{AT}[n]$, $\tilde{\beta}_{(1-\tau)T}[n]$ decline.

Baye, M. R., R. Gatti, P. Kattuman, and J. Morgan. 2002. Online Pricing and the Euro Changeover: Cross-Country Comparisons, Judge Institute of Management Research Paper in Management Studies 17/2002, University of Cambridge.

Benassy, J. P. 1996. Taste for variety and optimum production patterns in monopolistic competition. *Economic Letters*, 52: 41–47.

Bergin, P. R. and R. Glick. 2005. Tradability, productivity, and understanding international economic integration, NBER Working Paper No. 11637.

Bergin, P. R., R. Glick, and A. Taylor, 2006. Productivity, tradability, and the long-run price puzzle. *Journal of Monetary Economics*, 53: 2041–2066.

Burstein, A., J. Neves, and S. Rebelo. 2003. Distribution costs and real exchange rate dynamics during exchange-rate-based stabilizations. *Journal of Monetary Economics*, 50: 1189–1214.

Chaney, T. 2006. *Distorted Gravity: Heterogeneous Firms, Market Structure and the Geography of International Trade.* University of Chicago, Mimeo.

Corsetti, G. and L. Dedola. 2005. A macroeconomic model of international price discrimination. *Journal of International Economics*, 67: 129–155.

Crucini, M. J., C. I. Telmer, and M. Zachariadis. 2005. Understanding european real exchange rates. *American Economic Review*, 95: 724–738.

Dornbusch, R., S. Fisher, and P. Samuelson. 1977. Comparative Advantage, Trade, and Payments in a Ricardian Model with a Continuum of Goods. *American Economic Review*, 67: 823–839.

Engel, C. and J. H. Rogers. 2004. European product market integration after the Euro. *Economic Policy*, 39: 347–384.

European Commission. 2004. Single Market Review Series, Subseries II — Impact on Services, "Road and Freight Transport" (March) and "Air Transport" (May).

Feenstra, Robert. 1994. New product varieties and the measurement of international prices. *American Economic Review*, 84: 157–177.

Ghironi, F. and M. Melitz. 2005. International trade and macroeconomic dynamics with heterogeneous firms. *The Quarterly Journal of Economics*, 120: 865–915.

Goldberg, P. and F. Verboven. 2005. Market integration and convergence to the law of one price: Evidence from the European car market. *Journal of International Economics*, 65: 49–73.

Hummels, D. 1999. Toward a Geography of Trade Costs. Working Paper, Purdue University.

Hummels, D. 2001. Time as a Trade Barrier. Working Paper, Purdue University.

Imbs, J. and H. Mumtaz, R. O. Ravn, and H. Rey. 2004. *Price Convergence: What's on TV*? University of Chicago, Mimeo.

Kehoe, T. J. and K. J. Ruhl. 2002. How Important is the New Goods Margin in International Trade? Working Paper, University of Minnesota.

Lutz, M. 2002. Price Convergence under EMU? First Estimates, Working Paper, Institute of Economic, University of St. Gallen.

Melitz, M. 2003. The impact of trade on intra-industry reallocations and aggregate industry productivity. *Econometrica*, 71: 1695–1726.

Obstfeld, M. and K. Rogoff. 2000. The six major puzzles in international macroeconomics: Is there a common cause? in Bernanke, B. and Rogoff, K. (eds.), *NBER Macroeconomics Annual*, MIT Press, Cambridge, pp. 339–390.

Ruhl, K. J. 2003. *Solving the Elasticity Puzzle in International Economics.* Mimeo, University of Minnesota.

Section III

Global Integration of Asset Markets

CHAPTER 10

Interest Rates, Exchange Rates and Present Value Models of the Current Account*

Paul R. Bergin[†,§] and Steven M. Sheffrin[‡,¶]

[†] *Department of Economics, University of California at Davis, One Shields Ave., Davis, CA 95616, USA*

[‡] *College of Letters and Sciences, Deans Office, One Shields Avenue, University of California, Davis, CA 95616-8572*

[§] *prbergin@ucdavis.edu*

[¶] *smsheffrin@ucdavis.edu*

The relaxation of restrictions on international capital flows over the last several decades has greatly increased international integration in asset markets. One indication of this integration is the rise in capital flows used to finance current account deficits, and the resulting accumulation of substantial financial imbalances. Whether such imbalances are a matter of concern depends on the theoretical framework one uses to explain and interpret them. The intertemporal approach to the current account, in its simplest form, focuses on the optimal saving decision of a representative household as it smooths consumption. For example, considering a small open economy experiencing a temporary fall in output, the country would be expected to smooth consumption by borrowing in world capital markets and thereby run a current account deficit. This basic intertemporal model

*This article originally appeared in *The Economic Journal* (2000), 110(463), 535–558.

has been extended in many directions in the theoretical literature, to include investment, variable interest rates, nontraded goods, and even monetary policy.[1]

Empirical work on the intertemporal approach to the current account has lagged behind the theoretical literature. Simple intertemporal models focusing on consumption smoothing have been tested empirically in Sheffrin and Woo (1990a, 1990b), Otto (1992), Milbourne and Otto (1992), Otto and Voss (1995), and Ghosh (1995). Most of these studies adapt present value tests developed by Campbell (1987) and Campbell and Shiller (1987), originally developed to test consumption theory.

Present value tests are an approach that makes full use of the model's structure to derive testable hypotheses. The simple intertemporal model implies that a country's current account surplus should be equal to the present value of expected future declines in output, net of investment and government purchases. A vector autoregression (VAR) involving the current account and output can be used to compute a forecast of this present value, conditional on households' information. According to the theory, the VAR forecast of this present value should be equal to the current account. This implication can be evaluated formally using a Wald statistic, or informally by comparing the historical movements of the current account with those of the prediction from the VAR. Similar tests have been useful in studies of consumption behavior and government deficits.[2]

To date, the results of such tests applied to the current account are mixed at best. While the simple intertemporal current account model has often been found to work fairly well for large countries, it ironically tends to fail for many small open economies. This is surprising, inasmuch as one would expect the assumptions of the theory to be most appropriate in these cases. Small open economies can borrow from the rest of the world without inducing offsetting changes in other variables such as the equilibrium world real interest rate.

A likely explanation for this failure is that small economies may be affected strongly by external shocks, a factor not considered in the simple version of the intertemporal model tested previously. To explain the current

[1]See Obstfeld and Rogoff (1996) for a useful summary of this extensive literature.
[2]For example, see Huang Lin (1993).

account behavior of small open economies, it may be important not only to model shocks to domestic output, but also shocks arising in the country's larger neighbors or the world in general. These external shocks will generally affect the small open economy via movements in the interest rate or exchange rate. Just as individuals may adjust consumption and saving behavior in response to movements in real interest rates, countries may also adjust their current account in response to movements of the real interest rate in world capital markets.

Furthermore, Dornbusch (1983) has demonstrated that an anticipated rise in the relative price of internationally traded goods can raise the cost of borrowing from the rest of the world, when interest is paid in units of these goods. As a result, changes in the real exchange rate can induce substitution in consumption between periods, and it thus can have intertemporal effects on a country's current account similar to those of changes in the interest rate. In addition to these intertemporal effects, exchange rate changes of course can also have more standard *intra*temporal effects, by inducing substitution between internationally-traded goods and nontraded goods at a point in time.

This chapter expands earlier present value tests of the current account to allow for variations in the interest rate and exchange rate. The chapter derives a testable implication of an intertemporal model that allows for time varying interest rates as well as a distinction between tradable and nontradable goods. This testable implication is then subjected to present value tests, using quarterly data from three small open economies that have proved problematic in past studies: Australia, Canada, and the United Kingdom. In two of the three countries, it is found that including the interest rate and exchange rate significantly improves the fit of the model over a benchmark model which excludes them. These extensions allow the model prediction to better match the volatility of current account data, and they improve the model's ability to explain historical episodes of current account imbalance. However, the results suggest that the intratemporal elements of the theory, rather than the intertemporal elements, are primarily responsible for improving the fit.

The next section of the chapter outlines a theory of the current account for variable interest rates and exchange rates and develops the econometric framework. Section 3 discusses the data and parameter values. Section 4 presents results from the present value tests. Our conclusion highlights some additional issues in interpreting and extending intertemporal models of the current account.

1. Theory and Econometric Methods

Our extensions are based on log-linearization of the intertemporal budget constraint, following the lead of Campbell and Mankiw (1989) in their work on consumption and Huang and Lin (1993) in their work on fiscal deficits. Our log-linear intertemporal budget constraint for the open economy is combined with the appropriate Euler equation to derive a fundamental testable implication involving a transformation of the current account. This current account condition can be subjected to present value tests.

Following Dornbusch (1983), we consider a small country producing traded and nontraded goods. The country can borrow and lend with the rest of the world at a time-varying real interest rate. The representative household solves an intertemporal maximization problem, choosing a path of consumption and debt that maximizes discounted lifetime utility:

$$\max\ E_0 \sum_{t=0}^{\infty} \beta^t U(C_{Tt}, C_{Nt}) \tag{1}$$

$$s.t\ Y_t - (C_{Tt} + P_t C_{Nt}) - I_t - G_t + r_t B_{t-1} = B_t - B_{t-1}, \tag{2}$$

where

$$U(C_{Tt}, C_{Nt}) = \frac{1}{1-\sigma}(C_{Tt}^{a}\ C_{Nt}^{1-a})^{1-\sigma},$$

$$\sigma > 0, \quad \sigma \neq 1, \quad 0 < a < 1.$$

Consumption of the traded good is denoted C_{Tt}, and consumption of the nontraded good is C_{NTt}. Y_t denotes the value of current output, I_t is investment expenditure, and G_t is government spending on goods and services, all measured in terms of traded goods. The relative price of home nontraded goods in terms of traded goods is denoted P_t. The stock of external assets at the beginning of the period is denoted B_t. Finally, r_t is the net world real interest rate in terms of traded goods, which may vary exogenously over time. The left-hand side of this budget constraint may be interpreted as the current account. We may express total consumption expenditure in terms of traded goods as $C_t = C_{Tt} + P_t C_{Nt}$.

Appendix A derives the first-order conditions for this problem and uses them to derive the following optimal consumption profile:

$$1 = E_t \left[\beta^{\gamma} (1 + r_{t+1})^{\gamma} \left(\frac{C_t}{C_{t+1}} \right) \left(\frac{P_t}{P_{t+1}} \right)^{(\gamma-1)(1-a)} \right]. \tag{3}$$

In this condition, $\gamma = \frac{1}{\sigma}$ is the intertemporal elasticity of substitution. This derivation generally follows the well-known methods in Dornbusch (1983) and Obstfeld and Rogoff (1996). This involves defining a Cobb–Douglas consumption index corresponding to the utility function, and then finding a related price index. These are used to transform the optimization problem into a form involving a single composite good. The resulting intertemporal Euler equation then can be written in terms of this composite good and price index, or alternatively as condition (3) above, in terms of total consumption expenditure and the relative price of nontraded goods.

Assuming joint log normality and constant variances and covariances, condition (3) may be written in logs:

$$E_t \Delta c_{t+1} = \gamma E_t r^*_{t+1}, \tag{4}$$

where r^* is a consumption-based real interest rate defined by

$$r^*_t = r_t + \left[\frac{1-\gamma}{\gamma} (1-a) \right] \Delta p_t + \text{constant}. \tag{5}$$

We define $\Delta c_{t+1} = \log C_{t+1} - \log C_t$ and $\Delta p_t = \log P_{t+1} - \log P_t$. For the world real interest rate (defined in terms of traded goods), we use the approximation: $\log(1 + r_t) \approx r_t$.[3] The constant term at the end of the expression will drop out of the empirical model when we later demean the consumption-based real interest rate using (5).

This condition characterizes how the optimal consumption profile is influenced by the consumption-based real interest rate, r^*, which reflects both the interest rate r and the change in the relative price of nontraded goods, p. Previous empirical studies of the intertemporal approach to the

[3]Campbell (1998) discusses evidence that the variance and covariance terms in the constant term of Equation (5) may be time-varying. Existing evidence suggests this is mainly a problem for frequencies higher than that used in this study. Campbell also suggests that it may be important to consider the case of time-varying risk aversion. While such extensions are potentially useful, they are beyond the scope of the present chapter.

current account have not allowed for these variables.[4] Such models imply a consumption profile where the expected change in consumption is zero; households always try to smooth consumption over time by borrowing and lending with the rest of the world. In contrast, the representative consumer here may be induced to alter the consumption profile and "unsmooth" consumption, in the face of changes in the terms of such borrowing and lending. First, consider the interest rate. An increase in the conventional real interest rate, r, makes current consumption more expensive in terms of future consumption foregone, and induces substitution toward future consumption with elasticity γ.

A similar intertemporal effect can result from a change in the relative price of nontraded goods. If the price of traded goods is temporarily low and expected to rise, then the future repayment of a loan in traded goods has a higher cost in terms of the consumption bundle than in terms of traded goods alone. Thus, the consumption-based interest rate r^* rises above the conventional interest rate r, and lowers the current total consumption expenditure by elasticity $\gamma(1 - a)$.

In addition to this intertemporal substitution, a change in the relative price of nontraded goods also induces intratemporal substitution. Again if the price of traded goods is temporarily low relative to nontraded goods, households will substitute toward traded goods by the intratemporal elasticity, which is unity under a Cobb–Douglas specification. This raises total current consumption expenditure by elasticity $(1 - a)$. This intratemporal effect will be dominated by the intertemporal effect if the intertemporal elasticity, γ, is greater than unity.

The representative agent optimization problem above entails an intertemporal budget constraint. Define R_s as the market discount factor for date s consumption, so that $R_s = \frac{1}{\Pi_{j=1}^{s}(1+r_j)}$. Using the budget constraint of the optimization problem (Equation (2)), the current account (CA) may be written:

$$\mathrm{CA}_t = Y_t - (C_{Tt} + P_t C_{Nt}) - I_t - G_t + r_t B_{t-1} \quad (6)$$

[4]At the time of writing this chapter, Fahrion (1997) concurrently has developed a present value model which allows for variable interest rates; it does not consider nontraded goods.

or as

$$\mathrm{CA}_t = \mathrm{NO}_t - C_t + r_t B_{t-1}, \tag{7}$$

where we define net output as follows: $\mathrm{NO}_t = Y_t - I_t - G_t$. Summing over all periods of the infinite horizon, and imposing the following transversality condition:

$$\lim_{t \to \infty} E_0 \left(R_t \, B_t\right) = 0, \tag{8}$$

we may write an intertemporal budget constraint:

$$\sum_{t=0}^{\infty} E_0(R_t C_t) = \sum_{t=0}^{\infty} E_0(R_t \mathrm{NO}_t) + B_0, \tag{9}$$

where B_0 is initial net foreign assets. We log linearize this intertemporal budget constraint, following Campbell and Mankiw (1989) and Huang and Lin (1993). We show in Appendix B that Equation (9) may be log-linearized as follows:

$$-\sum_{t=1}^{\infty} \beta^t \left[\Delta \mathrm{no}_t - \frac{\Delta c_t}{\Omega} - \left(1 - \frac{1}{\Omega}\right) r_t\right] = \mathrm{no}_0 - \frac{c_0}{\Omega} + \left(1 - \frac{1}{\Omega}\right) b_0, \tag{10}$$

where lower case letters represent the logs of upper case counterparts except in the case of the world real interest rate, where we again use the approximation that $\log(1 + r_t) \approx r_t$. Here, Ω is a constant slightly less than one, $\Omega = 1 - \overline{B}/\sum_{t=0}^{\infty} R_t C_t$, where $\overline{B}$ is the steady state value of net foreign assets.

Next, take expectations of Equation (10) above and combine it with the Euler equation (4) to write:

$$-E_t \sum_{i=1}^{\infty} \beta^i \left[\Delta \mathrm{no}_{t+i} - \frac{\gamma}{\Omega} r^*_{t+i} - \left(1 - \frac{1}{\Omega}\right) r_t\right]$$

$$= \mathrm{no}_t - \frac{c_t}{\Omega} + \left(1 - \frac{1}{\Omega}\right) b_t. \tag{11}$$

The right side of this equation is similar to the definition of the current account in Equation (6), except that its components are in log terms. We label this transformed representation of the current account as CA*. We will follow the convention of choosing the steady state around which we linearize to be the one in which net foreign assets are zero. In this case, $\Omega = 1$ and the condition above may be written:[5]

$$\mathrm{CA}_t^* = -E_t \sum_{i=1}^{\infty} \beta^i \left(\Delta \mathrm{no}_{t+i} - \gamma r_{t+i}^*\right), \tag{12}$$

where

$$\mathrm{CA}_t^* \equiv \mathrm{no}_t - c_t. \tag{13}$$

This condition says that if net output is expected to fall, the current account will rise as the representative household smooths consumption. But the condition also says that aside from any change in domestic output, a rise in the consumption-based interest rate will raise the current account by inducing the representative household to lower consumption below its smoothed level. For comparison, we also test a simpler version of the intertemporal model, where the consumption-based interest rate is assumed to be constant, and consequently only the first of the two effects described above will occur. This amounts to testing a condition similar to Equation (12) above, where the second term in the brackets is not present.

This restriction in Equation (12) is tested using the approach of Sheffrin and Woo (1990b), augmented to consider the additional variable, r^*. To test the restriction that the current account depends on expected future values of net output and interest rate, we first must have proxies for these two sets of expected values. Under the null hypothesis of Equation (12), the current account itself should incorporate all of the consumers' information on future values of the linear combination of the interest rate and net output changes specified in that equation. This leads us to estimate a VAR to represent consumers' forecasts:

$$\begin{bmatrix} \Delta \mathrm{no} \\ \mathrm{CA}^* \\ r^* \end{bmatrix}_t = \begin{bmatrix} a_{11} & a_{12} & a_{13} \\ a_{21} & a_{22} & a_{23} \\ a_{31} & a_{32} & a_{33} \end{bmatrix} \begin{bmatrix} \Delta \mathrm{no} \\ \mathrm{CA}^* \\ r^* \end{bmatrix}_{t-1} + \begin{bmatrix} u_{1t} \\ u_{2t} \\ u_{3t} \end{bmatrix}. \tag{14}$$

Or written more compactly: $\mathbf{z}_t = \mathbf{A}\mathbf{z}_{t-1} + \mathbf{u}_t$, where $E(\mathbf{z}_{t+i}) = \mathbf{A}^i\mathbf{z}_t$. This may easily be generalized for higher orders of VAR by writing a pth order VAR in first order form. A test of the simpler model that holds interest rates

[5]Otto and Voss (1995) demonstrate it can be valuable to consider the net foreign asset position.

constant would involve a VAR that omits the third equation and the third variable, r^*.

Using (14), the restrictions on the current account in (12) can be expressed as

$$\mathbf{h}\,\mathbf{z}_t = -\sum_{i=1}^{\infty} \beta^i (\mathbf{g}_1 - \gamma \mathbf{g}_2)\mathbf{A}^i \mathbf{z}_t, \tag{15}$$

where $\mathbf{g}_1 = [1\ 0\ 0]$, $\mathbf{g}_2 = [0\ 0\ 1]$, and $\mathbf{h} = [0\ 1\ 0]$. (Again this can be generalized for a larger number of lags.) For a given $\mathbf{z}_t$, the right-hand side of Equation (15) can be expressed as

$$\widehat{\mathrm{CA}}_t^* = \mathbf{k}\,\mathbf{z}_t, \tag{16}$$

where

$$\mathbf{k} = -(\mathbf{g}_1' - \gamma \mathbf{g}_2')\beta \mathbf{A}(\mathbf{I} - \beta \mathbf{A})^{-1}.$$

This expression gives a model prediction of the current account variable consistent with the VAR and the restrictions of the intertemporal theory. This can be compared graphically with the actual data as an indication of how well the restrictions of the theory are satisfied. Note that $\mathbf{k}\ \mathbf{z}_t$ is not a forecast of the current account in the conventional sense, but rather is a representation of the model's restrictions.

In addition, if the restrictions of the theory were consistent with the data, such that $\widehat{\mathrm{CA}}_t^* = \mathrm{CA}_t^*$, then the vector $\mathbf{k}$ should equal [0 1 0]. This implies the model may then be tested statistically by using the delta method to calculate a χ^2 statistic for the hypothesis that $\mathbf{k} = [0\ 1\ 0]$. Let $\widetilde{\mathbf{k}}$ be the difference between the actual $\mathbf{k}$ and the hypothesised value. Then $\widetilde{\mathbf{k}}' \left(\frac{\partial \mathrm{k}}{\partial \mathrm{A}}\, \mathbf{V}\, \frac{\partial \mathrm{k}}{\partial \mathrm{A}}' \right)^{-1} \widetilde{\mathbf{k}}$ will be distributed chi-squared with three degrees of freedom, where $\mathbf{V}$ is the variance–covariance matrix of the underlying parameters in the VAR, and $\frac{\partial \mathrm{k}}{\partial \mathrm{A}}$ is the matrix of derivatives of the $\mathbf{k}$ vector with respect to these underlying parameters, which can be computed numerically.

2. Data and Parameter Values

We test Equation (12) using quarterly data from three countries: Canada, Australia, and the United Kingdom. Small open economies are of special interest, since these have been the most problematic in past studies. This is surprising, since the theory should be most applicable to a small open economy that can borrow without affecting international capital markets. Canada and the United Kingdom are studied because they were shown to be especially problematic for the intertemporal theory in the previous work of Sheffrin and Woo (1990b).[6] Australia was found to be problematic in work by Milbourne and Otto (1992). All three countries have long quarterly data for the required series. Tests using only annual data often are unable to reject the restrictions of the model, even though the estimates clearly do not coincide with the theory, simply because there is so much uncertainty around these estimates that almost no value can be rejected. All data are from the International Financial Statistics (IFS), seasonally adjusted at annual rates.

We compute a measure of the world real interest rate, r_t, following the method of Barro and Sala i Martin (1990). We collected short-term nominal interest rates, T-bill rates or the equivalent, on the G-7 economies. We use short-term interest rates because we wish to adjust for inflation expectations, which are much more reliably forecast over a short-time horizon. Inflation in each country is measured using that country's consumer price index, and expected inflation is forecast using a six-quarter autoregression. The nominal interest rate in each country then is adjusted by inflation expectations to compute an *ex-ante* real interest rate. An average real interest rate then is computed, using time-varying weights for each country based on its share of real gross domestic product (GDP) in the G-7 total. This same series is used for each of the three subject countries in the study.

The net output series, NO_t, was constructed for each of the three subject countries by subtracting investment and government purchases from GDP, adjusting by the 1990 GDP deflator and by national population. Equation (12) uses this in logged and differenced form, Δno_t. The series for the current account variable, CA_t^*, was constructed for each country by subtracting the log of consumption, adjusted for population and the 1990 GDP deflator, from the log of net output.

[6]Belgium and Denmark were also considered in this previous study, but the quarterly data was not available for the first of these countries and only available for the recent decade for the second.

We follow Rogoff (1992) in using as a proxy for P_t a measure of the real exchange rate derived from IFS. For Canada and the United Kingdom, the IFS computes an effective nominal exchange rate index based on unit labor costs. This is not available for Australia, so we instead use a market exchange rate index. These nominal indexes are converted to real terms using a consumption price index for industrial countries provided by IFS and a national price index for each subject country, respectively.[7] An *ex-ante* expected exchange rate appreciation is computed, $E_t\Delta p_{t+1}$, using a six-quarter autoregression, logging and differencing. Finally, the consumption-based real interest rate, r_t^*, is computed for each country using the common world real interest rate and the country-specific exchange rate series derived above, as specified by Equation (5). Because we are interested in the dynamic implications of the intertemporal model, the three series, Δno, CA* and r^* all are demeaned.

Tests of condition (12) are contingent on values for the parameters β, a, and γ. Previous studies that tested the simpler version of the intertemporal model needed to deal only with the first of these parameters, but we follow their strategy in considering a range of values for unknown parameters.

The present model has an advantage in assigning a value to β, the discount factor. Denoting as $\bar{r}$ the sample mean for the real interest rate in our data set, the model implies we may compute $\beta = \frac{1}{1+\bar{r}}$, which here equals approximately 0.94.

Regarding the share of traded goods in private final consumption, a, our data set is of little value for making any inference. So we turn to outside empirical studies. Stockman and Tesar (1995) estimate the share of tradables in two ways. First, using services as a proxy, they estimate the average share of nontradables over seven countries to be approximately one-half. A second method breaks down expenditure by categories used by Kravis, Heston, and Summers (1982), and uses expenditure on the following categories as a proxy for nontradables: rent, fuel, transportation, and communication. This method produces an average estimate of the traded share close to two-thirds. The present value tests below consider both values for the share parameter, though results are similar in both cases.

[7]Note that the real exchange rate measured here incorporates both the relative price of nontraded goods and the terms of trade, whereas the model is specified in terms of just the relative price of nontraded goods.

The intertemporal elasticity, γ, is the most problematic of the three parameters, in that outside empirical estimates range widely. Hall (1988) estimates the intertemporal elasticity to be small, concluding that it is unlikely to be much above 0.1 and it may well be zero. This is based on the observation that consumption tends to respond weakly to the real interest rate. On the other hand, the reciprocal of the intertemporal elasticity, σ, may be interpreted as the coefficient of relative risk aversion in the model. Mehra and Prescott (1985) have suggested that sensible values for σ should be less than 2.0, implying a value of γ greater than 0.5. These two concepts, though distinct, are linked as reciprocals because of the form of the utility function. Because the focus of this chapter is on the response of consumption to interest rates, rather than household attitudes toward risk, we are sympathetic to Hall's estimates.

Our tests consider a range of values for the intertemporal elasticity, but we focus attention on the case in which we estimate the elasticity in the context of our model. This estimation uses a method developed in an entirely analogous case by Campbell and Shiller (1989), in which the restrictions of the model are used to identify the parameter. Mechanically, we search for the value of γ that minimizes the $\chi 2$ statistic of the present value test. Campbell and Shiller (1989) demonstrate this can be interpreted as a method of moments estimation. However, when we eventually use the minimized $\chi 2$ statistic to evaluate a test of the overidentifying restrictions, a penalty must be imposed by reducing the degrees of freedom for the distribution by one.

As an alternative method of choosing parameter values, we experimented with conventional generalized method of moments (GMM) estimation of Equation (3), following Hansen and Singleton (1982). However, we found that these methods gave imprecise estimates of the three parameters with large standard errors, and estimates of the tradable goods share were outside the range permitted by the theory.[8]

Before we test the model, we must check the assumption that the variables in the VAR, CA*, r^* and Δno, are stationary. We run a standard

[8]Detailed GMM results are available from the authors.

procedure by regressing

$$\Delta CA_t^* = \sum_{i=1}^{n} b_i \, \Delta CA_{t-i}^* + cCA_{t-1}^* + \eta_t \tag{17}$$

and testing whether the coefficient c is negative and significantly different from zero using the appropriate Dickey–Fuller statistics.[9] We perform this test for a range of lags, n, on the differenced term. In addition, we test for nonstationarity by the Phillips–Perron test, which controls for higher-order serial correlation by making a correction to the t-statistic for the coefficient c, rather than adding a set of lagged difference terms as in the Dickey–Fuller tests. We use the Newey–West heteroskedasticity autocorrelation consistent estimate of the adjustment, and we consider a range of values for the number of periods of serial correlation. We perform these stationarity tests also for the two other variables used in our present value tests, the consumption-based real interest rate, r^*, and the change in net output, Δno_t. In computing r^* for the stationarity tests, we use a value for the parameter a of one-half, and for γ we use the values estimated using the method of Campbell and Shiller (1989), as discussed above. The results are reported in Table 1. For each of the three variables in each country, both the Dickey–Fuller test and the Phillips–Perron test reject the presence of a unit root at least at the 5% significance level for all numbers of lags considered.

3. Results

The results from present value tests are summarized in Tables 2–4. All tables have the same format, where each column represents an alternative specification of the model. The first and second columns are most important. The first column shows a benchmark model, which ignores changes in the interest rate and exchange rate. The second column shows a model augmented with these two variables, in which the intertemporal elasticity is estimated in the context of the model. Each column reports the estimated K-vector, as well as the associated χ^2 statistic and its p-value. Finally, the

[9] We do not include a time trend or constant in the above regression, because the three series have been demeaned, and they fluctuate around a level of zero without apparent trend throughout the sample period.

Table 1. Unit root tests

Nlags	1	3	5
Australia			
Current account (CA*):			
ADF	−2.599**	−3.126**	−3.160**
PP	−3.212**	−3.970**	−3.441**
Interest rate (r*):			
ADF	−7.421**	−5.515**	−4.327**
PP	−10.660**	−10.667**	−10.673**
Change in net output (Δno):			
ADF	−8.181**	−5.576**	−3.854**
PP	−14.153**	−14.242**	−14.377**
Share of traded goods = 0.5, intertemporal elasticity = 0.087, range: 1961-Q2 to 1996-Q2.			
Canada			
Current account (CA*):			
ADF	−2.768*	−2.661**	−2.388**
PP	−2.975**	−3.020**	−2.966**
Interest rate (r*):			
ADF	−6.697**	−5.119**	−4.435**
PP	−10.144**	−10.274**	−10.367**
Change in net output (Δno):			
ADF	−10.959**	−6.505**	−4.999**
PP	−15.255**	−15.734**	−15.911**
Share of traded goods = 0.5, intertemporal elasticity = 0.039, range: 1960-Q1 to 1996-Q2.			
United Kingdom			
Current account (CA*):			
ADF	−2.233*	−2.438*	−2.293*
PP	−2.396*	−2.502*	−2.553*
Interest rate (r*):			
ADF	−8.327**	−5.974**	−4.526**
PP	−11.873**	−11.876**	−11.872**
Change in net output (Δno):			
ADF	−9.191**	−4.995**	−4.587**
PP	−14.048**	−14.062**	−14.036**
Share of traded goods = 0.5, intertemporal elasticity = 0.085, range: 1960-Q1 to 1996-Q2.			

Notes: ADF indicates the augmented Dickey–Fuller test; PP indicates Phillips–Perron.

'*' indicates the test statistic is significant at the 5% significance level; '**' indicates the 1% significance level. Regressions do not include a constant or time trend.

Table 2. Australia present value tests

Cases:	Primary models: (1) Benchmark model (r^* constant)	Primary models: (2) Optimal model (γ chosen to minimize χ^2)	Alternative models: (3) γ chosen to match variance	Alternative models: (4) $\gamma = 0.5$	Alternative models: (5) $\gamma = 1.0$	Alternative models: (6) Just interest rate (exchange rate excluded)	Alternative models: (7) $a = 2/3$
γ	—	0.087	0.022	0.500	1.000	0.078	0.097
K-vector:							
no_t	0.308	0.048	0.048	−0.140	0.401	0.328	0.120
	(0.052)	(0.120)	(0.121)	(0.234)	(0.401)	(0.069)	(0.094)
no_{t-1}	0.059	0.124	0.124	0.288	0.212	0.084	0.108
	(0.030)	(0.071)	(0.071)	(0.137)	(0.236)	(0.041)	(0.055)
CA^*_t	0.406	0.934	0.988	1.008	1.063	0.523	0.749
	(0.105)	(0.231)	(0.234)	(0.413)	(0.772)	(0.134)	(0.180)
CA^*_{t-1}	0.206	−0.047	−0.034	−0.402	0.479	0.252	0.010
	(0.060)	(0.151)	(0.151)	(0.304)	(0.448)	(0.078)	(0.120)
r^*_t	—	0.009	0.001	1.169	12.945	1.841	0.021
		(0.013)	(0.003)	(0.357)	(3.280)	(0.568)	(0.018)
r^*_{t-1}	—	−0.004	−0.001	0.389	−5.680	−0.805	0.000
		(0.009)	(0.002)	(0.187)	(1.836)	(0.318)	(0.012)
χ^2-statistic	51.288	5.825	5.942	12.137	16.586	37.645	9.342
p-value	0.000	0.324*	0.312*	0.059	0.011	0.000*	0.096*
$\sigma_{CA^*}/\sigma_{CA^*}$	0.662	0.944	1.000	1.483	5.472	1.000	0.823

Notes: Standard errors in parentheses. Regressions are for 1961-Q4 to 1996-Q2. Share of tradables in consumption, a, is 0.5, unless otherwise stated. $\beta = 0.94$. * indicates degrees of freedom equal 5 in this case instead of 6 because of extra estimated parameter.

Table 3. Canada present value tests

	Primary models		Alternative models				
Cases:	(1) Benchmark model (r^* constant)	(2) Optimal model (γ chosen to minimize χ^2)	(3) γ Chosen to match variance	(4) $\gamma = 0.5$	(5) $\gamma = 1.0$	(6) Just interest rate (exchange rate excluded)	(7) $a = 2/3$
γ	—	0.039	0.177	0.500	1.000	3.740	0.397
K-vector:							
no_t	0.192	−0.196	−0.336	−0.304	0.813	2.105	−0.196
	(0.099)	(0.192)	(0.233)	(0.435)	(0.643)	(2.286)	(0.362)
no_{t-1}	0.068	0.011	−0.018	0.113	−0.052	−0.436	0.111
	(0.059)	(0.103)	(0.123)	(0.242)	(0.399)	(1.418)	(0.201)
CA_t^*	0.083	0.636	0.945	0.733	0.020	0.645	0.558
	(0.232)	(0.420)	(0.502)	(0.979)	(1.510)	(5.369)	(0.815)
CA_{t-1}^*	0.036	−0.208	−0.261	−0.528	0.128	0.325	−0.425
	(0.103)	(0.195)	(0.235)	(0.485)	(0.678)	(2.411)	(0.403)
r_t^*	—	0.021	0.209	2.969	8.587	49.050	2.459
		(0.010)	(0.070)	(0.853)	(2.070)	(12.469)	(0.708)
r_{t-1}^*	—	0.004	0.057	1.000	−2.066	−22.100	0.835
		(0.007)	(0.046)	(0.442)	(0.889)	(6.842)	(0.367)
χ^2-statistic	16.242	10.876	12.049	12.703	17.454	16.244	13.167
p-value	0.003	0.054*	0.034*	0.048	0.008	0.006*	0.022*
$\sigma_{CA^*}/\sigma_{CA^*}$	0.184	0.525	1.000	4.393	7.068	28.223	3.626

Notes: Standard errors in parentheses. Regressions are for 1960-Q3 to 1996-Q2. Share of tradables in consumption, a, is 0.5, unless otherwise stated. $\beta = 0.94$. * indicates degrees of freedom equal 5 in this case instead of 6 because of extra estimated parameter.

Table 4. United kingdom present value tests

Cases:	Primary models		Alternative models				
	(1) Benchmark model (r^* constant)	(2) Optimal model (γ chosen to minimize χ^2)	(3) γ Chosen to match variance	(4) $\gamma = 0.5$	(5) $\gamma = 1.0$	(6) Just interest rate (exchange rate excluded)	(7) $a = 2/3$
γ	—	0.085	0.458	0.500	1.000	0.049	0.429
K-vector:							
no_t	0.206	0.165	0.133	0.134	0.140	0.210	0.177
	(0.049)	(0.049)	(0.050)	(0.050)	(0.053)	(0.053)	(0.049)
CA_t^*	0.072	0.546	0.634	0.625	−0.128	0.001	0.396
	(0.202)	(0.203)	(0.205)	(0.206)	(0.217)	(0.217)	(0.203)
r_t^*	—	0.002	0.581	0.838	11.544	1.235	0.002
		(0.005)	(0.061)	(0.077)	(0.504)	(0.502)	(0.005)
χ^2-statistic	27.494	12.867	115.965	145.813	561.948	34.119	16.646
p-value	0.000	0.002*	0.000*	0.000	0.000	0.000*	0.000*
$\sigma_{CA^*}/\sigma_{CA^*}$	0.147	0.574	1.000	1.177	9.367	1.000	4.288

Notes: Standard errors in parentheses. Regressions are for 1960-Q2 to 1996-Q2. Share of tradables in consumption, a, is 0.5, unless otherwise stated. $\beta = 0.94$. * indicates degrees of freedom equal 2 in this case instead of 3 because of extra estimated parameter.

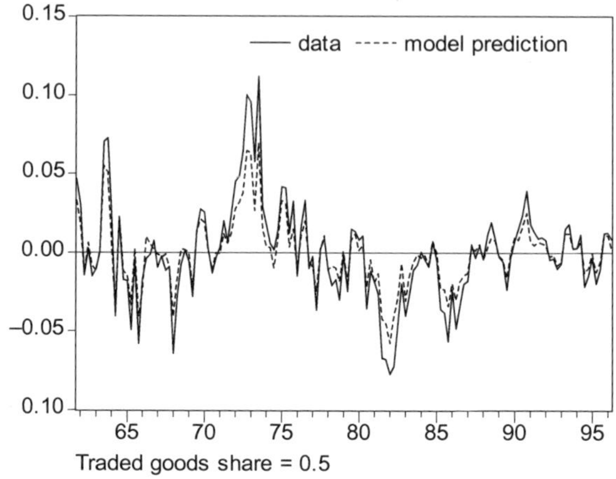

Figure 1. Australia: Current account variable excluding interest rate and exchange rate

volatility of the predicted current account is reported as a ratio to that for the actual data. Note that since the degrees of freedom vary by case, the χ^2 statistic is not comparable across cases, but the p-value is useful for such comparisons. To further illustrate how well the restrictions of the model are satisfied, Figures 1–6 plot the model prediction for the current account variable, derived using (16), and compare this to the data.[10]

To briefly preview the results discussed below in detail, the statistical test in all three countries rejects the benchmark model, which ignores changes in the interest rate and exchange rate. But for two of the countries, the model augmented with these variables is not rejected, and even in the third case, there appears to be improvement relative to the benchmark model.

3.1. *Australia*

In the case of Australia, the Akaike information criterion suggests that two lags be used.[11] Figure 1 shows the current account variable computed from the data and the prediction generated by the version of the

[10]Note that the figures do not offer a way to control for the number of variables or free parameters in the model. Therefore, in comparing alternative models, we will rely primarily on the statistical tests, and use the figures mainly for illustration.

[11]Similarly, Ghosh (1995) uses between 1 and 3 lags for his VARS on quarterly data.

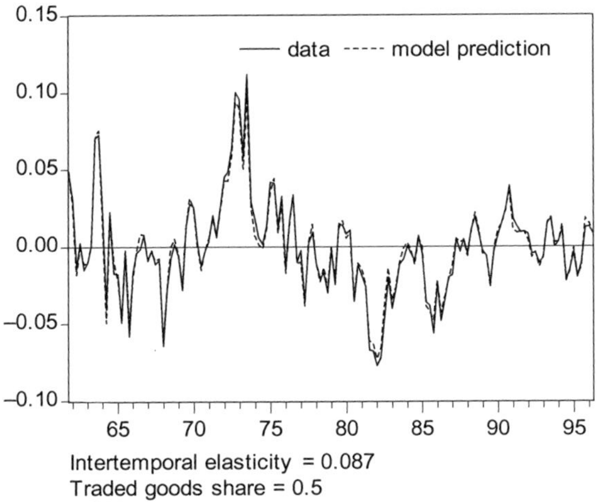

Figure 2. Australia: Current account variable including interest rate and exchange rate

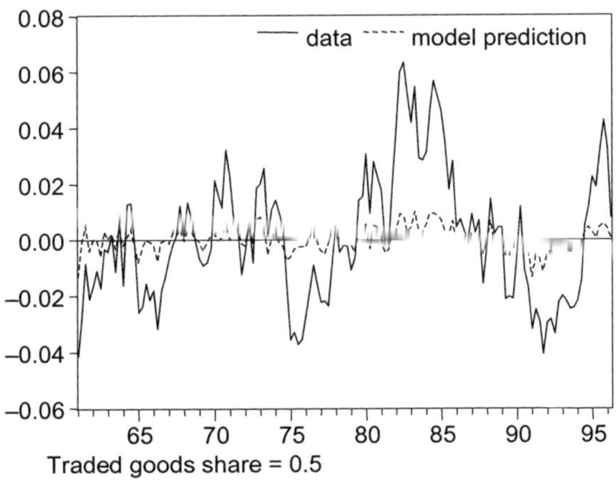

Figure 3. Canada: Current account variable excluding interest rate and exchange rate

intertemporal model that excludes interest rates and exchange rates, over the range 1961-Q4 to 1996-Q2. This simple model does fairly well in predicting the general direction of current account fluctuations, such as the run of sizable deficits in the early 1980s and another in the middle of the decade. Indeed, a cursory examination of output data for Australia suggests transitory dips in output roughly corresponding to these periods.

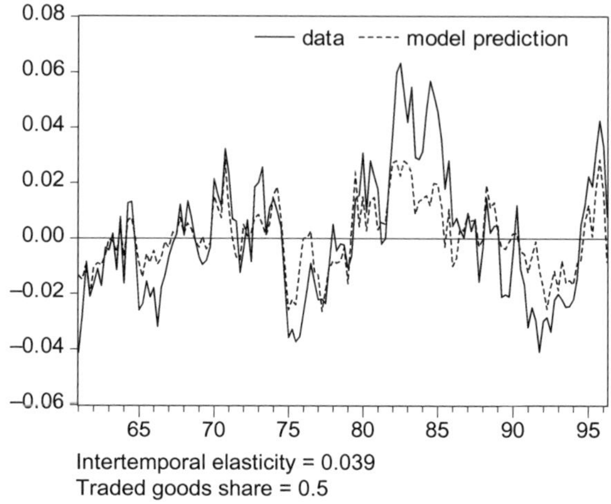

Figure 4. Canada: Current account variable including interest rate and exchange rate

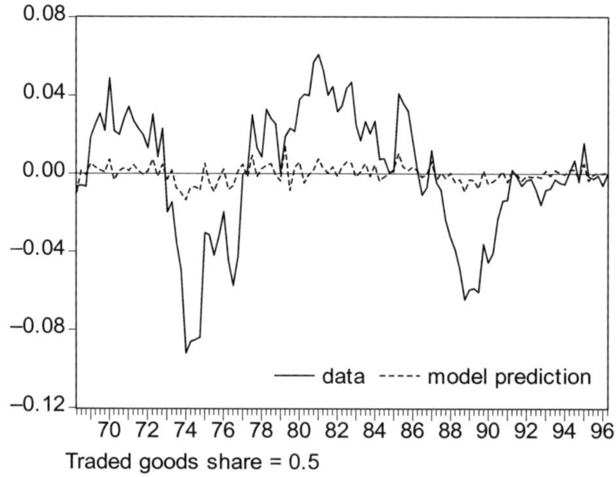

Figure 5. United Kingdom: Current account variable excluding interest rate and exchange rate

However, the statistical test presented in column (1) of Table 2, soundly rejects the model. The intertemporal theory suggests that with two lags and two variables the K-vector should be [0 0 1 0]. The **k**-vector coefficient on the current account at date t is 0.406, and while it is significantly different zero it also is significantly different from the value of unity suggested by

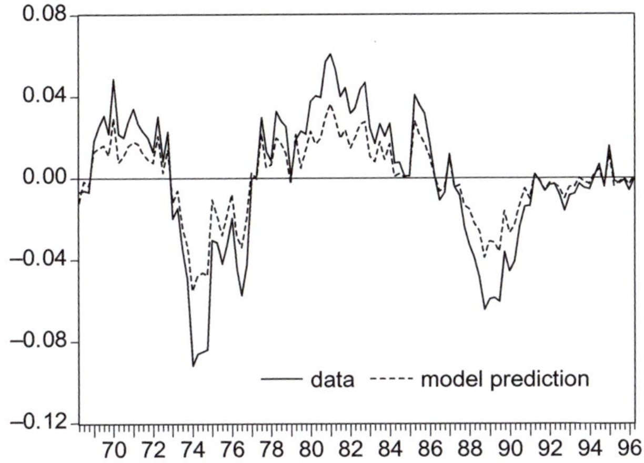

Figure 6. United Kingdom: Current account variable including interest rate and exchange rate

the theory. Further, the values on net output and lagged current account are significantly different from their theoretical values of zero. Overall, the χ^2 test strongly rejects the model, with a p-value of zero. This result is typical of most past tests in this area: While a simple graphical analysis suggests the simple intertemporal model can explain much, the model rarely satisfies statistical tests. The table shows that part of the problem is that the model prediction is only about two-thirds as volatile as the actual data. The graph confirms this; while the model captures the direction of most current account fluctuations, it repeatedly underpredicts the magnitudes.

Next consider an intertemporal model which includes a time-varying consumption-based real interest rate. We believe this partly explains some episodes of current account deficit in Australia, such as the middle 1980s, as the world real interest rate series computed here is unusually low during this period. We focus on the model in which we use the method of Campbell and Shiller (1989) to estimate the intertemporal elasticity. The resulting estimate for γ is 0.087, which is low but not out of line with estimates by Hall (1988) discussed in the previous section. Figure 2 shows that the model prediction is improved over that of the simpler model, mainly in that it better captures the magnitude of fluctuations. This improvement is confirmed in column (2) of Table 2. The intertemporal theory suggests that with two lags and three variables, the K-vector should be [0 0 1 0 0 0]. The coefficient on lagged current account is 0.934, significantly different from zero and not significantly different from the theoretically prescribed value of unity. All other coefficients are very small and insignificantly different from zero. The present value test is far from rejected, with a p-value of 0.324. We compute this p-value for a distribution of five rather than six degrees of freedom, to take into consideration the penalty for using one restriction to identify the elasticity we estimated. Confirming the impression from the figure, the table notes that the volatility of the current account forecast has risen, the standard error is now 94.4% of that for the actual data.

As an alternative, we consider a value for the intertemporal elasticity that enables the model to match the volatility of the current account data. The estimate for the elasticity again is small, 0.022. As shown in column (3) of Table 2, the K-vector coefficient on current account at date t is now 0.988, very close to the theoretically predicted value of unity. The statistical test again does not reject the model.

The other columns of Table 2 are included for sensitivity analysis. Columns (4) and (5) explore larger values for the intertemporal elasticity. As the intertemporal elasticity rises, the volatility of the current account rises in excess of the volatility of the actual data, and the fit of the model worsens. Next, column (6) considers a model in which the exchange rate is not permitted to vary, but the world real interest rate is. This is intended to distinguish the separate effects of the two components of our composite variable, r^*. The value of γ used here is that which matches the current account volatility, because the value which minimizes the value of the χ^2 statistic is negative. The model is rejected, suggesting that the exchange rate, rather than the interest rate, is primarily responsible for the improvement in the model's fit. Indeed, a relatively appreciated Australian real exchange rate at the beginning of the 1980s partly explains the current account deficit during this period. Column (7) tests sensitivity to the assumption of the share of nontraded goods. The experiment of column (2) is replicated under the assumption that $a = 2/3$ rather than $1/2$. The model performs somewhat less well, but the qualitative conclusions are unchanged.

Clearly, including the consumption-based interest rate improves the fit of the model to the data. In particular, it offers a way to increase the volatility of the model prediction for the current account to better match the data.

One interpretation of this result is that the new variable helps to capture important external shocks. These are transmitted to the home country through changes in the real interest rate and exchange rate, which then induce a response in consumption and hence fluctuations in the current account.

Small intertemporal elasticities appear to work best in the present model. This is consistent with outside estimates discussed earlier, which suggest that consumption responds only moderately to interest rate changes. The theory developed in this chapter implies that as the intertemporal elasticity grows small, so do the intertemporal effects of both the world real interest rate and the expected change in the relative price of nontraded goods. However, the theory implies that the relative price of nontraded goods also has an intratemporal effect, and this effect grows larger as the elasticity approaches zero. Our estimation of a low intertemporal elasticity suggests that it is mainly this intratemporal effect that is improving the fit of the model, more so than the additional intertemporal effects. Yet both sets of effects are consistent with the theoretical model. Note also that a small intertemporal elasticity means households aggressively smooth their consumption. So expected changes in net output, a central feature of the basic intertemporal current account theory, also plays a large role in our results.

3.2. *Canada*

The Akaike information criterion suggests that two lags be used in the case of Canada. Figure 3 shows the actual data for CA*, and the forecast based on the simple model that ignores changes in the interest rate and exchange rate. The model prediction is much less volatile than the actual data. While it shows some variability from quarter to quarter, the prediction misses the larger, medium-term swings of the current account away from balance. In particular, it misses the large surpluses in the early to mid 1980s and again in the middle of the next decade, toward the end of our sample. This poor prediction is reflected in the statistical test reported in column (1) of Table 3. The point estimate of the **k**-vector coefficient on the current account is 0.083, far from the value of unity prescribed by the theory. The χ^2 test rejects the hypothesis that the K-vector as a whole is [0 0 1 0], with a p-value of 0.003. The model also fails in that the forecast of the current account is only a fifth as volatile as the data.

Figure 4 suggests that the model prediction for the current account improves when the interest rate and exchange rate are included, and the statistical test in column (2) of the table confirms this. The intertemporal elasticity is estimated at 0.039, which minimizes the χ^2 statistic. Now the longer-run deviations of the current account from balance depicted in the figure are better captured by the model prediction, including the improvement in the early to mid 1980s and again in the middle of the 1990s. A plausible explanation may be that this pattern is due to shocks originating in the United States, whose current account follows a basically inverted pattern to that seen in Canada in those years. These external shocks are reflected in the effective Canadian exchange rate, which weights the US dollar heavily. The Canadian exchange rate depreciates in the early and mid 1980s and again in the mid 1990s. The theory implies that the current account surpluses could be generated by the intratemporal effect, in which it becomes more expensive to purchase tradable goods from abroad. In the table, the element of the **k**-vector corresponding to the current account is 0.636, an improvement over the benchmark model in column (1), but not as close to the theoretical value of unity as was the corresponding value for Australia. However, the other elements of the **k**-vector are close to zero, and the χ^2 test does not reject the hypothesis that the **k**-vector is [0 0 1 0 0 0] . The volatility of the current account prediction also is improved relative to the benchmark in column (1).

Column (3) shows the less successful result if the intertemporal elasticity is estimated to match the second moment of the current account data. The element of the **k**-vector corresponding to the current account is much improved, 0.95, but other elements of the K-vector are now significantly different from zero. The statistical test rejects, once the penalty is imposed for the fact we estimate the intertemporal elasticity. Columns (4)–(7) reiterate the conclusions from their counterparts for Australia in Table 2. Larger intertemporal elasticities generate excessive volatility. And consideration of a variable exchange rate is an essential component of the model's success.

3.3. *United Kingdom*

Results for the United Kingdom are less successful than in the previous two countries. The Akaike information criterion suggests only one lag be used. Figure 5 offers an especially dramatic example of how the benchmark model produces predictions that are much too flat. The model completely fails to predict the large swings in the current account, such as the large deficit in the start of the 1990s. The statistical tests in Table 4 confirm this: the test firmly rejects the intertemporal model restriction that $\mathbf{k} = [01]$.

One might again expect the intratemporal effect of exchange rates to be important here. For example, the United Kingdom real exchange rate is generally thought to be rather appreciated in the beginning of the 1990s as the UK fought to remain part of the Exchange Rate Mechanism in Europe. This may well have contributed to the low current account. Later, the devaluation in 1992 may have contributed to the return to current account balance. Figure 6 shows the prediction for the model augmented with a variable exchange rate and interest rate. The figure suggests the model prediction is strongly affected. It now begins to capture the medium-run swings from balance that were utterly absent previously. The statistical test shows that the *p*-value indeed is improved over that of the simple model. However, the fit still is quite poor, and the model still is rejected by the test.

4. Conclusion

This chapter has examined the question of why simple intertemporal models of the current account have not fared well in tests using data from small open economies. This failure is surprising, inasmuch as the underlying assumptions of the theory should apply especially well in these economies. We show that allowing both for a variable interest rate and exchange rate can improve the fit of the model. In some cases, movements in the interest rate and exchange rate can explain much of the medium-term movements of the current account from balance that had been unexplained under the simpler intertemporal theory used in earlier tests.

This chapter has offered an explanation for the explanatory power of these additional variables. The current account of a small open economy is likely to be affected not only by shocks to domestic output or government expenditure, but also by external shocks to the economies of large neighbors. Such external shocks should be expected to affect the domestic economy via changes in the world interest rate and the country's real exchange rate, both of which set the terms by which the small open economy can trade intertemporally with the rest of the world. The intertemporal theory implies that such changes in the interest rate and exchange rate affect the intertemporal profile of saving and hence the current account. However, the theory also allows for *intra*temporal effects arising from the presence of exchange rates, and it appears that these intratemporal effects are significantly responsible for the model's improved fit.

The intertemporal model, with its dynamic budget constraint and intertemporal trade-offs, is a useful starting point for current account analysis. The simplest versions of the intertemporal current account model admittedly are limited as positive descriptions of the data. But results here suggest that the model's descriptive power can be improved with modest extensions, notably the inclusion of certain *intra*temporal trade-offs. Future empirical work should consider further extensions of the basic model that have been considered in theoretical work, such as investment dynamics, a distinction between durable and nondurable goods, labor-supply decisions, and nominal rigidities.

Appendices

Appendix A: Deriving the optimal consumption profile

We follow Dornbusch (1983) and Obstfeld and Rogoff (1996) in deriving the optimal consumption profile. Define an index of total consumption, $C_t^* = C_{Tt}^a\, C_{Nt}^{1-a}$. Define also a consumption-based price index, P_t^*, as the minimum amount of consumption expenditure $C_t = C_{Tt} + P_t\, C_{Nt}$ such that $C_t^* = 1$, given P_t. Traded goods are the numeraire. The household problem (Equations (1) and (2)) implies $U_{Nt} = P_t U_{Tt}$ and hence the following allocation of expenditure between tradables and nontradables:

$$C_{Tt} = a\, C_t \quad \text{and} \quad C_{Nt} = (1-a)\,\frac{C_t}{P_t}. \tag{A1}$$

Substitute these into the definition of C_t^*

$$C_t^* = (aC_t)^a \left[(1-a)\frac{C_t}{P_t}\right]^{1-a} \tag{A2}$$

and use the definition of P^* to write

$$\left(aP_t^*\right)^a \left[(1-a)\frac{P_t^*}{P_t}\right]^{1-a} = 1. \tag{A3}$$

Solve this for the consumption-based price index:

$$P_t^* = P_t^{1-a}\left[a^{-a}(1-a)^{-(1-a)}\right]. \tag{A4}$$

This allows us to rewrite the budget constraint of the optimization problem (2) as

$$Y_t - P_t^* C_t^* - I_t - G_t + r_t B_{t-1} = B_t - B_{t-1} \tag{A5}$$

and the utility function as $U(C_t^*) = \frac{1}{1-\sigma}(C_t^*)^{1-\sigma}$. This implies an intertemporal Euler equation:

$$E_t\left[\beta(1+r_{t+1})\left(\frac{P_t^*}{P_{t+1}^*}\right)\left(\frac{C_t^*}{C_{t+1}^*}\right)^{\sigma}\right] = 1. \tag{A6}$$

To facilitate an empirical implementation, we rewrite this condition in terms of consumption expenditure and the relative price of nontraded goods:

$$E_t\left[\beta(1+r_{t+1})\left(\frac{C_t}{C_{t+1}}\right)^{\sigma}\left(\frac{P_t}{P_{t+1}}\right)^{(1-\sigma)(1-a)}\right] = 1. \tag{A7}$$

Assume joint log normality for the gross real world interest rate $(1 + r_{t+1})$, consumption growth rate $(\Delta c_{t+1} = \log C_{t+1} - \log C_t)$, and the % change in the relative price of nontraded goods $(\Delta p_t = \log P_{t+1} - \log P_t)$. Assume also that the variances and covariances between these variables are not time-varying. Then following conventional methods, the expression above may be written in log-linearized form:[12]

$$\begin{aligned} E_t\,\Delta c_{t+1} = \gamma E_t&\left[r_{t+1} + \frac{1-\gamma}{\gamma}(1-a)\Delta p_{t+1}\right] \\ &+\frac{1}{2}\left[\sigma_c^2 + \gamma^2\sigma_r^2 + (1-\gamma)^2(1-a)^2\sigma_p^2\right. \\ &\left.+2\gamma\sigma_{c,r} + 2(1-\gamma)(1-a)\sigma_{c,p} + 2\gamma(1-\gamma)(1-a)\sigma_{r,p}\right], \end{aligned} \tag{A8}$$

where the variances and covariances refer to the three variables defined above, and where $\gamma = 1/\sigma$. Use has been made of the approximation: $\log(1 + r_{t+1}) \approx r_{t+1}$. Defining the first bracketed set of terms on the right as a consumption based real interest rate, r_{t+1}^*, and noting that under our

[12]See Campbell, Lo, and MacKinlay (1997), pp. 306–307.

assumptions the second bracketed set of terms on the right is constant, this becomes the optimal consumption profile in the text (Equation 4).

Appendix B: Deriving the log-linearized intertemporal budget constraint

We can write the intertemporal budget constraint (9) as

$$\Phi_0 - \Psi_0 = B_0, \tag{B1}$$

where $\Phi_0 = C_0 + \sum_{t=1}^{\infty} R_t C_t$, and $\Psi_0 = \text{NO}_0 + \sum_{t=1}^{\infty} R_t \text{NO}_t$. Taking logs and following the linearization of Huang and Lin (1993), we have:

$$\phi_0 - \psi_0 = \left(1 - \frac{1}{\Omega}\right)(b_0 - \psi_0), \tag{B2}$$

where $\phi_0 = \log \Phi_0$, $\psi_0 = \log \Psi_0$, $b_0 = \log B_0$, and $\Omega = 1 - \frac{\overline{B}}{\Phi_0}$, where $\overline{B}$ is steady state net foreign assets. Now a further linearization yields:

$$c_0 - \phi_0 = \sum_{t=1}^{\infty} \rho^t (r_t - \Delta c_t), \tag{B3}$$

where $c_0 = \log C_0$, $\Delta c_t = \log C_t - \log C_{t-1}$, and $\rho = 1 - \frac{\overline{c}}{\phi_0}$ where $\overline{c}$ is the steady state value of the log of consumption. Similarly,

$$\text{no}_0 - \psi_0 = \sum_{t=1}^{\infty} \rho^t (r_t - \Delta \text{no}_t), \tag{B4}$$

where $\text{no}_0 = \log \text{NO}_0$, and $\Delta \text{no}_t = \log \text{NO}_t - \log \text{NO}_{t-1}$. Substitute Equations (B3) and (B4) into the intertemporal budget constraint, Equation (B2):

$$\begin{aligned} \text{no}_0 - \psi_0 &= \sum_{t=1}^{\infty} \rho^t (r_t - \Delta \text{no}_t) + \sum_{t=1}^{\infty} \rho^t (r_t - \Delta c_t) - c_0 \\ &= \left(1 - \frac{1}{\Omega}\right)(b_0 - \psi_0) + \left(1 - \frac{1}{\Omega}\right)\left[\sum_{t=1}^{\infty} \rho^t (r_t - \Delta c_t) - c_0\right], \end{aligned} \tag{B5}$$

which may be rewritten as Equation (10) in the text:

$$-\sum_{t=1}^{\infty}\beta^t\left[\Delta \text{no}_t - \frac{\Delta c_t}{\Omega} - \left(1-\frac{1}{\Omega}\right)r_t\right] = \text{no}_0 - \frac{c_0}{\Omega} + \left(1-\frac{1}{\Omega}\right)b_0. \tag{B6}$$

Acknowledgment

We would like to thank our colleagues Kevin Hoover and Wing Woo, as well as three anonymous referees and seminar participants at U.C. Berkeley, U.C. Davis, UCLA, and U.C. Santa Cruz for valuable comments.

References

Barro, R. J. and X. Sala i Martin. 1990. World real interest rates, in Blanchard, O. J. and Fischer, S. (eds.), *NBER Macroeconomics Annuals*, MIT Press, Cambridge, MA, pp. 15–61.

Campbell, J. Y. 1987. Does saving anticipate declining labor income? An alternative test of the permanent income hypothesis. *Econometrica*, 55(6): 1249–74.

Campbell, J. Y. 1998. Asset prices, consumption, and the business cycle. NBER Working Paper No. 6485 (March).

Campbell, J. Y., A. W. Lo, and A. C. MacKinlay, 1997. *The Econometrics of Financial Markets*, Princeton University Press, Princeton.

Campbell, J. Y. and N. G. Mankiw. 1989. Consumption, income, and interest rates: reinterpreting the time series evidence. in Blanchard, O. J. and Fischer, S. (eds.), *NBER Macroeconomics Annuals*, MIT Press, Cambridge, MA, pp. 185–244.

Campbell, J. Y. and R. Shiller 1987. Cointegration and tests of present value models. *Journal of Political Economy*, 95(5): 1062–1088.

Campbell, J. Y. and R. Shiller. 1989. The dividend-price ratio and expectations of future dividends and discount factors. *The Review of Financial Studies*, 1(3): 195–228.

Dornbusch, R. 1983. Real interest rates, home goods and optimal external borrowing. *Journal of Political Economy*, 91(1): 141–153.

Fahrion, M. 1997. The Current Account and Variable Interest Rates: Evidence From US, UK and Canadian Time Series. Mimeo, Department of Economics, Columbia University.

Ghosh, A. R. 1995. International capital mobility among the major industrialised countries: too little or too much? *Economic Journal*, 105(428): 107–128.

Hall, R. E. 1988. Intertemporal substitution in consumption, *Journal of Political Economy*, 96(2): 339–357.

Huang, C. and K. Lin. 1993. Deficits, government expenditures, and tax smoothing in the United States: 1929–1988. *Journal of Monetary Economics*, 31(3): 317–339.

Kravis, I., A. Heston, and R. Summers. 1982. *World Product and Income: International Comparisons and Real GDP*. Johns Hopkins University Press, Baltimore, MD.

Mehra, R. and E. Prescott. 1985. The equity premium: A Puzzle. *Journal of Monetary Economics*, 15(2): 145–161.

Milbourne, R. and G. Otto. 1992. Consumption smoothing and the current account. *Australian Economic Papers*, 31(59): 369–384.

Obstfeld, M. and K. Rogoff. 1996. *Foundations of International Macroeconomics*. The MIT Press, Cambridge, MA.

Otto, G. 1992. Testing a present value model of the current account: Evidence from U.S. and Canadian time series. *Journal of International Money and Finance*, 11(5): 414–430.

Otto, G. and G. M. Voss. 1995. Consumption, external assets and the real interest rate. *Journal of Macroeconomics*, 17(3): 471–494.

Rogoff, K. 1992. Traded goods consumption smoothing and the random walk behavior of the real exchange rate. *Bank of Japan Monetary and Economic Studies*, 10(2): 1–29.

Sheffrin, S. and W. T. Woo. 1990a. Testing an optimizing model of the current account via the consumption function. *Journal of International Money and Finance*, 9(2): 220–233.

Sheffrin, S. and W. T. Woo. 1990b. Present value tests of an intertemporal model of the current account. *Journal of International Economics*, 29(3–4): 237–253.

Stockman, A. C. and L. Tesar. 1995. Tastes and technology in a two-country model of the business cycle: Explaining international comovements. *American Economic Review*, 85(1): 168–185.

CHAPTER 11

Understanding International Portfolio Diversification and Turnover Rates*

Amir A. Amadi[†] and Paul R. Bergin[‡]

Department of Economics, University of California,
One Shields Ave., Davis, CA, 95616, USA
[†] *aamadi@ucdavis.edu*
[‡] *prbergin@ucdavis.edu*

1. Introduction

Data on international equity markets suggest a pair of stylized facts that have proved difficult to reconcile. One is home bias: despite the potentially significant gains from foreign diversification, investors hold a disproportionately small amount of foreign equity.[1] This would seem to offer evidence of imperfect international integration in asset markets. A second observation is that the turnover rate, the share of holdings bought or resold in a period of time, surprisingly is higher for assets held in a foreign market than for domestic assets. This would seem to offer evidence of a high level of international integration.

One intuitively appealing explanation for home bias raised initially in the literature is the presence of international transactions costs associated with purchasing an asset in a foreign market. But if transactions costs were

*This article originally appeared in *Journal of International Financial Markets* (2008), 18(2), 191–206.

[1] See French and Poterba (1991) and Tesar and Werner (1995).

the explanation for small foreign holdings, it should also lower turnover among foreign assets. Since the opposite appears to be true, the literature moved on to other types of explanations. Research within the open economy macroeconomics literature has focused on transactions costs in the international goods market, which limit the ability to reap the benefits of asset diversification.[2] Research within the finance literature has focused on information asymmetry between countries.[3]

However, while high foreign turnover might argue against trading costs of the usual proportional type, it does not rule out the presence of costs of a fixed type, that is, costs that are not proportional to the volume of trading. Recent research in the field of international trade theory has found that fixed costs of entry can be very useful in understanding aspects of international trade in goods markets.[4] This chapter studies theoretically if such fixed costs can be useful in understanding the puzzling aspects of international trade in equities markets, and what characteristics these costs would need to possess.

Interpretations of these fixed costs could include various types of establishment costs, like the need to deal with foreign languages and legal codes, or the costs of accessing information on a foreign firm. Amadi (2004a) finds empirical support for the idea that common language, distance and immigrant populations affect foreign investment.

In the context of a very simple portfolio allocation model, we find that a particular combination of fixed and proportional costs is able to generate the combination of stylized facts. The model includes proportional trading costs that are not heterogeneous between foreign and domestic assets, like those dismissed above, but instead are heterogeneous among agents within a country. Some agents have a cost advantage in executing financial trades, be it due to larger size, better technology, or expertise. In combination with uniform fixed costs of entering a foreign market, only

[2]See Tesar (1993) and Pesenti and van Wincoop (2002) for examples of nontraded goods arguments. See van Wincoop (1994) and Aizenman (1999) for preferences. See Obstfeld and Rogoff (2001) and Engel and Matsumoto (2004) for various types of goods market imperfections. Rowland and Tesar (2004) investigate the role of multinational firms as a substitute for portfolio diversification.

[3]See Ahearne, Griever, and Warnock (2004) for example.

[4]See Bernard and Jensen (2004) for example.

efficient agents with low per unit costs find it profitable to enter. Therefore, high cost agents remain solely in the domestic market, thereby resulting in a home bias. In addition, the agents with lower costs of trading naturally adjust their portfolio more often, resulting in a higher turnover rate. And since these agents are the only home-country agents active in the foreign market, this results in a relatively higher turnover rate in foreign investments.

The chapter also presents basic empirical work, arguing that despite recent increases in international diversification and despite measurement issues raised in Warnock (2002), the stylized facts are still broadly relevant in recent data. We also compare our explanation for the puzzle to that in Rowland (1999), which notes that the volume of trade between home and foreign equities is high when agents are in the initial stages of diversifying.

The next section examines recently improved international data on turnover to show that the basic stylized facts still are broadly relevant. Section 3 presents the portfolio allocation model, and Section 4 shows how it can generate results similar to the stylized facts. Section 5 explores the model's sensitivity to alternative parameter values and compares the model to alternative configurations of the trading costs. The final section summarizes results and draws implications for other related questions regarding international equity markets.

2. What Recent Data Have to Say

Results in Tables 1 and 2 verify that the puzzling stylized facts motivating our model are generally valid in current data. While the main focus is on turnover rates, we document first that there is still substantial home bias in equity holdings, as shown in Amadi (2004b). The first column of Table 1 reports the share of country portfolios in foreign equities by country and by date. The data on foreign equity positions are obtained from the International Monetary Fund's IFS database, compiled using both survey and capital flow data. Likewise, the first column of Table 2 reports the same variable but using equity holdings data from the IMF's coordinated portfolio investment survey, which uses purely survey data (see the data appendix for a more detailed discussion of the data sources). While one notes an interesting upward trend in the degree of diversification, it remains quite

Table 1. Turnover rates based on IFS data

Country	Year	Foreign diversification	Domestic turnover rate		Foreign turnover rate
Canada	1993	11.46	0.44		2.10
	1994	13.71	0.51		2.15
	1995	13.45	0.50		2.43
	1996	12.33	0.55		2.07
	1997	11.64	0.52		3.08
	1998	13.57	0.61		2.52
	1999	12.06	0.44		3.36
	2000	13.29	0.75		3.79
	2001	16.01	0.66		3.28
Germany	1993	23.75	0.65		1.61
	1994	28.21	0.98		1.11
	1995	26.24	0.99		0.99
	1996	26.11	1.17		1.51
	1997	27.44	0.65		3.03
	1998	31.55	0.70		3.15
	1999	32.41	0.57		1.49
	2000	37.22	0.84		2.44
	2001	39.65	1.32		1.96
Japan	1995	4.17	0.34		0.72
	1996	5.29	0.41		0.98
	1997	7.58	0.56		1.33
	1998	8.72	0.38		1.12
	1999	7.14	0.41		1.11
	2000	9.14	0.85		1.50
	2001	10.81	0.81		1.22
United States	1993	10.25	0.65*		1.51
	1994	11.85	0.70		1.31
	1995	10.96	0.74		0.95
	1996	11.38	0.84	0.55#	0.96
	1997	10.44	0.90	0.60	1.29
	1998	10.79	0.98	0.66	1.26
	1999	11.89	1.12	0.66	1.15
	2000	11.97	2.11	1.00	1.97
	2001	11.30	2.10	0.92	1.82

Notes: The foreign turnover rate is equal to the sum of the domestic country's purchases and sales of foreign equity within the year divided by the domestic country's foreign asset equity position at the end of the year. The domestic turnover rate is equal to the total transactions in the domestic market within the year divided by the domestic market's capitalization at

Table 1. (*Continued*)

the end of the year. Foreign diversification is equal to the foreign equity assets held by the country divided by the sum of its stock market capitalization and foreign equity assets adjusted for its foreign equity liabilities. *includes the NASDAQ, while #excludes the NASDAQ. Data on foreign transactions are from individual country sources. Data on foreign equity positions are from the International Monetary Fund's IFS database. Data on domestic transactions and capitalization are from the Standard and Poor's Global Stock Market Factbook. See data appendix for more detail.

small for most countries, and certainly it is smaller than the share implied by simple optimal portfolio models. The trend of rising diversification has also been noted in Amadi (2004b), Heathcote and Perri (2004), and Lane and Milesi-Ferretti (2003).

Table 2. Turnover rates based on CPIS data

Country	Year	Foreign diversification	Domestic turnover rate		Foreign turnover rate
Canada	1997	17.60	0.52		2.22
	2001	25.21	0.75		2.12
	2002	30.51	0.71		3.82
Germany	2001	32.31	1.32		2.62
	2002	39.61	1.80		2.38
Japan	1997	[illegible]	0.56		1.33
	2001	10.58	0.81		1.22
	2002	10.41	0.74		1.32
United States	1997	9.99	0.90*	0.60#	1.29
	2001	10.88	2.10	0.92	1.82
	2002	11.37	2.30	2.01	1.95

Notes: The foreign turnover rate is equal to the sum of the domestic country's purchases and sales of foreign equity within the year divided by the domestic country's foreign asset equity position at the end of the year. The domestic turnover rate is equal to the total transactions in the domestic market within the year divided by the domestic market's capitalization at the end of the year. Foreign diversification is equal to the foreign equity assets held by the country divided by the sum of its stock market capitalization and foreign equity assets adjusted for its foreign equity liabilities. *includes the NASDAQ, while #excludes the NASDAQ. Data on foreign transactions are from individual country sources. Data on foreign equity positions are from the International Monetary Fund's Coordinated Portfolio Investment Survey. Data on domestic transactions and capitalization are from the Standard and Poor's Global Stock Market Factbook. See data appendix for more detail.

The empirical literature defines the foreign turnover rate as the total foreign transactions that occur within a given year divided by the foreign asset position at the end of the year. The domestic turnover rate is defined as the total domestic market transactions in a year divided by the year-end domestic market's capitalization.[5] Tesar and Werner (1995) drew attention to the gap between home and foreign turnover rates for their data from 1989, finding a foreign turnover of 7.7 for Canada compared to a domestic turnover of only 0.61, and a foreign turnover of 2.5 for the US compared to 1.07 for domestic.

Table 1 shows updated turnover rates for Canada, Germany, Japan, and the United States for the last decade. The foreign turnover rates appear to be generally lower than those reported by Tesar and Werner, but nonetheless, they are almost uniformly higher than the corresponding domestic turnover rate. The only possible exception is for some recent years in the US, depending on whether Nasdaq values are included along with NYSE. Nasdaq reports notably higher turnover, though this may largely reflect a different convention for reporting turnover in this market.[6]

Warnock (2002) has correctly criticized Tesar and Werner's estimates for using data on foreign stock holdings that rely upon cumulated capital flows and estimated valuation adjustments. He finds that this leads to an underestimation of the holdings used in the denominator of the foreign turnover ratio, so the ratio itself is overestimated. To correct for this problem, he recommends using survey data. Such data have been available for the United States since 1989, and he constructs an estimate for Canada to use in comparisons with Tesar and Werner.

Following Warnock, Table 2 computes turnover rates[7] using data from the IMF's Coordinated Portfolio Investment Survey, which relies on survey

[5]The theoretical literature generally takes the values for the denominator from the midpoint of the year, rather than the end of the year. It is mainly due to the fact that asset position data are sometimes unavailable on a consistent annual basis that the empirical literature uses end of year values. The two definitions seem to produce similar results.

[6]Standard and Poor's 2003 Global Stock Markets Factbook notes that Nasdaq values include both sides of transactions when reporting "value traded," used in computing turnover (p. 29).

[7]Here the empirical definition for turnover rates are used since this survey data is not available on an annual basis.

data. The results are essentially the same as those in Warnock for 1997 (the year of survey data available to him).[8] We also report values for subsequent years of the surveys, which at times vary from the 1997 values substantially. Although the surveys are available for only a few years, we can compare the common entries for Tables 1 and 2. For the US and Japan, the turnover rates are unaffected, for Canada the adjusted ratios are indeed lower, but for Germany the adjusted ratio is higher. Overall, the ratios are very close to those reported in the larger data set of Table 1. Most importantly, the foreign turnover rates remain higher than their domestic counterparts in almost every case.

We conclude that the foreign turnover rates are generally lower than those reported in the initial empirical literature, but the puzzling stylized fact remains, in that there is a consistently positive gap between turnover rates in foreign compared to domestic equity holdings. This would seem to support the common wisdom that transaction costs cannot be important here as an explanation for home bias. After all, if buying foreign equities carried a higher cost than equities in one's own market, not only would one tend to accumulate a smaller stock of these foreign assets, but there likely would be a smaller flow of purchases. Clearly, this is not the case in the data.

Before turning to the theoretical model, it is worth noting that the turnover in foreign equities is greater than 100% of the stock of foreign equity holdings in almost all cases. Given that the growth in the stock of foreign holdings in Table 1 evolves fairly slowly in some countries, it would seem that the turnover cannot solely be in the form of net sales of home for foreign equities, as implied by the theoretical model of Rowland (1999). Either domestic participants in the foreign market are selling foreign equities back and forth to each other or, more likely, domestic participants in the foreign market are also tending to adjust their portfolio of foreign assets, trading one foreign asset for another. That is, we are seeing turnover within the foreign market as well as between home and foreign assets. This observation helps motivate the model below, which allows turnover within the foreign market between distinct foreign assets.

[8]The US domestic turnover rate that we reported is a composite of the NYSE and Nasdaq. Warnock (2002) presents the NYSE and Nasdaq rates separately.

3. A Simple Fixed Cost Portfolio Allocation Model

This study uses a Markowitz (1952) mean–variance model augmented with transactions costs, similar to that presented in Wang (2002). This class of models characterizes the optimal portfolio choice of individual investors, given asset returns that follow an exogenous stochastic process.[9] Our objective is to demonstrate that trading costs of a particular type can induce higher turnover in foreign markets among these agents, at the same time as inducing home bias in their equity holdings. Specifically the agent's utility function is expressed as

$$U(c) = E(c) - \frac{\lambda}{2}\mathrm{Var}(c), \tag{1}$$

where

$$E(c) = W\left(\sum_{i=1}^{4} R_i x_i + R_0 x_0 - \tau_{i,k}\sum_{i=1}^{4}|x_i - x_{i,t-1}|\right) - F\cdot z, \tag{2}$$

$$\mathrm{Var}(c) = W^2\left(\sum_{i=1}^{4}\sum_{j=1}^{4} x_i x_j \sigma_{ij}\right), \tag{3}$$

where W represents the agent's wealth, and c the agent's consumption. R_i represents the risky asset i's expected return, and λ a coefficient describing risk aversion. In the model, there are four risky assets ($i = 1, 2, 3, 4$), the first two are in the local market, while the latter two are in the foreign market. Modeling four assets allows for trading both between the domestic and foreign markets, as well as within the foreign market itself. Here, x_i represents the share of the agent's wealth devoted to asset i in the current period, while $x_{i,t-1}$ represents last period's share of wealth devoted to asset i. Similarly, x_0 and R_0 represent the share of wealth invested in the riskless asset and its return.

---

[9]The model examines the behavior of a group of agents who share similar beliefs; in actuality the trade between agents in equilibrium presumably arises from heterogeneity in beliefs regarding expected returns. Thus, this model does not attempt to provide a full equilibrium explanation for turnover in an entire market. However, the model's main mechanism applied here to a set of agents can, in principle, be incorporated into an aggregate analysis of the entire market.

Two key features of the model are the proportional transactions cost τ and the fixed foreign entry cost F. Specifically $\tau_{i,k}$ is the constant transaction cost associated with a per-unit change in the share of asset i by agent k. That is, it is associated with both the purchase and the sale of asset i. In this model, different agents incur inherently different trading costs. F represents the fixed cost associated with entering the foreign market, and therefore z is a dummy variable, equal to unity if $x_3 > 0$ or $x_4 > 0$.

The agent maximizes his or her utility based on the following constraints:

$$\sum_{i=1}^{4} x_i = 1 \quad \text{and} \quad x_i \geq 0. \tag{4}$$

That is, asset shares must sum to agent's wealth, and short sales are not permitted.

Such barriers as language, institutional, and legal differences might prevent entry into a foreign market. Amadi (2004a) and Grinblatt and Keloharju (2001) have shown that investors typically invest in markets that possess the same language, culture, or some other form of familiarity. One way of modeling this familiarity barrier is through a fixed cost. That is, one can assume that there is a fixed cost of operating in a foreign market, which represents the cost involved in acquiring equivalent information about that market. Also Ahearne, Griever, and Warnock (2004), as well as Martin and Rey (2000), find that cross listing significantly increases foreign diversification, which could be thought of as overcoming this fixed cost. Once again, this concept is not entirely new to the theoretical literature. Portfolio allocation models like Merton (1987) involve investors that pay "setup" or "receiver" costs in order to acquire detailed information regarding a firm's earnings or signals, although the models are applied in a domestic context.

The motivation for having different transactions costs is quite intuitive. Typically institutional investors and large brokerage houses face lower transactions costs than do average individual investors. These larger entities trade in significantly higher volumes, have access to less costly trading mechanisms, and typically have trade agreements that make their transactions relatively inexpensive. For example, many mutual fund companies charge reduced fees or no fees to investors who purchase a certain level of shares, typically in the millions. Again, in general, some agents have a cost advantage in executing financial trades, be it due to better technology or expertise. It is reasonable, therefore, to assume that different agents face different per-unit transactions costs.

The domestic and the foreign turnover rates, respectively, are measured as

$$\mathrm{TO}_D = \frac{\sum_{i=1}^{2} |x_i - x_{i,t-1}|}{\frac{1}{2}\sum_{i=1}^{2} (x_i + x_{i,t-1})} \tag{5}$$

and

$$\mathrm{TO}_F = \frac{\sum_{i=3}^{4} |x_i - x_{i,t-1}|}{\frac{1}{2}\sum_{i=3}^{4} (x_i + x_{i,t-1})}. \tag{6}$$

Here the numerator represents the total changes in the asset shares, while the denominator represents the average position in the assets between the beginning and the end of the period. To avoid conflating equity trades between periods with capital gains during period $t-1$, turnover is computed as the difference between the allocation at the beginning of period t and the allocation at the end of period $t-1$, after expected returns are realized.

Since it is difficult to draw analytical results from the first-order conditions of the maximization problem above, we will rely upon simulations and comparative static analysis in the next section to demonstrate the model characteristics. Nonetheless, the fundamental properties of the model are highly intuitive and are discussed here briefly. First, as t (proportional transaction cost) increases, the amount of transactions decreases. Second, as F (fixed foreign entry cost) increases, entry into the foreign market decreases. These results are obvious. Another implication is that as t decreases more agents will enter the foreign market. This is because agents with lower proportional costs gain more by entering the foreign market than agents with higher proportional costs, so they will be more likely to pay the fixed cost to enter the foreign market. Furthermore, agents with lower proportional trading costs naturally trade more actively and have higher turnover rates. Since we concluded that it is these agents that tend to be present in the foreign market, we should expect to find that foreign holdings have a higher turnover rate than domestic holdings, which are averaged over agents with both high and low trading costs.

In order to better grasp these implications, several simplifying assumptions are made, and a comparative static analysis is presented. First, it is assumed that agents have identical wealths normalized to unity. Second, with reference to the transactions costs, we only examine two types of agents, that of a “low cost” and a “high cost” agent. Furthermore, these two types of agents carry the same weight and therefore are distributed evenly. However, this could be extended to a model with a continuum of different types of agents with different weights. Finally, it is also assumed that all risky assets have the same market weight. Therefore, a fully diversified portfolio is one that would contain 50% foreign risky assets as a share of all risky assets. These simplifying assumptions help make the general implications of the model clearer.

This model is applied for two periods in a comparative static exercise in order to distinguish between the home bias and the turnover rate implications. In this analysis, returns are realized at the end of each period. In the first period, agents enter the asset market and optimize their portfolio based on the market’s characteristics and their own. One can imagine a case in which agents inherit wealth and would like to invest that wealth in the stock market, or a case in which agents would like to transfer money from their savings account into their investment account, and so this seems the most natural initial point for a model.[10] This period examines the extent to which agents diversify internationally. In the second period, the comparative static experiment considers the arrival of new information that shifts the expected returns of the assets. These agents thereby adjust their portfolios accordingly. This period examines the model’s implications with respect to the domestic and foreign turnover rates.

4. Deriving Benchmark Results

A numerical simulation is useful to explore the implications of the model. We use a simple comparative static exercise. For simplicity, assume that all risky asset returns are equal to 1.15, the riskless asset return is equal to 1.05, variances are equal to 0.2, and correlation coefficients are equal to 0.25. These numbers are within a reasonable range of actual parameter values for the past decade,[11] and in the sensitivity analysis section a wider range of numbers are presented for comparison. Also the parameter describing

[10] $x_{i,t-1} = 0$ in the first period.

[11] Specifically, the values were chosen based on the annualized returns, rolled over monthly, from 1994–2004 of Citigroup, Ford, Deutsch Bank, and Volkswagen. These large cap stocks make an appropriate representation of two domestic and foreign assets.

risk aversion is set equal to 2, which is common in the literature. As stated previously, the model only looks at two types of agents for simplicity; a low cost and a high cost agent. Suppose the low cost agent incurs a per-unit trading cost of 0.01, while the high cost agent incurs a per-unit trading cost of 0.03. These also represent reasonable values that are consistent with those used in other studies.[12]

Consider the first period problem optimizing over a cardinal utility function: Agents will enter the foreign market only if the extra utility they receive from the foreign market investment is greater than the fixed cost of entry. So in order to assess their decision, one needs to compare the maximum possible utility each type of agent receives if they chose to enter the foreign market versus if they chose to remain solely in the domestic market.

We solve the optimization problem for the high cost agent conditional on the two possible choices for international investment.[13] First, if the agent chooses to invest only in the domestic market, optimal portfolio shares at the end of period 1 are $x_i = 0.15$ for the domestic risky assets $i = 1, 2$, and $x_0 = 0.70$ for the riskless asset, with resulting utility level $U = 1.060$. Alternatively, if the agent enters the foreign market, optimal portfolio shares at the end of period 1 are $x_i = 0.11$ for the two domestic and the two foreign assets ($i = 1, 2, 3, 4$) and $x_0 = 0.56$ for the riskless asset, with resulting utility $U = 1.064$. Therefore, if the foreign fixed cost of entry is less than 0.004, the high cost agent in this example will optimally choose to enter the foreign market. Note that for period 1 we report portfolio shares for the end of the period, after expected capital gains have been realized.[14]

[12] Rowland (1999) uses similar values to differentiate between the costs associated with trading in the domestic and foreign markets.

[13] All computations performed in this study were done using Mathematica's Multiplier Method Algorithm.

[14] The corresponding beginning-of-period equity shares for period 1 for the high cost agent are as follows: $x_1 = x_2 = 0.14$ with $x_0 = 0.72$ for the purely domestic portfolio. To derive the end-of-period portfolio shares reported in the text and Table 3, beginning-of-period allocations are multiplied by the expected rates of return (1.15 for the equities and 1.05 for the riskless asset), and the values divided by the new value of the overall portfolio, so that shares again sum to unity. These end-of-period shares are more appropriate for comparison with beginning-of-period shares from period 2, as a measure of turnover. The change in portfolio shares between periods then represents the reallocation of shares in a portfolio with the same aggregate value, without conflating the sale of assets between periods with capital gains during period 1.

This is to facilitate later computation of turnover rates as the trade in equities between periods, without conflating this with capital gains during period 1.

Solving similarly for the low cost agent, the solution for domestic investment is $x_i = 0.19$ for both domestic assets 1 and 2, with utility $U = 1.066$. Entering the foreign market, the solution is $x_i = 0.13$ for all four assets, with utility $U = 1.073$, and so if the foreign fixed cost of entry is less than 0.007, the low cost agent will enter the foreign market.

Let us assume that the fixed cost of entry equals 0.005, so that only low cost agents invest in the foreign market.[15] Recall that both types of agents are given the same market weight. This implies an overall average foreign diversification among equity holdings of 32%, since the low cost agent is fully diversified, while the high cost agent remains solely in the domestic market and holds more of the riskless asset. These results are reported in Table 3, under the headings for model 1, period 1. Together these agents produce a degree of diversification close to the empirical values we reported for some countries. These values can also be adjusted downward, if desired, by assigning weights to the two groups.

In the second period, suppose that new information arrives that leads these agents to revise expected returns upward for one asset in each country and downward for the other asset in each country. In particular, suppose that the returns on assets 1 and 3 increase to 1.2, while the returns of assets 2 and 4 decrease to 1.1. This symmetric experiment is intended to represent the type of information received that might affect agents' expectations. Solving the optimization problem for this period, the portfolios are reallocated toward the higher-paying assets, and the resulting values at the beginning of period 2 are reported in Table 3, as model 1 and period 2. The agent that is able to execute trades at a lower cost naturally reallocates his portfolio more actively, both in the domestic and foreign markets. These reallocations allow us to compute a turnover rate for these agents with respect to the domestic and foreign

[15]Although this difference in the utility gains between the two agents might seem small, if this example is extended into a more realistic multiple periods, this difference would become relatively more significant.

Table 3. Simulation results for symmetric experiment

Model	Agent type	Period	Equity share x_1	x_2	x_3	x_4	Foreign divers.	Domestic turnover	Foreign turnover
1. Benchmark: heterog. prop. cost	Domestic	1	0.15	0.15					
		2	0.27	0.13					
	International	1	0.13	0.13	0.13	0.13			
		2	0.28	0.01	0.28	0.01			
	Combined	1					0.32		
		2					0.29	0.64	0.96
2. Uniform costs:	N/A	1	0.13	0.13	0.13	0.13	0.50		
		2	0.28	0.01	0.28	0.01	0.50	0.96	0.96
3. Heterog. fixed costs	Domestic	1	0.19	0.19					
		2	0.33	0.07					
	International	1	0.13	0.13	0.13	0.13			
		2	0.28	0.01	0.28	0.01			
	Combined	1					0.29		
		2					0.29	0.80	0.96
4. No fixed cost	N/A	1	0.16	0.16	0.08	0.08	0.35		
		2	0.28	0.01	0.21	0.08	0.50	0.90	0.59

Notes: In the first period, $R1 = R2 = R3 = R4 = 1.15$, $R0 = 1.05$, all variances = 0.2, all covariances = 0.05, and the risk aversion parameter equals 2. In the second period, **R1** = **R3** = 1.2, **R2** = **R4** = 1.1, $R0 = 1.05$, all variances = 0.2, all covariances = 0.05, and the risk aversion parameter equals 2. The equity allocations are taken from the beginning of each period. Period 1 equity shares reported are end-of-period values, after expected capital gains are realized. Period 2 equity shares reported are beginning-of-period values. To avoid conflating equity trades between periods with capital gains during period 1, turnover is computed as the difference between the allocation at the beginning of period 2 and the allocation at the end of period 1.

markets[16]:

$$\mathrm{TO}_D = \frac{|0.27 - 0.15| + |0.13 - 0.15| + |0.28 - 0.13| + |0.01 - 0.13|}{0.5((0.27 + 0.15) + (0.13 + 0.15) + (0.28 + 0.13) + (0.01 + 0.13))}$$
$$= 0.64^{17}$$

$$\mathrm{TO}_F = \frac{|0.28 - 0.13| + |0.01 - 0.13|}{0.5((0.28 + 0.13) + (0.01 + 0.13))} = 0.96$$

As one can see, the turnover rate is indeed higher for the foreign investments. This example demonstrates that the model can produce results similar to the two stylized facts that have been observed in the existing literature. First, fixed costs pose a hurdle for participating in the foreign market, and this hurdle will be prohibitive to those investors who also face high proportional trading costs in general, but it will not be prohibitive to agents with low proportional trading costs. So one implication is the desired result of 'home-bias.' But the second implication becomes obvious when we combine this with the fact that these low-cost traders have higher turnover in response to new information. Given that the foreign assets are held by these agents, average turnover for foreign assets will be relatively high. Turnover for domestic assets, however, is averaged over the high cost traders as well, and hence will be relatively low. Although this model is a highly simple example and cannot hope to explain all of the dynamics involved in portfolio allocation, it can provide a revealing and useful framework to help understand the key stylized facts.

5. Alternative Parameters and Cost Specifications

This section checks sensitivity of results to alternative calibrations in the numerical simulation. Figure 1 shows that as the variance of risky asset returns increases from 0.1 to 0.3, the two turnover rates fall together, as the agents hold a smaller portion of their portfolio in risky assets. Nonetheless, the foreign turnover rate remains higher. Figure 2 shows that as the coefficient of correlation rises from 0 to 0.5, initially the turnover rates spread

[16]Note that we follow the convention in the theoretical literature of using the midpoint of the asset holdings in the denominator of the turnover rate.

[17]Computations are based on numbers with higher precision than the two decimals reported in the chapter.

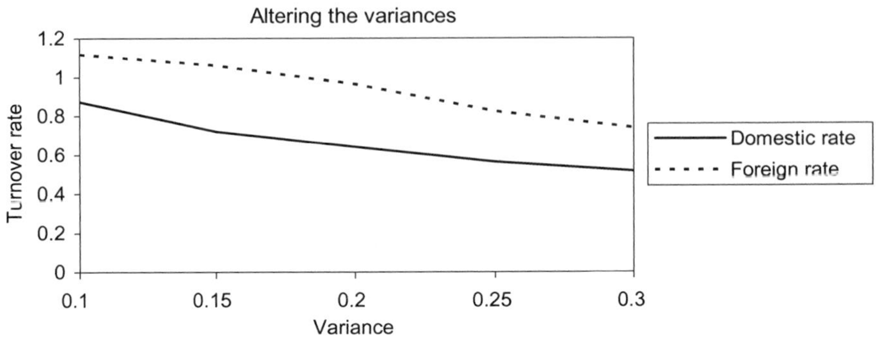

Figure 1. The effect of variance in risky returns on turnover rates

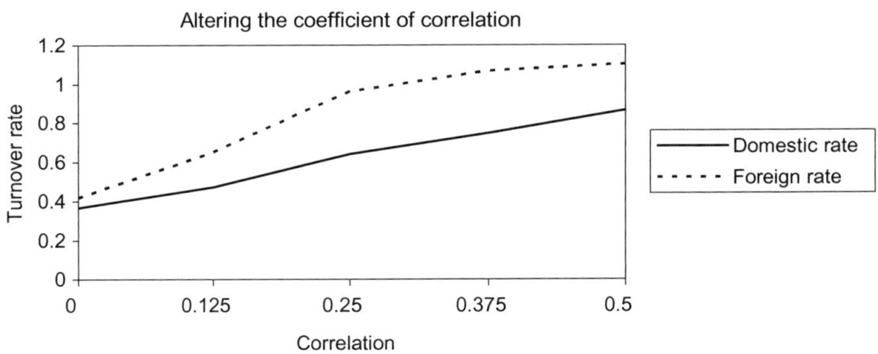

Figure 2. The effect of correlation in risky returns on turnover rates

apart, only to stabilize at higher correlations. This arises from the fact that a greater correlation across countries reduces the benefits of international diversification. Eventually agents will only invest in those assets with greater returns, thereby causing the investment behavior in the two markets to converge. Figure 3 shows that varying the risk aversion parameter from 1 to 3 has only small effects on the turnover rates. The robustness suggests that our mechanism for explaining high turnover could apply to a wide array of countries.

Next consider several alternative cost specifications. Table 3 reports results, and shows why the particular configuration of costs in Section 3 is needed to generate the desired results. The simplest alternative specifies proportional costs and fixed costs that are both homogenous across agents

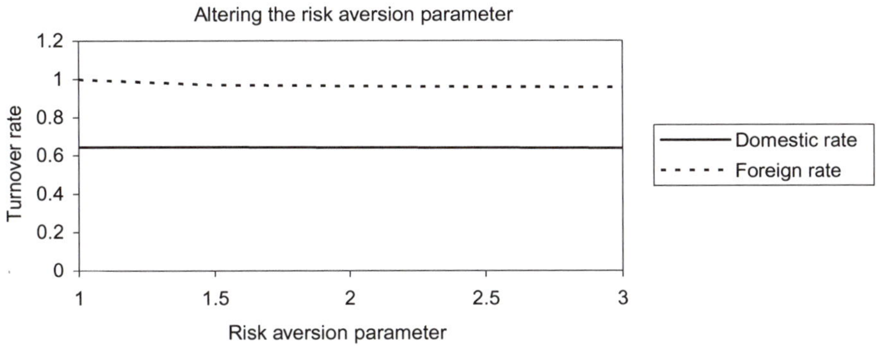

Figure 3. The effect of risk aversion parameter on turnover rates

and markets. Here, all agents are assumed to have a proportional trading cost equal to 0.01. Labeled as model 2, Table 3 shows that this case fails to replicate either stylized fact: there is no home bias, and domestic turnover equals foreign turnover. We conclude that the mere presence of fixed costs is not sufficient; some type of heterogeneity is needed.

The next alternative is to invert our benchmark case, with heterogeneity in fixed rather than proportional costs. All agents face a trading cost of 0.01, but different agents face different fixed costs of participating in the foreign market, such that only one group finds it beneficial to diversify internationally. Labeled model 3 in Table 3, there indeed is home bias in asset holdings, as well as a higher turnover abroad. While the gap in turnover rates is small compared to that in the benchmark case and to that in much of the data, it is surprising that foreign turnover exceeds domestic turnover at all in this case. Recall that the reason the benchmark case achieves higher foreign turnover is that the home agents in the foreign market by construction have lower trading costs — it was these lower proportional costs that lead them to enter the foreign market. But since proportional trading costs are uniform for all agents in this alternative case, what induces the agents in the foreign market to trade more aggressively in this experiment?

The reasoning for this case is a bit subtle. Recall that the experiment here is a symmetric rise in the expected returns of asset 1 in the home market and asset 3 in the foreign market. These agents would like to maximize the overall expected return of the portfolio by reallocating away from asset 2 and towards asset 1 in the home market, and away from asset 4 and towards asset 3 in the foreign market (for the agents who have invested in the foreign market). The cost of this less balanced portfolio, of course, is a rise in the overall risk (variance) of the portfolio. This tradeoff limits the degree of reallocation by investors, but the tradeoff is less severe for the agent with a portfolio diversified internationally. This is because the extra dimension of diversification gives the internationally diversified agent a lower overall risk (variance), which in turn gives the agent a greater flexibility in having a more unbalanced portfolio within each national market. Therefore, the international agent responds more to the shift in expected returns, resulting in a higher turnover. While interesting, we do not emphasize this configuration of costs as the most likely explanation for the turnover puzzle for several reasons. First, the magnitude of the turnover gap is small. Second, the result is not robust to alternative experiments with different shocks, as will be demonstrated shortly.

The last configuration of costs to consider posits no fixed cost at all, but just heterogeneous proportional trading costs among assets. In particular, suppose a trading cost of 0.01 for the domestic assets and a trading cost of 0.03 for the foreign. This case is considered, mainly because it formalizes the simple type of explanation considered and discarded in earlier research on home bias, such as Tesar and Werner (1995). Confirming earlier conjectures, model 4 of the table shows that such a configuration of costs can generate home bias, but it cannot replicate the turnover puzzle.

Some recent research on the issue of turnover has focused on a different type of experiment. Rather than a shift in expected returns of one home asset relative to another, it has considered a shift in expected returns of the foreign market relative to home.[18] Table 4 repeats the cost-configuration cases in Table 3 for this new type of experiment. The rise in foreign returns in this experiment naturally leads to a significant rise in foreign diversification in the second period of each case as agents shift toward foreign assets.

First is the benchmark case. Table 4 shows that this case continues to reproduce the stylized fact that foreign turnover is higher than domestic turnover. Thus, the benchmark theory is robust to the alternative experiment. Model 2 continues to fail to replicate the stylized facts, as was found

[18] In particular, Rowland (1999) naturally considers a shock of this type, as his model limits the number of risky assets to one representative asset in each country.

Table 4. Simulation results for alternative experiment

Model	Agent type	Period	Asset share				Foreign divers.	Domestic turnover	Foreign turnover
			x_1	x_2	x_3	x_4			
1. Benchmark: heterog. prop. cost	Domestic	1	0.15	0.15					
		2	0.14	0.14					
	International	1	0.13	0.13	0.13	0.13			
		2	0.01	0.01	0.29	0.29			
	Combined	1					0.32		
		2					0.66	0.61	0.74
2. Uniform costs:	N/A	1	0.13	0.13	0.13	0.13	0.50		
		2	0.01	0.01	0.29	0.29	0.97	1.74	0.74
3. Heterog. fixed costs	Domestic	1	0.19	0.19					
		2	0.12	0.12					
	International	1	0.13	0.13	0.13	0.13			
		2	0.01	0.01	0.29	0.29			
	Combined	1					0.29		
		2					0.59	0.86	0.74
4. No fixed cost	N/A	1	0.16	0.16	0.08	0.08	0.35		
		2	0.03	0.03	0.23	0.23	0.89	1.38	0.93

Notes: In the first period, $R1 = R2 = R3 = R4 = 1.15$, R0 = 1.05, all variances = 0.2, all covariances = 0.05, and the risk aversion parameter equals 2. In the second period, **R1** = **R2** = 1.1, **R3** = **R4** = 1.2, $R0 = 1.05$, all variances = 0.2, all covariances = 0.05, and the risk aversion parameter equals 2. Period 1 equity shares reported are end-of-period values, after expected capital gains are realized. Period 2 equity shares reported are beginning-of-period values. To avoid conflating equity trades between periods with capital gains during period 1, turnover is computed as the difference between the allocation at the beginning of period 2 and the allocation at the end of period 1.

for the previous experiment. More informative is the fact that model 3 also fails here. Although foreign turnover was higher than domestic for this case in Table 3, it is reversed here. We conclude that a heterogeneous fixed cost is not a very robust explanation for the puzzle.

Finally, model 4 again considers the case of higher proportional trading costs in the foreign market. This configuration is similar to that used in the theoretical model of Rowland (1999), and further, the experiment here of an asymmetric shock between regions is roughly patterned after his. Table 4 shows that this configuration still does not work to generate foreign turnover higher than domestic.

We think there is reason to prefer our mechanism as a general explanation. First, our explanation is consistent with the wide range in the degree of home bias among our sample countries, as it does not require turnover to be associated with the initial stages of diversification. In addition to Rowland's model, once the cost adjusted Sharpe ratio[19] of the foreign market exceeds that of the domestic market, home bias disappears and the domestic turnover rate becomes greater than the foreign rate. While reasonable for the US market in the 1980s, if we examine the Japanese market in the 1990s, the cost-adjusted Sharpe ratio of the world market likely exceeded that of the Japanese market.[20] However, as Tables 1 and 2 indicate, Japan still exhibits a substantial equity home bias, while maintaining higher foreign turnover rates.

6. Conclusion

The international economics literature continues to be puzzled by home bias in equity holdings, especially since turnover rates tend to be higher among foreign compared to domestic holdings. In contrast to the usual presumption in the literature, this study points to trading costs of a particular type in the asset market as a useful approach. It demonstrates this point in a portfolio choice model with heterogeneous per-unit transactions costs and a homogenous fixed foreign entry cost. First, using current data,

[19]The mean market return, adjusted for its transactions cost, divided by its standard deviation.

[20]In his highest cost difference example, adjusting for the costs produces the necessary results.

it shows that the foreign turnover rates are still notably higher than the domestic rate. Second, through its model, this chapter demonstrates that having agents that face inherently different trading costs produces a world in which there exists a notable home bias and higher foreign turnover rates. The fixed cost of entry presented in the model also compliments empirical evidence in the finance literature showing that the cross-listing of equity and factors such as a common language increase foreign diversification. While the model used to demonstrate these points is simple, we think it points out a useful direction for future research in international macro on this issue.

We conclude by noting another implication of our model. Recall from Tables 1 and 2 that there appears to be a trend over time of rising international diversification starting in the second half of the 1990s for many of the countries. Our model suggests that one explanation could be a fall in the fixed costs of participating in a foreign market. Such a fixed cost reduction might reflect harmonization of institutions across countries, increased access to information abroad, or the development of market institutions like mutual funds. We leave study of this question to future research.

Data Appendix

Foreign Equity Asset Holdings: One source is The International Monetary Fund's International Financial Statistics (IFS) database. This data is based on both survey and cumulated capital flows data. Valuations and estimation adjustments were made accordingly. The data for most nations runs 1993–2001. The second source is the International Monetary Fund's International Coordinated Portfolio Investment Survey. This survey was conducted in 1997, 2001, and 2002. It was performed after recommendations were put forth so that all participating countries provided accurate consistent data on asset holding.

Foreign Transactions: Foreign transactions include data on the sales and purchases of foreign equity. For the United States, the data comes from the Treasury Department's United States Transactions with Foreigners in Long-Term Securities. The Canadian data comes from Statistics Canada's International Transactions in Securities and Foreign Stocks. The data for Japan comes from The 2003 Tokyo Stock Exchange Fact Book Gross Capital Flow Data on Japanese Investment in Foreign Securities. The German data comes from Balance of Payments Statistical Supplement to the Monthly Report 3, Financial Transactions with Non-Residents.

Domestic Transactions and Market Capitalization: The Standard and Poor's Global Stock Markets Factbook. For the US, we report data both including and excluding transactions in the NASDAQ stock exchange, since the S&P Factbook states that academic studies have shown that the NASDAQ computes "both sides of a trade."

Acknowledgments

We thank Martine Quinzii and Frank Warnock for helpful comments. Remaining errors are our own.

References

Ahearne, A. G., W. L. Griever, and F. E. Warnock. 2004. Information costs and home bias: An analysis of US holdings of foreign equities. *Journal of International Economics*, 62: 313–336.

Aizenman, J. 1999. International portfolio diversification with generalized expected utility preferences. *Canadian Journal of Economics*, 32: 995–1008.

Amadi, A. A. 2004a. Does familiarity breed investment? An empirical analysis of foreign equity holdings. SSRN Working Papers Series.

Amadi, A. A. 2004b. *International Portfolio Diversification in a New Global Environment.* U.C. Davis Mimeo: Davis, California.

Bernard, A. B. and J. B. Jensen. 2004. Why some firms export. *The Review of Economics and Statistics*, 86: 561–569.

Engel, C. and Matsumoto, A. 2004. *Home Bias in Equities under New Open Economy Macroeconomics.* University of Wisconsin Mimeo: Madison, Wisconsin.

French, K. and J. Poterba. 1991. Investor diversification and international equity markets. *American Economic Review*, 81: 222–226.

Grinblatt, M. and M. Keloharju. 2001. How distance, language, and culture influence stockholdings and trades. *The Journal of Finance*, 56: 1053–1074.

Heathcote, J. and F. Perri. 2004. Financial globalization and real regionalization. *Journal of Economic Theory*, 119: 207–243.

Lane, P. and G. M. Milesi-Ferretti. 2003. International financial integration. *IMF Staff Papers*, 50: 82–113.

Markowitz, H. 1952. Portfolio selection. *The Journal of Finance*, 7: 77–91.

Martin, P. and H. Rey. 2000. Financial integration and asset returns. *European Economic Review*, 44: 1327–1350.

Merton, R. C. 1987. A simple model of capital market equilibrium with incomplete information. *The Journal of Finance*, 42: 483–510.

Obstfeld, M. and K. Rogoff. 2001. The six major puzzles in international macroeconomics: is there a common cause? In Bernanke, B. S., Rogoff, K. (eds.), *2000 NBER Macroeconomics Annual*. MIT Press: Cambridge.

Pesenti, P. and E. van Wincoop. 2002. Can nontradables generate substantial home bias? *Journal of Money Credit and Banking*, 34: 25–50.

Rowland, P. F. 1999. Transaction costs and international portfolio diversification. *Journal of International Economics*, 49: 145–170.

Rowland, P. F. and L. L. Tesar. 2004. Multinationals and the gains from international diversification. *Review of Economic Dynamics*, 7: 789–826.

Standard and Poor's. 2003. *Global Stock Markets Factbook*. McGraw-Hill Companies, New York.

Tesar, L. L. 1993. International risk-sharing and nontraded goods. *Journal of International Economics*, 35: 69–89.

Tesar, L. L. and I. M. Werner. 1995. Home bias and high turnover. *Journal of International Money and Finance*, 14: 467–492.

van Wincoop, E. 1994. Welfare gains from international risksharing. *Journal of Monetary Economics*, 34: 175–200.

Wang, S. 2002. *Portfolio Selection and Asset Pricing*. Springer, NY, New York.

Warnock, F. E. 2002. Home bias and high turnover reconsidered. *Journal of International Money and Finance*, 21: 795–805.

Section IV

International Dimensions of Macroeconomic Policy

CHAPTER 12

Fiscal Solvency and Price Level Determination in a Monetary Union*

Paul R. Bergin

Department of Economics, University of California at Davis, One Shields Ave., Davis, CA 95616, USA
prbergin@ucdavis.edu

1. Introduction

The establishment of Economic and Monetary Union in Europe (EMU) clearly forces cooperation in terms of monetary policy, as the monetary systems of the member countries are fully integrated. What might be less obvious is the restriction on the independence of fiscal policy implied by EMU. The primary objective of monetary policy at the European Central Bank is to maintain a stable price level. But a theory called the "fiscal theory of the price level" indicates that this objective depends upon the expectations regarding fiscal debts in all of the member countries.

A fiscal theory of the price level has been developed in Leeper (1991), Sims (1994) and Woodford (1994, 1995), and this has been extended to a various international contexts in Neumeyer and Yano (1996), Woodford (1996), Dupor (1997), and Sims (1997).[1] The purpose of this chapter is to apply the fiscal theory to the case of a monetary union. This provides an

*This article originally appeared in *Journal of Monetary Economics* (2000), 45(1), 37–53.

[1]Other discussions of the fiscal theory include Leeper (1993), Canzoneri *et al.* (1997), McCallum (1998), Schmitt-Grohé and Uribe (1997), and Cochrane (1998, 1999).

interesting context for studying the fiscal theory, in that a monetary union implies that a common price level prevails among multiple nations with multiple fiscal policies.

There is already a well-developed literature analyzing certain types of interactions between monetary and fiscal policies in a monetary union. Canzoneri and Diba (1991), Sibert (1992, 1994), and most recently Chari and Kehoe (1997) have demonstrated how a monetary union creates new incentives for national governments to increase debt as a means to acquire seigniorage revenue from the common central bank. While this literature is useful for characterizing the strategic interactions between fiscal and monetary authorities, it does not focus on the linkage between the increase in debt and the equilibrium price level. The fiscal theory is useful for characterizing this link, and this will be the focus of the present chapter.

The fiscal theory suggests that the price level is determined by the need to set a real value for nominal household wealth that is consistent with equilibrium. The household intertemporal budget constraint then is regarded as the condition that determines the equilibrium price level. In a closed economy, this condition for the household is identical to the intertemporal budget constraint for the government. In a monetary union, however, there are multiple household budget constraints that must be satisfied in equilibrium, and there is no longer a direct correspondence between the household and government budget constraint in each country. Nevertheless, the government budget constraints together still can be viewed as jointly determining the price level.

One implication of the fiscal theory is that even if seigniorage is small, the inflation tax on nominal bonds may be large if member governments have large debts. This suggests the focus by preceding literature on the issue of seigniorage may have been misplaced.

A second implication is that because the price level is determined jointly by the budget constraints of member governments, a rise in debt unbacked by future taxes of just one member government has the ability to raise the price level throughout the monetary union. This suggests a motivation for fiscal rules limiting debts of member governments.

A third implication is that fiscal solvency of all member governments is not strictly necessary to maintain a stable price level. This results from the ability of one government's surplus to offset another's debt, and is a feature not observed in a single-country setting. However, this conclusion requires strong assumptions about international risk sharing. Further, because the fiscal theory focuses on household wealth rather than government debt per se, to guarantee an equilibrium with a stable price level, we must also consider the distribution of private wealth between countries.

The chapter is organized as follows. The next section develops a simple model of a two-country monetary union. Section 3 draws several basic conclusions from examining the intertemporal budget constraints in this model. Section 4 develops examples to illustrate implications for the equilibrium price level.

2. The Model

This section constructs a simple framework for analyzing a hypothetical monetary union, in which two distinct countries share a common central bank. One notable element is that households are not assumed to be able to insure perfectly against asymmetric shocks.[2] Recent research has highlighted the apparent lack of international risk sharing.[3] Further, the perfect insurance assumption would severely limit the international character of the present model, in that it would blur the distinction between households across national borders.

Country one is populated by an infinitely-lived representative household, receiving a stochastic endowment of y_{1t} units of the common consumption good each period. The household chooses in period t a level of consumption, c_{1t}, nominal holdings of the common money, M_{1t}, and nominal bond holdings, B_{1t}. Bonds have gross nominal return, R_t. Real money balances, m_{1t}, are defined as the ratio of nominal money holdings to the common price level, p_t. The household pays τ_{1t} units of the consumption good in lump-sum taxes each period. Utility is discounted at the rate β.

The household solves the following problem:

$$\begin{aligned} \max \quad & E_0 \sum_{t=0}^{\infty} \beta^t U\left(c_{1t}, \frac{M_{1t}}{p_t}\right) \\ \text{s.t.} \quad & c_{1t} + \frac{M_{1t}}{p_t} + \frac{B_{1t}}{p_t} + \tau_{1t} = y_{1t} + \frac{M_{1t-1}}{p_t} + R_{t-1}\frac{B_{1t-1}}{p_t} \qquad (1) \\ \text{where} \quad & M_{1t} \geq 0, \; c_{1t} \geq 0. \end{aligned}$$

[2]This is in contrast to Woodford (1996).

[3]See Baxter and Jermann (1997).

Note that there is no nonnegativity restriction on the level of household holdings of bonds. However, there is a nonnegativity restriction on money, since this may be issued only by the government in the present model. Negative consumption is ruled out as nonsensical.

Optimizing behavior requires households plan to fully utilize their lifetime wealth. This is summarized in the transversality condition:

$$\lim_{T\to\infty}\left(\prod_{j=t}^{T-1} R_j^{-1}\right) W_{1T} = 0, \tag{2}$$

where nominal beginning of period wealth is defined:

$$W_{1t} = R_{t-1}B_{1t-1} + M_{1t-1}. \tag{3}$$

Violating (2) would contradict the assumption of optimizing behavior by households, by implying they could increase lifetime utility by consuming a portion of their unused wealth.[4]

If the single-period budget constraints for each period are summed over the infinite horizon, and we impose the transversality condition above, the result is the following household intertemporal budget constraint:

$$\frac{W_{1t}}{p_t} = \sum_{s=t}^{\infty}\left(\prod_{j=t}^{s-1} r_j^{-1}\right)\left[c_{1s} + \tau_{1s} - y_{1s} + \frac{R_s - 1}{R_s} m_{1s}\right]. \tag{4}$$

The real rate of return on bonds is represented by $r_t = R_t\left(p_t/p_{t+1}\right)$.

The household optimization problem also implies the conditions:

$$U_{c_{1,t}} = \left(\frac{R_t}{R_t - 1}\right) U_{m_{1,t}} \tag{5}$$

$$U_{c_{1,t}} = \beta R_t E_t\left[\frac{p_t}{p_{t+1}} U_{c_{1,t+1}}\right]. \tag{6}$$

[4]More precisely, optimization implies a one-sided inequality: $\lim_{T\to\infty}\left(\prod_{j=0}^{T-1} R_j^{-1}\right) W_{1T} \leq 0$. For the optimization problem to have a well-defined budget set, it is necessary to impose the constraint that households not accumulate debt beyond their ability to pay back eventually: $\lim_{T\to\infty}\left(\prod_{j=0}^{T-1} R_j^{-1}\right) W_{1T} \geq 0$. Combining this no-Ponzi condition with the inequality above produces the transversality condition presented in the text.

The household of country two faces an analogous problem, with corresponding intertemporal budget constraint and optimality conditions.

Now consider each of the two national governments. They have no control over the creation of money, but they do have control over direct lump-sum taxes. In country one, for example, taxes (τ_{1t}) along with real transfers from the common central bank (v_{1t}) and issues of nominal government debt (D_{1t}) are used to finance the constant level of real government purchases each period ($\overline{g}_1$), all subject to the following budget constraint:

$$\overline{g}_1 + R_{t-1}\left(\frac{D_{1t-1}}{p_t}\right) = \tau_{1t} + v_{1t} + \left(\frac{D_{1t}}{p_t}\right). \tag{7}$$

An analogous condition applies to the government of country two.

The common central bank is distinct from each of the national governments. It can control the issue of new money, M_t, through open market purchases of bonds, B_{mt}. The central bank does not issue debt itself, nor does it levy taxes. It has operating expenditures, g_{mt}. As suggested by the charter of the European Central Bank, the common central bank here is modeled as returning its interest income back to the national governments, in the form of rebates v_{1t} and v_{2t}. The central bank's budget constraint is as follows:

$$\frac{B_{mt}}{p_t} + v_{1t} + v_{2t} + g_{mt} = R_{t-1}\left(\frac{B_{mt-1}}{p_t}\right) + \frac{M_t - M_{t-1}}{p_t}. \tag{8}$$

It will be assumed that rebates are divided symmetrically between the two fiscal governments

$$v_{1t} = \frac{1}{2}\left(R_{t-1} - 1\right)\left(\frac{B_{mt-1}}{p_t}\right) \tag{9}$$

$$v_{2t} = v_{1t}. \tag{10}$$

Finally, market clearing in the goods, money and bond markets require:

$$c_{1t} + c_{2t} + \overline{g}_1 + \overline{g}_2 + g_{mt} = y_{1t} + y_{2t} \tag{11}$$

$$M_{1t} + M_{2t} = M_t \tag{12}$$

$$B_{1t} + B_{2t} + B_{mt} = D_{1t} + D_{2t}. \tag{13}$$

3. Fiscal Solvency and Household Transversality

A rational expectations equilibrium is here a collection of sequences $\{p_t, R_t, c_{1t}, c_{2t}, B_{1t}, B_{2t}, B_{mt}, D_{1t}, D_{2t}, M_{1t}, M_{2t}, M_t, \tau_{1t}, \tau_{2t}, v_{1t}, v_{2t}, g_{mt}, y_{1t}, y_{2t}\}$ that is consistent with 19 equilibrium conditions. These include the household intertemporal budget constraint (4) and its foreign counterpart, or equivalently, the household transversality condition in combination with the flow budget constraint (and foreign counterparts). Other equilibrium conditions are the fiscal policies of each fiscal government, the monetary policy of the common central bank, the two household optimality conditions (5 and 6) and foreign counterparts, the government flow budget constraint (7) and foreign counterpart, the budget constraint of the common central bank (8), the rebate allocation rules (9 and 10), market clearing for goods and money (11 and 12), and the exogenous sequence for outputs in the two countries and central bank expenditures (as well as the nonnegativity restrictions).

Note first that the household intertemporal budget constraint (4) treats bonds and money equally as elements of nominal wealth. If price rises, the inflation tax paid by the home household would cover holdings of bonds as well as money, and would equal the left-hand side of (4) multiplied by the inflation rate. A common rationale to dismiss the fiscal implications of monetary union is to note that seigniorage is typically very small. But consider for the moment a case where the national governments receive no seigniorage nor any income from the central bank; that is, let $g_{mt} = \frac{M_t - M_{t-1}}{p_t}$ and $B_{mt} = v_{1t} = v_{2t} = 0$ for all t. Government one still benefits from an inflation tax, equal to $\frac{p_{t+1} - p_t}{p_t} D_{1t}$, which may be large for governments with large nominal debt. Consequently, a high level of debt can create an incentive for national governments to lobby for inflation, regardless of the issue of seigniorage. This suggests that the focus of preceding monetary union research on the issue of seigniorage may have been misplaced.

Notice that while the household intertemporal budget constraints are necessary for equilibrium, no government intertemporal budget constraint or solvency condition is listed above as a necessary condition. Such a solvency condition for the government of country one would state that the present value of real outstanding government debt go to zero in the limit:

$$\lim_{T\to\infty}\left(\prod_{j=t}^{T-1} R_j^{-1}\right) D_{1T} = 0. \tag{14}$$

This solvency condition would imply a government intertemporal budget constraint, requiring the present discounted value of future tax and seigniorage revenues to cover expenditures and allow the government to pay back its outstanding debt:

$$R_{t-1}\left(\frac{D_{1t-1}}{p_t}\right) = \sum_{s=t}^{\infty}\left(\prod_{j=t}^{s-1} r_j^{-1}\right)\left[\tau_{1s} - \bar{g}_1 + v_{1s}\right]. \tag{15}$$

The analogous intertemporal budget constraint for government two would be

$$R_{t-1}\left(\frac{D_{2t-1}}{p_t}\right) = \sum_{s=t}^{\infty}\left(\prod_{j=t}^{s-1} r_j^{-1}\right)\left[\tau_{2s} - \bar{g}_2 + v_{2s}\right]. \tag{16}$$

The common central bank then also would have an analogous condition, concerning the issue of currency and the disbursement of income earned from its holdings of debt issued by the national governments:

$$\frac{M_{t-1} - R_{t-1}B_{mt-1}}{p_t} = \sum_{s=t}^{\infty}\left(\prod_{j=t}^{s-1} r_j^{-1}\right)\left[\frac{R_s - 1}{R_s} m_s - v_{1s} - v_{2s} - g_{ms}\right]. \tag{17}$$

These three intertemporal government constraints are not explicit in the list of necessary conditions for equilibrium, but they are nevertheless implied in consolidated form. If the household intertemporal budget constraint of country one (4) is summed with the analogous condition for the household in country two:

$$\frac{W_{2t}}{p_t} = \sum_{s=t}^{\infty}\left(\prod_{j=t}^{s-1} r_j^{-1}\right)\left[c_{2s} + \tau_{2s} - y_{2s} + \frac{R_s - 1}{R_s} m_{2s}\right] \tag{18}$$

the result is a condition that equals the sum of the intertemporal conditions for the three government entities (15)–(17):

$$\left(\frac{R_{t-1}\left(B_{1t-1}+B_{2t-1}\right)+M_{t-1}}{p_t}\right)$$
$$=\sum_{s=t}^{\infty}\left(\prod_{j=t}^{s-1} r_j^{-1}\right)\left[c_{1s}+c_{2s}+\tau_{1s}+\tau_{2s}-y_{1s}-y_{2s}+\frac{R_s-1}{R_s}m_s\right] \tag{19}$$

where market-clearing conditions have been used to simplify terms.

In a one-country model, the household intertemporal budget constraint would be identical to the consolidated government intertemporal budget constraint, and government solvency would indeed be required for an equilibrium. However, in a monetary union, these solvency conditions appear in a form that consolidates and then divides them along different lines, by household rather than by government. This has several implications for equilibrium.

First, it is not strictly necessary in an equilibrium that each government be solvent. As has been pointed out by Woodford (1996), if one government is insolvent because it has a debt growing at a rate greater than the interest rate, this need not violate equilibrium if the other government has assets growing at the same rate. In other words, if the second government purchases the expanding debt of the first indefinitely, there is no net effect on the household intertemporal budget constraints, and thus no violation of the equilibrium conditions.

However, by buying limitless amounts of debt without eventual repayment, the second government in effect would be transferring wealth abroad at the expense of its own citizens. This is not problematic if one assumes perfect insurance between home and foreign households, as in Woodford (1996). Insurance payments would then offset the effects of any such transfer and maintain a constant wealth distribution. While the assumption of perfect insurance is convenient for solving the model, it conceals the fact that home and foreign households are distinct entities with distinct interests, a fact central to much of international economics. Sims (1997) points out that the political economy of such an equilibrium would be unsustainable under imperfect insurance. This point is taken up further in a later section.

Further, once any attempt is made to justify such a government policy in terms of some government objective, government optimization would introduce a corresponding transversality condition. This would imply the set of three distinct government intertemporal budget constraints listed previously as necessary conditions for equilibrium. It may be argued that we do in fact observe significant transfers of wealth from rich members of the European Union to poorer members. But the case of direct transfers such as these can be consistent with a set of government transversality conditions, unlike the case of limitless purchases of debt never to be repaid.

A second implication of this model is that apart from government debt, equilibrium requires conditions on the distribution of private wealth between countries. This results from the fact that each of the two household intertemporal budget constraints is listed separately as a necessary condition for equilibrium. Suppose households of one country become indebted to those of the other country to a point that, for one reason or another, the debt is not expected to be repaid in present value out of future disposable income. It is not sufficient that the private sector as a whole in the monetary union would be solvent. Such a condition, often called "external imbalance," would violate each of the household transversality conditions taken separately.

4. Some Examples

The intertemporal budget constraints analyzed above have a significance beyond their role as necessary conditions for equilibrium; it is often useful to regard them as the conditions that determine the equilibrium price level. Some implications for the price level can be demonstrated by considering an example. Consider a quadratic utility function for households in country one:

$$U(c_{1t}, m_{1t}) = \left(c_{1t} - \frac{a}{2}c_{1t}^2\right) + \gamma\left(m_{1t} - \frac{b}{2}m_{1t}^2\right), \tag{20}$$

where $c_{1t} < \frac{1}{a}$ and $m_{1t} < \frac{1}{b}$ for all t.[5] The optimality conditions (5 and 6) then become:

$$(1 - ac_{1t}) = \gamma \left(\frac{R_t}{R_t - 1} \right) (1 - bm_{1t}) \tag{21}$$

$$(1 - ac_{1t}) = \beta R_t E_t \left[\frac{p_t}{p_{t+1}} (1 - ac_{1t+1}) \right]. \tag{22}$$

To highlight the role of imperfect insurance, consider the presence of transitory asymmetric output shocks. For simplicity, suppose these are offsetting across countries, so that there are no shocks to aggregate output:

$$y_{1t} = \overline{y}_1 + \varepsilon_t \tag{23}$$

$$y_{2t} = \overline{y}_2 - \varepsilon_t \tag{24}$$

$$\varepsilon_t \sim N(0, \sigma^2). \tag{25}$$

4.1. *Case 1: One bad apple*

It first will be demonstrated that fiscal irresponsibility by just one government can lead to a rise in the price level throughout the monetary union. Suppose that the government in country two is "fiscally responsible" in the following sense: it adjusts taxes, τ_{2s}, as necessary to guarantee its own solvency and satisfy (16) for any given value of central bank rebates, v_{2s}. On the other hand, suppose government one adopts a fiscal policy that pegs its tax at a given level, $\tau_{1s} = \overline{\tau}_1$, for each period s after the initial period t. This policy is regarded as "irresponsible," inasmuch as the government cannot guarantee its own solvency. Next suppose a monetary policy in which the common central bank pegs the nominal interest rate $R_t = \overline{R}$.[6] For simplicity, suppose a constant level of operating expenditures for the central bank, $g_{mt} = \overline{g_m}$.

If linearized around a symmetric, deterministic steady state and considered under the monetary policy rule, the *ex-ante* form of the household

[5]The satiation point is assumed to be sufficiently far away so as to not interfere with the transversality arguments made later.

[6]This reaction function could be viewed as arising from an optimizing central bank that has strong preferences for interest rate smoothing, as discussed in Barro (1989).

intertemporal budget constraint in country one (4) may be written:

$$\frac{\widetilde{W}_{1t}}{\overline{W}_1} - \frac{\widetilde{p}_t}{\overline{p}} = \left(\frac{\overline{W}_1}{\overline{p}}\right)^{-1} E_t \sum_{s=t}^{\infty} \beta^{s-t} \left[(\widetilde{c}_{1s} + \widetilde{\tau}_{1s} + (1-\beta)\widetilde{m}_{1s} - \widetilde{y}_{1s}) \right.$$
$$\left. + (1-\beta)\left(\frac{\overline{W}_1}{\overline{p}}\right) \sum_{j=t}^{s-1} \left(\frac{\widetilde{p}_{j+1}}{\overline{p}} - \frac{\widetilde{p}_j}{\overline{p}}\right) \right], \tag{26}$$

where overbars indicate steady state values, and tildes indicate deviations in levels from steady state. If we use the linearized form of the money demand optimality condition (21), $\widetilde{m}_t$ may be written in terms of $\widetilde{c}_t$ for each period. Then using the linearized intertemporal optimality condition (22), which expresses $E_t(\widetilde{c}_s)$ for $s > t$ as a function of $\widetilde{c}_t$, it is possible to solve recursively for current consumption: (see the appendix for details.)

$$\widetilde{c}_{1t} = \overline{\Phi} \left[\frac{\overline{W}_1}{\overline{p}} \left(\frac{\widetilde{W}_{1t}}{\overline{W}_1} - \frac{\widetilde{p}_t}{\overline{p}} \right) + E_t \sum_{s=t}^{\infty} \beta^{s-t} (\widetilde{y}_{1s} - \widetilde{\tau}_{1s}) \right], \tag{27}$$

where

$$\overline{\Phi} = (1-\beta)\left(1 + \frac{a}{b\gamma}(1-\beta)^2\right)^{-1}.$$

This condition states that changes in consumption are a function of changes in the household's expected intertemporal wealth, which is comprised of initial holdings of assets as well as the present discounted value of output net of taxes. In summary, the consumption decision is influenced by the relationship between outstanding government debt and anticipated future tax obligations.

To find the equilibrium, we sum the consumption functions of both countries (27 and its foreign counterpart), and impose the goods market clearing condition that joint consumption is constant. This produces

$$\frac{\widetilde{p}_t}{\overline{p}} = \frac{\widetilde{W}_t}{\overline{W}} - \left(\frac{\overline{W}}{\overline{p}}\right)^{-1} E_t \sum_{s=t}^{\infty} \beta^{s-t} (\widetilde{\tau}_{1s} + \widetilde{\tau}_{2s}), \tag{28}$$

where $W_t = W_{1t} + W_{2t}$, and likewise for steady state values.

Imposing the fiscal rules stated above for $\widetilde{\tau}_{1s}$ and $\widetilde{\tau}_{2s}$, and assuming that the economy starts at steady state in period $t-1$, the percent change in the price level in the period of the shock, t, may be written:

$$\frac{\widetilde{p}_t}{\overline{p}} = -\left(\frac{\overline{W}_1}{\overline{p}}\right)^{-1} \widetilde{\tau}_{1t}. \tag{29}$$

(See the appendix for details.) Consider an experiment in which the government of country one temporarily lowers taxes in period t, holding taxes fixed for periods $s > t$ as specified by the fiscal rule above. Condition (29) suggests the percentage rise in the price level will be proportional to the fall in taxes, the proportion depending on the initial wealth of the household in country one. The consumption function (27) suggests the following interpretation.[7] Without a price level rise, household wealth would rise in country one. Since the corresponding condition suggests consumption in household two would not fall, overall there would be excess demand in the goods market. A rise in the price level is needed to lower the real value of wealth to be consistent with goods market equilibrium.

Using the flow budget constraint of government one (7) and the definition of central bank rebates (9), condition (29) may also be written:

$$\frac{\widetilde{p}_t}{\overline{p}} = \frac{\widetilde{D}_{1t}}{\overline{D}_1}. \tag{30}$$

This states that under the preceding assumptions, the percent rise in price would equal the percent rise in outstanding debt of the fiscally "irresponsible" government. This makes clear that a rise in government debt in one country can lead directly to a rise in the overall price level throughout the monetary union.

Since consumption in country one is derived above using the household intertemporal budget constraint (26), it is simple to verify that this budget constraint holds not only jointly with the foreign counterpart, but also separately as required for equilibrium. The foreign counterpart must residually hold separately as well.

4.2. *Case 2: Maastricht scenario*

If the common central bank wishes to maintain price stability as its sole objective, it could specify the monetary policy rule $\widetilde{p}_t = 0$. Under this

[7]This argument is outlined in Woodford (1996).

policy rule, it can be shown that the deviations in the nominal interest rate will be zero for all periods, and the household intertemporal budget constraint in country one (4) may be written:

$$\frac{\widetilde{W}_{1t}}{\overline{W}_1} = \left(\frac{\overline{W}_1}{\overline{p}}\right)^{-1} E_t \left[\sum_{s=t}^{\infty} \beta^{s-t} \left(\widetilde{c}_{1s} + \widetilde{\tau}_{1s} + (1-\beta)\, \widetilde{m}_{1s} - \widetilde{y}_{1s} \right) \right]. \tag{31}$$

As in case 1 above, the Euler conditions may be used to substitute out money and solve recursively for consumption, and the consumption equations may be summed over both households and the goods market-clearing condition imposed. Note that since changes in total consumption and hence real money holdings are zero, under the current monetary policy rule so are changes in nominal money and hence central bank holdings of government debt. The result is

$$\frac{1}{\beta}(\widetilde{D}_{1t-1} + \widetilde{D}_{2t-1}) = \left(\frac{\overline{W}}{\overline{p}}\right)^{-1} E_t \sum_{s=t}^{\infty} \beta^{s-t} (\widetilde{\tau}_{1s} + \widetilde{\tau}_{2s}). \tag{32}$$

This condition requires that the two national governments be jointly fiscally responsible, as defined previously. Any change in the sum of outstanding government debt must be covered in present value terms by future joint tax revenues, without the need of additional transfers from the central bank.

Clearly one way to satisfy this condition is to require each government to set taxes so as to maintain its own solvency, satisfying (15) and (16) respectively. This conclusion offers some justification for the fiscal restrictions specified in the Maastricht Treaty for the European Monetary Union and in subsequent agreements. Note however that the condition of solvency in principle is much less restrictive than the debt ceilings imposed in practice.

Secondly, the usefulness of fiscal restrictions derives solely from their effect on household expectations about the future. Since price stability is a matter of household expectations about intertemporal wealth, neither tight monetary nor fiscal policies at the current time can guarantee price stability. What is needed is the ability to convince households that such policies will be maintained indefinitely in the future. For example, consider again the experiment of the previous section: A temporary cut in current taxes by government one with no offsetting change in future taxes. Even if the central bank pledges to maintain price stability, if the lack of tax response by fiscal authorities causes households to doubt such a tax response will come eventually, this will generate pressure for the current price level to rise.[8]

4.3. *Case 3: Fiscal bailout*

An equilibrium can be specified in which fiscal solvency is not necessary for each government individually. Consider a case in which the fiscal policy of each country fixes its tax rate, $\tau_{1t} = \overline{\tau}_1$ and $\tau_{2t} = \overline{\tau}_2$, and where the central bank pegs the nominal interest rate, $R_t = \overline{R}$. The possibility of such an equilibrium was noted first by Woodford (1996). The equilibrium resembles that for case 1 discussed previously: the joint household intertemporal budget constraint (26) holds, as do the consumption equation (27) and condition (28). But because of the new fiscal policy in country two, the equilibrium price conditions (29 and 30) pertaining to the period of the shock, t, are altered slightly to include the taxes and debt of country two:

$$\frac{\widetilde{p}_t}{\overline{p}} = -\left(\frac{\overline{W}}{\overline{p}}\right)^{-1} (\widetilde{\tau}_{1t} + \widetilde{\tau}_{2t}) \tag{33}$$

$$\frac{\widetilde{p}_t}{\overline{p}} = \frac{\widetilde{D}_{1t} + \widetilde{D}_{2t}}{\overline{D}_1 + \overline{D}_2}. \tag{34}$$

Consider again the fiscal experiment of the previous sections, involving a temporary tax cut and deficit which increases nominal debt of government one. Condition (34) implies the price level will rise enough to hold the aggregate level of real government debt constant. But this means the real value of debt of government one has risen, while that of government two has fallen in an offsetting way. In particular, substituting the price change from (33) into the linearized flow budget constraint of government one and assuming a symmetric steady state, the change in government one debt may be written:

$$\left(\frac{\widetilde{D}_{1t}}{\overline{D}_1} - \frac{\widetilde{p}_t}{\overline{p}}\right) = -\frac{1}{2}\left(\frac{\overline{D}_1}{\overline{p}}\right)^{-1} \widetilde{\tau}_{1t}. \tag{35}$$

[8]In a richer environment, there could be other possible resolutions to this dilemma, such as default by the irresponsible fiscal authority. Default could be viewed as another type of tax, levied on holders of debt.

So the tax cut raises the real debt of government one, despite the fact it is deflated using a higher price level.

The subsequent dynamics of real debt may be written using the flow budget constraint updated one period:[9]

$$E_t\left(\frac{\widetilde{D}_{1t+1}}{\overline{D}_1}-\frac{\widetilde{p}_t}{\overline{p}}\right)=\frac{1}{\beta}\left(\frac{\widetilde{D}_{1t}}{\overline{D}_1}-\frac{\widetilde{p}_t}{\overline{p}}\right). \tag{36}$$

Since the value in parentheses on the right is positive, we know the portion of real government debt in excess of the steady state level is growing explosively at the rate $\frac{1}{\beta}$. This violates the solvency condition and intertemporal budget constraint for government one, but neither is a necessary condition for equilibrium. Likewise, it may be shown that debt in country two changes according to

$$\left(\frac{\widetilde{D}_{2t}}{\overline{D}_2}-\frac{\widetilde{p}_t}{\overline{p}}\right)=\frac{1}{2}\left(\frac{\overline{D}_2}{\overline{p}}\right)^{-1}\widetilde{\tau}_{1t}. \tag{37}$$

The tax cut thus makes government two debt fall under the same conditions that it rises for government one. Since its dynamics are analogous to (36), its debt grows at the negative explosive rate $-\frac{1}{\beta}$.

Since the changes in government debt offset each other, there is no change in total household wealth, $\widetilde{W}_t=0$, and the joint household solvency condition is satisfied. It is again simple to show that the conditions for each household are also satisfied separately.

An interesting feature of this equilibrium is that the fiscal experiment affects the distribution of household wealth between the countries and thereby the individual levels of consumption. Using the consumption function (27), consumption in country one rises after the tax cut by

$$\widetilde{c}_{1t}=-\overline{\Phi}\frac{1}{2}\widetilde{\tau}_{1t}. \tag{38}$$

Using the goods market equilibrium condition, it is clear that consumption in country two falls by this same amount.

While the case above does describe an equilibrium, the implications for consumption call into question the government policies that underlie it. The equilibrium implies that government two purchases limitless amounts

[9]This uses the fact that price is not expected to move after the initial period of the fiscal shock.

of government one debt without any future repayment. This government policy lowers the wealth of households in country two, and consequently their consumption and welfare. If one views government policy as arising from a desire to optimize the welfare of a country's households, the policy described above is difficult to justify. As pointed out in Sims (1997), political pressure from households would surely discourage a government from pursuing such a policy.

4.4. *Case 4: External imbalance*

The present model with imperfect insurance offers one example where the distribution of private wealth could become unsustainable. Consider the effect of an asymmetric shock to output. A significant amount of research related to the European Monetary Union has analyzed the implications of such asymmetric output shocks for the objective of output stabilization. But the fiscal theory's focus on household wealth suggests that such shocks may have implications for the objective of price stabilization as well.

It has been argued widely that if output shocks are highly asymmetric across countries, the inability to tailor monetary policy to country-specific needs is costly. The present model implies that even without perfect insurance or independent monetary policy, households can smooth their consumption levels quite well. Consider a temporary shock to output in country one by amount ε_t. For simplicity, we consider the case where national shocks are offsetting, so total output in the monetary union is unaffected. Assume the monetary and fiscal policies of case one discussed previously, so the equilibrium conditions there hold also here. In particular, the consumption function (27) implies that consumption in periods t and $t+1$ are

$$\widetilde{c}_{1t} = \overline{\Phi}\varepsilon_t \tag{39}$$

$$E_t\widetilde{c}_{1t+1} = \overline{\Phi}E_t\left[\frac{\overline{W_1}}{\overline{p}}\left(\frac{\widetilde{W}_{1t+1}}{\overline{W}_1} - \frac{\widetilde{p}_{t+1}}{\overline{p}}\right)\right]. \tag{40}$$

Since $\overline{\Phi}$ is small for β close to unity, the impact on the household's consumption is small relative to the size of the shock. Consumption is smoothed by borrowing abroad, and thereafter consumption adjusts to the resulting change in household wealth.

The implications for household wealth in the periods after the shock may be derived from the linearized flow budget constraint of the household (1):

$$E_t\left(\frac{\widetilde{W}_{1t+1}}{\overline{W}_1} - \frac{\widetilde{p}_{t+1}}{\overline{p}}\right) = \left(\frac{\overline{W}_1}{\overline{p}}\right)^{-1} \varepsilon_t \tag{41}$$

$$E_t\left(\frac{\widetilde{W}_{1t+2}}{\overline{W}_1} - \frac{\widetilde{p}_{t+2}}{\overline{p}}\right) = E_t\left(\frac{\widetilde{W}_{1t+1}}{\overline{W}_1} - \frac{\widetilde{p}_{t+1}}{\overline{p}}\right). \tag{42}$$

These imply that a stochastic fall in current output of one country leads to a fall in the wealth of its households, and that any such change in wealth is expected to be permanent. The private debt in each country follows a random walk, implying that eventually private debt in one country could become so large that the solution to the consumption equation (27) would require a value of consumption less than zero.[10] If the nonnegativity restriction on consumption is not to be violated, the households will not be expected to be able to repay their debt in present value out of future income. This is a stylized example of how an unsustainable cross-country distribution of private wealth could undermine an equilibrium.

5. Conclusion

When applied to a monetary union, the fiscal theory of the price level suggests that the focus of past research on seigniorage is misplaced. Regardless of seigniorage, if government debt is large, a rise in the common price level can have large implications for government finance and household wealth through the inflation tax. Further, in the context of a monetary union, the fiscal theory takes on some new dimensions not observed in closed-economy contexts. For example, fiscal solvency may not be necessary for individual member governments. However, as long as international risk sharing is imperfect, this case is unlikely to arise. Future work could further explore the implications of imperfect insurance by considering explicitly optimizing governments and their strategic interactions in this context.

[10]Such a situation could be ruled out if precautionary saving were sufficiently strong; this is not true for quadratic utility.

Appendix

Listed here are omitted steps in the solution for equilibrium in case 1. Under the monetary policy that $R_t = \overline{R} = \frac{1}{\beta}$, a linear approximation of the money demand condition (21) implies

$$\widetilde{m}_{1t} = (1-\beta)\frac{a}{b\gamma}\widetilde{c}_{1t} \tag{A1}$$

where tildes indicate deviations from a steady state. This condition is used to substitute money balances out of the household intertemporal constraint (26).

Again under the monetary policy rule, the intertemporal optimality condition (22) may be linearized:

$$a\widetilde{c}_{1t} + (1-a\overline{c}_1)\frac{\widetilde{p}_t}{\overline{p}} = aE_t\widetilde{c}_{1t+1} + (1-a\overline{c}_1)E_t\frac{\widetilde{p}_{t+1}}{\overline{p}} \tag{A2}$$

where overbars indicate steady state values. An analogous condition applies to the household in country two. Summing over (A2) and the foreign counterpart, and imposing the linearized goods market clearing condition

$$\widetilde{c}_{1t} + \widetilde{c}_{2t} = 0 \tag{A3}$$

produces

$$E_t\frac{\widetilde{p}_{t+1}}{\overline{p}} = \frac{\widetilde{p}_t}{\overline{p}}. \tag{A4}$$

This condition implies that no future price changes are expected after the initial period, and it allows the term $E_t\sum_{s=t}^{\infty}\beta^{s-t-1}\left(\frac{\widetilde{p}_{s+1}}{\overline{p}} - \frac{\widetilde{p}_s}{\overline{p}}\right)$ in (26) to be eliminated.

Further, substituting (A4) back into (A2) implies

$$\widetilde{c}_{1t} = E_t\widetilde{c}_{1t+1}. \tag{A5}$$

Recursive substitution of (A5) into (26) produces the solution for current consumption shown in (27) in the text.

Next, sum this consumption function with its foreign counterpart, imposing goods market-clearing (A3) and the fact that $E_t\widetilde{y}_{1s} = 0$, for $s > t$, to produce (28) in the text. The fiscal rule for country one implies $E_t\sum_{s=t}^{\infty}\beta^{s-t}(\widetilde{\tau}_{1s}) = \widetilde{\tau}_{1t}$. Since the government of country two guarantees its own solvency, the present value of its stream of taxes is specified using the linearized government intertemporal budget constraint (16):

$$\sum_{s=t}^{\infty} \beta^{s-t}(\widetilde{\tau}_{2s}) = \frac{1}{\beta}\left(\frac{\overline{D}_2}{\overline{p}}\right)\left(\frac{\widetilde{D}_{2t-1}}{\overline{D}_2} - \frac{\widetilde{p}_t}{\overline{p}}\right) - \sum_{s=t}^{\infty} \beta^{s-t}(\widetilde{v}_{2s}). \tag{A6}$$

The last term in the expression above may be found using the linearized intertemporal budget constraint of the central bank (17):

$$\sum_{s=t}^{\infty} \beta^{s-t}(\widetilde{v}_{2s}) = -\frac{1}{2\overline{p}}\left[\widetilde{M}_{t-1} - \frac{1}{\beta}\widetilde{B}_{mt-1} - \left(\overline{M} - \frac{1}{\beta}\overline{B}_m\right)\frac{\widetilde{p}_t}{\overline{p}}\right]. \tag{A7}$$

Substituting (A6) and (A7) into (28) and regrouping terms produces expression (29) in the text.

Acknowledgment

I thank Kevin Hoover, Eric Leeper, Nouriel Roubini, Steven Sheffrin, Michael Woodford, and an anonymous referee for helpful comments. My special thanks go to Christopher Sims for his invaluable direction of my dissertation research.

References

Barro, R. J. 1989. Interest rate targeting. *Journal of Monetary Economics*, 23: 3–30.

Baxter, M. and U. J. Jermann. 1997. The international diversification puzzle is worse than you think. *American Economic Review*, 87: 170–180.

Chari, V. V. and P. J. Kehoe. 1997. On the need for fiscal constraints in a monetary union, Working paper, (Federal Reserve Bank of Minneapolis, Minneapolis, Minnesota).

Canzoneri, M. B. and B. T. Diba. 1991. Fiscal deficits, financial integration, and a central bank for Europe. *Journal of the Japanese and International Economies*, 5: 381–403.

Canzoneri, M. B., R. E. Cumby, and B. T. Diba. 1997. Is the price level determined by the needs of fiscal solvency? Manuscript, Georgetown University, Washington, D.C.

Cochrane, J. H. 1998. Long-term debt and optimal policy in the fiscal theory of the price level, Manuscript, University of Chicago, Chicago, Illinois.

Cochrane, J. H. 1999. A frictionless view of U.S. inflation. In Bernanke, B. S., Rotemberg, J. (eds.), *1998 NBER Macroeconomics Annual.* MIT Press: Cambridge, pp. 323–421.

Dupor, W. 1997. Exchange rates and the fiscal theory of the price level, Manuscript. Wharton School, Philadelphia, Pennsylvania.

Leeper, E. 1991. Equilibria under 'active' and 'passive' monetary and fiscal policies. *Journal of Monetary Economics*, 27: 129–147.

Leeper, E. 1993. The policy tango: Toward a holistic view of monetary and fiscal effects. *Economic Review of the Federal Reserve Bank of Atlanta*, 78: 1–27.

McCallum, B. T. 1998. Indeterminacy, bubbles, and the fiscal theory of price level determination, NBER Working Paper No. 6456.

Neumeyer, P. A. and M. Yano. 1996. Cross border nominal assets and international monetary interdependence, Manuscript, University of Southern California, Los Angeles, California.

Schmitt-Grohé, S. and M. Uribe. 1997. Price level determinacy and monetary policy under a balanced-budget requirement, Working paper, Board of Governors of the Federal Reserve System, Washington D.C.

Sibert, A. 1992. Government finance in a common currency area. *Journal of International Money and Finance*, 11: 567–578.

Sibert, A. 1994. The allocation of seigniorage in a common currency area. *Journal of International Economics*, 37: 111–122.

Sims, C. A. 1994. A simple model for study of the determination of the price level and the interaction of monetary and fiscal policy. *Economic Theory*, 4: 381–399.

Sims, C. A. 1997. Fiscal foundations of price stability in open economies, Manuscript, Yale University, New Haven, Connecticut.

Woodford, M. 1994. Monetary policy and price level determinacy in a cash-in-advance economy. *Economic Theory*, 4: 345–380.

Woodford, M. 1995. Price level determinacy without control of a monetary aggregate. *Carnegie-Rochester Conference Series on Public Policy*, 43: 1–46.

Woodford, M. 1996. Control of the public debt: A requirement for price stability? NBER Working Paper No. 5684.

CHAPTER 13

Does Exchange Rate Variability Matter for Welfare? A Quantitative Investigation of Stabilization Policies*

Paul R. Bergin,[†,¶] Hyung-Cheol Shin[‡], and Ivan Tchakarov[§]

[†]*Department of Economics, University of California at Davis, One Shields Ave., Davis, CA 95616, USA*
[‡]*Franklin Templeton Investments, One Franklin Parkway, San Mateo, CA 94403, USA*
[§]*Nomura Securities, 1 St Martin's Le Grand, London EC1A 4NP, UK*
[¶]*prbergin@ucdavis.edu*

1. Introduction

In an increasingly globalized economy, it might seem obvious that macroeconomic policy would need to take into consideration the global environment, including the exchange rate and policy of trading partners. However, much theory in international economics suggests that it is sufficient for policy makers to focus on domestic macroeconomic conditions. This chapter develops a theoretical model identifying characteristics of an economy that make it important for policy makers to focus on exchange rate stabilization, in addition to stabilizing domestic variables.

Several recent papers have employed analytically solvable models to characterize the implications of alternative monetary policy rules and

*This article originally appeared in *European Economic Review* (2007), 51(4), 1041–1058.

exchange rate arrangements in sticky price open economies. Bacchetta and van Wincoop (2000) demonstrate that monetary policy rules that stabilize the exchange rate do not necessarily increase household welfare or even trade, depending on the nature of preferences, the monetary policy rules, and the shocks.

Devereux and Engel (2003) show that the degree to which optimal policy lets the exchange rate fluctuate depends on the currency in which prices are sticky. Gali and Monacelli (2005) study classes of policy rules in the form of inflation targeting and Taylor-type rules.[1]

This chapter conducts a quantitative analysis of somewhat richer and more realistic economic environments, as permitted by calibration and numerical solution. For example, asset markets and preferences are not limited to cases that imply complete international risk sharing, which would imply the current account is restricted to zero balance. As a result, when the chapter computes the effects of exchange rate variability, it takes into consideration the potentially important effects that exchange rates have on a country's current account. This numerical analysis is made possible by the second-order solution method developed in Kim *et al.* (2003), which is also applied to an open economy setting in Kollmann (2002, 2004).[2] The analysis here differs from Kollmann in that it studies alternative economic environments, and pays special attention to the size of quantitative implications from policy choices.

The chapter begins by studying a generalized version of the standard model from the optimal policy literature, with calibrated parameters and augmented with incomplete asset markets. Experiments support the findings from simpler analytical models, in that the particular Taylor-type policy rule that is optimal prescribes aggressively stabilizing inflation. The optimized rule does not directly respond to exchange rate fluctuations, and it is optimal to let the exchange rate fluctuate in response to productivity shocks. However, the experiment highlights that the benefits from following an optimized stabilization policy are small in terms of representative household utility.

---

[1]For a sample of other related work, see Benigno (2004), Benigno and Benigno (2003), Carre and Collard (2003), Clarida *et al.* (2001), Corsetti and Pesenti (2001, 2004), Obstfeld and Rogoff (2002), and Sutherland (2005).

[2]Related solution algorithms have been proposed in Schmitt-Grohe and Uribe (2004a), and Collard and Juillard (2001).

The chapter goes on to study two new types of economic environments, where the utility benefits might be expected to be larger. The first of these cases is where household preferences exhibit habits. However, experiments indicate that the conclusions from the benchmark economy are little altered. Optimized policy continues to focus on inflation stabilization, and continues to allow substantial exchange rate variability. Further, while households with habits are by definition much more sensitive to certain types of variability, the utility gains from following an optimized stabilization policy increase only moderately.

The second alternative economic environment features one country unable to issue debt denominated in its own currency. Termed "original sin" in recent literature, this asset asymmetry makes it difficult for the country to respond to a stochastic environment through precautionary saving, since net foreign assets expose the country all the more to the effects of exchange rate variability. In this context, the optimized cooperative policy rule puts substantial weight on exchange rate stabilization and virtually eliminates exchange rate fluctuations. The size of the utility gain for the sin country is about four times that for the benchmark economy above.

The next section of the chapter presents the benchmark two-country model, calibration, and solution method. Section 3 presents results for the benchmark model and the two extensions. Section 4 concludes and makes suggestions for future research.

2. The Model

Consider a model of two countries, denoted home and foreign. Agents consume two final goods, where each country specializes in the production of one of these. Monopolistically competitive firms produce intermediates using capital and labor, and set prices sluggishly due to adjustment costs.

2.1. *Goods market structure*

Final goods (F) are a CES index over sub-indexes of the home (F_H) and foreign (F_F) intermediates. The aggregation technology for final goods is

$$F_t = \left[a^{\frac{1}{\mu}} F_{H,t}^{\frac{\mu-1}{\mu}} + (1-a)^{\frac{1}{\mu}} F_{F,t}^{\frac{\mu-1}{\mu}} \right]^{\frac{\mu}{\mu-1}}, \tag{1}$$

where

$$F_{H,t} = \left(\int_0^1 f_{H,t}(i)^{\frac{\lambda-1}{\lambda}} di \right)^{\frac{\lambda}{\lambda-1}}, \tag{2}$$

$$F_{F,t} = \left(\int_0^1 f_{F,t}(j)^{\frac{\lambda-1}{\lambda}} dj \right)^{\frac{\lambda}{\lambda-1}}, \tag{3}$$

where a lower case represents output of the individual firms.

Final goods producers behave competitively, maximizing profit each period:

$$\Pi_t = \max[P_t F_t - P_{H,t} F_{H,t} - P_{F,t} F_{F,t}], \tag{4}$$

where P is the overall price index of the final good, P_H is the price index of home goods in home currency units, and P_F of foreign goods in foreign currency units. The price indexes may be defined:

$$P_t = [a P_{H,t}^{1-\mu} + (1-a) P_{F,t}^{1-\mu}]^{\frac{1}{1-\mu}}, \tag{5}$$

where

$$P_{H,t} = \left(\int_0^1 p_{H,t}(i)^{1-\lambda} di \right)^{\frac{1}{1-\lambda}}, \tag{6}$$

$$P_{F,t} = \left(\int_0^1 p_{F,t}(j)^{1-\lambda} di \right)^{\frac{1}{1-\lambda}}. \tag{7}$$

Given the aggregation functions above, demand will be allocated between home and foreign goods according to

$$F_{H,t} = a \left(\frac{P_{H,t}}{P_t} \right)^{-\mu} F_t, \tag{8}$$

$$F_{F,t} = (1-a) \left(\frac{P_{F,t}}{P_t} \right)^{-\mu} F_t, \tag{9}$$

with demands for individual goods:

$$f_{H,t}(i) = \left(\frac{p_{H,t}(i)}{P_{H,t}} \right)^{-\lambda} F_{H,t}, \tag{10}$$

$$f_{F,t}(j) = \left(\frac{p_{F,t}(j)}{P_{F,t}} \right)^{-\lambda} F_{F,t}. \tag{11}$$

Analogous definitions apply to the foreign country.

2.2. *Home household problem*

The representative home household derives utility from consumption (C), real money balances (M/P), and labor (H). Households derive income by selling their labor (H) at the nominal wage rate (W), renting out capital to firms at the real rental rate (r), receiving real profits from home firms (Π), and from government transfers (T). In addition to money, households can hold a noncontingent nominal bond denominated in home currency (B_H) which pays an interest rate (i), or a bond denominated in foreign currency (B_F) which pays an interest rate (i^*), where S is the home currency price of a unit of foreign currency. The household determines capital accumulation (K), which involves a quadratic adjustment cost that depends upon the parameter ψ_I and a constant rate of depreciation (δ).

Household optimization for the home country may be written:

$$\max E_0 \sum_{t=0}^{\infty} \beta^t U\left(C_t, \frac{M_t}{P_t}, H_t\right)$$

subject to the budget constraint:

$$\begin{aligned} P_t C_t &+ P_t(K_{t+1} - (1-\delta)K_t) + P_t \mathrm{AC}_{I,t} + M_t + B_{H,t} + S_t B_{F,t} + \mathrm{AC}_{B,t} \\ &= (1+i_{t-1})B_{H,t-1} + S_t(1+i^*_{t-1})B_{F,t-1} + M_{t-1} + W_t H_t + P_t r_t K_t \\ &\quad + T_t + \Pi_t \end{aligned}$$

where

$$U_t = \frac{C_t^{1-\rho}}{1-\rho} + \frac{\chi_t}{1-\varepsilon}\left(\frac{M_t}{P_t}\right)^{1-\varepsilon} - \frac{H_t^{1+\psi}}{1+\psi} \tag{12}$$

and

$$\mathrm{AC}_{I,t} = \frac{\psi_I}{2}\frac{(K_{t+1}-K_t)^2}{K_t} \tag{13}$$

$$\mathrm{AC}_{B,t} = \frac{\psi_B}{2}\frac{(S_t(B_{F,t}-\bar{B}_F))^2}{P_{H,t}Y_t}.$$

Money demand shocks are represented by shifts in χ_t. There is a small adjustment cost on bond holdings, AC_B, to ensure stationarity in the net foreign asset position.[3] Later sections of the chapter will consider a more general form of preferences featuring habits. Later sections also consider an alternative asset market structure, limited to only one type of bond.

Optimization implies a money demand equation:

$$\frac{M_t}{P_t} = \frac{\chi_t^{1/\varepsilon} C_t^{\rho/\varepsilon}}{(1-d_t)^{1/\varepsilon}}, \tag{14}$$

a trade-off between consumption and leisure:

$$\frac{W_t}{P_t C_t^{\rho}} = H_t^{\psi}, \tag{15}$$

a consumption Euler equation:

$$d_t = \beta E_t \frac{P_t C_t^{\rho}}{P_{t+1} C_{t+1}^{\rho}}, \tag{16}$$

with the definition of d:

$$d_t = \frac{1}{1+i_t}, \tag{17}$$

an interest parity condition:

$$E_t\left[\frac{P_t C_t^{\rho}}{P_{t+1} C_{t+1}^{\rho}} \frac{S_{t+1}}{S_t}(1+i_t^*)\left(1+\frac{\psi_B S_t (B_{F,t}-\bar{B}_F)}{P_{H,t} Y_t}\right)^{-1}\right] = E_t\left[\frac{P_t C_t^{\rho}}{P_{t+1} C_{t+1}^{\rho}}(1+i_t)\right], \tag{18}$$

and finally

$$\left(1+\frac{\psi_I (K_{t+1}-K_t)}{K_t}\right) = \beta E_t\left[\frac{C_t^{\rho}}{C_{t+1}^{\rho}}\left(r_t + (1-\delta) + \left(\frac{1}{2}\psi_I \frac{K_{t+2}^2 - K_{t+1}^2}{K_{t+1}^2}\right)\right)\right] \tag{19}$$

[3]Home and foreign bonds are treated separately in this adjustment cost to ensure that there exists a determinate allocation between home and foreign currency bonds even in a first-order approximation to the system, as is required by the second-order accurate solution method.

equating the benefits and costs of capital accumulation. An analogous problem and first-order conditions apply to the foreign household.

2.3. *Home firm problem*

The benchmark model assumes producer currency pricing, so that firms set prices in their own currency both for sales domestically and sales abroad. They rent capital (K) at the rental rate r, and hire labor (H) at the nominal rate W. Prices are sticky because there is a quadratic cost to adjusting them. The home firm maximization problem is

$$\max E_0 \sum_{t=0}^{\infty} \xi_{t,t+n} \Pi_{H,t}(i), \tag{20}$$

where

$$\Pi_{H,t}(i) = (p_{H,t}(i) - \mathrm{MC}_t(i) - \mathrm{AC}_{P,t}(i))(f_{H,t}(i) + f^*_{H,t}(i)), \tag{21}$$

with the adjustment and marginal costs defined respectively as

$$\mathrm{AC}_{P,t}(i) = \frac{\psi_P}{2} \frac{(p_{H,t}(i) - p_{H,t-1}(i))^2}{p_{H,t-1}(i)}, \tag{22}$$

$$\mathrm{MC}_t = \frac{(r_t P_t)^{\alpha} W_t^{1-\alpha}}{\theta_t \alpha^{\alpha}(1-\alpha)^{1-\alpha}}, \tag{23}$$

and subject to the demand function for $f_{H,t}(i)$ from above and the production function specifying output $(y(i))$ as

$$f_{H,t}(i) + f^*_{H,t}(i) = y_t(i) = \theta_t K_t^{\alpha}(i) H_t^{1-\alpha}(i). \tag{24}$$

Here, θ_t represents technology common to all production firms in the country, and is subject to shocks. Lastly, $\xi_{t,t+n}$ is the pricing kernel used to value random date $t+n$ payoffs. Since firms are owned by the representative household, they are assumed to value future profits according to the household's intertemporal marginal rate of substitution in consumption, so that $\xi_{t,t+n} = \beta^n (U'_{C,t+n}/P_{t+n})(U'_{C,t+n}/P_t)$. An analogous problem applies to the foreign firm.

The optimization problem implies a trade-off between capital and labor inputs that depends on the relative cost of each:

$$P_t r_t K_t(i) = \frac{\alpha}{1-\alpha} W_t H_t(i), \tag{25}$$

and price setting behavior:

$$\begin{aligned} p_{H,t}(i) &= \frac{\lambda}{\lambda-1}(\mathrm{MC}_t + \mathrm{AC}_{P,t}) \\ &+ \frac{\psi_P}{\lambda-1} p_{H,t}(i)\left(1 - \frac{p_{H,t}(i)}{p_{H,t-1}(i)}\right) \\ &+ \frac{1}{2}\frac{\psi_P}{\lambda-1} p_{H,t}(i) E_t\left[\frac{\xi_{t,t+i+1}}{\xi_{t,t+i}}\left(1 - \frac{p^2_{H,t+1}(i)}{p^2_{H,t}(i)}\right)\frac{F_{H,t+1}}{F_{H,t}}\right]. \end{aligned} \tag{26}$$

Note that in the special case of no price stickiness ($\psi_P = 0$), price-setting is set as a simple markup over marginal costs: $p_{H,t}(i) = \frac{\lambda}{\lambda-1}\mathrm{MC}_t$. But in the presence of price adjustment costs, price-setting will deviate from this simple markup because of several additional terms. First, the resource cost of setting a price (AC_P) should be included along with the cost of production when computing the overall price of bringing a good to market. The next term in the expression above reflects the backward looking component of price setting: Firms are reluctant to make large changes in price due to the marginal adjustment cost. The final term reflects the forward-looking component of price setting. If a firm expects the need to change prices further in the next period, it will tend to change the price more today, to minimize future adjustment costs. Further, there is an additional reason to raise prices today, because a higher current price means that any future changes will be a smaller percentage change. Here, we see one reason for the monopolist to set a higher price on average, as a hedge against future price changes. Finally, note that in the symmetric equilibrium $p_{H,t}(i) = P_{H,t}$.

2.4. *Government*

Model experiments will consider three alternative policy rules. The first specifies a fixed exogenous money supply:

$$M_t = M_{t-1}. \tag{27}$$

This rule will be used as a benchmark for later comparisons, as it implies no endogenous response of policy to economic shocks or circumstances. The second rule pegs the exchange rate:

$$S_t = \overline{S}. \tag{28}$$

The third rule is a Taylor-type interest rate setting rule

$$i_t = \bar{i} + \Gamma_\pi \pi_t + \Gamma_Y \hat{Y}_t + \Gamma_s \Delta s_t \tag{29}$$

where $\bar{i}$ is steady state interest rate, π_t is inflation rate, $\hat{Y}_t = (Y_t - \bar{Y})/\bar{Y}$ is the output gap, and Δs_t is the percentage change in the nominal exchange rate.[4] It is assumed that central banks make a commitment to set these parameters at time-invariant values.

The government's budget constraint is

$$T_t = M_t - M_{t-1}. \tag{30}$$

2.5. *Market clearing and equilibrium*

Market clearing for the home goods market requires:

$$F_{H,t} + F^*_{H,t} = Y_t, \tag{31}$$

and for the home bond market:

$$B_{H,t} + B^*_{H,t} = 0. \tag{32}$$

Total home final goods demand must equal final goods supply:

$$\begin{aligned} F_t &= C_t + (K_{t+1} - (1-\delta)K_t) \\ &\quad + \mathrm{AC}_{I,t} + \frac{\mathrm{AC}_{B,t}}{P_t} + Y_t \frac{\int_0^1 [\mathrm{AC}_{P,t}(i)di]}{P_t}. \end{aligned} \tag{33}$$

The home balance of payments condition may be written:

$$\begin{aligned} &(B_{H,t} - B_{H,t-1}) + S_t(B_{F,t} - B_{F,t-1}) \\ &\quad = P_{H,t}Y_t + i_{t-1}B_{H,t-1} + S_t i^*_{t-1} B_{F,t-1} - P_t F_t. \end{aligned} \tag{34}$$

Equilibrium is a set of 37 sequences: C_t, C^*_t, $P_{H,t}$, $P_{F,t}$, P_t, P^*_t, S_t, W_t, W^*_t, H_t, H^*_t, Y_t, Y^*_t, F_t, F^*_t, $F_{H,t}$, $F^*_{H,t}$, $F_{F,t}$, $F^*_{F,t}$, K_t, K^*_t, r_t, r^*_t, d_t, d^*_t, MC_t, MC^*_t,

[4] For the foreign country's rule, the response coefficient to the exchange rate is the negative of that for the home country.

$B_{H,t}, B^*_{H,t}, B_{F,t}, B^*_{F,t}, \theta_t, \theta^*_t, M_t, M^*_t, i_t, i^*_t$. The 37 equilibrium conditions are comprised of the balance of payments constraint (34) and the following 18 equations combined with their analogous foreign counterparts: the definition of total demand (1), demand conditions for home and foreign goods (8 and 9), the overall price index (5), the price setting rule (26), the money supply rule (27, 28 or 29), labor-supply condition (15), capital–labor trade-off (25), money demand condition (14), the interest rate parity condition (18), production function (24), definition of marginal cost (23), definition of total demand (33), definition of d (17), consumption Euler equation (16), market clearing conditions for goods (31) and bonds (32), and capital accumulation (19).

The shocks, to technology and money demand in each country, will be log-normally distributed:

$$\begin{aligned}
(\log\theta_t - \log\bar{\theta}) &= \rho_1(\log\theta_{t-1} - \log\bar{\theta}) + \varepsilon_{1t} \\
(\log\theta^*_t - \log\bar{\theta}^*) &= \rho^*_1(\log\theta^*_{t-1} - \log\bar{\theta}^*) + \varepsilon^*_{1t} \\
(\log\chi_t - \log\bar{\chi}) &= \rho_2(\log\chi_{t-1} - \log\bar{\chi}) + \varepsilon_{2t} \\
(\log\chi^*_t - \log\bar{\chi}^*) &= \rho^*_2(\log\chi^*_{t-1} - \log\bar{\chi}^*) + \varepsilon^*_{2t}
\end{aligned} \tag{35}$$

$$[\varepsilon_{1t}, \varepsilon^*_{1t}, \varepsilon_{2t}\varepsilon^*_{2t}] \sim N(0, \Sigma).$$

To deal with the nonstationary nominal variables in this system, they will be transformed by dividing by their respective national price level. The nominal exchange rate will be dealt with in first differences in those cases where it is nonstationary in levels.[5]

2.6. *Solution method and welfare measure*

The model is solved numerically to a second-order approximation. See Kim *et al.* (2003) or Schmitt-Grohe and Uribe (2004a) for a detailed explanation of the methodology. This contrasts with the more standard method relying upon log-linear approximations of model equations, which would only capture the direct effects of exchange rate variability on utility through the fact that people dislike variance in consumption and leisure. A second-order approximation to the full set of model equations additionally picks

[5]The exchange rate is stationary under the fixed exchange rate rule (28) and the exogenous money supply rule with no shocks to money supply (27).

up the effects of variability on the means of consumption and leisure and hence utility. For example, firms may hedge against exchange rate variability by setting higher prices and lowering mean output, and households may engage in precautionary saving that affects mean consumption.

Although it is an imperfect measurement of welfare, we follow the literature in using a second-order Taylor expansion of the utility function of a representative household around the deterministic steady state, indicated here by overbars.[6] Using unconditional expectations:

$$EU(C_t, H_t) = \bar{U} + \bar{C}^{1-\rho}E(\hat{C}_t) - \frac{1}{2}\rho\bar{C}^{1-\rho}\text{var}(\hat{C}_t) - \bar{H}^{1+\psi}E(\hat{H}_t) - \frac{1}{2}\psi\bar{H}^{1+\psi}\text{var}(\hat{H}_t). \tag{36}$$

The unconditional loss is measured in terms of the share (u) of additional deterministic steady state consumption needed to equate the utility level of the unconditional expectation under uncertainty, defined above, with the deterministic steady state:

$$U((1+u)C, H) = EU(C_t, H_t). \tag{37}$$

This effect can be decomposed into the part due to the variance of uncertain consumption and leisure, and the part due to the effect of uncertainty on the means of these variables:

$$U((1+u^{var})C, H) = \bar{U} - \frac{1}{2}\rho C^{1-\rho}\text{var}(\hat{C}_t) - \frac{1}{2}\psi\bar{H}^{1+\psi}\text{var}(\hat{H}_t) \tag{38}$$

$$U((1+u^{\text{mean}})C, H) = \bar{U} + \bar{C}^{1-\rho}E(\hat{C}_t) - \bar{H}^{1+\psi}E(\hat{H}_t). \tag{39}$$

Tables also report conditional utility measures, which have the advantage of taking into consideration the transition dynamics following the implementation of a new policy rule. To compare the implications of adopting the set of alternative policy rules, the utility level is tracked as it starts out from the unconditional expectation implied by the exogenous money supply rule defined above, and evolves over time in response to the alternative rule under consideration. Utility implications are summarized analogously to the unconditional formulas above, except that it is the discounted sum of

[6]True welfare analysis is hampered by well-known problems of aggregation. As is standard in this literature, this chapter determines optimal policy in a model-consistent manner by maximizing the utility of a representative household.

expected utilities over time rather than the unconditional expectation that is reported. For example, the overall effect is computed:

$$U((1+u^{\text{conditional}})C,H)=(1-\beta)\sum_{t=0}^{\infty}\beta^{t}E_{0}U(C_{t},H_{t}). \qquad (40)$$

To solve for the reaction parameters in the policy rule (29) that are optimal, the sum of home and foreign unconditional utility levels is maximized. Since the benchmark case is symmetric, this is a fairly simple matter of choosing three policy parameters, Γ_{π}, Γ_{Y}, and Γ_{S}, which we accomplish by grid search.[7]

2.7. *Calibration*

Regarding behavioral parameters, the labor-supply elasticity is set at unity ($\psi=1$), following Christiano *et al.* (1997). Following Bergin and Feenstra (2001), we set $\varepsilon=\rho=4$, implying an interest elasticity of real money balances of 0.25 and an income elasticity of unity. Following estimates of the elasticity of substitution between home and foreign goods in Harrigan (1993) and Trefler and Lai (1999), μ is set at 5. A value of $\lambda=7$ implies an average price mark-up of 16%. The share of home goods in the home final goods aggregator, a, is set at 0.80, reflecting the 20% share of imports in GDP on average for the G-7 countries in the 1990:1–1998:4 period. $\beta=0.99$, where a period in the model is one quarter. For the depreciation rate, $\delta=0.025$, and for the capital share in production, $\alpha=0.36$.

Regarding adjustment costs, $\psi_{P}=50$, which implies that 95% of the price has adjusted four periods after a monetary shock. Investment adjustment cost, $\psi_{I}=4$, is calibrated such that investment is about three times more volatile than output. A small bond adjustment cost ($\psi_{B}=4\times10^{-6}$) is necessary to avoid a unit root associated with the incompleteness of the asset markets.

Regarding shocks, the variance and persistence of the technology shock is calibrated at standard values: $\text{var}(\varepsilon_{1})=\text{var}(\varepsilon_{1}^{*})=0.01^{2}$ and $\rho_{1}=\rho_{1}^{*}=0.90$, common values in the real business cycle literature. Money demand

[7]Search grids ranged from 1 to 5 for Γ_{π}, and from 0 to 5 for Γ_{Y} and Γ_{S}, with step size 0.25.

shocks are calibrated to replicate the variability and serial correlation of data on the bilateral exchange rate between the US and remaining G-7, HP-filtered, for the period 1973:1–2000:4.[8] To replicate these moments in the benchmark model for the exchange rate in levels form requires the calibration $\text{var}(\varepsilon_2) = \text{var}(\varepsilon_2^*) = 0.03^2$ and $\rho_1 = \rho_1^* = 0.99$. For simplicity, the shocks are specified as uncorrelated across countries.

3. Results

3.1. *Benchmark model*

Table 1 reports the results for the three types of policy rules. The optimized Taylor rule stresses inflation targeting, with inflation response $\Gamma_\pi = 5.0$, and with no effort to stabilize output or the exchange rate ($\Gamma_Y = 0.0, \Gamma_S = 0.0$).[9] This policy neutralizes the effects of money demand shocks, calling for shifts in money supply that accommodate shifts in money demand. And it responds procyclically to technology shocks, calling for a lower interest rate and higher money growth rate in the periods shortly following a productivity increase. This result corresponds to previous findings in the literature using simpler models (Devereux and Engel, 2003; Gali and Monacelli, 2005). Sticky prices prevent output and employment from rising fully in response to a rise in productivity, and a monetary expansion helps remedy this shortcoming.

Of special interest here is the implication of the optimal rule for exchange rate variability. Table 1 shows that while a large portion of exchange rate variance is offset, it is not optimal to eliminate all exchange rate variability. Impulse responses show that while the conditional variability following money demand shocks is fully eliminated, the monetary policy response to productivity shocks induces exchange rate fluctuations.

[8]While the search for an adequate theoretical explanation for exchange rate variability is itself the subject of ongoing research, the approach taken here follows on the example of the literature discussed in the introduction; Devereux and Engel (2003) and Bacchetta and van Wincoop (2000) each use money demand or money supply shocks to generate exchange rate variability. Bergin (2003) offers some empirical support for this approach.

[9]As in Schmitt-Grohe and Uribe (2004b), we found that the inflation parameter is at the upper bound of the range considered in the grid search. Allowing yet higher values of this parameter appears to have negligible effects on the equilibrium.

Table 1. Benchmark model

	Exogenous money supply	Fixed exchange rate	Optimized flexible exchange rate rule[3]
Standard deviations			
Consumption	1.24	1.21	1.20
Output	2.41	2.36	1.86
Investment	5.09	5.09	4.93
Inflation	0.70	0.48	0.02
Exchange rate depr.	1.44	0.00	0.20
Stochastic steady state deviations[1]			
Consumption	−0.036	−0.018	0.016
Leisure	0.012	0.017	0.026
Output	−0.015	0.007	0.046
Capital stock	−0.034	0.023	0.108
Interest rate	−1.481	−1.082	−0.324
Markup ratio	0.341	0.215	0.001
Home net assets	0.000	0.000	0.000
Trade volume	0.299	0.256	0.277
Unconditional welfare effects (as percentage of steady state consumption)[2]			
u-overall	−0.144	−0.113	−0.070
u-variance	−0.099	−0.082	−0.067
u-mean	−0.046	−0.031	−0.003
Conditional welfare effects (as percentage of steady state consumption)[2]			
u-overall	−0.144	−0.129	−0.109
u-variance	−0.099	−0.087	−0.070
u-mean	−0.046	−0.042	−0.039

Notes: [1]Percent difference between stochastic steady state and deterministic steady state.
[2]Difference between stochastic steady state and deterministic steady state, shown as a share of deterministic steady state consumption.
Foreign variables are identical to home in the cases shown here.
[3]The policy rule is $i_t = \bar{i} + 5.0\pi_t + 0.0\hat{Y}_t + 0.0\Delta s_t$.

This reflects the finding in preceding literature using simpler models, where exchange rate movements can help compensate for price stickiness, by promoting adjustment in international relative prices to productivity shocks. Figure 1 plots the dynamic response of the exchange rate to a 1% rise in home country productivity. The story above is reflected in a substantial home currency depreciation in the initial periods after the shock. But the dynamics also indicate there is a long-run currency appreciation

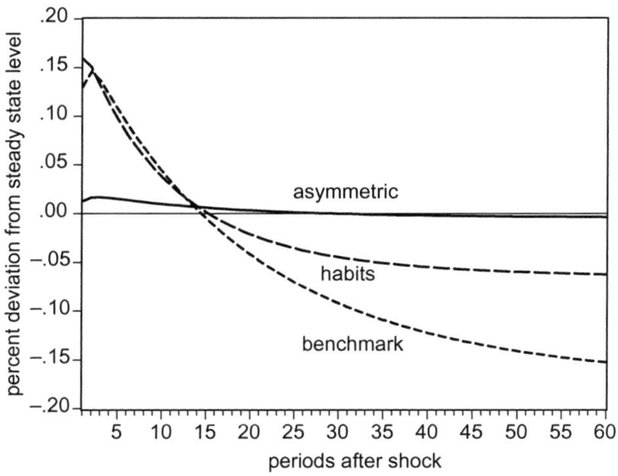

Figure 1. Exchange rate impulse responses following home productivity shock under optimized Taylor policy rules

implied by this rule following productivity gains.[10] As this implies a significant nonstationary component to the exchange rate movement, the table reports the variability for exchange rate depreciations rather than for the exchange rate level.

The table shows that the optimized policy rule eliminates any extra price markup ratio present under exogenous money supply and under the fixed exchange rate rules. This helps explain why the mean levels of output and consumption are higher under the optimized rule relative to the exogenous money rule (by 0.06% and 0.05%, respectively). This rule also raises unconditional utility of the representative household, by the equivalent of 0.07% of steady state consumption. The fixed exchange rate case is also inferior to the optimized rule, with lower output, consumption and utility. In particular, if this economy fixes the exchange rate, it lowers utility by 0.04% relative to the optimal policy.

While the optimal policy does generate positive gains relative to both alternatives here, it is worth noting that these gains are small in magnitude. As a useful comparison, Lucas (1987) measured the costs of business cycle fluctuations at 0.04% of annual consumption, concluding that this

[10]Gali and Monacelli (2005) find that a very similar permanent appreciation is implied by the various Taylor rules they consider.

was trivial. Lastly, we note that results based on conditional rather than unconditional measures are similar to those presented above.

The analysis of the benchmark model above indicates that some of the basic conclusions drawn in preceding literature in the context of simpler models continue to hold in the context of a more richly specified and more realistically calibrated model. However, a second lesson is that the gains in terms of utility remain quite small. The following two sections will consider further extensions to the basic model.

3.2. *Habits*

Past research on household consumption and asset choices has found that habits may be an essential part of household preferences.[11] Given that this literature has found households to be quite sensitive to variability in domestic equity markets, one might also expect them to be sensitive to variability in international asset markets. Yet research analyzing optimal monetary policy and exchange rate stabilization to date has not been able to consider this potentially important feature because it precludes the usual analytical solution.

To include habits in the model, we consider the utility function:

$$U_t = \frac{(C_t - \gamma C_{t-1})^{1-\rho}}{1-\rho} + \frac{\chi_t}{1-\varepsilon}\left(\frac{M_t}{P_t}\right)^{1-\varepsilon} - \frac{H_t^{1+\psi}}{1+\psi}, \tag{41}$$

which implies an intertemporal Euler equation:[12]

$$d_t = \beta E_t\left[\left(\frac{P_t}{P_{t+1}}\right)\frac{(C_{t+1} - \gamma C_t)^{-\rho} - \beta\gamma E_{t+1}(C_{t+2} - \gamma C_{t+1})^{-\rho}}{(C_t - \gamma C_{t-1})^{-\rho} - \beta\gamma E_t(C_{t+1} - \gamma C_t)^{-\rho}}\right]. \tag{42}$$

As γ goes to unity, households act to smooth changes in consumption rather than the level of consumption. We calibrate the habit persistence parameter at $\gamma = 0.8$, which is approximately what Deaton (1987) and Constantinides (1990) require in order to explain aggregate consumption smoothness and the equity premium puzzle.

[11]See, for example, Constantinides (1990) and Campbell and Cochrane (1999) regarding the equity premium puzzle, and see Deaton (1987) and Fuhrer (2000) for a discussion in the context of consumption behavior.

[12]The welfare formula is of course updated with the second-order expansion of the new utility function.

While it is common in calibrating habit persistence models to impose a large investment adjustment cost to keep the standard deviation of consumption from falling to implausibly low levels, this device does not work in an open economy where international borrowing breaks the link between domestic investment and saving. Instead, we augment the bond adjustment cost in the household budget constraint to penalize large changes in asset holding as well as large levels:

$$AC_{B,t} = \frac{\psi_B}{2} \frac{(S_t(B_{F,t} - \bar{B}_F))^2}{P_{H,t} Y_t} + \frac{\psi_{B2}}{2} \frac{(S_t(B_{F,t} - B_{F,t-1}))^2}{P_{H,t} Y_t}, \tag{43}$$

where ψ_{B2} is calibrated at 9×10^{-4}.

Results are reported in Table 2. The optimal policy parameters are the same as in the benchmark model above. It remains optimal to respond aggressively to stabilize the inflation rate, with no response to the exchange rate. Further, the optimal degree of variability of the exchange rate remains essentially the same as above, both in terms of unconditional variance, and in terms of the conditional response to shocks, as depicted in Fig. 1.

The welfare gains from optimal stabilization policy are increased slightly relative to the benchmark model. The optimized rule raises unconditional utility by the consumption equivalent of 0.13% relative to the exogenous money rule, which is around double the gain in the context of the benchmark economy. In contrast, the representative household in this habits economy would be willing to trade a more sizable 0.66% of steady state consumption if it were possible to eliminate all shocks from the economy, an amount which is more than four times that in the benchmark economy. So even if habits indicate that households are more concerned about certain types of variability, it appears that monetary policy has a limited ability to influence this impact on utility.

3.3. *"Original sin" in asset markets*

The implications of exchange rate variability can be shaped also by the structure of a country's asset market. Eichengreen and Hausmann (2005) has noted that perceptions in the international capital market make it impossible for many countries to issue international debt denominated in their own national currency. Given that such perceptions of untrustworthiness

Table 2. Habit persistence model

	Exogenous money supply	Fixed exchange rate	Optimized flexible exchange rate rule[3]
Standard deviations			
Consumption	1.25	1.24	1.25
Output	1.41	1.41	1.39
Investment	7.35	7.32	7.35
Inflation rate	0.73	0.50	0.14
Exchange rate depr.	1.20	0.00	0.23
Stochastic steady state deviations[1]			
Consumption	0.018	0.023	0.030
Leisure	−0.003	0.013	−0.020
Output	0.113	0.123	0.140
Capital stock	0.513	0.571	0.630
Interest rate	−8.235	−7.833	−8.560
Markup ratio	0.360	0.186	0.020
Home net assets	0.000	0.000	0.000
Trade volume	0.576	0.561	0.570
Unconditional welfare effects (as percentage of steady state consumption)[2]			
u-overall	−0.659	−0.580	−0.530
u-variance	−0.692	−0.674	−0.680
u-mean	0.033	0.095	0.150
Conditional welfare effects (as percentage of steady state consumption)[2]			
u-overall	−0.659	−0.655	−0.636
u-variance	−0.692	−0.688	−0.683
u-mean	0.033	0.032	0.047

Notes: [1]Percent difference between stochastic steady state and deterministic steady state.
[2]Difference between stochastic steady state and deterministic steady state, shown as a share of deterministic steady state consumption.
Foreign variables are identical to home in the cases shown here.
[3]The policy rule is $i_t = \bar{i} + 5.0\pi_t + 0.0\hat{Y}_t + 0.0\Delta s_t$.

may well be beyond the control of the country to change, but simply are a feature of the international capital market, the authors have termed this condition "original sin."

To study this feature, consider a version of the model where there is only one nominal bond that is traded internationally, denominated in the currency of the home country. This returns to the benchmark model above, except that B_{Ft} is set to zero in all periods. The home country in this model certainly is relevant for those countries whose currencies have the status of reserve currencies, such as the US, Japan, and EMU countries. And the foreign country in the model is relevant to some degree for any of the remaining countries, and most especially for developing countries.

Table 3 indicates that the equilibrium in the "original sin" model under the exogenous money supply policy is quite different from that in the benchmark model. The stochastic steady state deviations for endogenous variables are often a full order of magnitude larger. Further, they are asymmetric across countries, with consumption higher in the home country but lower abroad, and vice versa for production levels. Some intuition for this effect can be found by noting the large asymmetry in asset holdings, with net bond holdings by the home country rising 60% relative to the benchmark case, and hence that of the foreign country falling by 60%. This finding is precisely the inverse of that found by Kollmann (2002) in a small open economy model with a similar asset structure. That model indicated that the presence of uncertainty raised the desire for precautionary saving, which raised wealth and hence consumption. We show that moving from a small open economy to a two country general equilibrium model reverses this result. The distinction is that a small open economy model assumes that only agents in the small economy respond to the presence of shocks, while assuming the saving behavior of agents in the rest of the world and the equilibrium world interest rate are exogenous and remain unaffected.

In contrast, a two-country environment makes clear that if uncertainty encourages saving behavior of all households in the world, the world interest rate on bonds must fall to balance an excess demand for bonds. The presence of this effect in our model is confirmed by the fall in the interest rate in column (1) of Table 3. In equilibrium, the demand and supply of bonds are held equal by having the home (nonsin) country save more while the foreign (sin) country saves less. This appears to be due to an asymmetry in the saving options facing the two countries. Recall that the foreign country cannot accumulate a net positive asset position in its own currency. It may be that accumulating assets is a less attractive hedge against uncertainty, when the accumulation of foreign currency assets itself may increase exposure to the uncertainty of exchange rate fluctuations. As a result, the interest rate falls enough to more than compensate for the desired increase in precautionary saving in the sin country, and in equilibrium it holds fewer bonds.

Table 3. Asymmetric asset market model

	Exogenous money supply	Fixed exchange rate	Optimized rule: Joint welfare[3]	Optimized rule: Foreign welfare[4]
Standard deviations				
Consumption	1.31	1.28	1.36	1.34
Output	1.67	1.69	1.71	1.71
Investment	5.89	6.56	6.56	6.56
Inflation rate	0.57	0.39	0.08	0.26
Exchange rate depr.	1.04	0.00	0.02	0.01
Stochastic steady state deviations[1]				
Consumption (home)	0.157	0.079	0.122	0.109
Consumption (foreign)	−0.137	−0.031	−0.041	−0.036
Leisure (home)	−0.403	−0.088	−0.176	−0.148
Leisure (foreign)	0.595	0.287	0.376	0.345
Output (home)	−0.410	−0.094	−0.152	−0.130
Output (foreign)	0.534	0.261	0.371	0.336
Capital stock (home)	−0.389	−0.081	−0.086	−0.081
Capital stock (foreign)	0.431	0.227	0.369	0.324
Interest rate	−0.440	−0.218	−0.255	−0.477
Markup ratio	0.139	0.070	0.003	0.015
Home net assets	60.169	17.954	29.902	25.838
Trade volume	1.051	0.861	0.924	0.903
Unconditional welfare effects (as percentage of steady state consumption)[2]				
u-overall (home)	0.278	−0.030	0.079	0.046
u-overall (foreign)	−0.751	−0.416	−0.491	−0.462
u-variance	−0.177	−0.174	−0.173	−0.172
u-mean (home)	0.454	0.144	0.252	0.218
u-mean (foreign)	−0.575	−0.242	−0.318	−0.290
Conditional welfare effects (as percentage of steady state consumption)[2]				
u-overall (home)	0.278	0.288	0.298	0.299
u-overall (foreign)	−0.751	−0.736	−0.733	−0.731
u-variance	−0.177	−0.171	−0.168	−0.168
u-mean (home)	0.454	0.458	0.466	0.466
u-mean (foreign)	−0.575	−0.565	−0.565	−0.564

Notes: [1]Percent difference between stochastic steady state and deterministic steady state.
[2]Difference between stochastic steady state and deterministic steady state, shown as a share of deterministic steady state consumption.
[3]The policy rule is $i_t = \bar{i} + 2.0\pi_t + 0.0\hat{Y}_t + 5.0\Delta s_t$.
[4]The policy rule is $i_t = \bar{i} + 1.25\pi_t + 0.0\hat{Y}_t + 5.0\Delta s_t$.

A fixed exchange rate policy substantially offsets the asymmetries above. As column (2) indicates, the asymmetry in asset holdings is reduced by over two-thirds. Further, an optimized Taylor rule policy comes close to replicating the fixed exchange rate regime. When policy parameters are chosen to maximize the sum of home and foreign utility, as shown in column (3), the optimal exchange rate response is at the upper bound of the search grid and the response to inflation is reduced compared to previous cases ($\Gamma_\pi = 2.0$, $\Gamma_S = 5.0$).[13] As a result, the unconditional standard deviation of the exchange rate is reduced to only 0.02%, and the conditional response of the exchange rate to productivity shocks is nearly completely dampened, as shown in Fig. 1. Further, if one chooses policy parameters to maximize just the utility of the sin country alone, the response to inflation is reduced yet a bit further ($\Gamma_\pi = 1.25$, $\Gamma_S = 5.0$), leading to even greater exchange rate stabilization (as shown in column (4)).[14] Each country still offsets its own money demand shocks under these rules, even more so, as policy works to dampen the currency appreciation proceeding from a rise in money demand. Policy continues to respond procyclically to a productivity shock by lowering interest rates, but the degree of inflation stabilization is smaller under these policy rules.

The gains from stabilization policy for the sin country are somewhat larger than in the previous cases studied. The second of the optimized policies discussed above raises unconditional foreign utility by 0.29% over the exogenous policy, more than four times the gain from policy observed under the benchmark model.[15] The gains occur entirely in the mean component of utility, reflecting the effect of variability on the means of endogenous

[13]The grid search above is restricted to policy parameters symmetric across countries, implying that both countries work jointly to stabilize their bilateral exchange rate. Nonetheless, some ancillary experiments here with unilateral pegs indicated that the welfare of the foreign country can fall if it alone has $\Gamma_S > 0$.

[14]Figure 1 does not plot the response for the policy rule optimized for foreign welfare, as this is nearly identical to that for joint welfare discussed above.

[15]Note also that the conditional welfare effect is small despite the large unconditional effect. Adopting a new policy does not change the fact that the foreign economy is starting off with a low share of wealth. After the adoption of the new policy, the foreign country begins saving more, but this entails a lower consumption level during the lengthy transition period where it is building up its capital stock and assets.

variables, rather than in the variance component itself. The gain is even a bit larger under the fixed exchange rate rule (0.33%), suggesting that the gains from the optimized policy rule observed here are due to stabilizing the exchange rate and moderating the resulting asymmetries. We think this experiment is informative, indicating that economies of this type warrant further investigation in the theoretical literature.

4. Conclusions

This chapter performs a quantitative model-consistent evaluation of optimal policy rules in a two-country sticky-price model. The experiments focus on the important question of what degree of exchange rate variability is optimal for various types of open economies. The utility benefits of pursuing an optimized policy appear to be small for the types of simple economies typically studied in this literature. Developments in solving second-order approximations to dynamic stochastic models in principle open up the door to study much more varied and realistic economic environments.

The chapter finds that extending the environment to consider consumer habits has only minor effects on the conclusions standard in the literature. It remains optimal to aggressively stabilize inflation, while allowing the exchange rate to fluctuate in response to productivity shocks. Further, the utility benefits of pursuing optimized stabilization rules remain quite small. In contrast, an extension of the environment to consider asset markets exhibiting "original sin," does alter these conclusions. Since "original sin" appears to impose significant constraints on a country's precautionary saving, it becomes optimal, both from the perspective of the two-country world as well as from the sin country, in particular, to actively suppress exchange rate fluctuations. These results would seem to indicate that it is alternative economic environments such as this one, which most warrant further investigation in the theoretical literature.

Acknowledgment

We thank especially Michael Devereux, Robert Kollmann, and two anonymous referees for helpful comments. We also thank seminar participants at the Institute for Advanced Studies in Vienna, University of Bern, Central

European University, Simon Fraser University, and the University of British Columbia.

References

Bacchetta, P. and E. van Wincoop. 2000. Does exchange rate stability increase trade and welfare? *American Economic Review*, 90: 1093–1109.

Benigno, G. and P. Benigno. 2003. Price stability in open economies. *Review of Economic Studies*, 70: 743–764.

Benigno, P. 2004. Optimal monetary policy in a currency area. *Journal of International Economics*, 63: 293–320.

Bergin, P. and R. Feenstra. 2001. Pricing-to-market, staggered contracts, and real exchange rate persistence. *Journal of International Economics*, 54: 333–359.

Bergin, P. 2003. Putting the new open economy macroeconomics' to a test. *Journal of International Economics*, 60: 3–34.

Campbell, J. Y. and J. H. Cochrane. 1999. By force of habit: A consumption-based explanation of aggregate stock market behavior. *Journal of Political Economy*, 107: 205–251.

Carre, M. and F. Collard. 2003. Monetary union: A welfare based approach. *European Economic Review*, 47: 521–552.

Christiano, L. J., M. Eichenbaum, and C. Evans. 1997. Sticky price and limited participation models of money: A comparison. *European Economic Review*, 41: 1021–1049.

Clarida, R., J. Gali, and M. Gertler. 2001. Optimal monetary policy in open versus closed economies. *American Economic Review*, 91: 248–252.

Collard, F. and M. Juillard. 2001. Accuracy of stochastic perturbation methods: The case of asset pricing models. *Journal of Economic Dynamics and Control*, 25: 979–999.

Constantinides, G. M. 1990. Habit formation: A resolution of the equity premium puzzle. *Journal of Political Economy*, 98: 519–543.

Corsetti, G. and P. Pesenti. 2001. Welfare and macroeconomic interdependence. *Quarterly Journal of Economics*, 116: 421–445.

Corsetti, G. and P. Pesenti. 2004. International dimensions of optimal monetary policy. *Journal of Monetary Economics*, 52: 281–305.

Deaton, A. 1987. Life-cycle models of consumption: Is the evidence consistent with the theory? In: Bewley T. (ed.), *Advances in Econometrics Fifth World Congress*, vol. 2., Cambridge University Press, Cambridge, pp. 121–148.

Devereux, M. B. and C. Engel. 2003. Monetary policy in the open economy revisited: price setting and exchange rate flexibility. *Review of Economic Studies*, 70: 765–783.

Eichengreen, B. and R. Hausmann. 2005. *Other People's Money: Debt Denomination and Financial Instability in Emerging Market Economies.* University of Chicago Press, Chicago.

Fuhrer, J. C. 2000. Habit formation in consumption and its implications for monetary policy models. *American Economic Review*, 90: 367–390.

Gali, J. and T. Monacelli. 2005. Monetary policy and exchange rate volatility in a small open economy. *Review of Economic Studies*, 72: 707–734.

Harrigan, J. 1993. OECD imports and trade barriers in 1983. *Journal of International Economics*, 35: 91–111.

Kim, J. S., Kim, S. E. Schaumburg, and C. Sims. 2003. Calculating and using second order accurate solutions of discrete time dynamic equilibrium models. Mimeo, Princeton University.

Kollmann, R. 2002. Monetary policy rules in the open economy: Effects on welfare and business cycles. *Journal of Monetary Economics*, 49: 989–1015.

Kollmann, R. 2004. Welfare effects of a monetary union: The role of trade openness. *Journal of the European Economic Association*, 2: 289–301.

Lucas, R. E. 1987. *Models of Business Cycles.* Basil Blackwell, New York.

Obstfeld, M. and K. Rogoff. 2002. Global implications of self-oriented national monetary rules. *The Quarterly Journal of Economics*, 117: 503–535.

Schmitt-Grohe, S. and M. Uribe. 2004a. Solving dynamic general equilibrium models using a second-order approximation of the policy function. *Journal of Economic Dynamics and Control*, 28: 645–858.

Schmitt-Grohe, S. and M. Uribe. 2004b. Optimal simple and implementable monetary and fiscal rules. Mimeo, Duke University.

Sutherland, A. 2005. Incomplete pass-through and the welfare effects of exchange rate variability. *Journal of International Economics*, 65: 375–399.

Trefler, D. and H. Lai. 1999. The gains from trade: Standard errors with the CES monopolistic competition model. Mimeo, University of Toronto.

CHAPTER 14

Measuring Monetary Policy Interdependence*

Paul R. Bergin[†] and Òscar Jordà[‡]

Department of Economics, University of California at Davis,
One Shields Ave., Davis, CA 95616, USA
[†] *prbergin@ucdavis.edu*
[‡] *ojorda@ucdavis.edu*

1. Introduction

This chapter investigates the empirical regularities of monetary policy setting among a sample of 14 industrialized countries, with special focus on the international interdependence among these policies. A new empirical approach is proposed, which avoids the pitfalls implied by the VAR approach that traditionally has been used to address this issue. This approach allows us to look in a new way at the nature of policy coordination and the relative leadership roles played by the US Federal Reserve, the Bank of Japan, and the German Bundesbank.

International monetary policy coordination has become a subject of renewed interest of late. In particular, Obstfeld and Rogoff (2002) initiated a re-exploration of international policy coordination using models with microeconomic foundations, representing a significant methodological

*This article originally appeared in *Journal of International Money and Finance* (2004), 23(5), 761–783.

departure from past literature. They conclude that in this context the welfare gains of coordination are likely to be quantitatively small in comparison to the gains from domestic stabilization policy. In rebuttal, subsequent theoretical work has suggested a variety of economic features that could potentially generate greater motivation for nations to coordinate their monetary policies. See for example, Benigno (2002), Canzoneri *et al.* (2001), and Clarida *et al.* (2002). Given this theoretical controversy, it is natural to ask the empirical question of how much coordination we observe in actuality.

There is a history of empirical research on this question. Studies focusing on the major industrial countries generally find evidence that the US acts as a leader for policy makers in certain countries, but the mechanisms through which this coordination takes place are often unclear. (See Dominguez (1997), Furman and Leahy (1996), Chung (1993), Burdekin and Burkett (1992), Burdekin (1989), and Batten and Ott (1985)). Another branch has focused on coordination among European countries, generally finding that Germany had a limited leadership role among European countries prior to monetary union. (See Garcia-Herrero and Thorton, 1996; Katsimbris and Miller, 1993; Biltoft and Boersch, 1992; Karfakis and Moschos, 1990; von Hagen and Fratianni, 1990a, 1990b).

This chapter represents a significant methodological departure from the preceding empirical literature. We build upon the recently developed methodology of Hamilton and Jordà (2002), which has been successfully employed to study monetary policy in the US. We extend this methodology to a set of countries, and we explicitly allow for interdependence among these national policies. Our approach is based on a novel data set on overnight, interbank interest rate targets that central banks in our sample use to communicate and operationalize monetary policy.

Methodologically, we first argue against traditional time series techniques based on dynamic conditional correlations in semi-structural vector processes, which suffer from the common identification assumptions that mark the monetary vector autoregression (VAR) literature. Perhaps more importantly however, we show via Monte Carlo experimentation that the peculiar statistical properties that policy rate targeting imbue on market interest rates tend to severely distort these measures of association. In particular, these experiments demonstrate that, for example, Granger causality tests often will misrepresent the true nature of existing monetary policy linkages that are measured with market interest rate data.

These methodological pitfalls prompt us to pursue a more modest approach which is immune to the deficiencies described above. In particular, our goal is to determine whether G-3 policy moves help predict the timing of domestic policy adjustments and the direction in which interest rates are modified, all conditional on domestic macroeconomic conditions. Exploring these issues poses special econometric challenges that arise from the irregular nature in which policy rate targets are adjusted over time as well as the discrete nature in which these adjustments are made. Hence, we will use the autoregressive conditional hazard (ACH) model proposed in Hamilton and Jordà (2002) to tackle the predictability in the timing whereas a discrete ordered response model specification will permit us to deal with the discreteness of policy rate adjustments.

The empirical results are elucidating along several dimensions. First, our study can be seen as a broad investigation of individual central bank behavior, and in this sense, it provides important lessons to the literature that explores monetary policy rules. The special nature of the data and the particulars of our empirical design suggest that Taylor type rules do not universally describe monetary policy well, once the natural inertia of interest rates and macroeconomic data has been filtered. In particular, while US policy responds to inflation in a statically significant manner, we were unable to find similar evidence among any of the other countries, including Germany, which traditionally enjoyed a reputation for an aggressive stance against inflation. Further, while it is a current debate among monetary theorists whether it is optimal for policy rules to include the exchange rate, we find evidence that this variable has in practice played a very prominent role in the policy rules of many countries.

With regard to monetary policy interdependence, Germany emerges as a significant factor for a block of European countries, in agreement with most past work. This indicates that policy interdependence existed among this European core long before the creation of the explicit monetary union. Further, this European interdependence entailed more than simply responding to exchange rate movements, as required by the European Exchange Rate Mechanism (ERM), but appears to have involved direct responses by policy makers to changes in German policy.

We also find evidence that a limited number of countries respond to US policy changes. This list includes Germany and the UK, but in contrast to some past work, Japanese policy does not appear to respond in a significant way to the US.

2. Pitfalls of Interest-Rate Dynamic Correlations

It would be natural to explore the degree of monetary policy interdependence with vector time series techniques using interest rate data on the countries in our sample, as is done in Nogues and Grandes (2001), Bensidoun *et al.* (1997), and DeGennaro *et al.* (1994), for example. However, a large number of central banks in our sample operationalize monetary policy by targeting an overnight, interbank, interest rate. A consequence of this modus operandus is that interest rates in these countries have unusual statistical properties which make them unsuitable for conventional econometric analysis. This section briefly explains the nature of these problems with Monte Carlo experimentation and serves to motivate the empirical design in the remainder of the chapter.

Rudebusch (1995) demonstrated in a clever simulation that the manner the US Federal Reserve adjusts the federal funds rate target affects the statistical properties of traditional term structure regressions in a manner consistent with the poor results reported in that literature. We wish to extend Rudebusch's (1995) arguments to show that central bank interest-rate targeting behavior distorts conventional measures of dynamic covariation between interest rates of different countries.

Let r_t^A and r_t^B denote the overnight rate in countries A and B, respectively. Although central banks choose a target level for the overnight rate, they have only imperfect control over it. Therefore, the overnight rate tends to fluctuate around the target level. In the US, these deviations typically amount to only a few basis points and tend to be short lived (see Hamilton (1996)). Accordingly, we model the overnight rate as,

$$r_t^i = \overline{r}_t^i + \varepsilon_{it} \qquad \varepsilon_{it} \sim N(0, \sigma_i^2) \qquad i = A, B \tag{1}$$

where $\overline{r}_t^i$ denotes the target overnight rate. In practice, the residuals, ε_i, may be a general stationary sequence but to keep the exercise simple, we will simulate them as *i.i.d.* normal random variates. The variance of these residuals, σ_i^2, is a natural measure of the central bank's control over the interbank market. The process by which the target is adjusted is described by

$$\bar{r}_t^i = x_t^i \bar{r}_{t-1}^i + (1 - x_t^i)(\bar{r}_{t-1}^i + y_t^i) \tag{2}$$

where $x_t^i = 1$ if the target is changed in period t, 0 otherwise, and $y_t^i \in \{k_1, k_2, \ldots, k_m\}$, reflecting the fact that changes in the target are done in a small finite set of discrete increments. Each period, there is some probability that the target will be changed, $h_t^i = P(x_t^i = 1|\Omega_{t-1})$, which can be interpreted as a discrete time hazard. As usual, Ω_{t-1} represents the information set up to time $t-1$. Similarly, conditional on changing the target, the magnitude of the change, k_j, can be described by

$$P(y_t^i = k_j|x_t^i = 1, \Omega_{t-1}) = P(c_{j-1} < y_t^{i*} < c_j|x_t^i = 1, \Omega_{t-1})$$
$$j = 1, 2, \ldots, m \tag{3}$$

with $c_0 = -\infty$, $c_m = \infty$, and y_t^{i*} an auxiliary latent index that reflects the central bank's ideal for the overnight rate but which may be costly to attain in every single period. To complete the simulation, we specify a simple bivariate model for h_t^i that will capture the coordination in the timing between countries A and B, and a bivariate model for Δr_t^{i*} that will capture coordination in the direction of the change instead. First, note that h_t^i is a probability, hence a convenient way of ensuring $h_t^i \in [0, 1]$ is to take the following logistic transform

$$h_t^i = \frac{1}{1 + e^{\lambda_t^i}} \tag{4}$$

$$\begin{cases} \lambda_t^A = \omega_A + \rho_A \lambda_{t-1}^A + \beta \lambda_{t-1}^B + e_t^A \\ \lambda_t^B = \omega_B + \rho_B \lambda_{t-1}^B + e_t^B \end{cases} \qquad e_t^i \sim N(0, 0.1)$$

so that $x_t^i = 1$ if $h_t^i > u_t^i$, 0 otherwise, where u_t^i is a uniform [0, 1] random variable. The bivariate specification in (4) makes explicit two important features: (1) persistence in target changes, which as we shall see in later sections, is a common feature in our data set, and (2) policy setting in country A depends, via the parameter β, on country B's policy setting. If $\beta > 0$, the likelihood of a target change in A increases with the likelihood of a target change in country B, and vice versa. If $\beta = 0$, target setting occurs independently.

Similarly, to capture any coordination in the direction of changes in the target that may occur independently from coordinating the timing, consider the following bivariate model for the latent indices

$$\begin{cases} y_t^{A*} = \gamma_A y_{t-1}^{A*} + \psi y_{t-1}^{B*} + v_t^A \\ y_t^{B*} = \gamma_B y_{t-1}^{B*} + \quad + v_t^B \end{cases} \qquad v_t^i \sim N(0,1). \tag{5}$$

The parameters γ_i capture persistence in the direction of target changes, which is also a commonly observed feature of the data, and the parameter ψ makes explicit the correlation in the direction in which the targets in countries A and B are changed. If $\psi > 0$, countries A and B tend to change their targets in the same direction and vice versa, if $\psi = 0$, there is no relation.

The basic setup described in Equations (1)–(5) establishes a well-defined hierarchy: while decisions on country B's target are based completely on domestic information, country A's target timing and magnitude of changes depend on previous actions by country B whenever β and ψ are nonzero. In other words, *B Granger-causes A*. Table 1 contains the results of Monte Carlo experiments in which simulated overnight rates are generated for different parameter values, using Equations (1)–(5). For each combination of parameters, we generate 100 series of length 400, where the first 100 observations are deleted to avoid initialization problems. Then, on each of the series, we perform a standard Granger-causality test, collect the p-value of all these tests and report the Monte Carlo average. Figure 1 displays an example of what these simulated interest rate series look like to show they closely resemble the data in our study.

Several results deserve comment. The most immediately apparent is the extraordinary sensitivity of the Granger-causality test. Even in the quasi-ideal scenario in which there is substantial coordination in the timing ($\beta = 0.75$) as well as coordination in the direction ($\psi = 0.75$), Granger-causality tests will routinely fail to pick up these features whenever the frequency with which the target is changed is relatively low (below 30% of the time) and/or the central bank's control of the overnight rate around the target is poor ($\sigma_\varepsilon > 0.25$). Other features of the model appear to be less important in determining this sensitivity except perhaps the degree of persistence in the

Table 1. Monte Carlo experiments (a–e)

(a) Changing the frequency of target changes — No correlation in the timing, $\beta = 0$.

Theoretical frequency	Empirical frequency *A*/ and *B*	Directional correlation-ψ	*B* Granger-causes *A* p-value	*A* Granger-causes *B* p-value
0.4	0.403/0.400	0.99	0.0185	0.6570
		0.75	0.0393	0.6700
		0.50	0.1316	0.6927
		0.25	0.4045	0.7001
		0.00	0.6140	0.6894
0.3	0.304/0.301	0.99	0.0864	0.6264
		0.75	0.1280	0.6446
		0.50	0.2573	0.6679
		0.25	0.4982	0.6908
		0.00	0.6322	0.6768
0.2	0.202/0.199	0.99	0.2658	0.6306
		0.75	0.3302	0.6256
		0.50	0.4498	0.6363
		0.25	0.5989	0.6428
		0.00	0.6560	0.6348

Note: $\rho^A = \rho^B = 0.5, \gamma^A = \gamma^B = 0.5, \sigma_A = \sigma_B = 0.25$.

(b) Changing the correlation in the timing — Directional correlation $\psi = 0.75$.

Timing correlation-β	*B* Granger-causes *A* p-value	*A* Granger-causes *B* p-value	Empirical frequency *A*
0.25	0.0392	0.6638	0.403
0.5	0.0410	0.6553	0.402
0.75	0.0408	0.6488	0.401
0.99	0.0427	0.6453	0.401

Note: $\rho^A = \rho^B = 0.5$, $\gamma^A = \gamma^B = 0.5$, $\sigma_A = \sigma_B = 0.25$, Empirical Frequency for $B = 0.400$.

(*Continued*)

Table 1. (*Continued*)

(c) Changing the variance of the errors around the target — $\beta = 0.99$, $\psi = 0.99$.

$\sigma_A = \sigma_B =$	*B* Granger-causes *A*: *p*-value	*A* Granger-causes *B*: *p*-value
1	0.4387	0.5016
0.5	0.1583	0.5682
0.25	0.0207	0.6204
0.1	0.0151	0.6293

Note: $\rho^A = \rho^B = 0.5$, $\gamma^A = \gamma^B = 0.5$, $\sigma_A = \sigma_B = 0.25$, Empirical Frequency for $A = 0.400$, $B = 0.400$.

(d) Changing the autocorrelation of the timing process — $\beta = 0.75$, and $\psi = 0.75$.

$\rho^A = \rho^B =$	*B* Granger-causes *A* *p*-value	*A* Granger-causes *B* *p*-value	Empirical frequency *A*	Empirical frequency *B*
0.9	0.1227	0.5967	0.332	0.302
0.75	0.1304	0.6117	0.306	0.301
0.5	0.1231	0.6270	0.304	0.301
0.25	0.1225	0.6282	0.303	0.301
0	0.1325	0.6215	0.303	0.301

Note: $\gamma^A = \gamma^B = 0.5, \sigma_A = \sigma_B = 0.25$.

(e) Changing the autocorrelation of the directional process — $\beta = 0.75$, and $\psi = 0.75$.

$\gamma^A = \gamma^B =$	*B* Granger-causes *A*: *p*-value	*A* Granger-causes *B*: *p*-value
0.9	0.1084	0.4319
0.75	0.1096	0.5320
0.5	0.1231	0.6270
0.25	0.1941	0.6500
0	0.2374	0.6609

Note: $\rho^A = \rho^B = 0.5, \sigma_A = \sigma_B = 0.25$, Empirical Frequency for $A = 0.303$, $B = 0.301$.

(*Continued*)

Table 1. (*Continued*)

Equations of the Monte Carlo simulation

$$r_t^i = \bar{r}_t^i + \varepsilon_t^i \quad \varepsilon_t^i \sim N(0, \sigma_i^2) \quad i = A, B$$

$$\bar{r}_t^i = x_t^i \bar{r}_{t-1}^i + (1 - x_t^i)(\bar{r}_{t-1}^i + y_t^i)$$

$$P(y_t^i = k_j | x_t^i = 1, \Omega_{t-1}) = P(c_{j-1} < y_t^{i^*} < c_j | x_t^i = 1, \Omega_{t-1}) \quad j = 1, 2, \ldots, m$$

with $m = 5$, $k_1 = -0.50$; $k_2 = -0.25$; $k_3 = 0.25$; $k_4 = 0.50$; and $c_1 = -\infty$; $c_2 = -.75$; $c_3 = 0$; $c_4 = 0.75$; $c_5 = \infty$

Timing Model

$$h_t^i = \frac{1}{1 + e^{\lambda_t^i}}$$

$$\begin{cases} \lambda_t^A = \omega_A + \rho_A \lambda_{t-1}^A + \beta \lambda_{t-1}^B + e_t^A \\ \lambda_t^B = \omega_B + \rho_B \lambda_{t-1}^B + e_t^B \end{cases} \qquad e_t^i \sim N(0, 0.1)$$

$x_t^i = 1$ if $h_t^i > u_t^i$, 0 otherwise, where u_t^i is a uniform random variable in [0,1]

Directional Model

$$\begin{cases} y_t^{A*} = \gamma_A y_{t-1}^{A*} + \varphi y_{t-1}^{B*} + v_t^A \\ y_t^{B*} = \gamma_B y_{t-1}^{B*} + v_t^B \end{cases} \qquad v_t^i \sim N(0, 1)$$

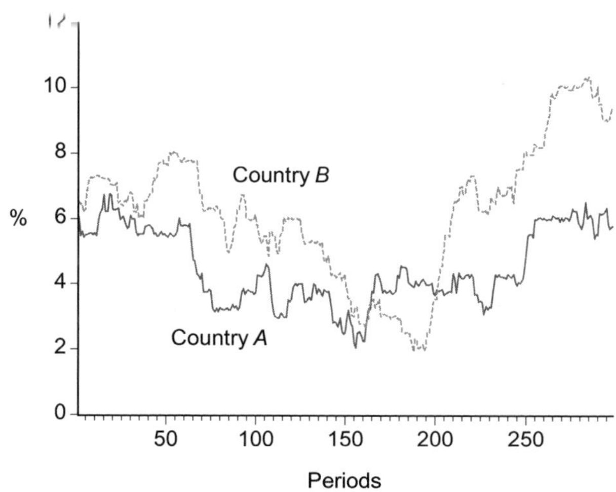

Figure 1. Simulated interest rates

direction of the target changes (γ^A and γ^B small). It is important to note that this failure of the Granger-causality test can occur under the most favorable of situations, with high values of the parameters β, and ψ, with a relatively precisely controlled overnight rate and with realistic parameters values. The Granger-causality test metric appears to be well suited to capture directional coordination since it will detect this type of coordination in the absence of coordination in the timing as long as the target is changed sufficiently often (40% of the time and above). However, even when the timing of target changes is strongly related ($\beta = 0.99$), as the value of ψ decreases, even slightly (from 0.75 to 0.5 and below), the Granger-causality test will fail to pick the relationship.

These results are strongly suggestive that conventional econometric techniques are unsuitable for the purposes of our analysis. Consequently, the remainder of the chapter devises an alternative empirical strategy which is based on the availability of an uncommon data set, whose properties we discuss in the next section.

3. A Novel Data Set on Policy Rate Targets

A significant aspect of our investigation on monetary policy linkages requires that we identify the policy stance of each country in our sample. As we discussed in the previous section, it is often common to do this by isolating the exogenous component of a monetary policy indicator based on a semi-structural VAR. However, in addition to the pitfalls discussed in the previous section, these measures of the policy stance are problematic since they depend on a number of untestable identifying assumptions and specification choices that can produce dramatically different outcomes (for a discussion on these issues see Rudebusch, 1998; Sims, 1998; and Evans and Kuttner, 1998).

We prefer to avoid this controversy altogether by pursuing a radically different approach. In an exhaustive survey from the Bank of International Settlements (BIS), entitled "Monetary Policy Operating Procedures in Industrial Countries," Claudio Borio[1] (1997) provides an in-depth

[1]We thank Greg Sutton and the Statistical Assistance Section of the Bank of International Settlements for providing us the data.

discussion on central bank operations for 14 major industrialized OECD countries, namely: Austria (AT), Australia (AU), Belgium (BE), Canada (CA), Switzerland (CH), Germany (DE), Spain (ES), France (FR), Italy (IT), Japan (JP), the Netherlands (NL), Sweden (SE), the United Kingdom (UK), and the United States (US).

Table 2 reports the specific variables and samples available for each country while Fig. 2 displays the policy target data along with the corresponding

Table 2. Summary of the data definitions

Country	Operational monetary data	Codes	Sample begins	Macro-international data	Freq.
Australia	Unofficial cash rate	ONAU	1/1/86	GDP, CPI, NEER	Q/M
	Target rate	***PRAU***	1/23/90		
Austria	Day-to-day money	ONAT	1/6/89	IP, CPI, NEER	M
	Short-term operations (GOMEX)	***PRAT***	6/5/85		
	Lombard rate	LRAT	1/24/80		
Belgium	Overnight interbank deposits	ONBE	1/2/91	IP, CPI, NEER	M
	Central rate	***PRBE***	1/29/91		
Canada	Overnight rate	ONCA	1/2/80	IP, CPI, NEER	M
	Operating target band	***PRCA***	4/15/94		
France	Day-to-day rate	ONFR	1/1/80	IP, CPI, NEER	M
	Tender rate	***PRFR***	1/4/8[illegible]		
	5–10 days repurchase facility	OCFR	10/12/88		
Germany	Day-to-day rate	ONDE	1/2/80	IP, CPI, NEER	M
	Repo rate	***PRDE***	4/1/80		
	Lombard rate	LRDE	1/1/80		
Italy	Overnight interbank deposits	ONIT	10/1/87	IP, CPI, NEER	M
	3-month interbank	M3IT	2/27/90		
	Tender rate	***LRIT***	5/13/91		
Japan	Overnight call money rate	ONJP	7/3/85	IP (up to 5/98), CPI, NEER	M
	Discount rate	***DRJP***	1/1/85		
Netherlands	Call money	ONNL	1/2/80	IP, CPI, NEER	M
	Rate on special advances	***PRNL***	1/2/80		
	Rate on advances (quota scheme)	DRNL	1/2/85		
Spain	Overnight interbank deposits	ONES	1/2/80	IP, CPI, NEER	M
	10-day repo purchases (marginal rate)	***PRES***	5/14/90		

(*Continued*)

Table 2. (*Continued*)

Country	Operational monetary data	Codes	Sample begins	Macro-international data	Freq.
Sweden	Day-to-day money	ONSE	11/21/88	IP, CPI, NEER	M
	Repo rate	***PRSE***	6/1/94		
Switzerland	Day-to-day money (tomorrow next)	ONCH	1/4/80	GDP, CPI, NEER	Q/M
	Flexible Lombard rate	***LRCH***	5/26/89		
UK	Overnight sterling interbank deposits	ONGB	1/2/80	IP (up to 7/98), CPI, NEER	M
	Band 1 bank bill purchases	***PRGB***	1/2/80		
US	Federal funds rate	ONUS	3/4/84	IP, CPI, NEER	M
	Federal funds rate target	***PRUS***	3/4/84		

Note: Target rates in bold and italic. NEER is the Nominal Effective Exchange Rate, IP is the Industrial Production Index, and CPI is the Consumer Price Index.

overnight interest rates. The countries in our sample fall into two broad groups: (1) Australia, Canada, Japan, and the US where the most representative policy variable is the overnight interbank rate; and (2) Austria, Belgium, Switzerland, Germany, Spain, France, Italy, the Netherlands, Sweden, and the UK in which the policy variable is usually a tender rate applicable mainly to repurchase agreements (repos) and whose maturity varies from one day to one month. Along with these data, we collected domestic macroeconomic data on inflation, output and exchange rates from the International Finance Statistics database produced by the IMF. The specifics for these data are also reported in Table 2.

It is instructive at this point to take a first look at our data. In particular, we ask whether the probability that domestic target rates are changed, depends on whether similar changes transpire in any of the G-3, regardless of the direction of the change. Thus, let $x_t = 1$ if in period t, the target was changed in a given country, 0 otherwise. We denote with $\mathbf{w}_t = (x_t^{\mathrm{DE}}, x_t^{\mathrm{JP}}, x_t^{\mathrm{US}})'$ the vector of explanatory variables that consists on the similarly defined x variables for each of the G-3 countries. The per-period probability conditional on the actions of the G-3 can be therefore be expressed as a discrete time hazard, $h_t = P(x_t = 1|\mathbf{w}_t)$. A simple way to

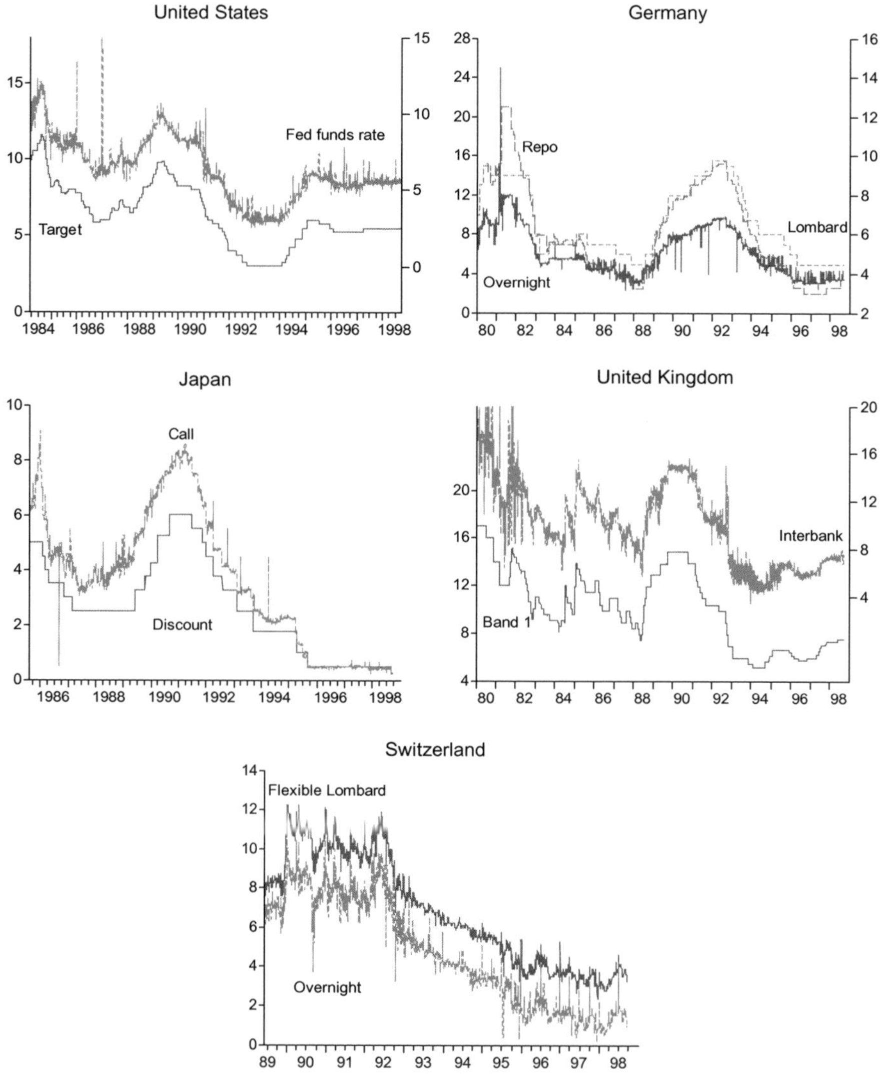

Figure 2. Policy target data and corresponding overnight interest rates

compute this hazard is with the logistic transform,

$$h_t = \frac{1}{1 + e^{\lambda_t}} \tag{6}$$

$$\lambda_t = \delta + \gamma' \mathbf{w}_t$$

with obvious log-likelihood

$$L(\theta) = \sum_{t=1}^{T} x_t^i \ln(h_t^i) + (1 - x_t^i) \ln(1 - h_t^i). \tag{7}$$

Table 3 reports for each country the baseline hazard and the hazard whenever there is a policy action in each of the corresponding G-3 targets. The data is organized at a monthly frequency with the double purpose of matching, the timing and length of the maintenance periods common in the countries that we consider, as well as the frequency at which our explanatory variables are available in the analysis reported below. The latter allows direct comparability with the results in Table 5.

A cursory look at Table 3 reveals perhaps familiar results. For example, Austria changes its target, on average, once every 10 months. However, if

Table 3. Hazard rates for policy rate adjustments as a function of adjustments in Germany, Japan and the US

	Austria	Australia	Belgium	Canada	Switz.	Germany	Spain
Baseline	0.12**	0.18**	0.17**	0.44	0.83**	0.48	0.38*
Germany	0.53**	0.14	0.70**	0.53	0.90	0.48	0.49
Japan	0.04*	0.32	0.13	0.99	0.87	0.69*	0.23
US	0.06*	0.30*	0.29	0.65	0.88	0.58	0.44
Obs.	111	98	89	48	111	150	94

	France	Italy	Japan	Nether.	Sweden	UK	US
Baseline	0.25**	0.27**	0.06**	0.35**	0.41	0.35**	0.38**
Germany	0.42**	0.33	0.22	0.73**	0.55	0.26	0.37*
Japan	0.16	0.28	0.06**	0.47	0.36	0.27	0.35
US	0.25	0.23	0.02**	0.25*	0.48	0.46	0.38**
Obs	118	91	144	150	48	147	150

Notes:

- Baseline: measures the probability that in any given month, the corresponding country's policy rate will be adjusted.
- Germany: measures the probability of a domestic adjustment when Germany adjusted its policy rate that month.
- Japan: measures the probability of domestic adjustment when Japan adjusted its policy rate that month.
- US: measures the probability of adjustment when US adjusted its policy rate that month.
- */** indicates significant at the 90%/95% confidence level.

there is a change in the German Lombard rate, the probability of a target change increases to a 1 in 2 chance for that month. The effect is more dramatic in Belgium (the baseline hazard is 17% but when Germany adjusts, the hazard increases to 70%), France and the Netherlands. Notice that although the effect of German policy on the US is statistically significant, it only represents a 1% decrease in the probability that the US will adjust the federal funds rate target that month. By contrast, although the effect in Spain is not significant, the hazard increases by more than 10% from a baseline level of 38%. With respect to Japan, it appears it is only influential with respect to German policy (the baseline is 48% but increases to 69% with a Japanese move). The effects of US policy appear to affect Austrian, Australian, Japanese, and Dutch policy but in every case the effects are not particularly strong.

Several results deserve comment. First is the fact that these are estimates of probabilities and therefore, highly nonlinear. Consequently, we have situations in which relations are statistically significant but economically weak (for example, the effect of US policy in Japan causes the baseline to decline from 6% to 2%, hardly an economically meaningful effect), and vice versa, effects that are economically noticeable but statistically weak (a move in Japanese policy causes the Australian baseline to almost double from 18 to 32%). Two more caveats to interpreting these results include (1) the effects that obviously omitted variables may have — domestic macroeconomic variables may explain away some of these relations or they make others become significant; and (2) the effect that omitted dynamics may have on the standard errors. Both of these issues are explored below.

Summarizing, it is not surprising that Germany's influence is felt in a list of countries that has often been characterized as the "European core." Italy's absence from this list may reflect the fact that our data sample for this country (September 1992–November 1996) is dominated by Italy's absence from the EMS following the 1992 crisis. The US influence does not appear very strong, which is at this stage, a surprising result. Other specific countries worthy of mention include Switzerland, whose measure of monetary policy is the flexible Lombard rate whereas in practice, the primary focus of the central bank is the volume of giro deposits. Borio (1997) thus suggests that "[. . .] interest rates are of limited significance in conveying policy intentions." (p. 17). Similarly, Japan is the only country that is still using a quantitative signal as a key mechanism for steering an interest rate operating target. Sweden uses a combination of a target for interest rate tenders with variable interest rate auctions when markets fluctuate around desirable levels (this mechanism is similar to that used by the Bundesbank).

Although these results are suggestive, it is difficult to discern at this point what motivates these interconnections. Our approach in the following sections will be to try to describe each central bank's policy rule and choice of response timing. If, after controlling for responses to a range of domestic macroeconomic factors, we are unable to control for the timing component, we will conclude that we have uncovered evidence of direct policy linkages. The next sections discuss the econometric aspects of this strategy.

4. Measuring Monetary Policy Interdependence

The Monte Carlo experiments in Section 2 and the preliminary evidence in Section 3 already provide a rough outline of the empirical strategy of the remainder of the chapter. In particular, we will measure monetary policy interdependence along two dimensions. On one hand, we will investigate to what extent the timing of policy rate adjustments is affected by actions of the G-3. On the other hand, we will examine whether domestic policy rate adjustments are made in the same direction as adjustments in the G-3, all conditional on domestic macroeconomic conditions. We begin by presenting the model specification of the timing model.

4.1. *The timing of policy rate adjustments*

Predicting when a central bank will adjust its policy rate next can be conceived as a discrete-time duration process, as we saw in the previous section in expression (6). However, unlike that specification, we wish to incorporate two new elements in the analysis: (1) adding explanatory variables on domestic macroeconomic conditions, and (2) allowing for a general dynamic specification. The first element is designed to rule out interdependence that is mediated by synchronized business cycles and exchange rate considerations while the second element is designed to account for serial dependence in target setting and to provide more accurate standard errors.

There is substantial agreement in the literature that the manner central banks determine the optimal level of their interest rate objectives can be well modeled by a Taylor rule (see Taylor, 1999, for an extensive survey). This monetary policy rule establishes the dependence of the policy instrument's optimal level on deviations of inflation from a target (usually 2% annual rate) and some measure of the output gap. In addition, small open economies also include a term related to the exchange rate variability. Therefore, it seems natural to assume that these variables would also determine the likelihood with which a central bank will decide to adjust its policy rate in time.

Based on this disquisition, we construct the following variables for each of the countries in our sample: The inflation variable π_t measured as the deviation of the annualized percentage change in the consumer price index from a 2% norm; the output variable g_t measured as the deviation of the annualized percentage change in the industrial production index from a 2.5% norm; and the exchange rate variable fx_t measured as the monthly percentage change in the nominal exchange rate weighted by the composition of each country's trading partners. All of these variables are added to the vector of explanatory variables $\mathbf{w}_t$ defined in Section 3 so that $\mathbf{w}_t = (\pi_{t-1}, g_{t-1}, fx_{t-1}, x_t^{\mathrm{DE}}, x_t^{\mathrm{JP}}, x_t^{\mathrm{US}})'$.

Several features of these variables deserve comment. First, to maintain the analysis at a monthly frequency rather than quarterly (for which we would not have had sufficient degrees of freedom), we had to compromise on the measures on the inflation and output variables commonly used elsewhere in the literature (typically consisting on the gross domestic product (GDP) deflator and the gap between GDP and some measure of potential GDP). Second, we preferred to avoid the well-known and controversial issue of measuring the output gap by using instead deviations from a 2.5% annual growth norm. Thirdly, these domestic macroeconomic variables are lagged to reflect the information available to the central bank at the time of decision. The final tally of the specific variables and sources can be found in Table 2.

The final element of the model's specification consists of endowing the process with dynamics that account for possible serial dependence in the timing of domestic policy rate adjustments. Hamilton and Jordà (2002) introduced the ACH model for this precise purpose in the context of US monetary policy setting. Thus, collecting all these elements together, the conditional probability that a country will adjust its policy rate at time t, presented in expression (6), can be expanded into a new version of the ACH model, namely

$$h_t = \frac{1}{1 + e^{\lambda_t}} \tag{8}$$

$$\lambda_t = \delta + \alpha u_{s(t-1)} + \beta \lambda_{t-1} + \gamma' |\mathbf{w}_t|$$

and where $u_{s(t-1)}$ denotes the amount of time elapsed between the two most recent policy rate changes as of date $t - 1$, and where λ_t now becomes a dynamic latent index whose structure is similar to that in an ARCH model. Notice that the explanatory variables $\mathbf{w}_t$ enter in absolute value since we are interested in the triggering mechanisms that prompt the central bank to adjust the policy rate and hence, this is likely to occur whenever these variables depart from above or from below their targeted values. We will call the version in expression (8) ACH(1,1) to refer to the fact that one lag of each the duration and the latent index enter the specification. The expression for this ACH(1,1) can be easily generalized to include longer lag lengths p and q and has the advantage of leaving the parameter space unrestricted.

The sum of the coefficients α and β provide a summary measure of the degree of serial dependence in addition to allowing the effect of the explanatory variables to be completely dynamic but parsimonious. To see this, notice that the difference equation of the latent index λ_t in expression (8) implies that the effect of the terms in the vector $\mathbf{w}_t$ is exponentially decaying over time at a rate β^t. The likelihood for the ACH model is the same as that in expression (7), which can be maximized by conventional numerical techniques.

4.2. *The direction of policy adjustments*

Conditional on the decision to adjust the policy rate, the central bank then needs to decide on the nature and magnitude of this adjustment. This is typically done in discrete increments (of 25 basis points in the US, for example) rather than continuously and therefore, it is natural to model this feature with a conventional ordered response model. Conditioning on $x_t = 1$ implies that the specification of the model is in *event time* rather than in the usual calendar time scale. This attribute has the considerable advantage of distilling demand fluctuations and other extraneous sources of variation from interest rate adjustments and into the actual nature of the intended policy moves.

Denote the magnitude of the policy rate adjustment when it happens by y_s. Since policy rates are adjusted in discrete increments, we think of y_s as taking a finite collection of values, $y_s \in \{k_1, \ldots, k_m\}$ and we make note that the index s refers to those periods in which $x_t = 1$ only. Therefore, the probabilistic model that determines the observation of the variable y_s can be written as

$$P(y_s = k_j | \Omega_{s(t-1)}) = P(c_{j-1} < y_s^* < c_j | \Omega_{s(t-1)}) \qquad (9)$$
$$y_s^* = \theta' \mathbf{w}_s + \varepsilon_s \qquad \varepsilon_s \sim N(0, 1)$$

where y_s^* is a latent index, the thresholds c_j, $j = 0, 1, \ldots, m$ are such that $c_0 = -\infty$, $c_{j-1} < c_j$, and $c_m = \infty$. $\mathbf{w}_s$ is the vector of explanatory variables defined in the previous section but where we replace the x_t^i, $i =$ DE, JP, US with y_t^i, $i =$ DE, JP, US so that $\mathbf{w}_s = (\pi_s, g_s, fx_s, y_s^{DE}, y_s^{JP}, y_s^{US})'$. $\Omega_{s(t-1)}$ denotes the information set available just before the sth event.

The parameter estimates of θ' are identified up to scale only, however, they are easily interpretable. For example, a positive value of $\widehat{\theta}_{DE}$ would suggest that domestic rates are more likely to be increased following a German increase and vice versa. The model in expression (9) has a well-known likelihood function (see Maddala, 1983) which can be maximized by conventional numerical techniques. Finally, we restrict the number of categories, k_j, to four to homogenize across the countries in our sample and to allow for better comparability. Hence, the four categories can be loosely interpreted as: $k_1 =$ strong decrease, $k_2 =$ decrease, $k_3 =$ increase, and $k_4 =$ strong increase.[2] Table 4 reports for each country the correspondence between this classification system and the specific discrete changes of each country. As an illustration, changes in the US federal funds rate target correspond to $k_1 = -0.50\%$, $k_2 = -0.25\%$, $k_3 = 0.25\%$, and $k_4 = 0.50\%$.

---

[2]The only exception to this reclassification is Switzerland. Due to the large number of observed values, it made more sense to proceed with a continuous model instead.

Table 4. Classification of target changes

Country	k_1 = strong decrease	k_2 = decrease	k_3 = increase	k_4 = strong increase
Australia	$\Delta\bar{r}_t < -0.75$	$-0.75 \leq \Delta\bar{r}_t \leq 0$	$0 < \Delta\bar{r}_t \leq 0.75$	$\Delta\bar{r}_t > 0.75$
Austria	$\Delta\bar{r}_t < -0.5$	$-0.5 \leq \Delta\bar{r}_t \leq 0$	$0 < \Delta\bar{r}_t \leq 0.5$	$\Delta\bar{r}_t > 0.5$
Belgium	$\Delta\bar{r}_t < -0.5$	$-0.5 \leq \Delta\bar{r}_t \leq 0$	$0 < \Delta\bar{r}_t \leq 0.5$	$\Delta\bar{r}_t > 0.5$
Canada	$\Delta\bar{r}_t \leq -0.5$	$-0.5 < \Delta\bar{r}_t \leq 0$	$0 < \Delta\bar{r}_t < 0.5$	$\Delta\bar{r}_t \geq 0.5$
France	$\Delta\bar{r}_t \leq -0.4$	$-0.4 < \Delta\bar{r}_t \leq 0$	$0 < \Delta\bar{r}_t \leq 0.4$	$\Delta\bar{r}_t > 0.4$
Germany	$\Delta\bar{r}_t \leq -0.4$	$-0.4 < \Delta\bar{r}_t \leq 0$	$0 < \Delta\bar{r}_t \leq 0.4$	$\Delta\bar{r}_t > 0.4$
Italy	$\Delta\bar{r}_t < -0.5$	$-0.5 \leq \Delta\bar{r}_t \leq 0$	$0 < \Delta\bar{r}_t \leq 0.5$	$\Delta\bar{r}_t > 0.5$
Japan	$\Delta\bar{r}_t < -0.5$	$-0.5 \leq \Delta\bar{r}_t \leq 0$	$0 < \Delta\bar{r}_t \leq 0.5$	$\Delta\bar{r}_t > 0.5$
Netherlands	$\Delta\bar{r}_t \leq -0.4$	$-0.4 < \Delta\bar{r}_t \leq 0$	$0 < \Delta\bar{r}_t \leq 0.4$	$\Delta\bar{r}_t > 0.4$
Spain	$\Delta\bar{r}_t < -0.5$	$-0.5 \leq \Delta\bar{r}_t \leq 0$	$0 < \Delta\bar{r}_t \leq 0.5$	$\Delta\bar{r}_t > 0.5$
Sweden	$\Delta\bar{r}_t \leq -0.3$	$-0.3 < \Delta\bar{r}_t \leq 0$	$0 < \Delta\bar{r}_t < 0.3$	$\Delta\bar{r}_t \geq 0.3$
UK	$\Delta\bar{r}_t < -0.5$	$-0.5 \leq \Delta\bar{r}_t \leq 0$	$0 < \Delta\bar{r}_t \leq 0.5$	$\Delta\bar{r}_t > 0.5$
US	$\Delta\bar{r}_t \leq -0.5$	$-0.5 < \Delta\bar{r}_t \leq 0$	$0 < \Delta\bar{r}_t < 0.5$	$\Delta\bar{r}_t \geq 0.5$

5. Results

5.1. *The timing model*

Table 5 displays the results of the ACH estimation of the timing model. For each country, the label *Constant* refers to the baseline hazard assuming that inflation and output are at their targeted levels (2% and 2.5%, respectively), that the exchange rate remained constant during the previous month, and that none of the G-3 central banks modified their policy rates during the month. The label *Inflation* refers to the hazard prevailing when inflation deviates by 1% from its targeted value. A similar experiment describes the entries associated with the labels *Growth* and *Ex. Rate.* The labels *Germany, Japan, US* correspond to the estimated hazards when these countries modify their policy rates that month. Finally, because the parameters α and β measure the degree of serial dependence in the timing data, we preferred to report the parameter estimates and their standard errors directly.

A first observation is that the standard Taylor rule variables, inflation and output growth, do not apply equally well to all countries. While inflation is an important variable for US policy, it does not appear as significant for any of the other countries. This is perhaps most surprising for Germany, given its traditional reputation for an aggressive stance toward inflation. Output growth is important for five of the countries, including Germany. Notably,

Table 5. ACH estimates: The timing model

	Austria	Australia	Belgium	Canada	Switz.	Germany	Spain
Constant	0.001**	0.86*	0.11**	0.45	0.79	0.05**	0.52
Inflation	0.001	0.85	0.08	0.58	0.86	0.06	0.47
growth	0.002	0.65**	0.12	0.38	0.81	0.07**	0.51
Ex. rate	0.99**	0.74	0.78**	0.39	0.31	0.69	0.68
Germany	0.10*	0.55**	0.58**	0.77*	0.82	0.05**	0.65
Japan	0.001	0.97**	0.09	0.45	0.99	0.65*	0.42
US	0.000	0.89	0.18	0.45	0.70	0.53**	0.60
α	0.08**	0.15**	0.09*		0.00	0.09**	0.25
	(0.04)	(0.04)	(0.06)		(0.1)	(0.04)	(0.33)
β	0.73**				0.63**	0.75**	
	(0.40)				(0.25)	(0.31)	
OBS.	99	86	77	36	99	138	83
Log-Lik.	−44.51	−34.44	−35.89	−23.03	−37.74	−75.17	−54.52

	France	Italy	Japan	Nether.	Sweden	UK	US
Constant	0.54	0.14	0.10**	0.05**	0.55	0.09*	0.38
Inflation	0.24**	0.15	0.06	0.05	0.61	0.09	0.54**
Growth	0.50	0.16**	0.10	0.05	0.49*	0.11*	0.36
Ex. Rate	0.72	0.18	0.16*	0.99**	0.49	0.36*	0.31
Germany	0.76*	0.14	0.33**	0.52**	0.60	0.02**	0.27
Japan	0.26	0.14	0.10**	0.07	0.55	0.01	0.24
US	0.62	0.10	0.05	0.01**	0.55	0.34*	0.38
α	0.07**		0.03*	0.00		0.00	0.12**
	(0.03)		(0.02)	(0.14)		(0.13)	(0.03)
β	0.26**			0.45**		0.67*	
	(0.12)			(0.17)		(0.48)	
OBS.	106	79	132	138	36	135	138
Log-Lik.	−61.31	−45.21	−39.40	−73.08	−23.15	−79.07	−79.16

Notes: Constant refers to the baseline hazard; Inflation, Growth, and Ex. Rate refer to the hazard when there is a 1% deviation in the corresponding variable from its norm; Germany, Japan, and US refer to the hazard when the corresponding G-3 bank adjusts its policy rate that month; α, β are the actual coefficient estimates from the ACH (standard errors in parenthesis); */** indicates significant at the 90%/95% confidence level; OBS. Is the number of observations, which differ from those reported in Table 3 because we loose the first 12 observations to compute annual growth rates of the explanatory variables; *Log-Lik* is the log-likelihood value.

the exchange rate also is important for five countries. So while monetary theorists have cast doubt on whether it is optimal to include the exchange rate in a country's monetary policy rule, our evidence suggests that quite a number of countries have done this in practice.

The next observation is that as in Table 3 previously, Table 5 shows a clear group of countries in the European core which respond to German policy. Note that this is in addition to the fact that these countries also respond in a significant manner to exchange rate movements. This appears to indicate a long-standing degree of policy dependence in Europe, one which is distinct from the demands of the ERM to respond to deviations in the exchange rate. In contrast, for countries usually thought to be in the European periphery, such as Spain and Italy, we do not discern a significant response to German policy. Also, Sweden and Switzerland, true to their reputations for independence, also appear to be independent of foreign influence in their monetary policies. The United Kingdom is an interesting case, in that the coefficient on German policy is statistically significant, but it is smaller than the baseline value. This indicates that once we control for British responses aimed at stabilizing its exchange rate, British policy makers appear to be actually less likely to change domestic monetary policy when the Germans have recently taken action.

Consider now the role of the US. While the US does not respond to Germany, German policy does respond to the US. One surprise, compared to previous literature, is that there is not clear evidence that Japan responds to US policy. The United Kingdom does respond to the US, which is interesting, given that we found above that the UK does not respond in a favorable way to German policy changes. It is worth noting that each of the relationships with the US listed above, inferred from the results in Table 5, is the opposite of that which one would infer from Table 3. Apparently, it is very important for judging the relationship with the US to account for the dynamics and Taylor rule variables, as is done for the results reported in Table 5. This was not the case for the relationships with Germany reported above; the core group of countries relating to Germany appears nearly the same in both Tables 3 and 5.

Considering lastly the influence of Japanese policy, this plays a role only for Germany and for Australia. It is interesting that Australian policy appears to have closer links to its neighbor in Asia, than its culturally more similar but geographically more remote trade partners in Europe and North America.

A final word on these results pertains to the dynamics captured by the ACH formulation. These are particularly important for Austria,

Switzerland, Germany, France, the Netherlands and the UK, where the sum $\alpha + \beta$ is, respectively: 0.81, 0.63, 0.84, 0.33, 0.45, and 0.67. They are somewhat less relevant but significant for Australia, Belgium, Japan, and the US where only α is significant and attains the values 0.15, 0.09, 0.03, and 0.12 respectively. The only countries for which the dynamics are not relevant are Canada, Spain, Italy and Sweden, although we have already remarked the lack of degrees of freedom for Canada and Sweden. Overall, these numbers confirm that accounting for serial correlation patterns in the data is beneficial for the majority of countries in our sample.

5.2. *The directional model*

Table 6 reports the ordered probit results, which directly display the coefficient estimates of the relevant parameters (along with the standard errors) since they are easily interpretable. We begin by remarking that, although the sample sizes are generally quite small (this is due to the fact that we conduct the analysis in event time and thus depend on the number of actual policy adjustments made by each central bank), the coefficients are rather precisely estimated and the overall fit of the models is quite good.

The estimates on the parameters of the domestic macroeconomic variables are generally consistent with the typical behavior one would expect of central banks and embodied in a typical Taylor rule. Inflation coefficients are positive and significant for Austria, Belgium, Switzerland, Germany, Spain, Japan, and the UK, indicating that a rise in inflation above the 2% target is tempered by an increase in the policy rate. Similarly, output deviations from the 2.5% norm cause interest rates to increase although this effect is measured significantly for Canada, Switzerland, and the US only. The exchange variable, which triggered central bank responses in many of the countries in the timing model, is significant for Canada, Germany, and the US only.

What about the pattern of responses to the G-3? The timing model suggested that Austria, Belgium, France, and the Netherlands responded significantly to the Bundesbank. The responses of the directional model are largely consistent with this view, with significant responses for Austria, Belgium, and France but in all cases of the correct sign: these countries adjust interest rates at the same time and in the same direction as Germany.

Table 6. Ordered probit estimates

	Austria	Australia	Belgium	Canada	Switz.†	Germany	Spain
Inflation	6.56	−1.38	12.14**	−0.54	0.32**	0.68**	10.10*
	(2.66)	(0.97)	(4.72)	(0.54)	(0.01)	(0.24)	(5.92)
Growth	0.53	2.84	0.34	5.20**	0.02**	−0.19*	−0.27
	(0.39)	(1.90)	(0.24)	(1.50)	(0.01)	(0.11)	(0.37)
Ex. Rate	2.23	−0.21	1.68	11.71**	−0.01	0.94**	−1.93
	(2.37)	(0.82)	(1.19)	(4.20)	(0.02)	(0.46)	(3.23)
Germany	5.75**		2.72*		−0.04		9.94*
	(2.91)		(1.64)		(0.06)		(5.70)
Japan	0.92	−3.80**	−0.44		−0.06**	1.16**	
	(4.05)	(1.96)	(0.79)		(0.03)	(0.32)	
US	1.16		−1.97		0.14**	0.22	0.73
	(1.81)		(1.63)		(0.04)	(0.41)	(1.93)
Log. Lik.	−9.65	−4.72	−12.22	−22.06	67.71	−54.90	−5.22
Pseudo R^2	0.48	0.57	0.59	0.29	0.89	0.25	0.80
Obs.	28	16	35	23	72	75	35
	France	**Italy**	**Japan**	**Nether.**	**Sweden**	**UK**	**US**
Inflation	39.39		3.80*	−1.66**	3.28	1.85**	0.37
	(31.20)		(2.03)	(0.36)	(3.65)	(0.41)	(0.32)
Growth	−0.78		0.59	−0.02	0.27	−0.56**	0.64**
	(0.76)		(0.39)	(0.08)	(0.35)	(0.20)	(0.14)
Ex. Rate	4.05		−0.30	−0.51	−0.04	0.15	0.32*
	(2.89)		(0.40)	(0.55)	(0.76)	(0.24)	(0.18)
Germany	12.10*			0.68·	1.06	0.87	
	(7.41)			(0.55)	(2.71)	(0.72)	
Japan	5.85			0.35		−0.32	−0.70
	(5.74)			(0.32)		(0.48)	(1.12)
US	4.00			0.86*		0.53	
	(3.25)			(0.46)		(0.61)	
Log. Lik.	−6.82		−6.33	−53.49	−10.24	−28.14	−69.74
Pseudo R^2	0.77		0.51	0.29	0.12	0.47	0.17
Obs.	36		13	72	14	43	64

Note: */** indicates significant at a 90%/95% confidence level. Standard Errors in parenthesis. † Switzerland's model estimated by OLS due to the large variation in policy adjustments. There were not enough observations on Italy to estimate a viable model.

Perhaps the only other pattern worth remarking is that of Australia. The timing model suggests that Australia responded strongly to Japan (the baseline hazard goes from 86% to 97%). The directional model also shows a strong response to Japan but in this case, it is in the direction of moving interest rates against the Bank of Japan.

5.3. *Robustness — The role of formal agreements*

The empirical experiments in the previous section demonstrate that there is a substantial amount of monetary policy interdependence. The relations existing between Germany and Austria, Belgium, France, and the Netherlands are likely to be a direct result of the formal ties that the European Monetary System (EMS) represented, now the European Monetary Union. By the same token, Italy's apparent lack of relation may be explained by its absence from the EMS from September 1992 to November 1996. Incidentally, the 1992 crisis in the EMS significantly affected Sweden although the sample available for this country only starts after 1994, well past this juncture. One may suspect that this particular episode may also adversely affect the results reported in the previous section. However, our methods are unaffected by this crisis since the logical consistency of our approach relies instead on the responsiveness of central banks in terms of timing and direction of adjustments made — an issue that would be clearly problematic had we taken the approach of using some measure of dynamic covariation. Nevertheless, to highlight that our results are not sensitive to the 1992 crisis, we experimented with a sample truncated in 1994. These experiments were broadly consistent with our findings in the previous section and therefore are not reported here to save space.

There is yet another dimension in which we experiment with the robustness of our findings. Interesting work by Dominguez (1997) explores the influence of formal international agreements. Dominguez (1997) studied the communiques produced from meetings of the G-7, G-5, and G-3 dating from 1975 to 1993, and identified when there was a call for a coordinated effort to reduce inflation or lower interest rates. Commitments to fight inflation coincide with periods where actual inflation is rather high, beginning with the first summit in 1975 through the London Summit in 1984, and again from mid 1988 to April 1989. The focus shifted to economic growth and commitments to lower interest rates in 1986, 1987, 1991, and 1992. Overall, Dominguez identifies in the sample 15 cases of commitments to lower inflation and 19 commitments to lower interest rates.

We experimented with the dates reported in Dominguez's (1997) study for the G-5 countries, namely Germany, France, Japan, the UK, and the US. This choice is primarily motivated by the length of the available samples for these countries and the overlap with the Dominguez (1997) sample. We specified complete timing models that included the domestic macroeconomic variables, the G-3 timing variables, a G-5/G-7 meeting dummy if that month corresponded to a meeting reported in Dominguez (1997), and the ACH dynamics. Rather than reporting a new table of estimates, we computed the baseline hazard and the hazard computed with the dummy variable for the G-5/G-7 meetings. The baselines for Germany, France, Japan, the UK and the US are 62%, 4%, 62%, 43%, and 70%, respectively. The G-5/G-7 meeting dummy was not significant for any country except for Japan. The corresponding values for these hazards are 60%, 2%, 25%, 50%, and 67% — virtually identical to the baselines except for Japan, where a month in which a G-5/G-7 meeting takes place is usually a month in which the Bank of Japan is half as likely to adjust its policy rate.

6. Implications

The contributions of this chapter span in several dimensions. At a methodological level, we demonstrated that interest rate targeting modifies the time series properties of market interest rate data in a manner that renders traditional vector time series techniques inapplicable. Our Monte Carlo evidence complements the results reported in Rudebusch (1995) regarding the effects of interest rate targeting on term structure regressions.

The solution we propose to this problem is based on an uncommon data set on policy rate target data and consists on decomposing central bank policy into the decision to adjust versus the actual type of adjustment. This strategy is based on previous work by Hamilton and Jordà (2002) for the US and is modified and used here for the first time on other countries to detect monetary policy interdependence.

This empirical design has several advantages that go beyond the econometric pitfalls discussed early on. In particular, recent research by Rudebusch (2002) and Van Gaasbeck (2002) suggest that Taylor rules may appear to accurately describe central bank behavior due to the inherent persistence in macroeconomic data. We completely dispense with this artifact by concentrating instead on the snap shots that target rate adjustments provide of actual central bank policy. Hence, our results are elucidating, not only with regard to the issue of monetary policy linkages, but also as an alternative analysis of domestic monetary policy in industrialized OECD countries.

We find evidence of a clear European core, that responded to German policy long before the creation of a formal monetary union. Further this interdependence seems to have involved more than just attempts to stabilize exchange rates, but instead involved more direct responses to German policy shifts. We also find evidence of a distinct European periphery, including Italy, Switzerland and the UK, which did not respond to German policy. Finally, some countries respond to US policy shifts, notably Germany and the UK. But we did not find any evidence that Japan responds to the US. Our results also shed light on the debate whether countries should include the exchange rate in their policy rules — quite a number of countries in practice do assign a very prominent weight on this variable.

Acknowledgments

The authors wish to thank Rob Feenstra, Greg Sutton, Alan Taylor and participants of the Macro/International Economics workshop at UC Davis for useful comments and suggestions. Selva Demiralp and Kristin Van Gaasbeck provided extraordinary research assistance. This research was funded by a grant from the Institute of Governmental Affairs at UC Davis.

References

Batten, D. S. and M. Ott. 1985. The interrelationship of monetary policies under floating exchange rates. *Journal of Money Credit and Banking*, 17(1): 103–110.

Benigno, P. 2002. A simple approach to international monetary policy coordination. *Journal of International Economics*, 57(1): 177–196.

Bensidoun, I., V. Coudert, and L. Neyman. 1997. Interest rates in east Asian countries: internal financial structures and international linkages. CEPII Working Paper 97/02.

Biltoft, K. and C. Boersch. 1992. Interest rate causality and asymmetry in the EMS. *Open Economies Review*, 3(3): 297–306.

Borio, C. E. V. 1997. Monetary policy operating procedures in industrial countries. *Bank for International Settlements*, Working Paper.

Burdekin, R. C. K. 1989. International transmission of U.S. macroeconomic policy and the inflation record of western Europe. *Journal of International Money and Finance*, 8(3): 401–423.

Burdekin, R. C. K. and P. Burkett. 1992. The impact of U.S. economic variables on bank of Canada policy: direct and indirect responses. *Journal of International Money and Finance*, 11(2): 162–187.

Canzoneri, M. B., R. E. Cumby, and B. T. Diba. 2001. *The Need for International Policy Coordination: What's Old, What's New, What's Yet to Come?* Georgetown University mimeo, Washington, D.C.

Chung, J. W. 1993. Monetary interdependence among G-3 countries. *Applied Economics*, 25(5): 681–688.

Clarida, R., J. Gali, and M. Gertler. 2002. A simple framework for international monetary policy analysis. NBER Working Paper No. 8870.

DeGennaro, R. P., R. A. Kunkel, and J. Lee. 1994. Modeling international long-term interest rates. *Financial Review*, 29(4): 577–597.

Dominguez, K. M. E. 1997. Do the G-3 countries coordinate monetary policy? In Cohen, B. J. (ed.), *International Trade and Finance: New Frontiers for Research: Essays in Honor of Peter B. Kenen*. Cambridge University Press, New York, pp. 280–315.

Evans, C. L. and K. N. Kuttner. 1998. Can VARs describe monetary policy? Federal Reserve Bank of Chicago Working Paper 98–119.

Furman, J. and J. Leahy. 1996. International transmission of monetary policy: The U.S. and Canada. Harvard University Discussion Paper.

Garcia-Herrero, A. and J. Thorton. 1996. Additional evidence on EMS interest rate linkages. IMF Working Paper.

Hamilton, J. D. 1996. The daily market for federal funds. *Journal of Political Economy*, 104(1): 26–56.

Hamilton, J. D. and Ò. Jordà. 2002. A model for the federal funds rate target. *Journal of Political Economy*, 110(5): 1135–1167.

Karfakis, C. J. and D. M. Moschos. 1990. Interest rate linkages within the European Monetary System: A time series analysis. *Journal of Money, Credit and Banking*, 22(3): 388–394.

Katsimbris, G. M. and S. M. Miller. 1993. Interest rate linkages within the European Monetary System: Further analysis. *Journal of Money Credit and Banking*, 25(4): 771–779.

Maddala, G. S. 1983. *Limited-Dependent and Qualitative Variables in Econometrics.* Cambridge University Press, New York.

Nogues, J. and M. Grandes. 2001. Country risk: Economic policy, contagion effect or political noise? *Journal of Applied Econometrics*, 4(1): 125–162.

Obstfeld, M. and K. Rogoff. 2002. Global implications of self-oriented national monetary rules. *Quarterly Journal of Economics*, 117(2): 503–535.

Rudebusch, G. D. 1995. Federal Reserve interest rate targeting, rational expectations and the term structure. *Journal of Monetary Economics*, 35(2): 245–274.

Rudebusch, G. D. 1998. Do measures of monetary policy in a VAR make sense? *International Economic Review*, 39(4): 907–931.

Rudebusch, G. D. 2002. Term structure evidence on interest rate smoothing and monetary policy inertia. *Journal of Monetary Economics*, 49: 1161–1187.

Sims, C. A. 1998. Comment on Glenn Rudebusch's 'do measures of monetary policy in a VAR make sense?' *International Economic Review*, 39(4): 933–941.

Taylor, J., (ed.), 1999. *Monetary Policy Rules.* University of Chicago Press: Chicago.

Van Gaasbeck, K. 2001. Is Timing Everything? Investigating U.S. Monetary Policy with Interest-Rate Rules. U.C. Davis mimeo, Davis, California.

von Hagen, J. and M. Fratianni. 1990a. German dominance in the EMS: The empirical evidence. *Open Economies Review*, 1(1), 67–87.

von Hagen, J. and M. Fratianni. 1990b. German dominance in the EMS: Evidence from interest rates. *Journal of International Money and Finance*, 9(4): 358–375.

Index

T

U

V

W